QUEERING CHRISTIAN WORSHIP

Reconstructing Liturgical Theology

BRYAN CONES, EDITOR

STEPHEN BURNS, W. SCOTT HALDEMAN,
AND SHARON FENNEMA,
CONTRIBUTING EDITORS

Copyright © 2023 by Bryan Cones

All rights reserved. No part of this book may be reproduced, stored in a retrieval system, or transmitted in any form or by any means, electronic or mechanical, including photocopying, recording, or otherwise, without the written permission of the publisher.

Scripture quotations are taken from the New Revised Standard Version Updated Edition. Copyright © 2021 National Council of Churches of Christ in the United States of America. Used by permission. All rights reserved worldwide.

Permissions
Gordon Lathrop, "*Ordo* and Coyote," *Worship*, Volume 80, Number 3, May 2006. Used by permission of Liturgical Press.

Siobhan Garrigan, "Queer Worship," *Theology and Sexuality* 15 (2009): 211–230. Reprinted by permission of Taylor & Francis Ltd, http://www.tandfonline.com.

Seabury Books
19 East 34th Street
New York, New York 10016

An imprint of Church Publishing Incorporated

Library of Congress Cataloging-in-Publication Data

Names: Cones, Bryan, editor.
Title: Queering Christian worship : reconstructing liturgical theology / Bryan Cones, editor, Stephen Burns, W. Scott Haldeman, and Sharon R. Fennema, contributing editors.
Description: New York, New York : Seabury Books, [2023] | Includes bibliographical references and index.
Identifiers: LCCN 2023027882 (print) | LCCN 2023027883 (ebook) | ISBN 9781640656499 (paperback) | ISBN 9781640656482 (hardcover) | ISBN 9781640656475 (ebook)
Subjects: LCSH: Queer theology. | Liturgics. | Church—History of doctrines. | Homosexuality—Religious aspects—Christianity. | Reformed Church—Liturgy. | Public worship—Reformed Church.
Classification: LCC BT83.65 .Q44 2023 (print) | LCC BT83.65 (ebook) | DDC 261.8/357—dc23/eng/20230808
LC record available at https://lccn.loc.gov/2023027882
LC ebook record available at https://lccn.loc.gov/2023027883

CONTENTS

Foreword v
Bryan Cones

Contributors ix

Part I: Listening 1
Interlude, Emilie M. Townes

1. **Cartographies of Queer Christian Practice** 3
   Mapping the Contours of Exclusion, Inclusion, and Disruption
   Sharon R. Fennema and Bryan Cones

2. ***Ordo* and Coyote** 21
   Further Reflections on Order, Disorder, and Meaning
   in Christian Worship
   Gordon W. Lathrop

3. **Queer Worship** 39
   Siobhan Garrigan

4. **Worshiping the Queer Jesus** 55
   Lisa Isherwood

5. **Celebrant** 69
   Sheezus Christa
   Stephen Burns

Part II: Practicing 85
Interlude, Emilie M. Townes

6. **"Forgive us our Kertervers"** 87
   A Church of England Theological College as Queer Liturgical Space
   Susannah Cornwall and Joel Love

7. **Queerpentecostal Worship** 99
   Karl Hand

8. Broken Readings—Queer (M)ending 111
   Bertram J. Schirr

9. Redeeming Pleasure in Worship 123
   An Annotated Liturgical Play
   Lis Valle-Ruiz

10. Under the Preacher's Robes 143
    A Queer Embodied Homiletic
    Lucas Hergert

11. Queer Congregational Song 153
    Past Celebrations, Current Resources, and Hopes for the Future
    Stephanie A. Budwey

12. The Queer Art of Worship 167
    Rod Pattenden

13. Untitled (Holy Mysteries) 177
    Motifs of Containment, Presence, and Reservation in
    Liturgical Imagination
    Rebekah Pryor

Part III: Proposals 189
   Interlude, Emilie M. Townes

14. "Holy Abomination, Batman!" 191
    Questions about Ordination from a Gay Lay Scholar
    W. Scott Haldeman

15. An Indecent Proposal 203
    Love Is Not Love
    Bryan Cones

16. Funerals and Vigils 221
    Aspects of Queer Grief
    Florence Häneke

17. Bury Me in the Struggle for Freedom 237
    Lament as the Queer Apophatic Practice of Failure toward a New World
    Sharon R. Fennema

Index 245

FOREWORD

Bryan Cones

Queering Christian Worship: Reconstructing Liturgical Theology has been in the works for over a decade and was first conceived by the Queering Liturgy Seminar of the North American Academy of Liturgy. The existence of that seminar from 2009 signaled that scholarship once excluded from, or overlooked by, the academy was already having an effect on Christian practice in some assemblies. Indeed, the fact that there was anything to study at all is a testament to daring forebears, who, rather than abandoning a tradition that excluded them, took prayer into their own hands, negotiating love, commitment, and with the AIDS crisis, grief through unfolding queer lenses. The introduction to this volume sketches the contours of that new revelation, which has laid the groundwork for the essays that follow.

That is not to say that the disruption at the heart of queer theorizing was absent from academic and pastoral reflection on Christian practice. The introduction opens a moment of "listening" to what has come before by sketching a historical map documenting a journey from invisibility, to a search for acceptance, to a full-throated insistence on the graced presence of queer persons in the churches, along with rituals to mark their lives. Two previously published essays, both of which influenced many of the original essays in this volume, provide further starting points. Gordon Lathrop's reflection on "coyote" in liturgy—unscripted moments that disrupt the standard *ordo* of common prayer—provides one such pathway toward queering worship. Siobhan Garrigan's aptly titled "Queer Worship" is more direct in its subject matter, particularly by not shying away from the whole range of queer expression, sexual and interpersonal.

Any queer reflection on liturgy must acknowledge a debt to its allied foremothers in the various waves of theological feminism. Not only did these pioneers interrogate how God is named in common prayers, they also contested hierarchical ritual patterns and insisted on recasting received prayer—Eucharist, baptism—as well as creating new ritual from scratch. Lisa Isherwood brings this work to bear on the mystery of Christ as it appears in the liturgy, while Stephen Burns tracks the progressive appearance of images of Christa in places of prayer—while acknowledging that her images remain absent from most Christian assemblies.

One obstacle to queered worship lies in the limits of those who prepare it—and the unwillingness of theological schools and seminaries to try on queer patterns. Opening a section on queered practice of prayer, Susannah Cornwall and Joel Love document a curious controversy in a UK Anglican theological college over the use of Polari, a queer slang once common in the UK, in a chapel evensong. The scale of the reaction from the college head signaled just how fraught any attempts to include queer voicing in chapel worship can be—likely forming those trained there to step cautiously in any experiments, if at all. Not all queering happens in seminaries, of course—and it sometimes appears in unexpected places. Karl Hand writes of his own queering of his received Pentecostal tradition, a Spirit-filled encounter which led him eventually to pastor a queer church with a Pentecostal style of worship. He then turns his queer Pentecostal eye to liturgical studies, which have often excluded Pentecostal forms of common prayer, opening new lenses on what liturgy can be.

Successive chapters lean further into queered liturgy, not only in its verbal and performative dimensions but also through the use of art and objects, which themselves reflect and refract what happens in the assembly. Betram Schirr interrogates the practice of reading scripture in many assemblies, troubling any fixed meaning or even text via queer lenses on text, reading, and performance. Performance also figures prominently in Liz Valle-Ruiz's chapter, which extends Schirr's approach to performativity in proclamation to the entire worship event, which in her case becomes a kind of extended sermon on queer identity and self-acceptance through Christian and other lenses. Lucas Hergert explores the erotics of preaching, arguing that the preaching event is as much about the preacher's body as about their voice. Voice appears also in Stephanie Budwey's account of queered hymnody, both in how it names what is human and how it praises what is divine. Rod Pattenden and Rebekah Pryor add further dimension, exploring in different ways how art in the place of prayer transforms what happens there in queer ways.

The final essays, with an eye to queer "proposals," engage work yet to be done even where queer bodies and identities have begun to appear in the churches, whether as ordained persons, committed households, or communities of grief. Scott Haldeman extends the conversation begun by Cornwall and Love to ordination practice itself. Many churches now ordain queer bodies, but whether the offices they hold or the institutions they serve will be queered by their ministry, and how, remains to be seen. Bryan Cones wonders what queer and other households have been lost, or erased, in the movement for legal and liturgical "marriage equality." Through the lens of his own committed partnership, he sketches a wedding liturgy that might suggest paths for a queerer variety of households to appear in an assembly's practice. Florence Häneke unpacks the unique dimensions of queer grief and its ritualizations in vigils and funeral, while Sharon Fennema proposes patterns of apophatic lament to capture "queer failure." The fundamental open-endedness of Fennema's reflections signals the length of the journey still ahead.

While we who have worked on this project hoped to capture the widest range of the international queer rainbow as we could, we nevertheless ran up against limits. Black and brown scholars are not well represented in this collection as compared to white, and the European, North American, and Australian voices here lack counterpoint from scholars of the global South. The difference we have managed to capture, however, can be found in ecclesial diversity, along with the varying patterns of prayer each of them offers. Among Pentecostal and Unitarian, Reformed and Congregational, Anglican/Episcopal and Roman Catholic, Lutheran and Evangelical, one should not expect to find a consistent account of liturgy, worship, or common prayer—or what it means to "queer" any of it. If disrupting received norms and contesting binaries and their embedded hierarchies lies deep in queer theory, identity, and practice, then a volume on queering worship cannot propose any new norm. It is then with full awareness that we offer this collection as a new moment in an ongoing conversation that, we hope, will find new partners to both critique and enrich. We also offer our thanks to those who have preceded us, named and unnamed, some remembered, many forgotten, who have paved the way. This collection spans a decade. We can look to the next years with both trepidation and hope: trepidation in the face of new and increasing resistance to the full flourishing of gender diversity; hope that the Spirit will continue to speak in new voices and bodies. This work has only just begun.

CONTRIBUTORS

Stephanie A. Budwey is the Luce Dean's Faculty Fellow Assistant Professor of the History and Practice of Christian Worship and the Arts, and the Director of the Religion in the Arts and Contemporary Culture Program at Vanderbilt University Divinity School in Nashville, TN, USA. Her teaching and research focus on the relationships between social justice issues, liturgy, and the arts. In addition to articles and book chapters published on such topics as intersex and theology, Marian congregational song, queer congregational song, and Saint Wilgefortis, she has published two monographs: *Religion and Intersex: Perspectives from Science, Law, Culture, and Theology* (Routledge, 2023) and *Sing of Mary: Giving Voice to Marian Theology and Devotion* (Liturgical Press, 2014). She has also co-edited *In Spirit and Truth: A Vision of Episcopal Worship* (Church Publishing, 2020). A member of the Episcopal Church, she currently serves as Organist/Parish Musician at St. David's Episcopal Church in Nashville.

Stephen Burns (contributing editor) is a professor of liturgical and practical theology at Pilgrim Theological College, University of Divinity, Melbourne, Australia. His publications include *Liturgy with a Difference* (ed. with Bryan Cones, SCM Press, 2019), *Twentieth Century Anglican Theologians* (ed. with Bryan Cones and James Tengatenga, Wiley, 2020), *Feminist Theology: Interstices and Fractures* (ed. with Rebekah Pryor, Fortress Academic Press, 2022), *From Shores of Silence: Explorations in Feminist Practical Theology* (ed. with Ash Cocksworth and Rachel Starr, SCM Press, 2022), *Conversations about Divine Mystery* (ed. with HyeRan Kim-Cragg, Fortress Academic Press, 2023), and *Speaking of Christ, Christa, and Christx* (ed. with Janice McRandal, SCM Press, forthcoming).

Bryan Cones (editor) holds a PhD in liturgical and practical theology from the University of Divinity in Melbourne, Australia, and is an honorary postdoctoral researcher at Pilgrim Theological College/University of Divinity. He is the author of *This Assembly of Believers: The Gifts of Difference in the Church at Prayer* (SCM Press, 2020) and co-editor (with Stephen Burns) of *Liturgy with a Difference: Beyond Inclusion in the Christian Assembly* (SCM, 2019).

Susannah Cornwall is Professor of Constructive Theologies at the University of Exeter, UK. Her books on theology, sex, gender and sexuality include *Constructive Theology and Gender Variance: Transformative Creatures* (Cambridge University Press, 2022), *Un/familiar Theology: Reconceiving Sex, Reproduction, and Generativity* (Bloomsbury, 2017), *Controversies in Queer Theology* (SCM, 2011), and *Sex and Uncertainty in the Body of Christ: Intersex Conditions and Christian Theology* (Routledge, 2010). She edited *Intersex, Theology and the Bible: Troubling Bodies in Church, Text and Society* (Palgrave Macmillan, 2015), and, with John Bradbury, *Thinking Again About Marriage: Key Theological Questions* (SCM, 2016).

Sharon R. Fennema (contributing editor) is Join the Movement curator and storyteller for the United Churches of Christ (UCC), leading the denomination's antiracism initiative using stories as both inspiration and lessons for cultivating a life of practices that move us toward racial justice. Prior to joining the UCC national staff, she was Assistant Professor of Worship and Director of Worship Life at the Pacific School of Religion and the Graduate Theological Union in Berkeley, California, where she taught classes in antiracist and decolonial spiritual formation, organization leadership as care work, mourning as resistance, and ritual, trauma and social change. Recent articles and essays include: "Christian (De)Formation: Gender Theory and Per/forming Identity in Christian Worship," in *Practical Matters* 7.2 (2014); "Postcolonial Whiteness: Being With in Worship," in *Only One is Holy: Liturgy in Postcolonial Perspectives* (Palgrave Macmillan, 2015); and "The Forgetfulness of Gentrification and the Pilgrimage of Protest: Re-Membering the Body of Christ," in *Review & Expositor* 115 (2018). She is also a worship consultant and lay leader in the United Church of Christ.

Siobhán Garrigan is Loyola Chair of Theology at Trinity College, Dublin. Her best known book is *The Real Peace Process: Worship, Politics and the End of Sectarianism*, a study of the work yet to be done to change hearts and minds regarding the Irish–British conflict. Her next two projects are *A Theology of Home in a Time of Homelessness*, a theoretical response to the practical experience of contemporary homelessness, and *Theology and Song*, a study of the sonic theologies of Irish traditional music.

W. Scott Haldeman (contributing editor) is an associate professor of Worship at Chicago Theological Seminary. Specializing in the history, theology, and practice of US Protestant worship, Haldeman is also interested in the less formal ways human beings ritualize themselves in relation to various categories of identity, such as race/ethnicity, gender, and sexuality. In queer religious studies, examples of his work include: "'In the Name of . . .': Baptismal Incorporation in a Gender-Fluid Age," in *Call to Worship: Liturgy, Music, Preaching, and the Arts* (Office of Theology and Worship of the Presbyterian Church [USA], Summer 2019); and, "Sacraments and Queer Theory," in Martha Moore-Keish and James Farwell (editors), *T&T Clark Handbook of Sacraments and Sacramentality* (New York: T&T Clark, 2023), 390–404.

Karl Hand is an ordained pastor in Metropolitan Community Churches, an affirming and liberating faith movement which originated among LGBTQIA+ folk in the 1960s. Karl is the pastor of Crave Church on Gadigal Land (Sydney, Australia), where he has served since 2007. He holds a PhD from Charles Sturt University and has taught subjects in New Testament Exegesis and New Testament Greek at Charles Sturt University, the University of Newcastle, and Australian Catholic University. Karl wrote the chapter on "Ephesians" in *The Queer Bible Commentary* (volume 2).

Florence Häneke holds a PhD in practical theology from the University of Basel in Switzerland with an empirical study on Queer Pastoral Identification in

Germany. Florence is interested in researching and exploring realms of the in-between and the shifting, combining academic fields such as theology, sociology, and queer theory as well as arts, practice, and theory. They serve as ordained parish minister in Brandenburg near Berlin, Germany and currently hold a position as postdoctoral researcher in Practical Theology at the University of Erlangen, Germany.

Lucas Hergert holds a D.Min in Preaching from the Pacific School of Religion and an M.Div from Harvard Divinity School. He teaches ethics and preaching at Meadville Lombard Theological School and also serves as a congregational minister. He lives with his husband in Deerfield, Illinois.

Lisa Isherwood is a professor of practice at the University of Wales-Trinity Saint David. Her work explores the nature of incarnation within a contemporary context and includes areas such as the body, gender, sexuality, and eco-theology. She is extensively published and has lectured across Europe, India, USA, Australia, and Canada. In 2009, she was the vice president of the European Society of Women in Theological Research. Between 2017 and 2019, she built a research website entitled "Theological Wanderings in the Cosmos," which brought together scientific, mythological, and theological disciplines to create a conversation between the new cosmologies and ecofeminist theologies.

Gordon W. Lathrop has served as a parish pastor, a professor of liturgy at Wartburg Theological Seminary and the Lutheran Theological Seminary at Philadelphia, and a visiting professor at Yale Divinity School, the Virginia Theological Seminary, the University of Iceland, the University of Uppsala in Sweden, and the Pontifical Thomas Aquinas University in Rome. His books from Fortress Press include *Holy Things: A Liturgical Theology* (1993), *Saving Images: The Presence of the Bible in Christian Liturgy* (2017), and *The Assembly: A Spirituality* (2022). He has been president of both the North American Academy of Liturgy and the International Societas Liturgica.

Joel Love was raised in a North American Baptist tradition and is now a parish priest in the Church of England. After teaching modern languages and a career in translation, Joel studied theology at Westcott House in Cambridge. Joel Love is a gay man, an uncle, and a godparent.

Rod Pattenden is a recently retired as minister of the Adamstown Uniting Church, Australia, where he led the development of a dynamic performing and visual arts program. He holds a PhD from the University of Sydney and has lectured and written widely on the arts and spirituality in Australia, and is a painter and liturgical artist. He is co-editor of *Imagination in an Age of Crisis: Soundings from the Arts and Theology* (Pickwick, 2022). He was for many years the Chair of the Blake Prize for Religious Art, and co-creator of InterPlay Australia, an embodied practice based in the theater arts. He has had extensive experience as a curator, developing exhibitions by a range of leading Australian artists, including "George Gittoes: on being there." Rod Pattenden is a visiting Fellow of the Australian Centre for Christianity and Culture.

Rebekah Pryor (www.rebekahpryor.com) is an artist and a writer who specializes in representations of the body in feminist theology and contemporary art. She is an honorary researcher at Pilgrim Theological College, University of Divinity, Melbourne, Australia and author of *Motherly: Reimagining the Maternal Body in Feminist Theology and Contemporary Art* (SCM Press, 2022) and co-editor (with Kerrie Handasyde and Cathryn McKinney) of *Contemporary Feminist Theologies: Power, Authority, Love* (Routledge, 2021), and (with Stephen Burns) of *Feminist Theologies: Interstices and Fractures* (Lexington Books/Fortress Press, 2023).

Bertram J. Schirr holds a PhD in practical theology from the University of Goettingen, Germany, and an MTh in Applied Theology from the University of Oxford. Bertram serves as an ordained parish minister in South Berlin and is an adjunct lecturer at the Protestant University of Applied Sciences, Berlin. He is the author of *Intercessory Prayers as Religious Performance—A theological-ethnographic analysis of three contrasting worship cultures in Berlin* (*Fürbitten als religiöse Performance—eine theologisch-ethnographische Untersuchung in drei kontrastierenden Berliner Gottesdienstkulturen*, EVA 2018).

The Rev. Dr. Emilie M. Townes, a distinguished scholar and leader in theological education, is dean *emerita* of Vanderbilt Divinity School and University Distinguished Professor of Womanist Ethics and Society and Women and Gender Studies.

The Rev. Lis Valle-Ruiz is Assistant Professor of Homiletics and Worship and Director of Community Worship Life at McCormick Theological Seminary, Chicago. She earned her PhD in Homiletics and Liturgics from Vanderbilt University, Nashville, Tennessee, where she also studied gender and sexuality. Her research interests lie at the intersection of preaching, worship, and performance studies. Rev. Valle received a ThM in Homiletics from Princeton Theological Seminary and an MDiv from Louisville Presbyterian Theological Seminary. She also holds a JD and a BA in Education from the University of Puerto Rico. Theater is her lifelong passion.

PART I

LISTENING

perhaps a murmur turned to singing
    coming low and soft to an ear
inviting a place of comfort . . . or was that confrontation
    that comes a-winding as we sit
        or stand
        or bow
        or kneel
listen softly with large hearts
    open spirits
        and swinging lo like chariots

CHAPTER ONE

CARTOGRAPHIES OF QUEER CHRISTIAN PRACTICE

Mapping the Contours of Exclusion, Inclusion, and Disruption

Sharon R. Fennema and Bryan Cones

In Macky Alston's film *Love Free or Die*,[1] which documents the life and character of Episcopal Bishop Gene Robinson, Bishop Barbara Harris quips, "Get real. Gene Robinson is certainly not the first gay bishop in the church. He may be the first one who's openly gay, but you know, give me a break." As much as that is likely the case for the hierarchy of the Episcopal Church, it certainly is also true for the entire Christian tradition. Even though gay, lesbian, bisexual, transgender, intersex, queer, two-spirit, and allied (hereafter LGBTQIA2S+) theologies are more recent additions to Christian theological discourse, queer characters have been part of the story all along. What is more, persons with non-normative gender and sexual identities, expressions and embodiments have been worshiping and leading worship in communities of faith as long as two or three have gathered in Christ's name. Queering Christian Worship centers on explorations of the dynamics of exclusion, inclusion, and disruption that characterize the theological performances known as "liturgy" when we acknowledge the truth of these claims and foreground the presence, participation, insights, and reflections of queer characters who have so often been ignored or made invisible.

For many, the word "queer" elicits memories of taunting jeers, vicious mocking, and hostility. In the mid- to late-twentieth century, queer was most often used as a disparaging term for a same-gender-loving or gender-variant person. Its force was intended to shame, express contempt, do violence with its naming. Yet, toward the end of the century, political groups began to reclaim the word as a source of defiant pride. Chants of "we're here, we're queer, get used to it," and groups like Queer Nation created a new sense of queer by reversing the efforts to shame and enact violence around the term, and instead creating a rallying point and crying for political action. Our use of "queer" in this volume continues that act of linguistic reclamation that began nearly four decades ago.

---

1. https://lovefreeordiemovie.com/ [accessed 7 March 2023].

As the political movements for recognition and equal rights continued to develop, the diversity of experience within these movements began to be recognized, each named with its own unique experiences, needs, and goals. "Lesbian" was added to "gay," and later, "bisexual" and even later, "transgender." As this much-needed specificity created an ever-growing list of identities—a list that continues to unfold as gender-diverse persons gain greater freedom of expression—"queer" also became a convenient shorthand for a way of characterizing all those whose sexual or gender expression places them in opposition to the current idea of "normal." Though we are cautious about the erasure of particularity that comes with this use of the term "queer," its important conceptual contribution to the work of this volume comes in its recognition of these identities as non-normative, outside the mainstream, and often marginalized.

The move toward not only a collective way of naming these identities but also toward a coalitional politics based on the opposition to normativity, especially in the wake of the HIV/AIDS epidemic in the United States, birthed a political and theological movement aimed at identifying, questioning, challenging, and changing what society considers "normal" in reference to gender and sexuality. With queer politics and queer theory came the understanding of queer not only as a "being" but, more importantly, as a "doing." Queer becomes a verb designating acts that deviate from the expected or what is considered normal. As the title to this volume suggests, this use of the word queer is at the heart of our inquiry, where the doing of, or performance of, "queer" becomes a bridge to the doing of, or performance of, "worship" across a range of traditions.

The meaning of the term queer, as almost every person who attempts to define it points out, is complex and contested. Like the concepts it seeks to capture—identity, sexuality, relationship creation, gender performance, even theory—"queer" remains a slippery term, ever resistant to being pinned down. Anything "queer," however, will relentlessly interrogate binary concepts, both to disrupt their boundaries and to unveil the "excluded middle" they obscure. Each of the authors in this collection will use the term differently and may employ any number of meanings, or another set of meanings altogether. The point of offering these understandings of the term queer is not to constrain its utility for the authors of this volume or for those who will continue to contribute to this dialogue, but rather, to point toward the trajectory that this volume of essays seeks to contribute to and develop. Fundamentally, the authors in this collection explore the question: When queer is a verb, what does it mean to worship God?

Though the reality of queers *in* Christian worship is as old as Christianity itself, the notion of queering Christian worship that forms the heart of this volume reflects more recent developments at the intersections of theology, queer theory, critical discourses around sexuality and gender, LGBTQIA2S+ religious practices, and Christian worship. These developments begin with the initiation of gay theological discourses. From the start, the unfolding movements of LGBTQIA2S+ political advocacy simultaneously birthed both theologies and practices engaged in the deconstruction of heteronormativity and the reconstruction of homo-generis/ous spiritual expressions.

Foundations: Mapping New Territories: The Development of Homo-Theo-Logos

While every telling of historical development is subject to contestations, most scholars who trace the development of gay and lesbian theological thought point to the Stonewall riots of June 1969 as the symbolic starting point of both a social movement and new trajectories in Christian theology. This event begins the formation of a "gay self" by creating a public space for those who reject heteronormativity and the construction of homosexuality as a disease or deviance. The visibility and collectivity associated with Stonewall brings into being gay characters who embrace homosexuality as a primary marker of identity that can (and should) be accepted and celebrated with pride, creating the modern gay person. Even though the Stonewall riots were initiated primarily by transsexuals and transvestites who resisted the violence of police raids on a bar in the Greenwich Village section of New York City, they became a symbol for gay people claiming both voice and place, that is, of subjectivity, moral agency, and the right to self-determination in a public arena. In this context, "coming out" became the primary act of entering the political movement of gay pride.

It is within this historical context that gay and lesbian theological thought developed. At its beginnings, what Mary Hunt calls the "homosexual stage,"[2] gay theologies tended to embrace the voice- and place-claiming impetuses of the contemporaneous political action, acknowledging the theological significance of homosexuality, and bringing the insights of same-sex love into the theological conversation. These theologians inspired the development of denominational support and advocacy groups, but generally elaborated views of homosexuality that were normatively male.

The earliest gay and lesbian theological thought took on the methods of liberal theology. What Elizabeth Stuart names "gay liberal theology" had primarily an apologetic task: to affirm the goodness of gay people and their spiritual worth, while convincing Christian communities to accept gay people and their relationships in the churches. Theologians such as John McNeill,[3] Malcolm Macourt,[4] John Fortunato,[5] and later,

---

2. Mary Hunt describes three stages of development, discussed below, in *Fierce Tenderness: A Feminist Theology of Friendship* (New York: Crossroad Publishing, 2004), 151–153.

3. See, for example, John McNeill, *The Church and the Homosexual* (Boston: Beacon Press, 1976) and *Taking a Chance on God: Liberating Theology for Gays, Lesbians, and Their Lovers, Families, and Friends* (Boston: Beacon Press, 1988).

4. See, for example, Malcolm Macourt, ed., *Towards a Theology of Gay Liberation* (London: SCM Press, 1977).

5. See, for example, John Fortunato, *Embracing the Exile: Healing Journeys of Gay Christians* (New York: Seabury Press, 1982).

Chris Glaser,⁶ endeavored to take the dominant discourse regarding homosexuality as deviant, dangerous, and sick and transform it into something positive and gay-affirming, a project Patrick Cheng has called "the struggle for acceptance."⁷ These theologians reconstructed the gay self as the primary source of authority, using it to interrogate a largely heterosexist tradition. The theological argument goes something like this: Gay is good because love is the point of contact between God and the human self. In a context where the goodness of the gay self is denied, the focus must then be on creating self-love and an authentic self through which to encounter the divine. Gay wisdom and insight, the authority of the gay self, can displace the authority of the tradition. This theology revolves around a strong sense of the gay self with clearly defined patterns of relating and distinctive experiences which must be placed at the heart of any future reflection on theology and sexuality.

In the early years of the 1970s, the newly formed gay political movement adopted a radical social agenda aimed at the deconstruction of gender and sexuality, particularly as they were shaped by heteronormativity and homophobia. By the middle of the decade, the focus of the movement shifted to the center on integration into the social order through demands for equal rights, which Cheng has described as a "struggle for equality."⁸ In this form, the movement took on an ethnic minority-based model of identity and political action. Though distinct from the primarily male-focused gay pride movement, the lesbian feminist movement shares a similar developmental history. In the early 1970s, lesbian identity was viewed as a defiant way of being in a patriarchal world. By the middle of the decade, lesbians began to develop a more equal rights-based approach as well, and writings of the time begin to set limits for proper lesbian identity.⁹

We can recognize a similar shift and demarcation in what Hunt calls the "lesbian/gay/bisexual stage" of homo-theo-logos, where more attention is paid to the particularity of male and female experiences. Gay male theology, developing in a liberation theology-influenced ethos, highlights the experience of exile and exodus and places more emphasis on sexuality as a point of contact between gay people and the divine. Exemplified by Michael Clark,¹⁰ Gary David Comstock,¹¹

---

6. See, for example, Chris Glaser, *Come Home! Reclaiming Spirituality and Community as Gay Men and Lesbians* (San Francisco: HarperSanFrancisco, 1990) and *Coming Out as Sacrament* (Cleveland: Pilgrim Press, 1998).

7. See Patrick Cheng, *From Sin to Amazing Grace: Discovering the Queer Christ* (Cleveland: Pilgrim Press, 2012), Kindle edition, 15–24.

8. See Cheng, *From Sin*, 25–35.

9. See, for example, Mary Hunt, "Lesbianism as Religious Practice," *Journal of the American Academy of Religion* 67:3 (1999): 585–601.

10. See, for example, J. Michael Clark, *Defying the Darkness: Gay Theology in the Shadows* (Cleveland: Pilgrim Press, 1997).

11. See, for example, Gary David Comstock, *Gay Theology without Apology* (Cleveland: Pilgrim Press, 1993) and *Unrepentant, Self-Affirming, Practicing: Lesbian/Bisexual/Gay People within Organized Religion* (New York: Continuum, 1996).

and Richard Cleaver,[12] among others, these theologies ground themselves in the experience of oppression, described by Cheng as a "struggle for liberation."[13] They are critical and interrogating of some aspects of culture and tradition which perpetuate this oppression and build on the "see, judge, act" liberation methodology to identify and address oppression within both the culture and the Christian tradition, and create practices, both political and liturgical, of transformation.

In contrast, lesbian theologies, developing in a feminist-theology-influenced ethos, rely heavily on Audre Lorde's identification of the divine with the erotic,[14] or the deep inner cravings for joy and satisfaction encountered in sexual relations but also in many other ways as the empowerment of creative energy. Resisting the opposition of the spiritual and the erotic (and the political), these theologies see them as inextricably linked. Exemplified in the work of Carter Heyward,[15] Mary Hunt,[16] and Elizabeth Stuart,[17] they explore the power, joy, and creativity that come from a deep, erotic connection with self and with others. This emphasis yields theological formulations of friendship as a theological paradigm for right relationships based on mutuality and equality.

Parallel to work of predominantly white gay and feminist scholars, scholars of color, some also inspired by Lorde's work, provided the beginnings of sustained attention to the overlapping oppressions related to sexuality, gender, race, and migration, among others. Horace Griffin documents the religious life of African American lesbian and gay Christians and the responses of their churches through this period.[18] Black feminist and womanist scholars, such as Katie Cannon,[19]

---

12. See, for example, Richard Cleaver, *Know My Name: A Gay Liberation Theology* (Louisville, KY: Westminster John Knox Press, 1996).

13. See Cheng, *From Sin*, 36–46.

14. Audre Lorde, "Uses of the Erotic: The Erotic as Power," in *Sister Outsider: Essays and Speeches* (Berkeley: Crossing Press, 2007), 53–59.

15. See, for example, Carter Heyward, *Touching Our Strength: The Erotic as Power and the Love of God* (New York: Harper & Row, 1989), and Stephen Burns and Bryan Cones, "Carter Heyward (1945–)" in *Twentieth Century Anglican Theologians: From Evelyn Underhill to Esther Mombo*, eds. Stephen Burns, Bryan Cones, and James Tengatenga (Chichester, UK: Wiley Blackwell, 2021), 175–184.

16. In addition to her many writings, Hunt was a founder of the Women's Alliance for Theology, Ethics, and Ritual: https://www.waterwomensalliance.org/ [accessed 7 March 2023]. See Hunt, "WATER as a Locus for Feminist Liberation Theology," *Journal of Feminist Studies in Religion* 18:1 (Spring 2002): 107–110.

17. See, for example, Elizabeth Stuart, *Just Good Friends? Towards a Lesbian and Gay Theology of Relationships* (London: Mowbray, 1995) and *Gay and Lesbian Theologies: Repetitions with Critical Differences* (London: Ashgate, 2003).

18. Horace L. Griffin, *Their Own Receive Them Not: African American Lesbians and Gays in Black Churches* (Louisville: Westminster John Knox Press, 2006).

19. See, for example, Katie G. Cannon, "The Emergence of Black Feminist Consciousness," in *This Bridge Called My Back: Writings by Radical Women of Color*, eds. Cherríe Moraga and Gloria Anzaldúa, 36–44 (New York: Kitchen Table: Women of Color Press, 1983); and Katie G. Cannon, *Black Womanist Ethics* (Atlanta: Scholars Press, 1988).

Emilie M. Townes,[20] and Dolores Williams,[21] among others, highlighted the intersections of race, gender, and sexuality, emphasizing how their interactions both enriched and complicated the lives of Black woman especially. Gloria Anzaldúa's *Borderlands/La Frontera: The New Mestiza*,[22] among other writings, drew attention the overlapping realities of migration, colonization, and heteronormativity through the lens of her life at the Texas border.

In the 1980s, the HIV/AIDS crisis intervened in the parallel developments of lesbian and gay politics and theologies. In the words of Stuart, "Death hung like a pall over the lesbian and gay communities,"[23] as thousands of gay men were dying each year. By 1999, 425,000 people, the vast majority being gay men, had died of the disease in the United States alone. The cultural conflation of gay-AIDS-death and the inaction of the government, medical communities, and social service agencies brought about coalitions of lesbians, gay men, and transgender people under the blanket of queer activism, resulting in the unity of groups that had previously emphasized their difference and the creation of a "queer" politicized identity.

From the queer activism and coalitional politics initiated by the AIDS crisis and the radical refusal of gender essentialism in third-wave feminism, "queer theory" emerges in the work of scholars, such as Eve Kosofsky Sedgwick[24] and Judith Butler[25] in the 1990s. In its earliest stages, what would later be called queer theory revolves around the idea that modern constructions of sexuality and gender are not stable but incoherent and contested. Indeed, sexuality and gender are performative, that is, not expressive of some inner nature, but a performance of certain actions, gestures, and styles. Butler argues that gender requires an enactment that is repeated, a repetition of acts which constitute and reinscribe gender on the body. Yet, within the repetition of gender identities as performances there exists the possibility of subversive repetitions that call into question the regulatory practice of identity. Embedded within the discourse of queer theory is a call for such subversive actions to proliferate in the hopes of transformation.

---

20. See, for example, Emilie M. Townes, *In a Blaze of Glory: Womanist Spirituality as Social Witness* (Nashville: Abingdon Press, 1995); and "Womanist Theology: Black Women's Experience as a Source for Doing Theology," in *The Cambridge Companion to Liberation Theology*, ed. Christopher Rowland, 2nd ed., 156–171 (Cambridge: Cambridge University Press, 2007).

21. See, for example, Delores S. Williams, *Sisters in the Wilderness: The Challenge of Womanist God-Talk* (Maryknoll, NY: Orbis Books, 1993).

22. Gloria Anzaldúa, *Borderlands/La Frontera: The New Mestiza* (San Francisco: Aunt Lute Books, 1987).

23. See Elizabeth Stuart, "AIDS and the Failure of Gay and Lesbian Theology" in *Gay and Lesbian Theologies*, 65–78.

24. See, for example, Eve Kosofsky Sedgwick, *Epistemology of the Closet* (Berkeley: University of California Press, 1990) and *Tendencies* (Durham: Duke University Press, 1993).

25. See, for example, Judith Butler, *Gender Trouble: Feminism and the Subversion of Identity* (New York: Routledge, 1990) and *Bodies That Matter: On the Discursive Limits of Sex* (New York: Routledge, 1993).

Likewise, queer theology emerged from the collapse of gay liberal, gay liberation, and lesbian feminist theologies under the weight of the HIV/AIDS epidemic, which revealed the inadequacy of modern conceptions of sexual identity, disrupted sensibilities of the gay self/subject and created the "queer" as an activist. Heavily influenced by the work of Judith Butler and the philosopher Michel Foucault, these theologies generally reject the metaphysics of substance. Gender and sexual identities are deconstructed sociologically, with the performative understanding of Butler, and theologically in the light of baptismal identity and incorporation into the body of Christ, which is interpreted as the "queerest" identity of all.

Developing a methodology of "queering the tradition," queer theologians, including Marcella Althaus-Reid,[26] Justin Tanis,[27] Laurel Schneider,[28] Pamela Lightsey,[29] and Linn Tonstad,[30] among others, highlight the ways in which the Christian tradition is itself queer, while developing theological themes of the queer Christ and taking an activist and performative approach to theology. Though beginning with sexuality, queer theology is not necessarily about sexuality per se, but about subversive and disruptive performances both as they have already occurred within the Christian tradition and as they continue to be imagined. Queer theologies point toward the ways in which the already subversive message of the gospel might be performed now and in the future to disrupt the disciplinary constraints of normativity, be they theological, sexual, or otherwise.

Exclusions: Mapping the Starting Points— Finding Homo-Liturgicus

Within the geography of gay, lesbian, and queer theologies, queering Christian worship emerges as a possibility. From, in and with each stage in this theological development, approaches to the study and practice of worship emerge that become starting points for new trajectories of liturgical theology. Though their evolution is chronologically messy, to say the least, it is possible to identify where

---

26. Marcella Althaus-Reid, *Indecent Theology: Theological Perversions in Sex, Gender and Politics* (London: Routledge, 2000) and *The Queer God* (London: Routledge, 2003). See also Mark Jordan and Lisa Isherwood, eds. *Dancing Theology in Fetish Boots: Essays in Honour of Marcella Althaus-Reid* (Eugene, OR: Pickwick Publications, 2010).

27. Justin Tanis, *Trans-Gendered: Theology, Ministry, and Communities of Faith* (Cleveland: Pilgrim Press, 2003).

28. See, for example, Laurel Schneider, *Beyond Monotheism: A Theology of Multiplicity* (London: Routledge, 2008) and Laurel Schneider, ed., *Polydoxy: Theology of Multiplicity and Relation* (New York: Routledge, 2010).

29. Pamela R. Lightsey, *Our Lives Matter: A Womanist Queer Theology* (Eugene, OR: Pickwick Publications, 2015).

30. Linn Marie Tonstad, *Queer Theology: Beyond Apologetics* (Eugene, OR: Cascade Books, 2018). See also W. Scott Haldeman, "Sacraments and Queer Theory," in James W. Farwell and Martha Moore-Keish, eds., *T&T Clark Handbook of Sacraments and Sacramentality* (London: T&T Clark, 2023), 392–406.

some streams of inquiry begin, and to trace how those trajectories develop. We begin with one of the first such streams, connecting to the voice- and place-claiming impetuses of early gay activism and gay liberal theology, striving to create Christian theologies that affirmed: "gay is good."

Perhaps the earliest work in "queering" Christian worship can be traced to the scholarship of historians who sought to foreground the same-sex relationships, love, and eroticism present, if invisible for the most part, in the history of Christianity. The work of John Boswell and Bernadette Brooten exemplify this strand of scholarly inquiry. Brooten's foundational study, *Love Between Women: Early Christian Responses to Female Homoeroticism*[31] explores the thesis that condemnations and prohibitions of sexual love between women found in historical documents, artifacts, and writing offer proof that there was widespread awareness of female homoeroticism in the ancient Roman world. Brooten argues that these condemnations were based on an understanding of what is "natural" with regards to sexual activity and social order, and women's passive and submissive relationship to men, which comprised a worldview shared by early Christians and their Roman neighbors. Where Brooten's study intersects with Christian worship is in the resources she uses to make her arguments. From sermons by John Chrysostom and Augustine to descriptions of woman–woman marriage in second-century Alexandria and in Clement of Alexandria's treatises, Brooten claims a place for female homoeroticism in the earliest Christian liturgical practices, recognizing a certain level of tolerance for such love even as it is condemned based on the gender role transgression it involves.

In contrast to Brooten's focus on the condemnation of homoeroticism, John Boswell's work[32] suggests that the homophobia associated with Christianity is a later accrual to the Christian tradition. Focused primarily on male homoeroticism (though he does not always acknowledge that fact), the thesis that Boswell develops in several of his historical works is fourfold: (1) Christianity came into existence in an atmosphere of Greek and Roman tolerance for same-sex eroticism; (2) nothing in the Christian scriptures or early tradition required a hostile assessment of homosexuality, rather, such assessments represent a misreading of scripture; (3) medieval Christians showed no real animosity toward same-sex eroticism; (4) it was only in the twelfth and thirteenth centuries that Christian writers formulated a significant hostility toward homosexuality and then read that hostility back into their scriptures and early traditions.

In his book, *Same-Sex Unions in Premodern Europe*, Boswell develops the implications of that thesis in connection to liturgical practices. He suggests that certain rites called *adelphopoiesis* describe ceremonies of same-sex union, which

---

31. Bernadette Brooten, *Love Between Women: Early Christian Responses to Female Homoeroticism* (Chicago: University of Chicago Press, 1996).

32. John Boswell, *Christianity, Social Tolerance, and Homosexuality: Gay People in Western Europe from the Beginning of the Christian Era to the Fourteenth Century* (Chicago: University of Chicago Press, 1980) and *Same-Sex Unions in Premodern Europe* (New York: Villard Books, 1994).

"functioned in the past as a gay marriage ceremony."[33] Boswell's study presents an initial attempt to both re-read and analyze texts from the liturgical traditions of the Christian church with a perspective that presumes the existence of homosexuals and homoeroticism as part of that history and does not assume that Christianity is and has always been anti-gay and homophobic. In doing so, he offered one of the first contributions to the queering of Christian worship by creating the possibility of a history of remembering same-sex relationships in liturgical practices.

These early historical works helped find the *homo liturgicus*, that is, the queers in the liturgical tradition, particularly in relation to their exclusion, both through condemnation or prohibition and willful forgetting. In fact, the history of worship practices related to same-sex relationships, as it came to be known in the work of scholars like Brooten and Boswell, came into view primarily in relation to their exclusion. In a similar way, the creation of LGBTQIA2S+-specific worship resources and studies of and reflections on these worship practices simultaneously established gay-affirming liturgical traditions while also revealing the exclusions of such characters from the ritual life of Christian worshiping communities. These practice-oriented works form another important part of this strand of queering Christian worship.

Inclusions: Mapping the Road Less Traveled—Worship in LGBTQIA2S+ Theologies

LGBTQIA2S+ liberation theologies and queer theologies also talk about worship. For example, in *Jesus Acted Up: A Gay and Lesbian Manifesto*,[34] Robert Goss talks about the practical implications of a queer Christology and critical practices in queer communities as part of his overall project of creating a gay and lesbian liberation theological discourse that resists the homophobic and oppressive deployment of Christianity. In particular he explores adjustments to Eucharist to reconceive it as a "holy feast" that welcomes the marginalized, and the creation of new rituals specific to queer life cycles, such as coming out, gender transition, and queer family creation. In a similar way, Marcella Althaus-Reid's *The Queer God*[35] uses ritual and liturgy as sources for theology, at one point contrasting the practice and effects of Eucharistic celebrations with the indigenous religious celebrations, particularly of bisexuality, in Moya, Peru, as models of reciprocity and poly-fidelity more appropriate to both trinitarian and Eucharistic practices and theologies.[36] For most LGBTQIA2S+ liberation theologians, worship (in its ideal sense) functions as a practice of resistance to oppression, and a way in which lib-

---

33. John Boswell, *Same-Sex Unions in Premodern Europe*, 280–281.

34. Robert Goss, *Jesus Acted Up: A Gay and Lesbian Manifesto* (San Francisco: HarperSanFrancisco, 1994), especially 69–108.

35. Marcella Althaus-Reid, *The Queer God* (London: Routledge, 2003).

36. Althaus-Reid, *The Queer God*, 117–123.

eration can be enacted. Theirs is a deconstruction aimed at inclusion and equality. For queer theologians, liturgy is the space of performativity, the generative and oppressive space that holds the possibility for the transformative performance of repetition with critical difference.

The embrace of the voice- and place-claiming impetuses of political action in early gay liberal theologies—by asserting the theological significance of homosexuality and bringing the insights of same-sex love into the theological conversation—lead to the development of denominational support and advocacy groups.[37] At the same time, they also lead to the development of new worship resources and identity-specific worshiping communities and for LGBTQIA2S+ Christians. With the increasing visibility of gay and lesbian people in the society following the watershed moment of the Stonewall riots and subsequent political advocacy, came the more vehement, public and articulated exclusion both from positions of leadership and full membership in Christian communities. Recognition of the need for gay-affirming and gay-particular liturgical language, music and ritual also emerged from both the increasing visibility and exclusion. So communities began to compile and publish such resources.

One of the earliest of these published collections was titled *Equal Rites: Lesbian and Gay Worship Ceremonies and Celebrations*[38] and was edited by MCC pastor Kittredge Cherry and Episcopal priest Zalmon Sherwood. There are echoes of the foundations of their work in the gay liberal theologies of the time in the book's introduction:

> Authentic spiritual expression is a basic human need. People long for times and places in which relationships are restored, the meaning of life is regained, and the divine is made real. Worship, a word that means "to make worthy" or "to respect," has the power to affirm our whole selves, body, mind and spirit. . . . The time is ripe for a collection of worship services, ceremonies and celebrations created by lesbian and gay people for use in communities that affirm them. On the one hand, the need is overwhelming. Established churches have systematically condemned lesbians and gay men for centuries on moral, biblical, and theological grounds. The result is a tremendous hunger for worship services that

---

37. These groups have existed across denominations, including DignityUSA (Roman Catholic), http://www.dignityusa.org/; Integrity USA (Episcopal) (http://www.integrityusa.org/), Lutherans Concerned (now ReconcilingWorks, https://www.reconcilingworks.org/), More Light Presbyterians (https://mlp.org/), and the United Methodist Reconciling Ministries Network (https://rmnetwork.org/); and The Evangelical Network (https://www.ten.lgbt/) [all websites accessed 12 March 2023]. These groups were often incubators for queering rituals that eventually worked their way into the collections described below and, in the case of marriage rites, into denominational resources. See, for example, Bryan Cones, *This Assembly of Believers: The Gifts of Difference in the Church at Prayer* (London: SCM Press, 2020), 70–74; and Elizabeth Smith, "How Do We Get It? Pray for It! Liturgical Resources for a Long Journey," in *Kaleidoscope of Pieces: Anglican Studies on Sexuality*, Alan H. Cadwaller, ed. (Adelaide, SA: ATF Theology, 2016), 183–200.

38. Kittredge Cherry and Zalmon Sherwood, eds., *Equal Rites: Lesbian and Gay Worship, Ceremonies and Celebrations* (Louisville: Westminster John Knox Press, 1995).

honor lesbian and gay experiences. On the other hand, the need is already beginning to be filled. Lesbians and gay men are forming their own faith communities inside and outside the established churches, and ever-increasing numbers of mainline churches are proclaiming that they welcome all people. . . . *Equal Rites* is designed for lesbian and gay people, as well as for anyone seeking to experience and affirm the full diversity of God's creation in worship.[39]

In this collection, different rites are contextualized, located in their particularity, and situated within the communities that created and performed them or for which they were imagined or intended in order that they might be recontextualized for use in other worshiping communities. They are, in that way, a sharing in "what works" from one community to another to satisfy the hunger for affirming practices in the midst of the experience of exclusion.

This collection, like many at the time,[40] includes a variety of different complete worship services and individual worship elements that both reconfigure traditional Christian rituals such as baptism, communion, confession, footwashing, funerals, and marriage, and create new rituals to embody and address moments of significance particular to queer characters, such as rituals for coming out, for dialogue amidst difference, for healing from gay/lesbian bashing, for gender transition, and for lesbian and gay pride celebrations. These two strategies of ritualization come to dominate the development of worship resources like this in general. First, they embody strategies that revolve around reimagining liturgical practices in such a way that gay lives and loves may be experienced as theologically significant and generative sources of insight and interpretation. Take, for example, Chris Glaser's worship resources for Advent in *Equal Rites* that make use of the image of the closet as a metaphor for the yearning and anticipation of the traditional liturgical season:

Call to Worship

One: How long, dear God, how long?
Many: Our longing cries to thee.

One: Come out of your distant closet,
Many: Our yearning beckons thee.

One: Reveal thyself to us, in us, with us in this age,
Many: Make known thy love for us . . .

---

39. Cherry and Sherwood, "Introduction," *Equal Rites*, xi.

40. See also for example, Kelly Turney, ed., *Shaping Sanctuary: Proclaiming God's Love in an Inclusive Church* (Chicago: Reconciling Congregation Program, 2000) and Geoffrey Duncan, ed., *Courage to Love: Liturgies for the Lesbian, Gay, Bisexual and Transgender Community* (London: Dartman, Longman, and Todd, 2002).

Prayer

One: In the fertile darkness of soil, the green of life bursts out of its shell; in the fertilized darkness of womb, the flesh of life builds cell upon cell.

Many: Those born in darkness have seen life.

One: The closet may be a fertile place: creativity bursts out of a lonely hell, from a closet fertilized with hope, the spirit leaps from a monastic cell.

Many: Those born in darkness have seen life . . . [41]

Second, they employ strategies that consist of creating newly conceived rites to accompany and enable moments of significance particular to LGBTQIA2S+ lives. These rituals recognize the unique spiritual needs of queer Christians and claim a voice for them within the worship life of Christian communities. Liturgies like the one created for an evening prayer celebration of Gay Pride by the Pride Interfaith Coalition at Harvard articulate the ways in which the particularities of LGBTQIA2S+ lives are made invisible by their exclusion as they maintain a place for them to be honored and celebrated.

> Creator God, we gather to thank you for your countless gifts to us. We are ever grateful for your love, compassion and faithfulness. But we also thank you for our history, our sexuality, our families of choice, and our uniqueness—all truly special gifts to us and our gay, lesbian, bisexual and transgender communities of faith. We praise you and bless you, this night and every night. Amen.[42]

The addition of worship resources like these to the activism already a part of Christian faith communities offered concrete embodiments of the gay-affirming theologies that had begun to appear. At the same time, they began to critically engage Christian liturgical traditions both through their re-imaginings of traditional liturgy with a "queer eye" and through their assertion of the need for rituals specific to LGBTQIA2S+ lives and experiences.

With the growing number of LGBTQIA2S+-affirming and particular worshiping communities also comes the scholarly inquiry into the sociocultural dynamics and religious impact of such practices and communities. While not primarily concerned with developing theological meanings, these studies take practices into account in a way that connects them with both the historical research and worship resources characteristic of this stream in queering Christian worship. In some of these resources, worship is analyzed as one part of the larger social dynamics of a religious community, as in Dawne Moon's *God, Sex and Politics: Homosexuality and Everyday*

---

41. Chris Glaser, "Rite for Advent," in *Equal Rites*, 76–77. Used with permission.
42. Turney, *Shaping Sanctuary*, 239. Used with permission.

Theologies,⁴³ where Moon explores the impact that the languages and activities of worship have on forming participants' belief about God and justice, and how these beliefs impact their everyday thoughts, interactions, and political decision-making around issues related to sexual and gender expression.⁴⁴

Others in this genre focus on ritual activity in LGBTQIA2S+ communities in particular, for example, the case study of lesbian/gay worship in Siobhán Garrigan's *Beyond Ritual: Sacramental Theology after Habermas*,⁴⁵ or several of the essays in Scott Thumma and Edward Gray's collection of essays, *Gay Religion*. As the forward to that volume explains, these studies mark:

> a watershed in the study of lesbian, gay, bisexual, and transgender (LGBT) religious experience in contemporary . . . society. Rather than understanding the relationship between LGBT people and religion as a problem to be debated, which so much other literature seems to assume, this volume recognizes the richly diverse religious experiences of gay people as a new and as yet unmapped resource in the history of . . . religious expression.⁴⁶

As such, they too participate in the voice- and place-claiming impulses of gay liberal theology, but in a descriptive way rather than a prescriptive one. They offer analysis of the beliefs, understandings, and ideas actually being performed in LGBTQIA2S+ communities of faith and in gay-affirming communities in general, contributing anthropological and sociological lenses to the work of queering Christian worship. Part Four of the *The Edge of God: New Liturgical Texts and Contexts in Conversation*⁴⁷ presents a combination of approaches, offering both actual liturgical texts and worship resources, as well as theological, sociological, and even psychological reflection on those resources, giving them both a practical emphasis and a theological impact.

As Christian denominations become increasingly accepting and affirming of LGBTQIA2S+ members and leaders, resources for the practice of worship that address and incorporate LGBTQIA2S+ lives continue to be developed. For example, denominational resources for same-sex marriage can now be found in several

---

43. Dawne Moon, *God, Sex, and Politics: Homosexuality and Everyday Theologies* (Chicago: University of Chicago Press, 2004).

44. Another fine example in this genre is Melissa Wilcox's study of members in two MCC churches, *Coming Out in Christianity: Religion, Identity and Community* (Bloomington: Indiana University Press, 2003).

45. Siobhán Garrigan, *Beyond Ritual: Sacramental Theology after Habermas* (Aldershot, UK: Ashgate, 2004).

46. "Foreword," in Scott Thumma and Edward Gray, eds., *Gay Religion* (Walnut Creek, CA: AltaMira Press, 2005), ix.

47. Stephen Burns, Nicola Slee, and Michael N. Jagessar, *The Edge of God: New Liturgical Texts and Contexts in Conversation* (London: Epworth, 2008).

denominational worship directories, such as that found in The Episcopal Church's *Witnessing and Blessing of a Lifelong Covenant*.[48] With the advent of legal same-gender marriage in the United States, same-gender couples now have access to the same marriage liturgies once reserved for different-gender couples. Beyond marriage, more and more gay-particular liturgies are included as one aspect or theme in a more general collection of worship resources. Recent additions to this stream also include more resources that point specifically to transgender and (less so) bisexual lives and experiences. Perhaps the most leading edge of this stream of queering Christian worship are those scholars and practitioners who marshal the resources of the Christian tradition to create practices that reveal the ways in which Christianity and Christian worship practices are already queer, like this liturgy by Elizabeth Stuart for coming out.

A Liturgy for Coming Out

The room should be darkened.

The person coming out:

As Eve came out of Adam, as the people of Israel came out of slavery into freedom, as the exiled Israelites came out of Babylon back to their home, as Lazarus came out of the tomb into new life, I come out—out of my desert into the garden, out of the darkness into the light, out of exile into my home, out of lies into truth, out of denial into affirmation. I name myself as lesbian/gay/bisexual/transgendered. Blessed be God who has made me.

All: Blessed be God who made you so.

The person coming out lights a candle and all present light their candles from it. Flowers are brought in. Music is played. The whole room is gradually filled with light, color and music. Bread and wine are then shared.[49]

These approaches to developing resources for and analysis of the practice of worship begin to break out of the dynamics of exclusion and inclusion into a more complex engagement with the spectrums of normativity and its disruption. Yet, with the memory of exclusion still present and shaping worshiping communities of LGBTQIA2S+ persons and others, and the persistent need and desire to claim a

---

48. This and other resources are explored in Cones, *This Assembly*, 162–196. See also Kimberly Bracken Long and David Maxwell, eds., *Inclusive Marriage Services: A Wedding Sourcebook* (Louisville, KY: Westminster John Knox Press, 2015).

49. Duncan, *Courage to Love* (Pilgrim Press edition, 2002), 279. Used with permission.

voice and a place within Christian communities, it remains a revolutionary act to find, interpret, and address the homo-liturgicus, that queer Christian worshiper rendered voiceless and placeless by Christian homophobia and heterosexism.

Disruptions: Mapping Excursions—Subversions and Perversions of Queering Liturgy

Drawing on the complexity of gender proposed by third-wave feminists, the coalitional and performative politics of the HIV/AIDS crisis, and developments in critical theories of sexuality and gender, queer theory launched gay and lesbian theologies into new landscapes. Rather than a geography of inclusion and exclusion, theologies that are informed by queer theory traverse the terrain of disruption and disorder. It is the land of parody, where the normative is revealed to be both constituted by its repetitive performance and subject to subversion, or the failure to repeat. It is this failure to repeat, this potential for a performance of the normative that goes awry, which opens up the possibility for transformation, or at least, proliferation of what is understood as normative. In it, we find ourselves moving beyond the normal binaries to the multidirectional dynamic interplay between those genders, sexualities, and desires that are understood as binary pairs in opposition to one another.

Out of the shifting landscape of queer theories and theologies emerges generative potential for the understanding, interpretation, and analysis of Christian worship. The performative notions of gender and sexuality characteristic of queer theory become a bridge for notions of liturgy as performance, recognizing liturgy as a place in which gender scripts are inscribed, performed, and subverted. Furthermore, the context of liturgy frames these performances in a peculiarly theological way, opening up new ways of thinking and acting, liturgically and theologically, and discovering new insights that have the potential to challenge and change understandings of Christian identity, worship, and theology. In a like manner, the idea of performative identities frames the theological interpretation of worship in a peculiarly queer way. The combination of these subjects and approaches, this queering of liturgy, yields productive analyses of subversive performances in the context of worship.

In this area, the gender of the presider as a "representative person" in Christian liturgy has become a productive site of queer reflection on liturgical performance, particularly as women, transgender, nonbinary persons have been ordained in greater numbers. Taking feminist reflection on the presider's role and its connection to the "person of Christ/a" in some traditions as a starting point,[50] queer practitioners

---

50. See, for example, Sarah Coakley, "The Woman at the Altar: Cosmological Disturbance or Gender Subversion," *Anglican Theological Review* 86:1 (Winter 2004): 75–44; Anita Monro, "'And ain't I a woman': the phonetic dramaturgy of feeding the family," in Nicola Slee and Stephen Burns, eds., *Presiding Like a Woman* (London: SPCK, 2010), 123–132, along with other essays in that volume.

have begun to unpack a gender-queer dimension to Christx as performed in the liturgy, such that the presider reflects and refracts the queer reality of the gathered assembly itself. As trans priest and presider Rachel Mann puts it, "Trans subjects like me who happen to be priests expose the performative structure of priestly identity; we suggest that the priest (and the church and God whom she/he/they represent) works in queered time and space rather than univocal, authoritarian time and space."[51] W. Scott Haldeman has further applied the performativity of gender to marriage rites celebrated by same-gender couples, unveiling dimensions of both continuity and disruption.[52]

Recognizing that the implications of queer theory for the study of liturgy go beyond analyzing gender and sexuality in the context of worship, the work of a few scholars who have occupied this generative intersection moves away from the apologetic task of gay and lesbian liberal theologies and the equality-seeking justice orientation of LGBTQIA2S+ liberation theologies to the disruptive and constructive potential of queer theory. In this way, "queering liturgy" is found to signify not only identifying and situating gay and lesbian experiences within Christian worship practices, but also further, showing the queerness of Christian worship practices. Queer theory yields insights for theologies of Christian worship which takes into consideration both the formation of identity and the disruption of identity that occurs in the context of worship. The revelatory potential of subversive performances that it proposes lends itself to the theological study of worship and offers a theoretical foundation for the analysis and interpretation of disruption in worship.

While feminist liturgical scholars have brought critical gender theory to the study of worship,[53] and a few liturgical scholars have written on the topic of disruption in worship,[54] the ideas of queer theory and theology were slower to enter the field of liturgical studies, though the past decade has witnessed more scholarly effort at "queering Christian worship."[55] Among the earliest was theologian Elizabeth Stuart, whose work has been both prolific and groundbreaking.

---

51. Rachel Mann, "'The Performance of Queerness': Trans Priesthood as a Gesture Towards a Queered Liturgical Assembly," in Bryan Cones and Stephen Burns, eds., *Liturgy with a Difference: Beyond Inclusion in the Liturgical Assembly* (London: SCM Press, 2019), 35–46, at 44. See also, Cones, "'Christ Is Present in *His* Church'? Gender, Presiding, and the Primary Symbol," *This Assembly*, 103–133.

52. See W. Scott Haldeman, "The Queer Body in the Wedding," in *Liturgy with a Difference*, 61–78.

53. See Teresa Berger, *Gender Differences and the Making of Liturgical History: Lifting a Veil on Liturgy's Past* (Farnham, UK: Ashgate, 2011).

54. See Gordon Lathrop, "*Ordo* and Coyote: Further Reflections on Order, Disorder, and Meaning in Christian Worship," *Worship* 80:194-212; and Dirk Lange, *Trauma Recalled: Liturgy, Disruption, and Theology* (Minneapolis, MN: Fortress Press, 2010).

55. See, for example, Cones, *This Assembly*, especially regarding a queer account of baptism (70–102), of the presider and eucharistic assembly (103–133), and of marriage (162–196). Other examples include essays by Mann and Haldeman in *Liturgy with a Difference* noted above, as well as Susannah Cornwall's "All Things to All: Requeering Stuart's Eucharistic Erasure of Priestly Sex" (47–60), and Frank Senn's "I Had to Do It for My Son: The Story of a Same-Sex Wedding" (79–98).

As early as 2000, Stuart published "A Queer Death: The Funeral of Diana, Princess of Wales,"[56] making use of queer theory as an analytical tool to highlight the ways in which the funeral of Princess Diana could be understood as disrupting the sense of death as natural by displaying the tragedy of death, which in turn allowed for more authentic expressions of hope and resurrection. She also noted the ways in which oppositional binaries (of sacred/secular, popular/ecclesiastical, Anglican/Catholic, for example) were blurred, creating a queer space that echoed Princess Diana's subversive life. For Stuart, what is at the heart of queer theory, namely the deconstruction of binary oppositions, the instabilities of identities, and the disruptive potential of subversive performances, is also at the heart of Christian worship. In this way, worship, and the Christian tradition in general, is fundamentally queer. Stuart continues to explore these themes, perhaps nowhere more compellingly than in her "Making No Sense: Liturgy as Queer Space"[57] in the collection *Dancing Theology in Fetish Boots* in honor of Marcella Althaus-Reid.

Stuart argues that what is queer about the Christian tradition is the ways in which practices such as Eucharist and baptism erase, subvert, or make nonsense out of the normative identities that shape human living. In baptism, Christians are formed as neither Jew nor Greek, slave or free, male or female, rendering all such binary oppositions and identities unstable and meaningless. In Eucharist, the Body of Christ is formed, with its tremendous diversity of sexes, sexualities, races, genders, classes, and so on, and even the gender of the priest is erased by the eschatological practice which anticipates and performs the end of all divisions. She contends:

> When I take part in the celebration of the eucharist I enter a space that makes a non-sense of the scripts to which I am expected to conform by the culture in which I live. My baptized self is re-membered in a dynamic of mutual donation and return, which reflects the pulse of the cosmos emanating from a divine from whom a new creation emerges that reflects the divine confounding of gender. I partake in a sacred space in which bodies are queered and made holy, flesh becomes one, and all are rendered indecent. And all of this is just a prefiguring of what is to come.[58]

For Stuart, queering Christian worship means understanding the ways in which binary oppositions are erased, and identities are revealed to be unstable through the disruptive practices of liturgies that echo the disruptive qualities of

---

56. Elizabeth Stuart, "A Queer Death: The Funeral of Diana, Princess of Wales," *Theology and Sexuality* 7 (2000): 77–91, https://doi.org/10.1177/135583580000701307.

57. Elizabeth Stuart, "Making No Sense: Liturgy as Queer Space," in Lisa Isherwood and Mark Jordan, eds., *Dancing Theology in Fetish Boots: Essays in Honour of Marcella Althaus-Reid* (London: SCM Press, 2010), 113–123.

58. Stuart, "Making No Sense," 123.

God's grace revealed in Jesus Christ in anticipation of the foretaste of the queer feast to come.

Nevertheless, Stuart's "erasure" has not gone unanswered, with both Susannah Cornwall[59] and Bryan Cones asserting that, rather than erase, queer lenses on Christian liturgy also refract and extend the performative diversity present in the gathered assembly. As Cones writes of baptism:

> This ritual action embodied by a "body" made up of so many embodied human differences, not least gender, cultural heritage, and sexual orientation, opens to Christian affirmation the almost limitless possibilities through which [the one baptized] may embody Christ, or rather Christa and/or Christx. . . . Seen in this light, the incorporation into a queer, hybrid body of Christ is not entrance into a fixed, static, or uniform body, in which "there is no Jew or Greek, slave or free, male or female." On the contrary, in this body male and female are but two possibilities in a fundamentally open-ended collection of bodies, each nevertheless equal in dignity and integrity.[60]

Futures: Mapping the Intersections—Queer and . . .

More recent developments in the intersection of Christian worship and queer theological reflection have drawn further attention to "intersections," that is, the ways minoritized identities related to gender, race and/or ethnicity, cultural heritage, ability, and sexual orientation, among others, overlap in ways that make the bearers of such difference both more vulnerable to oppression and locations of unique and productive theological reflection. At the annual meeting of the North American Academy of Liturgy in 2009, the Queering Liturgy seminar was born. Its initiation marked significant developments in the fields of both liturgical studies and LGBTQIA2S+ studies in religion, bringing "queer" into the study of Christian worship, and worship practices into the study of queer religion and theology. This collection of essays is the next step in the continued unfolding of the trajectories brought together by that seminar and mapped here. To this ever-evolving geography, we now turn.

---

59. Cornwall, "All Things to All?," 47–60.
60. Cones, *This Assembly*, 85.

CHAPTER TWO

ORDO AND COYOTE

Further Reflections on Order, Disorder, and Meaning in Christian Worship[1]

Gordon W. Lathrop

This essay was originally published in the journal Worship *(May 2006) and is reprinted here with permission.*

The concern of the liturgical movement, I would argue, is the well-being, well-meaning, and well-doing of communally enacted public religious symbols. *Well-being* because such symbols, capable of great cosmic, social, and personal resonance, can also be shrunk, dismissed, over-controlled, made ugly, and static; *well-meaning* because of the sense that we cannot speak of, encounter, or trust the mystery of God without such symbols, but even then, our speech and encounter remain fragile and capable of malformation; and *well-doing* because we think that these very symbols can do—or at least can propose—great good, but that they can also—even if made large and beautiful, participatory, and meaningful—do great ill. These matters—liturgical aesthetics, liturgical theology, and liturgical ethics, one could say—might rightly occupy anyone involved with the liturgical movement, engaging them in mutual conversation and mutual encouragement. You might not quite put it that way. But, in this paper, let me try to explore these assertions.

Not least because you are reading this journal, I hope you might also have some engagement with the remarkable convergences and enthusiasms of the ecumenical liturgical movement. Liturgical study, born of that movement, has now existed long enough to have seen the maturing of its field of study, the proliferation of its subdisciplines, the growth in its sophisticated uses of ancillary disciplines, and the beginnings of better attention to actual practices in diverse communities. Then, as time went on, liturgical study has also experienced the

---

1. This paper is a revised version of a lecture first given in response to the Berakah Award at the annual meeting of the North American Academy of Liturgy in San Diego, CA, on January 8, 2006, and then again at the Institute of Sacred Music in New Haven, CT, on January 30, 2006. The original version is published in the *Proceedings* of the NAAL. This version of this paper appeared in *Worship* 80:3 (May 2006), 194–212, and is used here with permission. The concluding postscript was written for this volume.

cycles of academic and institutional-religious acceptance and rejection, the loss of any easy sense of liturgical triumph, and sometimes even an abandoning of hope for any movement at all. The latter has been the case especially when those engaged in the study and the movement have not known what to do in facing postmodern fragmentation, the dispersal of what we once thought were common definitions, the ascendancy instead of a certain kind of Christian evangelical–fundamentalism as the established, even the *imperial* religion of this time, and the painful application in at least one major church of an official and secretive suppression of much remarkable and admired liturgical work, crafted over the years. In such a situation, it might seem that only the disinterested *study* of the phenomena of public worship, a study without any proposals or reforming intentions at all, might be the safest place for any fascination with the subject.

Still, I remain convinced that *reforming care* for communally enacted symbols, for their well-being, well-meaning, and well-doing continues to call us. I continue to think that such care for aesthetics, theology, and ethics continues to be a good reason for me—but also for you—to be involved with liturgy. I suppose I hope you see that, in a time of pluralism, fundamentalism, and trivialized religion, liturgical symbols are still an important public portal to transcendence and its meaning. One way to articulate such reforming care is this: I think that we have hoped to respond to the challenge made years ago by Susanne Langer: there is indeed a profound, present human need for public symbols capable of holding and orienting our lives in the environmental and social realities that surround us, capable of giving new grounds for hope and a social context for the healthy functioning of the individual mind.[2] Unlike Langer, however, we have believed that the classic enacted symbols of public worship are not yet exhausted. Far from it. Unshrunk, made larger, as Robert Hovda used to say, made accessible, inclusive, participatory, and self-critical, given away and not protected, they can indeed so hold us. And, I think, they can do so freely, openly, without becoming the material of an imposed and potentially tyrannical sacred canopy, a putative theory of everything.

Let me express this hope for liturgical symbols "holding and orienting us," as Langer says the matter more concretely and more personally. When I was an eight- or nine-year-old boy, my pastor asked me to be an acolyte. Vested in a cassock and surplice, I lit and extinguished the candles, received the offering plates, and held the small bowl of water at baptisms. I was the font. I also stood inside the communion rail and picked up the small glasses that were used in the communion practice of that struggling Lutheran mission. It was, of course, in those late 1940s, a practice of enacted symbols pretty far from what I might hope for today, but it was nonetheless a practice seriously engaging for this boy. After all, I could see the faces of the communicants, watch them closely in

---

2. Susanne K. Langer, *Philosophy in a New Key* (Cambridge, MA: Harvard, 1978), 288–289.

their joy and their sorrow and their numbness, even before I was a communicant myself. And right above the altar, around which they all knelt, was a crucifix, an image of the crucified Jesus, arms extended, as if that image were gathering the small assembly into safety and hope, or at least into company with other sufferers, outside of this circle. What I will especially never forget from that time is this: once—or was it more than once? was it several times?—I looked up to see my stepfather weeping; my stepfather, a good man carrying the burden of too many jobs in order to feed his family, a man of failed inventions worked in the garage at night, a man of a first wife too-early-dead, a man of long confinements in a mental hospital, a man of sweet gentleness, and sudden, for me, inexplicable rage, a man of both fierce arguments with my mother and of long, loving mutual care—my stepfather, weeping. There was nothing I could do. Merely pick up his glass. But I knew this already; there was room for his sorrow, room for him, in that enacted symbol. Moreover, there was room for me, for my family, for all the little half-circle at the rail, potentially perhaps even for anyone who would come. Now I might say it in these words: the enacted symbol—including, of course, not just that moment but all the words and songs and art and environment and theological proposals to which that moment was juxtaposed—the *enacted, communal symbol* told the truth, gave him and me grounds for hope, for thought in social context, for mutual forgiveness, and held and re-oriented us all toward seeing the world through mercy. The symbol had no immediate answers. But its very repeated formality held our inarticulate traumas, unresolved but also unhidden, in an open order, as if in the arms of God.

Sometimes I think that my whole vocation has been to continue to be that acolyte, simply working to make the font and the drinking vessel—and maybe the words and the circle—a little larger, a little more generous, more clearly welcoming. But there have been for me many, many other such encounters with the symbols that hold and orient. There was my first Easter Vigil, celebrated at a Benedictine priory in the California desert, where I watched fierce, truth-telling Dorothy Day, candle-illuminated across the *versus populum* altar, bringing her passion for social justice to that ancient world-proposing liturgy. The fire, the moonlit night, the stories of salvation, the dialogue mass—all had room for the as yet unrealized hope for justice. Or there were the monks of the community of Taizé singing the psalms of Joseph Gelineau in the old Cluniac Romanesque church, led by the since-murdered frère Roger Schutz and even then trying to welcome all who came, including me, including ultimately, and in another space also—to their own hurt—a woman from Romania with her own agonies: "be reconciled, all who enter here." Then there was a little, low communion table I once saw in a tin-sided, thatched-roofed, dirt-floored village church in Cameroon, a table that doubled as a stand for a blackboard used in literacy lessons. The table that had held the simple Eucharist also had room to hold the blackboard and the remains of those empowering words, standing there now in the dusty beams of light playing through the thatch. Or there was also the preacher whooping the praise of Jesus in his Philadelphia pulpit and bringing his congregation—and me—to shout and sing with him, the moment holding us in a taste of freedom, but only after we heard the preacher tell us: "no celebration without education." Or there was the time that Lawrence Hoffman got us two tickets to Yom Kippur liturgy at Central Synagogue, so that when the congregation heard Max Bruch's astonishing, cello-played *Kol Nidrei*, it held also us as mercifully, paradoxically, even scandalously free from all those many, many deadly, self-imposed obligations we cannot possibly meet. Or there has been the little congregation to which I currently belong, holding us in both honesty and hope when it calls out the names of its dead on All Saints Sunday and sings, hauntingly, "All of us go down to the dust, yet even at the grave we make our song: Alleluia."

There have been many other such occasions and there have been other places of symbolic integrity and depth. Such moments and places have been for me astonishing gifts, symbols that hold and orient a community in the real world. They were never perfect, never complete. But they were a reason—or illustrations of the reasons—to go on with work for the well-being of symbols.

I hope that you will have your own lists. And I hope that some of the events and places on your list may be why you are involved in liturgy at all. The point, however, ought not be that we seek to get other people to replicate our own personal experiences. I only mean to ask you to consider the existential sources and the reasons for your passion for liturgical study. We, too, have been held into meaning and hope.

For some of us, those existential reasons may best be told in fiction. John Steinbeck's astonishing novel *The Grapes of Wrath* includes an image of westward traveling migrant families, refugees from the American dust-bowl and the American industrialization of farming in the 1930s, making camp each night and so making a world:

> Thus it might be that one family camped near a spring, and another camped for the spring and for company, and a third because two families had pioneered the place and found it good. And when the sun went down perhaps twenty families and twenty cars were there. In the evening a strange thing happened: the twenty families became one family, the children were the children of all. The loss of home became one loss, and the golden time in the West was one dream. And it might be that a sick child threw despair into the hearts of twenty families, of a hundred people; that a birth there in a tent kept a hundred people quiet and awestruck through the night and filled a hundred people with birth-joy in the morning. A family which the night before had been lost and fearful might search its goods to find a present for a new baby. In the evening, sitting about the fires, the twenty were one. They grew to be units of the camps, units of the evenings and the nights. A guitar unwrapped from a blanket and tuned—and the songs, which were all of the people, were

sung in the nights. Men sang the words, and women hummed the tunes. Every night a world created, complete with furniture—friends made and enemies established; a world complete with braggarts and with cowards, with quiet men, with humble men, with kindly men. Every night relationships that make a world, established; and every morning the world torn down like a circus. At first the families were timid in the building and tumbling worlds, but gradually the technique of building worlds became their technique. . . . The families learned what rights must be observed—the right of privacy in the tent; the right to keep the past . . . hidden in the heart; the right to talk and to listen; the right to refuse help or to accept, to offer help or to decline it; the right of the son to court and the daughter to be courted; the right of the hungry to be fed; the right of the pregnant and the sick to transcend all other rights. And the families learned, although no one told them, what rights are monstrous and must be destroyed: the right to intrude upon privacy, the right to be noisy while the camp slept, the right of seduction or rape, the right of adultery and theft and murder. These rights were crushed, because the little worlds could not exist for even a night with such rights alive.[3]

For Steinbeck, the spring, the fires, the guitar, the songs, the birth-gift were tools of the communal world-making technique, of course. They were symbols of the temporary but all-important, desperately needed, all-holding *world*, the grounds on which the loss and the dream could be indirectly but openly shared, on which the rights could be discovered. I have sometimes imagined that the concern of the liturgical movement has been a care for something like the spring, the fires, the guitar, and the songs amid the cars and tents in the temporary camps of our times. We do not make up the spring. We do not own all the fires. We may not even bring the guitar. But, with others of the campers, we can care about the well-being of these symbols and about what they do, especially in a time when shared fires and common song are all too rare.

Less widely known is the remarkable British film, *A Month in the Country*, based on the novel of the same name by J. L. Carr. The film tells of a seriously battle-traumatized World War I veteran, Tom Birkin, who finds symbols—symbols to hold his unspeakable sorrow and to remake his world—in a medieval mural of the last judgment, a Yorkshire village church painting that he is uncovering and restoring. He himself intimately knows the hell he is discovering, the hell with its yawning, soul-devouring mouth, and he begins to recognize, angrily at first, the one in the middle who comes "with wundes red to judge the living and the dead." He is perhaps also slowly beginning to know that those wounds are the source of the life in the other half of the mural, indeed that this judge in the middle is seated upon the rainbow. These symbols become especially available to him as his encounter

---

3. John Steinbeck, *The Grapes of Wrath* (New York: Viking Bantam, 1946), 172.

with the slowly uncovered painting is also combined with local Methodist hospitality, with current stories of pain not his own, and with the loyal friendship of an also-traumatized gay man (*Moon*, he is called) who nonetheless remains unincluded anywhere, except perhaps in awkward friendship with Birkin. Sometimes I have thought that my whole vocation must be to try to be like that painting-restorer: hoping to uncover old, classic symbols that have long been white-washed but that can still hold us, can still heal us, can still do at least part of the job amid our current stories of pain and exclusion.

Perhaps you too have thought of some metaphoric way to imagine your liturgical work, some story or image to hold you meaningfully in a thing you cannot quite say. I hope so.

Still, how, exactly, do symbols "hold and orient?" And how does such holding avoid becoming an imposed, exclusionary order? And what enacted, ritual symbols shall these be? What shall be our mural, our spring and fires and songs? These are questions that matter urgently to our common study now, if we would wish to attend to the aesthetics, theology, and ethics of the symbols.

I have elsewhere tried to propose that in many Christian assemblies certain central symbols do indeed pull ourselves and our communal hopes into their interactions. I have argued that these symbols, arising from the center of the tradition—this bath and table, prayer and word, to use one summary list—come into meaning especially as they are juxtaposed to each other in mutually interpretive and mutually critical ways, as they become again and again the center of open assemblies, and as they then propose to us ways of re-reading our understandings of the world. In order to see these central symbols as set next to each other and as communally enacted, it became useful for me to call the classic patterns of their juxtapositions by the old Latin word *ordo*. Actually, the Orthodox scholar Alexander Schmemann made that word available to us again when he proposed, as the solution to his "problem of the *ordo*," the meaning and practice that he believed early occurred when the Christian resurrection meal of the eighth day was set next to the religious observances of the week, one thing against the other.[4] Whether or not one would today easily agree with Schmemann's constructions of Jewish and Christian liturgical history, his use of the idea of *ordo*, from the outset, was interestingly filled with the critical and reinterpretive tensions of *one thing against another*, perhaps even *one thing against another across a silence*, as John Ciardi might say.[5]

I have thought that a certain space is created when one thing is held in tension with another and perhaps another—word with sign and silence, or bath with prayer with table, or Sunday meeting with the flow of the week, or thanksgiving with lament, or people with pastor with stranger, or strong center with open door, or here with not-here—matters and tensions with which classic liturgy is filled. I have thought that this space can enable our enacted symbols to hold us,

---

4. Alexander Schmemann *Introduction to Liturgical Theology* (Leighton Buzzard: Faith, 1966), 47.
5. John Ciardi *How Does a Poem Mean?* (Boston: Houghton Miflin, 1959), 995.

our losses, and our dreams, and, from that place of holding, to propose to us both re-readings of the world and consequent actions for justice. I have thought that certain classic things, received from the tradition as if from God, with ongoing cosmic, social, and oneiric resonances—as Paul Ricoeur would say[6]—are the most likely candidates to create this space. And I have thought that this space will be the clearer, the more welcoming, and paradoxically, the less constraining, if each of those contrasting things is made larger, more generous, more beautiful, more true, more clearly in tension with the others. It is as if the space at the table of the Roublev icon of the holy Trinity, the welcoming space between the flowing yet contrasting three, or the space between the facing cherubim on the ark cover as Exodus pictures it, the mercy seat—or, let us say, the space between the saved and the damned on the judgment mural, or the space amid the fires in the temporary migrants-camp beside the spring—*is the very space* we find between the burning candles surrounding the holy table or surrounding the ambo or the bema, or *is the very space* between us as we face each other, singing. And it is as if this space were a space capable of holding, for a moment, an unconstrained event that is of immense significance for everything.

The *ordo*, then, is the scheduling of that space as a temporary event, here in our camp for the night. The *ordo* is a marking of time that makes it possible for us to begin to experience in time a thing that is otherwise incomprehensible, inaccessible. More simply, the *ordo* is the list of the matters that are set side-by-side, in tension with each other, according to the continually rediscovered tradition of our community. The *ordo* is the list of our community's central symbols, as they are scheduled, set in action, enacted. The *ordo* is what we hope to do with the symbols as we care about their well-being, well-meaning, well-doing. In that sense, the *ordo* is indeed an "order"—the "order of service," we say. And, I have argued, this order is capable of proposing order to our chaos.

Ah, order. Now we need to be careful. "Whose order?" we may ask. And who or what gets left out? Even if we argue that the "order" of the *ordo* is itself marked by critical tensions, by the opposite of a consequent system, by Heraclitean paradoxes, by immensely subtle layering, it is still an order, and it can tempt us to forget its origins in one thing against another. We can deal with *ordo* as if it were a consequent, harmonious whole, meaning one single thing, and in need of being enforced. Liturgists, alas, have sometimes been noted as enforcers. Mark C. Taylor was surely right when he wrote, on the occasion of the death of Jacques Derrida:

> . . . every structure—be it literary, psychological, social, economic, political or religious—that organizes our experience is constituted and maintained through acts of exclusion. In the process of creating something, something else inevitably gets left out. These exclusive structures can become repressive—and that repression comes with consequences.[7]

---

6. Paul Ricoeur *Symbolism of Evil* (Boston: Beacon, 1969), 10–14.

7. Mark C. Taylor, *New York Times,* October 14, 2004, A29.

In honor of Derrida, Taylor went on to appeal, among other things, for religious practice aware of limits and contradictions, open to the unsettling and revision of every construction—open to the return of the repressed, we might say—and tempered by doubt. Can this appeal be addressed to the construction called the *ordo*?

Here is another way to put the question. I know a young playwright, a playwright who had a remarkable one-act in last year's Philadelphia Fringe Festival, who wrote to me recently, in a letter:

> A few weeks ago, I forget the context, I started thinking [again] about the role of the Trickster in communal belief systems and mythologies. Your reference . . . to Coyote, the unbalancer, restarted my thought process. I am curious to know from . . . you what you think about my perception that this element (the Trickster) has somehow been run over roughshod by the Christian church. I, of course, can easily see some element of the Trickster in Jesus, in many of the parables, for instance, or in the role of unbalance. . . . But [that] seems to me half of the essence of the Trickster. . . . I do not wish for humor above all, though perhaps I do feel that this is an element more under-appreciated than not in Christian practice. More precisely . . . I would hope that the Trickster is neither completely magnanimous, nor unduly pernicious. In essence, I long for something more capricious—some thing or person who sometimes acts for our enlightenment and sometimes for our downfall. Somewhere along the line . . . I feel that western Christianity, perhaps western theology, separated the unity of our cosmology by dividing these responsibilities among two sets of characters. Put simply, Jesus is, as popularly presented at least, too nice, too earnest perhaps, too loving, dare I say. At the same time, Lucifer . . . is too shady altogether. Please understand that I know that these are great simplifications, but simplifications which are omnipresent in our culture, at the least, as well as in many manifestations of Christianity. Basically, I am curious why, besides the obvious assistance it gave and gives to the church in rules, judgment, etc., what should to me be represented in one figure is split so irreparably into two. In my humble opinion . . . a church would perform more ably in the world were this division overcome. At the very least, I personally would be . . . able to make stronger connections to Christ as the Trickster. . . .[8]

At the time, fascinated by the query, I haltingly wrote back a beginning attempt at a response. I talked about the Lutheran conception of the "masks of God," I think—and about the so-called "left and right hands" of God, about "law and

---

8. J. Arthur Blyth, in a personal communication, February 11, 2004.

gospel." I talked more about the parables, or at least the earliest parables, the ones most likely attributable to Jesus. And I hope I argued that healthy Christian liturgy, in its tensions, ought never be taken to mean a single, ideological, nice, un-dangerous thing. But the question has stuck with me, has refused to go away. For one thing, I have found myself wishing to God that more preachers would realize that people like this playwright are—at least sometimes—trying to be in their congregations. But for another thing, for me Coyote has kept yipping, even howling, at the edge of the *ordo*.

Coyote, of course, is one of the great trickster figures of North American mythology, showing up to do his unbalancing work in many otherwise quite diverse cultures of the western first peoples of this continent. In other places, the trickster has many other names: *Raven* or *Glooskap*, for example, in other parts of North America; *Anansi* in some parts of Africa; *Loki* among the Norse of the Eddas. But Coyote continues to fascinate me, not least, I suppose, because he has

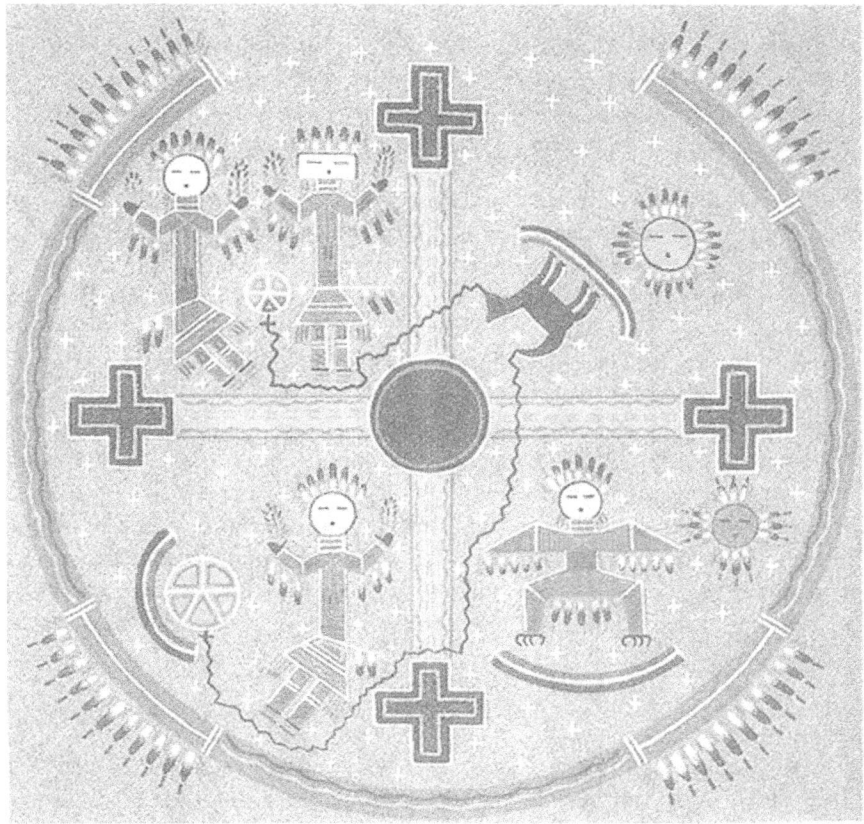

"Coyote Steals Fire: Navajo Sandpainting," personal collection of the author.

a ritual role. The Navajo have had a healing ceremonial actually called "Coyoteway."[9] And Coyote's stealing of fire, to the benefit of First Man and First Woman, makes up one of the important ritual sandpaintings of traditional singers.

Interestingly, Coyote can sometimes be merely a fool. In the Zuñi tales,[10] Coyote is clever, but he does not dance well, cannot sing, meddles stupidly with matters that do not concern him, and finally is simply foolish and funny, easily tricked himself and easily dismissed. I have wondered if the strong relationship between ritual and order among the Zuñi has excluded a more seriously important Coyote, or, more likely, if the significant role of the clown in Zuñi ritual has made Coyote less important. But among the Navajo, Coyote plays an important part in the very creation of the world. Coyote is sometimes a minor nuisance, sometimes a joker, often a major danger. But this same Coyote introduces the people to the importance of death as making place for life, the importance of difference of opinion as making place for thinking. Coyote interprets the diverse times of the day, the diverse colors of the world and their contrasts. Indeed, as John Farella says:

> there is beauty and ugliness in this and in all things, and a side that is beautiful and a side that is ugly in all beings. Entities are never one-sided, and entitivity is defined essentially by that two-sidedness that is completeness. Coyote alone is wise enough to see and express this.[11]

But one should be careful here. Traditional Navajo are no dualists, as if there were an absolute or universal source for moral ambiguity. On the contrary, Coyote is not equal to Changing Woman, nor to Mother Earth and Father Sky, nor—in the sand painting of the stealing of fire—to Black God, the Sun and its Guardian Eagle, the Moon, First Man and First Woman. It is simply that Coyote does indeed walk a crooked line, dribbling embers, across the perfectly proportioned, world-representing quadrants of the sand painting, guilefully stealing fire from the *Yé'ii*, but thus also delivering it to the people. Without that crooked line, without that stolen fire, the four quadrants would not so much be the world. They would be more like an intolerable prison. Coyote is immensely important to "walking in beauty," as both ethics and ritual observance may be called by the traditional Navajo, perhaps precisely because Coyote can symbolize the importance of what may be called the "ceremonial break" in Navajo adaptive practice[12] as well as the importance of "difference" in Navajo worldview and Navajo ethics.

---

9. Karl W. Luckert, *Coyoteway: a Navajo Holyway Healing Ceremonial* (Tucson: University of Arizona Press, 1979).

10. See Frank Hamilton Cushing, *Zuñi Folk Tales* (Tucson: University of Arizona, 1901).

11. John R. Farella, *The Main Stalk: A Synthesis of Navajo Philosophy* (Tucson: University of Arizona, 1984), 62.

12. Farella, *The Main Stalk*, 196.

It is *this* Coyote—this crooked line, this ceremonial break—I find howling near the *ordo*. In saying that, I know that I am neither asking a Navajo question nor reflecting very profoundly on Navajo religion. But there is such wisdom in this image that, used respectfully, I hope it may help us all to think about liturgical symbols. So, I find Coyote howling near the *ordo*.

What do I mean? Well, there is that letter I received. First, there is my correspondent's acknowledgment, "I know that these are great simplifications, but simplifications which are omnipresent in our culture, at the least, as well as in many manifestations of Christianity." Does the *ordo* belong to these simplifications? More, there is that phrase, "I am curious why, besides the obvious assistance it gave and gives to the church in rules, judgment, etc. . . ." *Besides!* Are not such "rules, judgments, etc." enough to raise the question? If the "rules, judgments, etc.," are something like Steinbeck's "rights," communally arising in the campground, among the fires, that may be one thing. But if they are a universally asserted, universally imposed code, if they are the unbroken quadrants, or if they are simply the *status quo*, that is another. Which does the *ordo* support? I do not mean to say that I know. I simply mean to say that I hope to hear the question and the search of this young playwright and to hear it precisely as a *liturgist*, as one who cares for the well-being, well-meaning, well-doing of public, communally enacted symbols.

St. Gregory's Mass," Medieval paintings by Albertus Pictor. Härkeberga kyrka/church. Diocese of Uppsala, Enköping, Sweden. Photograph by Xauxa Håkan Svensson. (Creative Commons)

Let me say this more clearly with another image. In the Härkeberga parish church in central Sweden there is preserved one of the most complete and most astonishing interior mural painting programs of all of late-medieval Christianity. The painter was the famous Albertus Pictor, Albert the Painter, whose fifteenth-century workshop in Stockholm was responsible for a whole series of painted churches in Sweden and probably also in what is now southern Finland. The program in the nave and chancel was largely drawn from the typological pairs of the *Biblia Pauperum*, with stunning results. But the narthex is another matter. There in the "weapon-house," as it is called in Swedish—the place to leave your sword or club when you come to church—there are beasts and witches and warlocks, the devil at work in tempting a woman, and a man falling off the wheel of life. And, on one side, at the top of the eastern vault, there is a beautiful painted image of St. Gregory's mass. The great bishop of Rome, so associated with the western Christian liturgy, is kneeling before the chalice on the altar, surrounded by candle-holding servers, and beholding behind the chalice the figure of the wounded Christ appearing to him and holding the instruments with which he was beaten. Scholars have studied this image as a key both to details of fifteenth century liturgical practice and to fifteenth century accounts of visions associated with the elements of the Eucharist. Above the image of the mass, on two side vaults, are images of Adam and Eve, each still holding the apple, just after the fall, as if the mass is the answer to the fall, the chalice to the apple. But—and here is the point—between Adam and Eve and just above the altar and the Christ of Gregory's mass, the central junction of the ribs of the vaulting has become the location of a large, ugly, Punch-like head, looking down at the mass and pulling open its mouth and sticking out its tongue. Perpetually, as the visitor to the Härkeberga church comes to mass, there on the margins of the celebration in the church is that face. Some people may think that it is just the humor of the artist, set free a little in the looser possibilities of the narthex. Others may think that, in the misogynist or antisemitic environment of the late middle ages, it is a stylized witch or a caricatured Jew, forever mocking the mass. I think it is Coyote, howling. Not literally Coyote, of course, but I think the artist knew that the ordered program of this remarkable church needed instances of ceremonial breaking, instances of the ritual order unable to contain the whole world of experience, lest it become false order and prison. Furthermore, I think that evidences of this artistic wisdom can be found in yet other painted churches of the time.

If that is true, then the question remains, "Where is Coyote for us?"

I think that this question is indeed for all of us. Perhaps the answer is simple. You have encountered Coyote when, in your most beautiful liturgical moment, your voice broke, you lost your place, the wrong sermon really *was* before you on the ambo, as you feared. Or your community has encountered Coyote when that homeless man who is frequently on the street outside of the building, actually came inside, sort-of joining in the singing, speaking an odd petition in the prayers, presenting himself for communion, none of it in the way you all ordinarily do these things. A wonderful story is told of an officiant in the San Francisco Episcopal cathedral.

According to the tale, once, when a woman came into the chancel during the Magnificat of evening prayer and proceeded to undress while she danced to the music of the chant—perhaps indeed enacting an idea quite appropriate to the song—this liturgist had the presence of mind gently to clothe her in his cope as she finished. One may not exactly welcome Coyote, but that presider was at least at ease with the howl. Perhaps genuinely attending to the significant importance of these ceremonial breaks, these failures, these crooked lines or even this mocking face, is enough.

But then, I think Coyote was already there, in fact, in several of the images I have used for liturgy so far in this paper, and not only in the head above Gregory's mass. My stepfather's weeping at the communion rail was unanswered. The mouth of hell in the mural was unclosed, and for all of Birkin's slow resolutions, Moon was unreceived, still falling. Those undisclosed pasts of Steinbeck's migrants cast large shadows on the shared fires. And Steinbeck's reader knows—dreads—that the western dreams of golden times, shared by the campers and expressed in their songs, are sure to be cruelly disappointed. These serious matters hold the ritual order open to a thing beyond its possibilities. Coyote stalks crookedly, dangerously across the quadrants and is by no means always funny. Ritual may be only a pretense at order, perhaps even a false order, without those crooked lines. Of course, in good ritual, the quadrants must be strikingly beautiful. But they must also be broken.

Indeed, I wonder if Coyote does not helpfully yip—even howl—at the edge of our symbolic practice in some of the phenomena of postmodernism: the decay of easy universals and shared definitions, the distrust in modern theories of progress, the end of the sacred canopy and the meta-narrative. I certainly think that Coyote howls nearby when we turn our ritual enacting to support only the well-being of the *human* community—perhaps even just *this* ritual community, just *us*, or perhaps only our interests or our armies—forgetting the surrounding and aching world and all the nonhuman creatures. How do our enacted public religious symbols also welcome or at least acknowledge Coyote? I think this question is for all of us, Christian and Jew, Protestant and Catholic, traditionalist, revivalist, restorationist or emerging ritualist, as we care about the well-being, well-meaning and well-doing of liturgical symbols.

In this paper, I have mostly wanted simply to put the ideas of *ordo* and Coyote side by side, believing that this further juxtaposition might be fruitful. I have not wanted to answer the question. I have wanted to say that I hope to keep thinking about it.

But my correspondent wonders more. He himself is no dualist, no polytheist. He wonders if *Jesus Christ* might be seen as the Trickster. I am a Christian—indeed, a Lutheran Christian, a pastor committed to the idea of word and sacraments at the heart of a participating community as the most helpful idea of church, and a self-confessed continuing participant in the liturgical movement who still believes in that movement and the astonishing beauty and layered subtlety of its central symbols. So I should dare to say yet a little more, by way of responding to the question of Coyote, a question I have said is put to us all. You will understand that what I write now, I write only as my response today and I write as a Christian.

What can most hold the liturgy of a *Christian* community open to a reality larger than it can contain, proposing a greater order than it can enact, is not so much Coyote on the porch nor even Coyote wandering across the ritual practice—as interesting and as helpful as those images may be—but Jesus Christ at the center of the meeting and the Spirit in the body of the people. The enacted doctrine of the Trinity—that is what I think Christian liturgy ought to be—already has something of Coyote about it. At best, the center of a Christian meeting can be continually eccentric, the one at the center of the meeting, encountered in word and sacrament, being the very one who identifies with the wretched, the disordered, the war-torn, the unincluded and the poor, who shares all still-hidden trauma, outside of this meeting, and whose story entails this diverse, wounded earth as holy ground. Furthermore, at best, the Spirit enlivening the meeting can be the very Spirit poured out from the cross, en-spiriting an unlikely people and still blowing where it will in the world. Here is a focused, ordered meeting, with disorder and away-from-here at its heart. Here is a ritual pattern which includes cross, Spirit and reference to those left out as part of its essential center.

In Gregory's mass, more astonishing yet than the grimacing Punch-head sticking out its tongue, more dangerous to some easy order of the mass, is the appearance of the tortured Christ, at least if we conceive of that appearance as a surprise to the liturgists and not somehow under their control. The one who sits upon the rainbow in Birkin's judgment mural, indeed the one who *judges*, is also a nearly naked wretch, one who may be just as well a candidate for that gaping mouth. That one—that Jesus—goes away with Moon, wherever he goes. Only so, does the surprise and grace of the story of Matthew 25, the story on which the judgment image was based, reach us. In other paintings of the time, other church-mural programs from the school of Albertus Pictor, it is this very naked wretch, the crucified-risen one, who is now pulling folks out of the mouth of hell. And right above the altar, where I picked up the glasses, where I watched my stepfather weep, was a crucifix, arms extended, as if that image were gathering the small assembly into safety and hope, or at least into company with other sufferers, outside of this half circle.

When the Spirit makes use of the central matters of Christian liturgy, its work will not be unlike the wisdom of Coyote. I have hoped to propose[13] that the *ordo* itself is made up of local, ordinary matters of daily life—matters often

---

13. Most recently in "Bath, Word, Prayer, Table: Reflections on Doing the Liturgical *Ordo* in a Postmodern Time," in eds. Dirk G. Lange and Dwight W. Vogel, *Ordo: Bath, Word, Prayer, Table* (Akron: OSL, 2005), 221–223.

used by us to organize our ordinary, local worlds—now used in critical and re-orienting association with Jesus: with his reversals of religious meaning and his attack on religious boundaries, with his death and the communal practice of his resurrection, and with the life-giving, uncontained Spirit poured out in the world from these events. So water flows locally, in many ways organizing our boundaried worlds. But in the four gospels of that resurrection practice, water is a sign of the reign of God now present in the world, all water, even wounded water, now holy, transcending boundaries. So, local words tell local stories with conventional endings. But in the four gospels, traditional stories are given surprising, mercy-filled endings. So, in need, prayers arise from practically every set of local lips, to anything that might be regarded as being able to help. But in the four gospels, the community is invited to pray for *others* beyond this ordered circle, to pray for the earth itself, and to pray in Jesus' eccentric name. So, communal meals are a universally local phenomenon, in which our small group assures itself of its own survival and passes on its own culture. But in the four gospels and the letters of Paul, commensality with Jesus is combined with an open door to the outsider and the sending of food to the poor. A liturgy that seeks to enable the inviting and beautiful centrality of bath, word, prayers and table, should also seek to go the way of the four gospels, the way of the Spirit, and seek to let its order constantly be broken open to matters that are far beyond its ordering ability. Such a liturgy means to reorient local practice and local perceptions of world so as to invite us again and again to walk in this world in the way of faith, not control. Indeed, such a liturgy invites us to the active criticism of both the religion and the politics of control.

I have hoped that something like this was what I meant when I wrote about *ordo*. If I did not, then I hereby wish to adopt the pose of the head above Gregory's mass, lips pulled apart, tongue out.

But I am not yet done with my work, I hope. No, dear reader of *Worship*, *we* are not done—with reform, with care for the well-being of publicly enacted symbols, with liturgical aesthetics, liturgical theology or liturgical ethics. For one thing, I want to keep thinking about *ordo* and Coyote. The point is not to turn the order of liturgy into a mess, but, as Catherine Keller says, in her remarkable chaos theology,[14] to suggest a better order. I hope you might think with me.

Postscript for *Queering Christian Worship*

The article you have just read proposes a number of images for the ways in which ritual symbols may hold and orient us in the real world, drawing from my own experiences but also using a traditional Navajo sand painting, a late medieval narthex fresco, the trenchant questions of a young playwright, and two pieces of

---

14. Catherine Keller, *Face of the Deep* (London and New York: Routledge, 2003), 23.

narrative fiction. One of those narratives is J. L. Carr's remarkable novel, *A Month in the Country*, and perhaps even the more remarkable film by the same name, based on the novel. Note that in the novel and its film, Moon is a brilliant archeologist and World War I veteran who is also queer. He is a man marked by deep hurt, worked in him by the bloody horror of the trenches, but also by the fact that in the middle of the war he had been imprisoned for his homosexuality, in spite of his immense personal bravery, his well-earned *Military Cross*. As one unsympathetic officer puts it, viciously describing an act of love, Moon was caught "buggering his batman."

In the Yorkshire village where the story plays out, after the war and after the military prison-term, Moon is supposed to be looking for the medieval burial site of someone who was refused a place in the consecrated church graveyard. He is also uncovering the ruins of a Saxon basilica. He finds them both, while the principal protagonist of the story, Birkin, is simultaneously uncovering a medieval painting of the Judgment in the nearby church.

Both men find some healing in their work—especially Birkin, as my article describes. Moon finally goes away, disappears, unincluded in anybody's world. Still, Moon has found the excluded body and he has discovered, by the presence of a crescent moon marking this body, that the man was probably a Muslim, rejected in medieval England. Meanwhile, Birkin's discoveries suggest that this Muslim man was actually the very painter of the Judgment who died just before its completion. While Moon finds no place for his own woundedness in the central image of the painting, he is profoundly identified with the painter himself. Indeed, it is he who first characterizes the figure of Christ as the one "who shall com with woundes red" and first sees the parallel between the scene of the Judgment and the battlefields the two veterans have so recently left. The rejected and dead painter, Moon himself, and Jesus Christ all provide queer counter-signs, "ceremonial breaks," "difference," to the status quo of the world of the village.

You will see that I wrote, "Jesus . . . goes away with Moon, wherever he goes." I still think that is true.

Just as the Anglican Church—or, at least its rector—would rather not have the distracting painting in the midst of the stately ecclesial rituals, so Moon is not welcome there. He is also not welcome at the Sunday School picnic of the Methodist chapel. Draw a line to exclude, as a professor friend of mine used to say, and Jesus Christ is always on the other side of that line. If ritual order proposes a closed world, as if it contained all of reality within its coded enactments, that order is in need of Coyote—or of a painting of the Judgment.

This book is about queerness in Christian liturgy. In pursuing that question, as I wrote in the article, I think we need to attend to Christ himself as the "trickster" and to the untamable Spirit that blows where it will from the proclamation of Christ's death and resurrection in word and sacrament in assembly.

I first delivered this article as a lecture in 2006 in response to the Berakah award of the North American Academy of Liturgy. I am honored to have it included here, 17 years later, now in dialogue with many other ways to think about ritual holding and orienting. I hope it joins those other ways in warning against such ritual "holding" when it becomes false order, in celebrating those occasions when ritual queerness becomes one way of orienting us to a world larger than our symbols can actually contain, and in working toward our ritual order always welcoming difference.

But, one way or another, Jesus goes with Moon. Moreover, where Jesus is, Moon also belongs.

Gordon Lathrop
February 2023

CHAPTER THREE

QUEER WORSHIP[1]

Siobhan Garrigan

This essay was originally printed in the journal Theology and Sexuality *(2009); some references refer to a period before civil or religious same-gender marriage was legal in many contexts.*

Introduction

The past twenty years have witnessed a great deal of discussion about the place of lesbian, gay, bisexual, and transgendered (LGBT) people in the church, particularly through two sets of debates: one on whether and under what circumstances LGBT people should be ordained and another on whether and under what circumstances LGBT people should have their marital unions blessed. Substantially different positions are held within as well as across denominations, and the process of resolving these issues will likely take many years. In the meantime, LGBT Christians, like all Christians, need to go to church on Sunday and have the key events of their lives tie into the life of the community of faith. In response to this situation, an increasing number of congregations have let it be known, explicitly or implicitly, that they are "open and affirming" to LGBT people even as their denominational bodies wait for consensus before making such a statement.[2] Some congregations put a sign at the door, hang a flag on the outside of the church building, or put a note at the top of every bulletin that announces the fact that LGBT people are welcome there. Others use these same media to indicate that they subscribe to their denomination's pro-LGBT lobby. And yet others, particularly among Roman Catholic Churches, communicate by more subtle, but nonetheless unambiguous, means that LGBT people are invited to their congregation, for example, a sign posted on the front wall of a Roman Catholic Church in New York City reads: "*ALL* are welcome, *ALL* in this Village."

---

1. This essay originally appeared in the journal *Theology and Sexuality* 15 (2009): 211–230, and is reprinted here with permission.

2. This essay considers the mainstream Christian denominations in America, but not the Metropolitan Community Church, which was founded specifically to minister to lesbian and gay people. While some individual bishops/congregations will ordain LGBT people and some individual pastors will bless same-sex unions, so far The United Church of Christ is the only denomination to have (since 2005) polity supporting "inclusive marriage" and, with the Disciples of Christ, polity affirming equal access to ordained ministry for sexually active LGBT people.

The past 20 years have also witnessed the creation and dissemination of various liturgical materials responsive to the needs of LGBT people. Some can be found via the websites of advocacy groups for LGBT people within denominations,[3] and others have been published as resources for an ecumenical readership.[4] A common focus among these publications has been on developing worship services capable of hosting key events in LGBT people's lives, events which are crucial to a person's life and faith but for which there were no existing rites in public worship. Thus, there has emerged a wide range of materials for what ritual scholars might identify as "rites of passage"; coming-out services, trans-naming ceremonies, house blessings, and, by far the one that has been given most attention, weddings, or, as some prefer to call them, blessings of same-sex unions.

Coming-out, renaming, and house-blessing ceremonies were found to be needed by people in many different places as a way of living into their identities, and, moreover, living into those identities alongside the pain of ecclesial rejection at either the congregational or institutional level, or both.[5] While such rites specifically for LGBT people are no doubt "new" in the canon of the church's liturgical practices,[6] a liturgical detective can usually trace a cornucopia of elements from traditional rites implicit within their forms and language, Christian baptism and confirmation especially. And rites for the blessing of same-sex unions rarely even require much detective work, because they usually

---

3. These are Association of Welcoming and Affirming Baptists (American Baptist Churches and the Alliance of Baptists); Dignity (Roman Catholic Church); Gay and Lesbian Acceptance (Community of Christ); More Light Presbyterians (Presbyterian Church USA); Open and Affirming Ministry (Christian Church (Disciples of Christ); Open and Affirming Program (United Church of Christ); Reconciling in Christ (Evangelical Lutheran Church in America); Reconciling Ministries Network (United Methodist Church); Room for All (Reformed Church in America); Supportive Congregation Network of the Brethren Mennonite Council for LGBT Interests (Brethren Mennonite).

4. See Cherry Kittredge and Sherwood Zalmon, *Equal Rites: Lesbian and Gay Worship, Ceremonies, and Celebrations* (Louisville KY: Westminster John Knox, 1995); Paul V. Marshall, *Same-Sex Unions: Stories and Rites* (New York: Church Publishing, 2004); Elizabeth Stuart, ed., *Daring to Speak Love's Name: A Gay and Lesbian Prayer Book* (London: Hamish Hamilton, 1992); plus resources available from the Lesbian Gay Christian Movement (lgcm.org.uk) and WATER (https://www.waterwomensalliance.org/mary-e-hunt/).

5. There are strong and varied theologies as well as pastoral concerns at play in each of these ceremonies for which there is no space to explore here: briefly, coming out services create a public space which enables the individual to come out to themselves and their community (with the theological understanding that God created this person and loves this person and calls the community to support their flourishing). Re-naming services allow a trans-gendered person to claim a new name, a name that allows them to live fully in their realized identity and to be recognized (we are all called to new life in God, and we are all being always transformed by God). House blessings developed mostly in Jewish lesbian and gay households and were co-opted by same-sex Christian couples as a way of having their relationship—and its material forms—blessed by God in sight of friends and family (some argue this substituted for marriage, some that it was a unique blessing in its own right).

6. "Queer liturgies in general and same-sex weddings most particularly should be regarded as serious points of liturgical innovation. The innovation raises fresh questions about what liturgies are, how they mean, and what social reforms they can produce." Mark D. Jordan, *Blessing Same-Sex Unions: The Perils of Queer Romance and the Confusions of Christian Marriage* (Chicago: University of Chicago Press, 2005), 152.

explicitly mimic the standard marriage rites of Jewish and Christian traditions in form and symbolic structure, if not in words.[7]

Where "queer worship" is discussed, it is often the issues attending to this brief history that are at stake: how the church responds to the unique rites of passage in an LGBT person's life, if at all? How should the church be responsive to the great variety of experience in LGBT people's lives? (i.e., some people need or want coming-out services, renaming services, house blessings and marital unions, but others do not.) Are queer people's lives so very different from other people's lives that they need special rites for key events? Are the forms of services for Christian marriage truly only appropriate for heterosexual unions or do they work for people of all genders? How far can you change an ecclesial rite and still have it count as an ecclesial rite? Who performs these rites, and if not an ordained minister, then by what authority are they performed? Who witnesses these rites, and if not the whole assembly, then how are these rites related to wider church life?

In my judgment, such rites are needed, they should be available for those who want them, they should ideally happen within the whole assembly, and more time and energy should be spent in developing them. By performing gender in its moments of most acute transformation and expression, these services make queer life visible in a way that quieter, less contested moments of queer life cannot. Furthermore, it construed and developed as the public liturgical worship of an assembly, and not as the private, pastoral concern of the LGBT individual, they will, over time, contribute substantially to the queering of worship—and therefore of the church.

However, I worry that by concentrating on these occasional and extraordinary events in a person and a community's life as "queer worship" (with its double sense of both "unusual worship" and "worship for LGBT people"), we are neglecting the myriad ways in which day-to-day worship is, and is not, queer. Far greater attention remains to be given to the varied ways in which the questions articulated above impact on not just the occasional needs of LGBT people but their daily access to liturgical life. It is my experience that there are a large number of churches in which the sign on the door announces an *open and affirming* congregation every Sunday morning while most aspects of the liturgy remain closed and detracting or, if not actually detracting, then simply indifferent. (Out of the closet and into the armoire?) The question this essay asks, therefore, is whether and under what circumstances everyday worship in LGBT-friendly congregations can be "queer."

How many times have you heard sermons in which the stories told are about LGBT people's lives? If a sermon illustration is given about a couple, how often is it about a same-sex couple? How often are the complexities of relationships

---

7. Even though attempts to use existing rites (for marriage) were often found not to work, because they were perceived to be too heterosexually oriented in their language or gestures, or both, much of the language, form, and rhythm of the traditional rite was nonetheless echoed.

mentioned by the multiple, diverse and unexpected ways we love and are loved? How often have you heard stories told during sermons of a transgendered person's journey, a lesbian's coming-out process, a gay man's adoption of a child, a teenager's exploration of their sexuality, or a queer family's baptism? And I mean neither as a "special" illustration nor on the Sunday that coincides with the PRIDE parade in your town, but as happenstance, obvious, exemplars, just the way that stories from supposedly straightforward and recognizable heterosexual couples and their family lives pepper most sermons most weeks.

How many times have you heard transgendered pronouns used in worship? How many times have you heard intercessions for specifically lesbian, gay, bisexual, or transgendered needs lifted up during the prayers of the people? During open prayer, if you have it, do the LGBT people speak up? How many times have you seen same-sex couples sitting hand in hand in church? Or couples with a transgendered partner? How are deceased LGBT members remembered in your church? If you are from a tradition that honors saints, have you been led in devotion to those who can model lives of Christian witness for people who are neither heterosexual nor celibate?

As you sing with the faithful in all times and all places, how often have you sang in terms that were not based on heterosexist binaries—father and mother, male, and female? And are you invited to sing as "sopranos and altos/tenors and basses" or just as "women/men," regardless of the voice God gave you? How is sexual diversity talked about and otherwise imaged in your worship? How do you recognize the one in every 2,000 babies born with "indeterminate" sex organs? How many prayers begin only, "Brothers and Sisters"? How many of the worship leader's well-meaning remarks class people as "gay or straight," as if they were the only options? How are bisexual people represented in your church, if at all? Are bisexual people mis-portrayed as "straight" if they are in a male–female relationship?

Indeed there are congregations who, either through the minister's leadership or the congregation's commitment, or both, have given years of sustained consideration to these and other related matters as they pertain specifically to their liturgy, but they are a minority. Most of the LGBT people with whom I have worked in classes or workshops on enlivening worship report that they can count on one hand the number of times in their whole lives, if ever, that their particular way of being in the world was reflected in an ordinary worship service, and many report that they have never encountered any form of recognition of their sexuality or affirmation of their gender behavior in church at all.

The Problem of Heteronormativity

Of course, some LGBT people are happy with things this way: for them, worship needs no renovation on their account. They claim that the liturgy is simply the liturgy: it is by its nature neutral and being gay, straight, or anything else is irrelevant when it comes to how one worships. It would seem that this view is legitimated by many liturgical studies.[8] While open to critical debate about particular matters, such as the impact of the global South, the field frequently persists in a presumption of a generalized site ("the liturgy") with a core that pertains across cultures and is neutral regarding gender. As Teresa Berger has recently made plain, this has distorting consequences for theological reflection; if, as she demonstrates from a historical perspective, "gender remains unacknowledged as a fundamental marker both of the liturgical past and of authorizing claims to it,"[9] then, "the integrity of claims to this theological site becomes questionable."[10]

Where Berger's primary concern is with the false-absence of not just women from the *lex orandi*[11] but also a broader gender-critique from the "liturgical tradition,"[12] mine is with present-day rites in English-speaking churches, but it is based on the same point: worship is, like any other public arena, gendered, and gendering. What is perceived as "neutral" in worship is in fact a constant negotiation and establishment (through its very performance) of particular and specific power relations based on a particular and specific understanding of gender, and this has consequences for all aspects of church life, including theological reflection. Furthermore, due to the inevitable restrictions of any person's conceptual frames prior to the hard work of deconstruction, LGBT people insisting that worship is "neutral" regarding gender are either blind to or in denial about the extent to which Christian liturgy is not only gendered but, moreover, usually heteronormative (just as others claiming its neutrality are blind to its habitual misogyny).[13]

Heteronormativity in worship is when the norms of behavior that govern the liturgical agency of the assembly are based solely on heterosexual categories,

---

8. There remains an understanding of "liturgy" and "liturgical tradition" which imagines public worship as a normative, stable, inherently nonoppressive site of human–divine communication and, in some accounts, divine revelation. This view has already had significant critics. In addition to feminist works, see, for example, Paul Bradshaw, "Difficulties in Doing Liturgical Theology," *Pacifica* 11 (1998): 181–184.

9. Teresa Berger, "The Challenge of Gender for Liturgical Tradition" in *Worship* 82:3 (May 2008): 243.

10. Berger, "The Challenge of Gender," 245.

11. Teresa Berger, "Prayers and Practices of Women: Lex Orandi Reconfigured" in Susan Roll, Annette Esser and Brigitte Enzner-Probst eds., *Women, Ritual and Liturgy* (Leuven: Peeters, 2001), 63–77.

12. Berger's work investigates a multitude of historical and contemporary liturgical practices, demonstrating the ways in which they are gendered, from menstrual taboos in mediaeval Europe to the conception of sacred space; see Berger, "The Challenge of Gender," 243–261.

13. The phrase "heteronormativity" was coined by Michael Warner (see his introduction to *Fear of a Queer Planet*, 1993). Initially used to refer mainly to the marginalizing effects of a "heterosexual imaginary" (the title of Chris Ingraham's 1994 book), the term has since been excavated for its ability to refer to those institutions and practices that, as Cathy Cohen puts it, "legitimize and privilege heterosexuality and heterosexual relationships as fundamental and 'natural' within society" especially regarding the co-production of race and class with gender. Cathy J. Cohen. "Punks, bulldaggers, and welfare queens: The radical potential of queer politics?" in E. Patrick Johnson and Mae G. Henderson, eds., *Black Queer Studies* (Durham, NC: Duke University Press, 2005), 24.

central to which is the notion that the "natural" (i.e., divinely created) way for human beings to be in the world is for one man to marry one woman. Most worship habituates this code in every aspect of its human behavior and speech, from the way people are expected to dress, to where they are expected to sit, to who serves in leadership roles, to how God is addressed (including what words are used) in prayers. As Mary McClintock Fulkerson remarks, simply including LGBT people in church life is insufficient to redress (and it may even mask) the gendering of worship according to a heterosexual worldview that conditions the imagination of all aspects of life.

> The discourse of inclusion of lesbian and gay persons . . . does some important work: it names as good what has been branded as inherently sinful in church traditions; this discourse, however, does not expose the constructed and unstable nature of all sexual configuration. . . . Reproduction of heterosexuality has produced the illusion that subjects are constituted by a real, sexed essence which is naturally or unnaturally expressed by practice. Given the strength of that construction, and the productive as well as the juridical nature of power, the only way to contest compulsory heterosexuality is performance of gender that calls the security of that regime into question.[14]

In the remainder of this article, I will explore possible avenues of such performance, asking who and how, exactly, can perform gender in worship in such a way as to dismantle the heteronormative regime. But it would be a mistake to conceive of contesting the "secure regime" of heteronormativity in worship as an entirely immanent enterprise: it is part of a web of civic and religious interests in which the theological stakes of the nation-state system are acutely exposed. As Janet Jakobsen and Ann Pellegrini remark, "From tax relief and inheritance rights to preferential treatment in immigration cases, state-sanctioned heterosexuality confers a host of material benefits and rewards. And all this, in addition to the heterosexual couple's symbolic role as the nation's anchor, with the heterosexual family representing the body politic on a smaller scale."[15] Heteronormativity is embedded in American civic life just as, and perhaps because, it is embedded in American religious life and one of the main ways in which it is continuously embedding in American religious life is through worship.

Furthermore, because of the dominance given to Christianity in American civic life, Christian sexual ethics and heteronormativity are virtually synonymous in the public imagination: the result being the dominant expectation of what

---

14. Mary McClintock Fulkerson, "Gender—Being It or Doing It? The Church, Homosexuality and the Politics of Identity" in Gary D. Comstock and Susan E. Henking, eds., *Que(er)ying Religion: A Critical Anthology* (New York: Continuum, 1997), 39.

15. Janet R. Jakobsen and Ann Pellegrini, *Love The Sin: Sexual Regulation and the Limits of Religious Tolerance* (New York: New York University Press), 122.

constitutes "respectable" behavior and, therefore, "respectability" in social status. Many commentators have already shown how such an ordering of reality (and the mere definition of respectability along such lines) has harmed women, but it is only now being revealed how it is the same ordering that harms queer people. In his study of the theological arguments made by conservative Christians against same-sex unions, Ludger Viefhues-Bailey identifies "respectability" as the core concern motivating heteronormative religious regulation. While the object of his study is right-wing media organizations, on this matter of respectability he taps a prevailing norm in broader Christian life that, as I want to suggest, pervades many *open and affirming* congregations just as uncritically as it does those who promote the literature of *Focus on the Family*. Speaking of "*the* ideal heterosexual gender and sexuality difference" he argues that, "The strategy of declaring same-sex desire to be outside of the purview of respectable sexuality helps to maintain this ideal—and with it the implied power differences between men and women."[16] Moreover, as he goes on to demonstrate, via the same strategy (casting same sex-desire as outside seemingly basic or purportedly natural notions of respectability) this ideal heterosexual difference not only makes sure that female submits to male in domestic and civic arrangements, but it also insures an essentialist imaging of God as male. It is for this reason, as we will see, that queer worship is at its most controversial not when it proposes the acceptability of people coming to worship dressed in leather but when it suggests calling God something other than Father.

The Problem of Tolerance

While some LGBT people perceive liturgy as "neutral" and do not want "queer" changes, many other LGBT people can identify the "respectability" conditions of their liturgical community and adapt to them; they do not perceive liturgy as immutable, yet nevertheless see it as a game with certain rules and understand that they have to act a certain way in order to be allowed to play the game. It is not that they have to pretend to be straight—on the contrary, they know they are welcome to attend as an LGBT person—it is, rather, that they know they have to not "flaunt it" or expect "special treatment" because of their LGBT identity; for example, when leading worship for a national ecumenical gathering, one of the cathedral staff discretely asked me to tell my colleague not to wear a pink shirt. When I asked why, the argument went, "It's a hard enough time for those of us pushing for full gay acceptance [it was right after Gene Robinson's ordination] that we can't afford to have him rubbing the church leaders' noses in it." My colleague did not own a pink shirt, and had never worn a pink shirt, but the organizer had obviously imagined him doing so and felt strongly enough about it to say: "He is a fabulous gay man and we love him; he does not need to flaunt it."

---

16. Ludger Viefhues-Bailey, *Between a Man and a Woman: Making Sense of Christian Opposition to Same-Sex Love* (New York: Columbia University Press, 2009), 122.

Another example is a couple of lesbian friends with two children who had attended the same *open and affirming* congregation for a decade. When the time came to baptize their young children they decided to do so at a "private" service on a Sunday afternoon and not at the morning service, which is the service at which all infant baptisms in the parish usually occur. The pastor had apparently advised them that it was ultimately their choice but he felt that the afternoon option would be "less stressful" for them; they said they would love the whole assembly to be present, and they would love to do it the normal way, but they would feel odd standing there "as two moms" on a Sunday morning and so it was better to go for the afternoon—it was still baptism, after all, wasn't it?

Both these anecdotes are examples of something which happens every Sunday in much supposedly open and affirming worship: the welcome is honestly given, but the LGBT person is required, or feels a need, to "mute" their behavior in subtle ways in order to participate; muting in the sense of not drawing attention to their LGBT-ness. Writing about manifold ways in which such "muting" is subtly required of people across a whole range of arenas of public life, from employment or entertainment to the negotiations between a couple about whether or not to hold hands in at a social gathering, the lawyer Kenji Yoshino has coined the term "covering." Not limiting his theory to the issue of gay rights, but rather demonstrating how gender, race, sexuality and socioeconomic status are coproduced, he contends:

> The covering demand is the civil rights issue of our time. It hurts not only our most vulnerable citizens but our most valuable commitments. For if we believe a commitment against racism is about equal respect for all races, we are not fulfilling that commitment if [for example] we protect only racial minorities who conform to historically white norms.[17]

Likewise, a commitment against homophobia is about equal respect for people of all sexes, so we are not fulfilling that commitment if we protect only LGBT people who conform to heterosexual norms. We in the church are not *open and affirming* of LGBT people if the "respectability" of our worship is based on heteronormative foundations, so that "two moms" would "stand out" were their children to be baptized in the Sunday morning service.

As it conditions the behavior of LGBT people, Yoshino distinguishes covering from "converting" (lesbian and gay people trying to transform themselves into straight people) and from "passing" (LGBT people accepting their sexuality privately, but pretending to be straight in public), arguing that while it is now widely accepted that conversion and passing are both harmful behaviors to require of LGBT people, "covering" is far more contested, and there is a great range

---

17. Kenji Yoshino, *Covering: The Hidden Assault on Our Civil Rights* (New York: Random House, 2007), 23.

of opinion in LGBT communities as well as in society at large about whether and to what extent people should in fact "cover." "We remain riven," he writes, "by questions of covering—how much individuals should assimilate into the mainstream *after* coming out as gay. Should gays 'act straight,' or embrace gender atypicality? Should we be discreet about our sexuality, or 'flaunt' it?"[18] This is the key question that LGBT people face in *open and affirming* worship—meaning, this is the question that confronts LGBT people as they come before God, just as it needs to be navigated in every other interaction in their lives.

Yoshino characterizes the basic difference of opinion in the LGBT communities about this as a tension between "normals" and "queers." According to this typology, normals are those, like the lesbian couple, who are openly non-heterosexual but who are willing to fit into those forms of behavior that are most easily acceptable to the community in which they find themselves; queers are those who would wear the pink shirt when working in the cathedral (not meaning to implicate the bishop, of course!) or who would insist on standing as two moms while their children are baptized in the full assembly: those who "flaunt" their LGBT-ness. Some—not all—but some of the congregations that welcome LGBT people think their worship is already "queer" because it allows LGBT people to participate in it. They have long objected to any suggestion that LGBT people should convert and argue vehemently against any implication of Christian theology in ongoing arguments for conversion. Furthermore, they are appalled at the idea anyone would have to "pass" as straight to come to their church: they want people to come "openly" as LGBT people. And yet they have no idea why they are unattractive to LGBT people when they think they are being so welcoming. Nor do LGBT people have any idea why they go to "gay friendly" churches only to feel dissatisfied, or even marginalized, without knowing why—and so blaming themselves for not being sufficiently Christianly "aligned." I suggest it is because of this subtle "covering" demand regarding gender performance, the way it requires "normal" (meaning straight) behavior, and the way it combines with racial and other status markers.[19]

In these reactions, both the "open" church folks and their queer co-worshipers are mimicking the tendency of liberal social theory to confuse "toleration" with "integration." Writing about the law and related arenas of public life, Jakobsen and Pellegrini argue that, while obviously preferable to hatred, tolerance does not permit an actual re-ordering of a world along non-hate-based lines. Tolerance, they argue, "maintains the very structures of hierarchy and discrimination on which hatred is based [because it] establishes a hierarchical relation between a dominant center

---

18. Yoshino, *Covering*, 77.

19. A very significant one of which is poverty. See Marcella Althaus Reid, *Indecent Proposals: Theological Perversions in Sex, Gender and Politics* (New York: Routledge, 2000). The intersection of queer and poor in relation to liturgical expression demands far greater attention and study.

and its margins. . . . it sets up an us-them relation in which 'we' tolerate 'them'."[20] This us-them relation helps to explain why LGBT people are required to "cover" in supposedly "welcoming" congregations: because the notion of tolerance that has permitted their admission casts LGBT people forever as a "them" in relation to the "us" of the community. A "them" that allows LGBT people to be "part of" it (hence the desire to cover, to remain a part of), but never fully or authentically "us" (wherein authentic behavior is entirely unexceptional).

Philosophically, tolerance is based upon a fundamentally individualistic paradigm, and it is therefore no wonder that the odd queer who calls out intercessions for their specifically queer needs during open prayer is perceived to be a queer individual within a normal worship service rather than a participant in a queered and queering community's worship. This move whereby an individual who makes explicit their "themness" and is remarked as "exceptional," even as they have been welcomed, is a direct result of framing their inclusion in the first place as a matter of tolerance and not of mutual integration. In the effort to not hate anyone, and to avoid the charge of being involved in an institution's hate, LGBT people in churches are "tolerated," gladly, but their *behavior as LGBT people* remains coded as odd or outrageous; hence the need for covering. Jakobsen and Pellegrini identify this as the phenomenon of the creation of "extremism" and argue it is the inevitable result of the way we in modern democracies conceive of the opposite of "hate" as "inclusion."

> In a public organized around tolerance, the question is not whether we as a society have created unjust (and violent) social hierarchies, but whether we as individuals hate anyone. This disabling structure of tolerance has important implications for participatory democracy [and, I contend, public worship] because it puts those who take up political activism in any form at risk for charges of extremism.[21]

So when my lesbian friends are worried that they would "stand out" if they opted to baptize their children on a Sunday morning, they were correct: they would indeed "stand out." Their LGBT-open church, because of the terms on which it had welcomed them (toleration), would inevitably find their behavior "as two moms" to be extreme. The covering was thus required of them.

I am not of the opinion that acting as "queers" and not as "normals" would have solved anything in this case, or in so many other cases of ordinary Sunday worship where LGBT people feel the need to mute their behavior or speech. On the one hand, to act "queer" might reinforce rather than challenge the "us" and "them" dynamic and this might put the individuals at risk; or, on

---

20. Jakobsen and Pellegrini, *Love the Sin*, 50.
21. Jakobsen and Pellegrini, *Love the Sin*, 58

the other hand, if the individual is adored for their flaunting, a motif of "isn't it fabulous to be extremist" (or "isn't it fabulous to have some extremists in *our* church," like a badge of honor) might arise, and such is at odds with Christian ecclesiology, with its emphasis on equality, reciprocity, and service. Neither outcome diminishes the covering demand; in fact both isolate the "queer" and thus reinforce the respectability of the "us" through the counter-example of the "them." But this takes us to the heart of the problem: the covering demand is not a problem any individual can fix (this is what makes the "rivenness" of the queer community over this issue especially unfair: it is not a problem *individuals* can address, and yet it has most impact at an individual level). Furthermore, church is just not a place where the challenge of the solo queer will work: the basic ethic of being church is too non-individualistic to allow for the success of such a model.

Performing gender differently is, as McClintock Fulkerson argued, the only way to destabilize the "secure regime" of heteronormativity in church, but, given the above discussion about the covering demands made on those who would perform gender differently, I contend that it has to be the whole congregation, and not any queer individual, who has to do the work of queering worship. It is one thing for worship to be open to LGBT people, but it is quite another for it to be queer. In order to remove the risk of "standing out," the burden of "queering" worship must fall to the congregation as a whole and not to LGBT individuals within it. By this I mean that LGBT people must not be the only people having to choose to do an "unusual" thing, a thing that exposes them and their relationships in ways that others never have to experience. Perhaps Judith Butler's now-classic formulation about the nature of queer change—". . . the normative focus for gay and lesbian practice ought to be on the subversive and parodic redeployment of power rather than on the impossible fantasy of its full-scale transcendence"[22]—can be read/lived/imagined as the performance of a group and not of an individual or sub-set of individuals. Thus, the congregation would have to create the conditions of possibility of two moms presenting their infant children for baptism in the Sunday morning service, conditions that take away the need for the parents to make a spectacle of themselves. By enabling full (and unpredictable[23]) LGBT participation, the whole church and its worship become "queer," instead of a picture where the church is normal—where, in other words, normal behavior is suggested of all who wish to feel accepted within it—while those who would stand up "as two moms" are considered queer as individuals within a technically "accepting" community.

---

22. Judith Butler, *Gender Trouble: Feminism and the Subversion of Identity* (New York: Routledge), 158.

23. I hope it is obvious by now that I am not requiring all gay men to wear pink shirts to church; that would be a form of "reverse-covering"; an equally oppressive social demand "that individuals act according to the stereotypes associated with their group" (Yoshino, *Covering*, 23).

The Queerness of Christian Liturgy

So far, in considering the possibility of "queer worship," I have considered two claims. The first claim is that liturgy need not be queer because it is neutral regarding gender (heteronormativity), and this was clearly inadequate. The second claim is that one ought to mute one's LGBT behavior in order to conform to the liturgy's norms (covering). I turn now to a third claim that "the liturgy is by its nature already queer," a claim that typically arises in two quite different venues.

The first is a gay man who has grown up in a conservative denomination and now attends an *open and affirming* Anglo-Catholic Church. Finally being able to be part of a Christian community, being loved *as a gay man* by the church people, and enjoying a liturgical form that affirms the body and its senses (bowing, moving, censing, singing, touching, eating, drinking) are all profoundly "affirming" experiences and, indeed, undeniably queer compared to the locked-down, body-suspicious, gay-bashing alternative to which it is being compared. Furthermore, the demographics of the vestries of such churches reveal that their gay members play an integral, vital, indispensable role in the administration of the church, and so the charge of the perils of "toleration" with its inevitable "us/them" community do not apply. Moreover, openly gay people in such a venue can usually undertake all liturgical leadership roles and when they speak up in authentically (and identifiably) queer ways, as in the prayers of the people, they are seen as "part of" what's going on, and not "extremist."

However, while thus accomplishing much of what was identified above as being necessary for queer worship, there remains a problem with the queerness of such worship. The lesbian couple mentioned above attended such a church. As did another female couple who, in their fifties, were thrilled to finally find a church that accepted them as a couple. Yet, after many years, including a stint on the vestry, they decided to leave because none of the three pastors would even listen to their requests for occasional use of non-masculine terms of address to God. They were not asking for any changes to authorized texts, just for expansion in the vocabulary used for God in the prayers or in the homily, or occasional reference to the Holy Spirit as "she." It is often the churches that are most gay-friendly in some regards that are most resistant to challenging patriarchy, such as in their language; and "queer" issues are not just about being "gay," they are also about dismantling the mechanisms that continue to enforce heteronormativity.[24]

Week in, week out in gay-loving, highly ritualized churches, God is addressed as nothing but Father (with all its progenitorial weight) by men who cense and bow to the image of His Son on the cross in the main space, while the Lady Chapel sits there, off to the side, adorned with sparkly things. It is as if they

---

24. Many of which come in the form of words, but also include other things, such as space arrangements and the ways symbols are used.

are chopping nice smelling wood (but not getting sweaty) with their Almighty Father while Mom is off out of sight in the kitchen. Far from being queer worship, this is gynophobia run amok, the fear of the female body and contempt for the female gaze expressed and simultaneously masked by the robes, spatial configurations, words and gestures of the praying public. Gynophobia is precisely what we saw with the two lesbian couples mentioned above: with the baptizers, women's bodies were put out of sight (supposedly for their own "comfort" or "stress reduction"); with the couple in their fifties, women found it almost impossible to have their voices heard by those in leadership, and non-gendered or even feminine vocabulary and imagery could never be used in worship. Such high-church Anglo-Catholic worship[25] may be queerer than most but we have to be careful not to settle for a version of queer that harbors contempt for the female body and voice.

The second location in which the claim to liturgy's inherent queerness arises is the theoretical theological community, and it furnishes an abstracted but nonetheless compelling understanding of "queer worship." According to this view, worship can be claimed as queer by its very character as a perennially countercultural force, one of the key mechanisms whereby the endlessly changing divine–human alliance is established and developed, contested and investigated in this world. How can such an eschatological performance, with its acknowledgement of all that is, shot-through with redemption of all that has been (suffering especially), and simultaneous orientation toward a future of eternal freedom, be anything other than queer? In its essential resistance to normalization (via its claim always to allow for God's Spirit to inspire all that happens), worship can be conceived as being *inevitably* queer. Michael Warner has remarked that: "For both academics and activists, 'queer' gets a critical edge by defining itself against the normal rather than the heterosexual. . . . The insistence on 'queer' . . . has the effect of pointing out a wide field of normalization, rather than simple intolerance, as the site of violence."[26] And theologians can recognize in Warner's formulation a way of expressing what we know to be true of worship's queering power: far from being limited to an undoing of the oppressions of heteronormativity, worship is also committed to the undoing of any and every site of supposedly established worldly power.

Although few theologians have yet explicitly used queer theory to reflect on the liturgy, much of the most exciting contemporary liturgical theology seems to me to be saying something quite similar: that is, claiming the need for a space that can "queer" supposed norms of power and play in this world in favor of an emancipatory vision of human being. For example, borrowing from Navajo narrative, Gordon Lathrop describes the coyote who transgresses borders and by so doing

---

25. Which is by no means typical of all Anglo-Catholic parishes.

26. Michael Warner, *Fear of a Queer Planet: Queer Politics and Social Theory* (Minneapolis: University of Minnesota Press, 1993), xxvi.

makes access, who speaks of death and by so doing enriches life, and who is not a force in the world but without whom the world's order doesn't truly come into being. "It is *this* coyote—this crooked line, this ceremonial break—I find howling near the *ordo*"[27] (the *ordo* being the pattern produced by the various juxtapositions of word, bath, table, prayer and people that he sees as the deep structure of all Christian worship). If the juxtapositions of the *ordo* ensure faithfulness, then coyote ensures the pattern of faithfulness can never be rendered "normal." And in such a combination of coyote and howl and *ordo*, I discern a description of what in other quarters might be claimed as queer life.

Realizing the genre of worship as a structurally queer site in human living, privileges it as a legitimate site for queer theological reflection. But of course for worship to be queer it has to function not merely like Lathrop's coyote; it also has to be LGBT-cognizant. In these days when so much of the church remains enmeshed in "a wide field of normalization as the site of violence" regarding sex and gender, including simple intolerance of queers, it is not enough to talk about how Christian worship queers the pitch of a consumerist culture or even just of a self-satisfied queer ritual ethic: that is to spin the word queer out too poetically, if not to wholly appropriate it.[28] Claiming worship as queer has to prioritize the fact that queer is a praxis and not a theory (or a theory only insofar as theory is seen as praxis), and that queerness is ineluctably about sex, and thus worship cannot truly be queer in this culture unless it integrates sex, unless it stems from the life experiences of those whose sexed lives entail their acceptance of the label queer (whether happily or as an imposition) in this culture.

Taking queer sex seriously as a source for the structuring of worship plays out in two ways: direct and indirect (or substantive and consequential). The first way is fairly simple: it involves naming it, and naming it not as a transgression of any supposed straight norm. LGBT dating and union-making, threesomes, bathhouses, periodic celibacy, open relationships, adoptive families, and self-insemination need to be talked about, just as straight dating and marriage, monogamy, nuclear families, nursing home romance, and immaculate conceptions (!) are.[29] Obviously, the church should not be open to and affirming of all behaviors: the church's job is as much, if not more, to challenge as to affirm. Adultery is as sinful for the lesbian,

---

27. Gordon Lathrop, "*Ordo* and Coyote: Further Reflections on Order, Disorder and Meaning in Christian Worship" in *Worship* 80:3 (May 2006): 194–212 (206).

28. It is helpful to refer to Gloria Anzaldua's distinction between appropriation and proliferation in the use of "queer" as a term: *"the difference between appropriation and proliferation is that the first steals and harms; the second helps heal breaches of knowledge."* Gloria Anzaldua, "Haciendo cara: una entrada" in Gloria Anzaldua, ed., *Making Face, Making Soul/Haciendo Caras: Creative and Critical Perspectives by Feminists of Color* (San Francisco: Aunt Lute Books, 1990), xxi.

29. For a recent attempt to construct a ritual theology and Christian sexual ethic using gay experience as a resource, see W. Scott Haldeman, "A Queer Fidelity: Reinventing Christian Marriage" in *Theology and Sexuality* 13:2 (2007): 137–152.

greedy investment is as sinful for the gay man, apathy about global poverty is as sinful for the LGBT community as they are sinful for anyone else. My point is that queer worship demands actually talking about things that the church has in general not talked about. The church has had to learn to talk about divorce, cohabitation, multiple marriages, abortion, and many other sorts of sexual matters from straight life that it considered taboo even a generation ago, so it will not be impossible to learn to talk about the things that its LGBT members are doing.

The second way is more complex; it involves naming the ways in which queer sex produces non-normative social forms, and to name these as graced, as parts of God's ongoing work of creation and redemption in the world is basically, as of-God. This raises the question of the theological implications of what I have suggested above and I hope there will be time to think these through in future work because it is beyond the limits of this particular article. But, in preparation for that, it is vital that we consider what becomes of "the Body of Christ" after Judith Butler. Meaning, no single body can be the body of Christ: it is a singular ("the" body) of plurals ("we are one body") and thus it is the point at which the individualized language of modernity breaks down. It is the point at which our corporate nature is most apparent and our private lives most publicly blessed. And yet, we are each in our body alone and our body performs us in the world. For a queer person, the risk this involves—and the lack to date of a thought-through ecclesiology to which to belong—are so great as to be prohibitive for full functioning in the life of the church. Nevertheless, the insight of the queer Christian (just like that of queer worship) is that God is no more the author of heteronormativity than he or she is the victim of it: once worship is queered, God is too. God is thus restored to the Being that tradition has long worshipped; beyond gender, beyond binaries (Three in One), confounding of descriptive capabilities, but very much knowable—through loving. Perhaps, even, through acts of queer sex.

Conclusion

When working in those *open and affirming* churches who understand that the inherent queerness of worship as a social force can only be fulfilled by integrating lives that are actually queer, I am often asked for a list of things one can do to move beyond toleration to queer worship. The list of questions generated in the Introduction might serve as a starting point, but only a starting point, because without a depth of understanding on the congregation's part such acts could quite easily sate only the hunger for inclusion based on tolerance. In general, the goal is to create the conditions of possibility of non-heteronormative behavior and speech for all persons including LGBT people, and a summary might include such things as: having LBGT people as leaders of the rites; making positive reference to LGBT people in prayers, etc.; always praying for those awaiting adoption as well as the birth of a child; referring to "parents" not "mother and father"; using queer hermeneutics in textual interpretation;[30] and naming and drawing on aspects of LGBT lives and lifestyles as sources for expression and as sources of theology. It also, importantly, necessitates talking about the myriad ways in which heterosexual relationships vary.

But I would caution strongly against approaching the subject solely this way. Seen reductively, it can become the "add gay and stir" method, and it does not work for at least two reasons: first, worship is contextual, and so there are no readymade recipes for what will constitute queer worship in any given place (and relatedly, the "normal" that is being queered is different in every given place); thus, a particular set of queer prayers are transformational in one place and utterly cringe-inducing in the next. Second, queering worship is long, slow work and it involves the transformation of the congregation (and not, as discussed above, the promotion of an individual or their exceptional rights). Admittedly, there is a chicken and egg component here; by introducing measures like the ones just suggested, the congregation's experience will indeed change. Conversely though, such measures will feel false unless they stem from the congregation's changed expectations.

Queer worship, like all genuine worship, is a work only ever in progress: that's why it's called "liturgy." As many liturgics teachers remind us, the root "urg" means work in the sense of being wrought, and just as ore is wrought from iron in metallurgy, so "lit", the people, is what is wrought by the work of liturgy. But, unlike the ore analogy, worship is a time and space in which we are only wrought, never completed and held up as a finished product.[31] Liturgy is by its nature inevitably *the work of a group*; and this is why the individualized notions of openness mentioned above, with their concomitant experiences of extremism, prove ultimately self-sabotaging for the *open and affirming* congregation. Only by slow, hard work, only by being wrought, will queer worship be accomplished. A quick drag act will not do it.

For LGBT people to be fully accepted and not merely (caught in a web of being) tolerated in churches, worship needs to be shaped by their experiences and needs, their symbol-structures and language-games as much as by anybody else's. Queer worship envisions not only the creation of a church in which LGBT Christians are beloved, but a church in which all Christians, of all sexualities, can grow into fullness of life by the grace of God; a church which, as such, can be a sign of God's realm on earth.

---

30. One useful resource for this is *Out in Scripture*: http://www.hrc.org/scripture/.

31. As Mark Jordan puts it, "any liturgy, as text or performance, necessarily fails to represent what it enacts." *Blessing Same-Sex Unions*, 142.

CHAPTER FOUR

WORSHIPING THE QUEER JESUS

Lisa Isherwood

I have come to believe that an effort to do Christology in classic terms (Was Jesus divine? Was he human?) is much like trying to draw fresh milk from a very sick, tired, dry, sacred and as it turns out male goat. Christian feminists and others committed not only to the work of justice but also to holding our theologies and Christologies accountable to this work must set new terms for our faith, including and especially new terms for what we preach and teach about Jesus/Christ and for how we live in relation to the Jesus story and its Christic meaning.[1]

What is it that Christians believe they are doing when they take part in liturgies, particularly the Eucharist? This question has increasingly given me cause for concern over the years, as my research has uncovered how many queer Christians feel disempowered by taking part in church liturgy. Indeed, many others do not feel welcome at the table set by Jesus, a table at which even his betrayer was welcome. Is it that churches are full of unwelcoming people? This is hopefully not the answer. I think there is a deeper theological reason, and in this chapter I will explore that reason and offer alternatives to it.

Addressing the question of how Jesus the inclusive became Christ the exclusive is a challenging endeavor. When Jesus offered the hospitality of his own body through the bread he broke with his friends, he included all. We would not have expected less given the stories we have of his inclusion of those placed outside the society of his day. So how is it, then, that we hear stories of alienation from queer Christians, many of whom no longer feel welcome at the table? One young man said that if he did attend church he felt like a resident alien hiding in plain sight. That is a feeling I think many of us have in the sense that the whole of our embodiment cannot be present. I suggest that most of the answers lie with the image of "the Christ" that the churches have constructed over the centuries, an image that increasingly stood for disembodied control and

---

1. Carter Heyward, *Speaking of Christ. A Lesbian Feminist Voice* (New York: Pilgrim Press, 1989), 21.

power rather than inclusion. This is the image that was weighed down by Greek dualistic metaphysics, leading to a removed figure, fully divine, perfect, male, and celibate rather than the incarnate, flesh-and-blood, messy outpouring of the divine. It is this perfect male image after all, this Christ, we have been called to worship in most Christian liturgy.

So Who Do They Say I Am/We Are?

Christology in the twentieth century was a very exciting affair. It witnessed huge shifts in method and representation, and saw the emergence of a rainbow of Christs which lit our Christian landscapes throughout the globe. It does seem to be true that, despite this theological work, very little has found its way into church worship, and so the old dualisms remain and exclude just as before.

In the 1980s, queer feminist theologian Carter Heyward[2] made a close analysis of Mark's gospel in which she reread the meaning of, as she saw it, two significant words throughout the gospel. These words were *exousia* and *dunamis*. *Exousia*, she noted, meant "power over" and was routinely rejected by Jesus throughout the gospel. However, she concluded that *dunamis* is an inborn erotic energy, the birthright of us all that draws us to others and the world. Erotic in this sense may be sexual but is also that exuberant energy in all that lives. It propels us forward and is the energy of relationality, even across species, as we shall see. This human–divine energy makes us friends, not servants, of God and so enables Jesus to include us with him in what are traditionally understood as Trinitarian words, "In that day you will know that I am in my Father and you in me and I in you" (John 14:20). The scholarly consensus that the gospel according to Mark did not originally include a resurrection narrative or any post-resurrection appearance narratives further enables a greater understanding of *dunamis* as a birthright of us all. I suggest that it was no mistake by the author of the gospel according to Mark to alert us to our innate potential and then leave us standing at an empty tomb. The story continues with us in the human–divine nature we are now part of. We are pilgrims and resurrection people in the here and now, for all generations.

This approach highlights that we are part of a multidimensional divinity. The reality of the divine is neither removed to another realm nor is it an outpouring from above. It is within and between us. For Heyward, *dunamis* significantly destabilizes dualistic metaphysics and yields new understanding. For her, transcendence carries a new understanding and has no hint of the "above and beyond" within it. Rather it signals movement across and within, opening to new views and locations, among different companions, all engaged in this dance of embodied transcendence. Heyward does hold on to a difference between our

---

2. Carter Heyward, *The Redemption of God: A Theology of Mutual Relation* (New York: University of America Press, 1982).

divine incarnation and that of Jesus, but this difference is nothing more than a breath, not the large chasm and the absolute model of purity and perfection that dualistic metaphysics produces.

I am indebted to Heyward as her work enables me to further develop a queer theological method through her development of what she calls "godding"—which I prefer to call radical incarnation—as the birthright of all. "Godding" is a process, just as is radical incarnation, and it carries a spiraling element in it. While we have *dunamis* as a birthright, we grow toward greater fullness through life and experience, just as Jesus did. Heyward's insights have helped me to understand more acutely the flesh made word/s. Once we acknowledge the innate indwelling of *dunamis* as our birthright, then indeed our flesh and that of others become the outpouring of incarnational possibilities. The flesh-made word enables us to find a voice and to make our desires known. This radical incarnation enables a discourse which impacts matter and shapes it because matter is already discursive. With the reversal of word-made flesh to flesh-made word, bodies have a voice rather than being flesh that has the one and only divine imprint on one body, that is of Jesus. All bodies are now part of the divine becoming flesh with multiple outcomes and no one divine script.

The body speaks and often screams! This is radical materialism,[3] which due to its discursive nature, spells a future that we set through our actions, limited or otherwise in the present.

Received western theology has it that the only enfleshment required to satisfy the divine taking flesh came in the shape of Jesus. This brings us to the implications of the Word dwelling among us, or in the words of the gospel according to John, the Word pitching its tent among us. A pitched tent allows for an entirely different meaning from a preformed almighty divinity coming among us and bombarding flesh as it inhabits it or stamping itself on flesh. A tent is a structure that, while being staked and often tethered to the ground, is also malleable, adaptable, and portable. A tent can be moved to different locations with relative ease to adjust to the changing needs. Divinity imagined in this way has multiple sites of becoming, rather than only a single fixed expression. The flesh thus carried and placed among different realities is softened and appears more malleable rather than rigid, static, and unyielding. It is expansive and embracing; therefore, Christians may not project the abject, those things they feel are ungodly or even sinful which more often than not reside in themselves and their communities. Nor may they consume difference under the cloak of holy sameness but should rather be open to change through the adventure of expanding incarnation, an incarnation that is breaking out from the heavens and the narrowing dictatorial voice.

---

3. Ward Blanton, Clayton Crockett, Jeffrey Robbins, and Noelle Vahanian, *An Insurrectionist Manifesto: Four New Gospels for a Radical Politics* (New York, Columbia Press, 2016).

Thinking of Jesus as simply one incarnation of the divine in flesh pushes against traditional understandings and opens a whole new range of human experience to positive theological exploration. The body is no longer sidelined as fallen flesh and sinful humanity but can be seen as God-bearing in its multiple forms and expressions. Rather than being present on altars in liturgical celebration as wafers opening paths to redemption, a radical incarnate Christ appears as lives that enrich our understanding of the divine, within and between us, as we commune/ingest Eucharistic food.

However, lines are drawn around the body when the body gets too vocal in the creation of Christology. It has to be silenced and brought into line; there are edges and they narrow the body's shape. We can, perhaps, just about cope with a female Christ as long as we are not asked to look at questions of gender. A nice suffering, contained figure is acceptable, but a kick-arse, leather clad-lesbian warrior is quite another thing. This is Xena,[4] lesbian warrior, who declares she will climb off the cross to save the woman she loves, who is hanging next to her, and to do so she will kill those who have put them there. This is no passive woman giving up her soul to a distant God. She is willing to fight, to be passionate, and to change the narrative.

For me this graphic novel character demonstrates that we have lost the truly transformative power of incarnation; we have contained the glorious passion of the outpouring of the divine within a frame that makes it impotent. Would it be blasphemous to set this image before us as we celebrate the Eucharist? Is she so far removed from Jesus, who after all was quite often violently angry with both money lenders and fig trees? Christ's admonition to turn the other cheek and forgive those who hurt us has erased anger as a virtue, and thus made it difficult for the outsider to fully express the depth of pain that damages their divine becoming. The dualistic Christ has removed from Jesus' followers the ability to protest vehemently against the blasphemy committed against their human–divine natures. In worship, then, I am asking for more realism for the bodies of the marginalized to be present not simply as glorified sufferers but also as complex bearers of incarnation. I am asking that these bodies be not simply in the congregations but on the altars as objects that reflect diverse areas of queer life and expression. Contemplate them as part of the diverse becoming of divine life and receive with joy. This then becomes an act of communion in harmony with the glorious array of divine becoming gathered together.

Is it too outrageous to suggest such worship when we realize that the life of Jesus, only one among the enfleshed divine, presents us with a reading of rupture, that is, his life challenges the accepted norms of his day? His whole story kicks a hole in what was considered reality. Through the sharing of *dunamis*, he desires us to make it bigger. This is not done by believing in promised kingdoms and perfect

---

4. Wagner, Chin, and Wong, *Xena Warrior Princess* (Milwaukee: Dark Horse Comics, September 1999).

eschatons but by living in the flesh as an ongoing process of imagination and creative engagement with those considered to be on the margins or unclean. It is not the task of theologians, therefore, to heal the rupture that the divine incarnate makes; rather it is our task to continue the discontinuity as we embrace our own incarnate flesh. This is a very different understanding to the one that received theologies have upheld as they seek to close down and control the divine energy that flows in our veins and pulsates in every fiber of our being.

Marcella Althaus-Reid offers more to this breaking through of reality by urging countercultural politics, which she sees fully enacted in the life of Jesus. Here was a man who becomes the Messiah through walking with marginalized communities and individuals, which she understands to be a political act. Those with whom Jesus engaged were the outcasts, not simply the marginalized, and in some cases, were unclean according to the laws of the day. I would like to add to Althaus-Reid's insights by saying that even the genealogy of the man Jesus shows that his incarnation was entangled with many marginalized persons, prostitutes, foreigners, and others not seen fit by the creeds and words of his day. I have always understood the rupture that Althaus-Reid speaks about as that proposed between heaven and earth, now no longer separated by notions of absolute divinity. It is further a rupture in what is considered normal and acceptable religion and society through the outpouring of the human–divine, as we, in each generation, engage with and unfold the multiple possibilities that lie in each moment of existence, pressing always for wider vistas and encompassing understandings. Incarnation speaks, not just from the head, but through the whole body, and it is this voice that returns the power of incarnation to people.

Marcella Althaus-Reid[5] also spoke of an obscene Christ, and by this she meant that obscenity uncovers what needs to be made visible. For example, she says that the Black and feminist Christs are obscene as they uncover both the racism and sexism inherent in Christology. Even these images cause concern in some circles, where it is often claimed that the white male Christ does not lead to any exclusions or biases. Therefore, the entrance of queer bodies as the enfleshed realities "of Christ" are no less alarming for some Christians but that does not make them unnecessary for the inclusive church.

Speaking of the necessity of "uncovering" Christ, Althaus-Reid says, "any uncovering of Christ needs to follow that pattern of obscenity at the same time because Christ and his symbolic construction continue in our history, according to our own moment of historical consciousness."[6] In our own time, it is a matter of theological deceit and even falsehood if we continue to construct Christologies on the old knowledges. Dualistic metaphysics have no part to play in how we understand Jesus who became a Christ. The queered Christ heralds a full,

---

5. Marcella Althaus-Reid, *Indecent Theology. Theological Perversions in Sex, Gender and Politics* (London: Routledge, 2001).

6. Althaus-Reid, *Indecent Theology*, 111.

glorious, and unexpected embodiment of the divine as it aims to make manifest the gloriously passionate, promiscuous love affair with all flesh that is the incarnation. If Christology is indeed rooted in the erotic, as Heyward understands it, then Christian theologians will have to think again about their naïve division of the deeply human, deeply divine elements of humanity, and how to represent this in the central Christian sacrament, the Eucharist.

Elizabeth Stuart[7] has an interesting take on the Eucharist, which she believes helps inclusion in the church. She argues that this central sacrament of Christian church stands as an embodied practice, suggesting erasure of gender and sex. It takes both to a symbolic level and displaces them. By this sacramental enactment, we move through a range of identities, all of which are unstable, to the point of erasure. Therefore, as a welcoming community, the church gathered in this communal meal should never accept any identity as final.

I have no difficulty with the idea that the church should see no identity as fixed, but where I depart from Stuart is in moving to a symbolic realm before total erasure. This makes my heart sink. The symbolic world, which for Stuart is metaphysical, is the world in which Lacan[8] tells that women, and even queers, have no place, since the symbolic is wholly and purely male and is conveyed through language and culture which necessarily excludes all but heterosexual males. Why then would those excluded from it see the symbolic as a powerful dwelling place? This highlights a dilemma; in that symbolic world there can be no subjectivity until women find a place in the constructed male culture, since this belonging gives psychic leverage to our personhood. This dilemma is equally true for queers, perhaps historically even more so in both a church and a world that has not offered a sense of their belonging as whole persons. I believe that bodies can be radically subverting of culture when they find their voice beyond the fixed language and meaning of the master's discourses. However, we do need those bodies and not have them erased in a symbolic realm which many queer people would say has been their experience within churches. We have to find new ways of being by thinking through the body. The connection of body and being is crucial for those who have suffered under the dualistic metaphysics of church doctrine.

Roman Catholic theologian Gerard Loughlin sees things very differently from Stuart and states:

> The body of the Church which is most clearly visible in the Eucharist is startling. It is composed of many diverse bodies and is yet also one body which is both human and divine, being the body of Christ. At the same time it is a maternal body with enough substance for everyone; while also a nuptial body where each is brought together through desire of the other,

---

7. Elizabeth Stuart, "The Priest at the Altar: The Eucharistic Erasure of Sex," in Lisa Isherwood and Marcella Althaus-Reid, *Trans/Formations* (London, SCM Press, 2009), 127–138.

8. Jacques Lacan, *Ecrits: A Selection* (London: Routledge, 2001).

attracted by the beauty and allure of Christ's body. As bride and mother the Church is properly sexed as female but as composed of many bodies she is also multi-sexed, as male and female, gay and straight and as all other variations and dispositions. Thus part of what it is for the Church to speak her sex is to say, for example, that she is a woman or that she is a lesbian.[9]

There is no call here for erasure but rather for an embrace of the multi-sexed possibilities based on the words and ways the church has and does understand itself. The celebration of the Eucharist then becomes a celebration of this extraordinary body of Christ. It becomes possible to argue that the celebrants should also display this remarkable kaleidoscope of being in and through their physical representation and through the objects on the altar, which could reflect the queer lives of those gathered to worship. There is also a change in emphasis from ingesting Christ for remission of sin and a path to heaven to party time, allowing Eucharist to become a vibrant celebration of the diversity of life and the *dunamis* within all creation.

Graham Ward's[10] reflections on the gendered body of Jesus lend further strength to this argument. He claims that the gospels themselves tell stories of shape and location change as salvation history. From the outset the male body of Jesus is peculiar; it springs solely from the body of his mother and so is materially unstable. Even if virgin birth were possible, parthenogenesis would result in a female child. Therefore, right from the start, materiality is becoming metaphorical, a movement expanded in the gospel accounts where the man walks on water, is transfigured, ascends bodily into heaven, and is said to be present in the breaking of bread. In each of these scenarios the body of Jesus is displaced and, according to Ward, the sexed body becomes problematized and eroticized.

Ward suggests that the gendered body of Jesus is malleable and capable of transposition and that the gospels chart this course of increasing destabilization and many transformations. Each of these makes manifest more of the divine glory. The important point to notice, for Ward, is that it is not the gendered body that does this but the flesh-and-blood body free of categorization that demonstrates how these boundaries can be pushed. Ward not only challenges gender but also corporeality, noting that the gospels see no limits for it. Taking incarnation as more than the person of Jesus, as much feminist work suggests, this presents a challenge to us all. In my view it also opens the way for multiple incarnations to be present on and around altars, all open to change through the instability of the divine nature.

---

9. Gerard Loughlin, "Sex After Natural Law," in *The Sexual Theologian: Essays on Sex, God and Politics*, eds. Marcella Althaus-Reid and Lisa Isherwood (London, T&T Clark, 2004), 86–98.

10. Graham Ward, "On the Politics of Embodiment and the Mystery of All Flesh," in Althaus-Reid and Isherwood, *The Sexual Theologian*, 71–85.

Before moving to a wider vista, I wish to return to Heyward for a moment. She acknowledges that the power of *dunamis* infuses the whole of creation and as such invites us into mutually empowering and vulnerable relationships with all that exists. When she suggested that a horse could be a priest,[11] based on her observations in the therapeutic riding school she founded, some thought she had gone too far. Here was an Episcopal priest suggesting that a horse performed the same Eucharistic function as she did. For Heyward the argument was a logical one: If God is the wellspring of all, if the *dunamis* that enlivens us is the stuff of all life, then a horse can be the one who helps us in our godding and opens us to sacred energy. And riding a horse, like the Eucharist, "can be an occasion of thanksgiving in which creaturely and human divine life are united through mutual participation in the holiest of sacrifices—God's giving up of control in order to be with us."[12] She says that therapeutic riding demonstrates our capacity "to give ourselves over to empowering one another and other creatures to go together in right, more fully mutual relationship, in which we move together, more nearly as one, creatures united."[13] The sacredness of this action is the sharing, in this case across species, giving an agency to the nonhuman. Here is a Christology that is not simply anthropocentric and power-laden; it is a truly liberating narrative that opens us to life in abundance. In my view, it is creative and empowering, and finds a way for Christian theology to move with the cosmic celebration of *dunamis*.

Queer in the Cosmos

As we have seen, incarnation, rather than the constructed body of Christ, is no abstract concept. The work of Catherine Keller points further toward the queering of incarnation. While Keller herself does not deal with queer theology, her work proposes a larger vista with implications for queer bodies and Christian Eucharist.

Keller[14] introduces us to cosmic beginnings, to void and chaos, and we are asked to make our theology from that ground, that is, to understand who we are and who we might be from *tohu vabohu*, the depth veiled in darkness. Keller's use of beginnings here is important because *beginnings* are always relative, contested, and historical, whereas *origins* are absolute and power-laden. The absolute and the power it bestows are two concepts that have contributed to the narrow theology we now encounter. However, beginnings give theologians the chance to decolonize the space of origins in creation and the inevitable creator who sits apart. They allow us to challenge, as Keller, puts it "the great supernatural surge of

---

11. Carter Heyward, *God in the Balance: Christian Spirituality in Times of Terror* (Cleveland: Pilgrim Press, 2002).

12. Heyward, *God in the Balance*, 93.

13. Heyward, *God in the Balance*, 93.

14. Catherine Keller, *The Face of the Deep: A Theology of Becoming* (New York: Routledge, 2003).

father power, a world appearing zap out of the void and mankind ruling the world in our manly creator's image."[15]

Once we give agency to void and chaos there can be no creation out of nothing as our power-laden dualistic origin. Creation ceases to be a unilateral act, and the divine speech in the pages of Genesis is no longer understood as a command uttered by the Lord and warrior King who rules over creation. On the contrary, as Keller tells us, "let there be" is a whisper of desire, and what comes forth emanates from all there is, rather than appearing from above and beyond. In this shift we also see the possibility for incarnation to be understood as the rule of creation rather than its exception because the whisper desires enfleshment.

Keller enables us to move from a bounded and narrow monotheism through an investigation of the Deep, which is the very ground of who we are but has no fixed identity relying on the One. It is a Deep situated in the cosmos itself that gives the lie to *creatio ex nihilio* and opens before us the God who is of intimate/infinite entanglements.[16] This is the God who is the "all in all" of First Corinthians, not beyond, not distant, but entangled. Keller visits Paul's writings in First Corinthians on the body of Christ, noting the use of *energeia* in 12:4–6 when Paul describes human differences but asserts it is the same God who is in all. For Keller this disables any theology of distance and separation: God is not above, nor is the divine simply androcentric. Rather the scripture itself declares God to be eco-centric, "all in all."

Energy is then not something we have but something we are,[17] and it is the same energy that gives life to all. It is the stuff of entanglement. Keller writes, "feeling the pulsations of our bodies in our planet and the pulsations of the planet in its universe our earthly interactions are rendered simultaneously intimate and virtually infinite."[18] This is the energy of incarnation which comes from the free flow of these energies uninhibited by repression, exploitation, and denial. Just as Heyward accused theology of making us less than what we are by dampening and denying desire within us, so Keller suggests that exploitation and denial of entanglement blocks energy, which leads to depression and lack of meaning. As Keller puts it, "God in heaven who we create without a body to do work for us and who in the name of religion represses the rhythms of the human body and pulsations of desire"[19] leaves us adrift. I would argue it is this God without a real body that we find represented on altars; that God needs to be replaced by the diverse incarnational realities assembled.

---

15. Keller, *The Face of the Deep*, 6.

16. Catherine Keller, "The Energy We Are: A Meditation in Seven Pulsations," in eds. Donna Bowman and Clayton Crockett, *Cosmology, Ecology and the Energy of God* (New York: Fordham University Press, 2012), 11–25.

17. Keller, "The Energy We Are," 12.

18. Keller, "The Energy We Are," 13.

19. Keller, "The Energy We Are," 15.

Importantly, Keller argues the cosmos did not emerge from Platonic forms but rather from tehomic chaos. There was no set-in-stone blueprint but rather glorious outpourings of surprise and novelty. This unformed future is made up of repetition but from very early in cosmic development, this repetition always adds something new. In every repetition is a transgression: Our bodies and that of the cosmos are in constant flux; as they regenerate they change. They are then in essence transgressive, so our earthly home is a place where stable identities and categories cannot find an eternal home. Keller allows us to take a large step forward in terms of destabilizing notions of identity while remaining within God's creation, namely the cosmos.

I am sure some may wish to argue at this point that bread and wine on the altar represent as much as any these transformations from grain/seed to wheat/grapes, then to bread and wine, and of course to the body and blood of Christ. However, while Eucharist represents the transformations of these elements, it does not address those issues of exclusion so prevalent in churches today. Such accounts of Eucharistic transformation remain too abstract and the leap appears too far to make for embodied beings.

We therefore have to return intentionality and agency to matter, moving it from the background of consciousness to the foreground, from silent to speaking, and from the ordinary to the extraordinary, to the wonderful, and to the sacred. This move is needed if we truly understand that incarnation is the rule not the exception: All that lives is part of the ongoing unfolding of the divine. We need to develop cultural/ liturgical practices that re-inscribe the material with everyday wonder and this includes the human body and material labor. Christian Eucharist has, to some degree, included this by making central bread and wine, but perhaps moves too far by turning them into the body and blood of Christ rather than recognizing in the elements themselves part of the glorious array of divine incarnation. This is surely miraculous enough. It is, however, very hard to see any celebration of the earth's incarnational potential in these days of sanitized offerings.

However, if we go back a few centuries, the possibilities do become brighter, as there was no emphasis on blood sacrifice. None of what was brought to the altar by the community could signify blood or death: so, no meat or even red wine. In this way the story is significantly changed from one of worshipping the sacrifice of one man to a celebration of all life. Macrina, sister of Basil the Great, argued strongly that there should be no element on the table that suggested death or blood.[20] However, she also advised that it was not just what was on the altar that mattered but the surroundings. Art should be fecund, full of life and flourishing, plants, animals all basking in the glory and their *dunamis*-infused divine creation. Death and suffering should have no place. In this way, Jesus is not seen as dying for us but rather as living for and with us in a revolutionary way,

---

20. Rita Nakashima Brock and Rebecca Ann Parker, *Saving Paradise: How Christianity Traded Love of this World for Crucifixion and Empire* (Boston, Beacon Press, 2008), 151.

a countercultural form of life lifting up the abused and ostracized but nonetheless rejoicing in the divine glory of all that lives. Based on the theology of Heyward and Keller, I would suggest we embrace Macrina's approach and create fecund Eucharistic tables expressing the flourishing of life, not death and suffering. For many queer folk in the congregation, this would be a profoundly liberating visual message, since so many queer lives are filled with repression and suffering, both external and internal.

What's on the Altar?

Many theologians have given time and thought to the elements as they are and the implications for embodied lives. Monica Hellwig[21] argues that the way in which we view the "hunger of the world" should always be within the context of the Last Supper, which was, as she sees it, the foundational meal of Christianity. The context was one of oppression, and the act of communal eating was a commitment of ultimate fellowship that would be embodied through continued acts of eating and radical praxis. I would like to suggest that what one ingested was the "passion of Christ" understood not as a final sacrifice but as a radical way of living countercultural praxis through the skin. We are fed with incarnational possibilities and sustained to ever widen the boundaries of this contained patriarchal order that does nothing to embrace and allow for the flourishing of our divine–human reality. Hunger, Hellwig tells us, is a powerful experience that drives us to action.

Some years ago, theologian Tissa Balasuriya[22] urged Catholics to suspend the celebration of the Eucharist until such time as all were equal at the table. He argued that around that table we proclaim the inclusion and equality of all in a world that in reality is unequal and excluding. His solution was a suspension, a political act akin to individual hunger strikes, in order to bring to the attention of world governments the need for radical change. He focused on economic inequality, but would such a suggestion work also for the queer community? Would it be possible to get churches to suspend the Eucharist in solidarity with queer communities? Probably not, so what impact would a political walkout by queer members have? I imagine if they were priests, bishops, and cardinals, some impact would be felt. But the thousands of queer folks who have walked away so far has had little to no impact at all. Might assemblies entertain an occasional suspension of the Eucharist named as an action in solidarity with queer communities?

The stories about Jesus propose eating as a celebratory and revolutionary step, a proclamation of the kingdom of God through eating and drinking with

---

21. Monica Hellwig, in Lisa Isherwood, *The Fat Jesus. Feminist Explorations in Boundaries and Bodies* (London: DLT, 2007).

22. Tissa Balasuriya, *The Eucharist and Human Liberation* (London: SPCK, 1988).

the outcasts of his day. Here then was a statement about the world he asks us to commit to when sharing his table. I think this has other implications too which are fundamental to who we are. We fail to see that our appetites can be an asset since they reveal to us the centrality of desire in our full functioning as human persons. With Heyward, I believe desire is at the heart of our divine–human reality because it most fully connects us with ourselves and also propels us outward into relationality, mutuality, and vulnerability. It is then something to be embraced. The distinction between one's desire for God and one's desire for the "things of the world" has been false and damaging. Desire is rooted in our *dunamis*, our erotic/divine natures, and as such needs to be acknowledged and celebrated in a Christian life.

The attempt to control passion within Christian theology and religious practice has badly backfired by cutting us off from our deepest passions, disconnecting us from each other. In the area of sexuality this has meant that the behaviors that the churches meant to stop have in many cases simply increased and become even more meaningless. We are not rooted in who we are; it is as though we are in a dream and simply inhabiting our bodies rather than fully living in them. Or worse, as queer people, that we are so at odds with our desires that we see ourselves as dirty, sinful, perverted, and worthless. The Eucharistic table should connect people with passion in all areas of life in order to understand it as the divine spark which makes us fully human and enables us to move away from the superficiality so prevalent in many aspects of our lives, from sexual relations to shopping. When we are disconnected, we are always in need of something or somebody else to fill the ache in our guts.

For an incarnational theologian, this disconnection signals the degree to which we continue to believe that the heavens have not been collapsed by incarnation. We are still not at home in our flesh and so we fail to live the radical cocreative implications of that reality. We will not fully commit to flesh, and so we live as though we truly are meant to inhabit somewhere else. Once incarnation, rather than Christology, is at the center of the Eucharistic actions, the fleshy reality of our community becomes apparent. We are not engaging with someone or something that descends to enter the elements but rather a divine reality that dwells in bread and wine and us all, which is being drawn out by community presence.

Communion in this sense is then the coming together of multiple incarnational possibilities and the life they give rise to. This is far removed from viewing this table and indeed every table as filled with "stuff" that simply performs a function. We can be instead drawn into an ecological relationship with the bread and wine as well as those who labor to make it. In this light, the Eucharist also carries an economic demand that all share of the one bread and cup. This radical critique of global capitalism in turn has implications for the use and abuse of the earth's resources including human labor. We do not eat "my bread" but "our bread" and the "our" now includes not just the hands that made it but the soil, sun, water that infuse it.

The notion of "our bread" also includes all gathered and should be a celebration in gratitude for the richness of the bodies and lives brought together in this revolutionary act of equality. Could we envisage the Eucharist naming the communities gathered by the use of various kinds of bread and wine from diverse communities, rather than the sterile hosts so popular today? Doing so could make a greater variety of those who are embodiments of *dunamis* visible, rather than "the Christ," who regardless of intention has become exclusionary.

Now that markets target the excess income of some queer communities (the so-called "pink pound" in the UK), it is worth making the point that how such excess is spent affects global communities. While queer people ask for inclusion, it is good to reflect on inclusion into what and what for? It is understandable that there should be celebration of those who appear to "make it" and thus have resources that many queer folk never thought was possible. Many still do not have such resources in many parts of the world. Those who gather at the Eucharistic table should also reflect on their impact on others. Queer theology as a liberation theology does not simply seek access to power and money for queer communities but rather for all.

Conclusion

Nelle Morton writes that our journey home proceeds under the weight of a disempowering rhetoric about sexuality and gender. We need a journey back to our bodies, to a place of once again inhabiting this vacant flesh that holds within it the divine incarnate. We are asked to touch and revel in our passions and desires, to touch, taste, and see it is good. This invitation is laid out before us at the Eucharistic table, a table that has become sterile and bounded but that in its inception was the radical space of sensuous engagement and commitment. Here the exchange model of a patriarchal society was challenged by the sharing of bread. The politics of such a meal ensured that patriarchy would always be challenged through this radical sharing. It is in the Eucharist that we are invited to refuse the assumption of norms and to instead find countercultural ways of radical praxis of living as if the fullness of divine–human incarnation was already enfleshed. It is through these repeated incarnational performances that cocreation and liberation become lived realities in and between us. We are bringing our incarnate lives and celebrating the birth of something bigger than the sum of the parts; we dare to dream of a new world which we commit to creating together.

Christian liturgies demonstrate "incarnation" in word and action, with "incarnation" understood as the in-born energies of the universe that we all share. Incarnation is the empowerment and shared human–nonhuman heritage of *dunamis* where raw energy attracts us to the world and all that is in it. Liturgies then should be based on and express the entanglement of the human–nonhuman–divine. Energy is, as Keller tells us, not something we have but something we are,[23] and it is the same energy that gives life to all. Keller is deeply influenced by Nicolas of Cusa who himself understood "every creature is, as it were, a finite, infinity or created God."[24] God incarnate is not confined to one body in space and time; rather, the divine is equally distributed.

Nevertheless, we inhibit ourselves because we have stopped telling our stories as though they spoke of our birthright and have given them away by interpreting them as a tales of hero-gods and their power to save us through their actions, in the Christian case, through the death of one man. We and the whole of the cosmos are disempowered. We also place "the man" as the pinnacle of humanity as well as divinity, and once in the hands of clerics, this becomes a power game of exclusions. The churches are able to view the humanity of Jesus in any way they wish, yet with each imagining he excludes more people.

I believe that if we wish to move from queering theology to having a truly queer theology of worship, then abandoning the God who appears as the unmoving figure in an ever-becoming cosmos for the God who becomes is a crucial step. It is this God of becoming who should be central to Christian worship. This could be the very nature of incarnation: a form of divinity expressed in John's Gospel that pitched its tent among us, a moveable structure whose strength lies in its ability to move with the wind, to change shape, to be pitched in many different locations, and to be permeable. This is the God of the Hebrew Bible who declared, "I will become what I will become," rather than, "I am what I am." This is a queer God who manifests in diverse locations and bodies, and should be celebrated in all.

So how would I wish to see the future of Christian worship that embraced queerness? For me the first step is embracing the risk of our incarnation rather than finding comfort in the suffering and death of one man, who in life was inclusive and in death became exclusionary. Incarnation was a risk for the God who dwelt beyond, and it is risk we are called to enter into as we embrace the glorious array of lives in their fullness. It is this celebratory risk I would welcome seeing enacted.

---

23. Catherine Keller, "The Energy We Are," 11–25.

24. Nicolas of Cusa quoted in Catherine Keller, *The Cloud of the Impossible. Negative Theology and Planetary Embodiment* (New York: Columbia University Press, 2014), 118.

CHAPTER FIVE

CELEBRANT

Sheezus Christa

Stephen Burns

The following reflections consider glimpses of Christa. Beginning with ways in which she queers the gender of Christ in art, they move to how she appears in theology, before finally imagining her queering Christian worship.

Christa in Art

One is more likely to be introduced to Christa in artistic depictions of a female Christ than to find her in an introductory text on Christology.[1] At least one Christa image has received widespread attention, and in recent years it has come to reside in an ecclesial context: Edwina Sandys' *Christa*. An interview with the artist revealed that "though she is not a religious person, she felt the need to represent women within what's often considered the most important image: Jesus on the cross." She then stated that the sculpture "showed the suffering of women."[2] Sandys' *Christa* wears some sort of head-dress—flowers, a crown, a twine of thorns?—but is otherwise naked. Her body twists in so far as it is able, fixed at hands and feet to the plinth, and her face expresses pain, "suffering but compassionate," in Sandys' words. And in other words, bar that this victim of torture is female, the iconography is close to countless numbers of more traditional crucifixes.

While it was created in 1974 for the United Nations Decade for Women: Equality, Development and Peace (1976–1985), Sandys' *Christa* was first exhibited in a gallery setting in London in 1975. It later traveled not only to other galleries but also to universities and notably to at least one religious setting,[3] the Cathedral of St. John the Divine in New York, an Episcopal Church building, turning up there toward the end of the "decade for women" in Holy Week 1984.

---

1. Julie Clague, "The Christa: Symbolizing My Humanity and My Pain," *Feminist Theology* 14 (2005): 83–108; Nicola Slee, "Visualizing, Conceptualizing, Imagining and Praying the Christa: In Search of Her Risen Forms," *Feminist Theology* 21 (2012): 71–90.

2. https://en.wikipedia.org/wiki/Edwina_Sandys.

3. https://feminismandreligion.com/2015/10/06/christa-interview-with-edwina-sandys-by-nettie-reynolds/.

The sculpture met some very mixed opinions—such as the cathedral dean seeing it as "a positive message to women" while the suffragan bishop of the diocese started a campaign to get people to write in complaints. In time, the dean's view prevailed, as the sculpture returned to St. John the Divine in 2016, now on a permanent basis. So it has found a liturgical context, as an "altar cross" in the reredos of a grand Eucharistic table and thereby was made part of the ceremonial scene of at least some of the worship offered at the cathedral. Notably, the sculpture's return to the building was made in the context of another exhibition, *The Christa Project*, a project on "divine bodies" involving 21 other images by a range of artists.[4]

Another well-known Christa image from the 1970s is James Murphy's *Christine on the Cross*, which was exhibited in the chapel of Union Theological Seminary, and interestingly in Eastertide 1984 when Sandys' *Christa* was across Central Park at St. John the Divine. There seems to be no record of one use emboldening the other, if that was the case. In any event, Murphy's sculpture was used in worship led by the Episcopal biblical scholar Phylis Trible, then a teacher at the seminary. Trible had just published what was quickly to be recognized as a "classic" of feminist biblical scholarship, *Texts of Terror*, with its unflinching look at the abuse of women in certain Hebrew Bible narratives, replete with sketches of the "tombstones" bearing the women's names (that is, where known: Hagar, Tamar, the daughter of Jephthah), and with its striking statement, "sad stories do not have happy endings."[5] *Texts of Terror* was also a key part of the liturgy on the occasion *Christine on the Cross* appeared, and for his part, Murphy, a minister in the United Church of Christ, had to be convinced by Trible of the aptness of the sculpture's use in a liturgical setting.

Despite Murphy's view that "the world's rejection and hatred of women culminates in crucifying the female Christ,"[6] his reserve seems to have related to his intent to "confront . . . issues of sexuality and spirituality" and how these in turn "relate in the context of people of the opposite-sex relating to one another in the Christian Church."[7] His own rationale for *Christine* was to explore in art "men's sexual excitement at the female body" in connection to "traditional church teachings [that] made them feel guilty and confused."

So *Christine* is fixed on an upside-down cross, spread-eagled. Exploring his own unease with aspects of the sculpture, Murphy—notably also a psychiatrist as well as minister—came to the view that "men's rejection of the idea of a female God or Christ-figure has been based as much on their sexual anxiety and guilt as on their

---

4. Cathedral of St John the Divine, *The Christa Project: Manifesting Divine Bodies* (Catalogue 2016). See also Nicola Slee, *Fragments for Fractured Times* (London: SCM Press, 2020), 234.

5. Phylis Trible, *Texts of Terror* (Philadelphia: Fortress Press, 1984), 2.

6. Clague, "The Christa," 93.

7. Clague, "The Christa," 94.

theological disagreements with the idea."[8] Curiously, Phylis Trible does not seem to have put into print any of her own reflection on the sculpture, presumably because she has nothing to add about this "Christian" image to what she had already said about violence toward women in the Hebrew Bible in *Texts of Terror*.

A third well-known Christa image from the 1970s is *Crucified Woman* by Almuth Lutkenhaus-Lackey, a German-Canadian. Like Murphy with his *Christine*, Lutkenhaus-Lackey had misgivings about the use of her art in worship. She nevertheless permitted its use when asked to lend the sculpture to the Bloor Street United Church of Canada in downtown Toronto to feature in a service on "battered wives" on Good Friday 1979. As with Sandys' *Christa*, responses were mixed, but clear among reactions to these crucified women was an extraordinary level of appreciation from some. Indeed, "deeply touched by the many women who told me that for the first time they had felt close to Christ, seeing suffering expressed in a female body,"[9] Lutkenhaus-Lackey donated the work to Emmanuel College in the University of Toronto, the United Church of Canada's seminary in that city. The work remains there and over time it came to be particularly associated not just with "soft" misogyny in the university sector but a very specific act of violence. In 1989, a failed male student in a Montreal polytechnic opened fire and fatally shot 14 women (and then himself, while wounding a further 13 persons), the women having found their way into the study which he himself had flunked. Hence, this Christa has found wide resonance across Canada's education sector.

There are numerous other Christa images from other times and places, including at least one under the auspices of the World Council of Churches (WCC): Margaret Argyll's *Bosnian Christa* which was used at Manchester (UK) Cathedral in 1993, mid-way through WCC's "Decade for Churches in Solidarity of Women." Argyll's image of a crucified woman is suspended at the center of a vulva-like opening, meant to evoke the "obscenity of rape" in the warzone of the former Yugoslavia—a conflict with horrors on all sides, but certainly including the systematic assault of Muslim Bosnian women by Christian Serb soldiers.

From Australian contexts, we might note several further images. Arthur Boyd's *Crucifixion, Shoalhaven* (1979–1980) sets a cross in the middle of Shoalhaven River, New South Wales, with a backdrop of a bleak scree but with some trees growing on it that jut up from the earth at the same angle as the cross in the water. The deep river and the dry bank behind it suggest both flood and drought common in Australian experience, as might the "big sky" of blue and harsh light on the whole scene. Boyd seemingly crafted his image in ways meant to reflect a western tradition of art on the dying and dead Jesus, but intentionally recast in

---

8. Clague, "The Christa," 94–95.

9. Clague, "The Christa," 89.

"an alien antipodean landscape," talking back to "the attempt of Europeans to force upon the land of the Aboriginal an alien culture."[10]

Along with that disjunction comes, perhaps, its most obvious one: that the figure on the cross is female, with Boyd giving the reason for this as being that it is "not enough to say *he* [Jesus Christ] represented all of us," or to allow "just the male to be seen" in depictions of suffering.[11] Sally Douglas suggests that Boyd's female Jesus is "possibly pregnant," "shimmering with potency."[12] Lee Meina Skye's work on Aboriginal women's Christology underscores that, given that two key figures in First People's spirituality—Earth Mother and Creator Spirit—are females. Aboriginal women do not struggle to "see God as both He and She," Skye suggests, and even if they see Jesus as "He" they do not "have a problem . . . that Christ was one with this female God."[13]

Also from Australia, Jill Ansell's *Tribute to Matthias* is a reworking of the risen one in Matthias Grünewald's famous Isenheim altarpiece, but with Christ depicted as a female.[14] Reg Mombassa's "ambiguous and anxiety-making" image of Christ, *Australian Jesus stripped bare*, depicts Jesus as bearded with a wooden body shaped like a cross. The body is "transgendered,"[15] with breasts and a penis. As Rod Pattenden notes, the image was painted at a time when marriage equality was being fiercely debated in Australian society, and this Jesus reminds viewers of "the role of religion in reinforcing dualistic notions of gender."[16] *Australian Jesus stripped bare* was entered in the Blake Prize, an Australian initiative in "spiritual art," the same year as Zara Sullivan's *Sheezus*.[17]

A further Australian Christa is John Tansey's "Deterrence," a sculpture twined from barbed wire of three crucified bodies—a man, a woman, and a child—with each of their crosses sporting an inscription naming offshore detention centers for migrants found at sea in Australian waters, a hideous part of the country's "stop the boats" policy which designates vulnerable persons risking life

---

10. Rosemary Crumlin, *Beyond Belief: Modern Art and the Religious Imagination* (Melbourne: National Gallery of Australia, 1998), 140–141.

11. Clague, "The Christa," 91.

12. Sally Douglas, *Early Church Understandings of Jesus as Female* (London: Bloomsbury, 2016), 185.

13. Lee Meina Skye, *Kerygmatics of the New Millennium: A Study of Australian Aboriginal Women's Christology* (Delhi: ISPCK, 2007), 45.

14. Kittridge Cherry, *Art That Dares: Gay Jesus, Woman Christ, and More* (Berkeley: AndroGyne Press, 2007), 24. Cherry notes that Ansell was born in the United States; she migrated to Australia.

15. Jason Goroncy, "'A Pretty Decent Sort of Bloke': Towards the Quest for an Australian Jesus," *HTS Teologiese Studies/Theological Studies* 75:4 (2019): a5545: 1–10, at 3.

16. Rod Pattenden, "Images of Jesus and Masculinity in the Work of Reg Mombassa," in *Theological and Hermeneutical Explorations from Australia: Horizons of Contextuality*, ed. by Jione Havea (Lanham: Lexington, 2020), 113–124, at 120, on which page the image is also found.

17. Goroncy, "A Pretty Decent Sort of Bloke," 3. See https://issuu.com/casulapowerhouseartscentre9/docs/cpac0027_blake_prize_catalogue_hr, with Sullivan's "Sheezus" at 172–173 and Mombassa's "Jesus Stripped Bare," at 40–41.

and limb to arrive on safer shores "illegal maritime arrivals."[18] A much brighter work not made but found in Australia is that of Filipino artist Emmanuel Garibay.[19] His *Emmaus* adorns the Paddington Uniting Church.[20] This Christa is not on a cross, but rather in a tavern, and she is not alone, but in company, and she is not suffering, but laughing. She is drinking with friends, and happy about it. Only the mark of the nails on her hands gives away her identity (though her bright red dress might also be meant to suggest blood, albeit in this vibrant scene, as lifeforce). Furthermore, the title of the painting gives the clue that this is a post-resurrection Eucharistic scene (Luke 24:13–52), while also recalling gospel memories of slurs against Jesus as "glutton and drunkard" (cf. Luke 7:34). This Christa is evidently content at a table.

In fact, Christa of *Emmaus* is one of several variants of the same scene, with the same name, by Garibay. So as well as being found in a Uniting Church building (the only liturgical use of the image, so far as I know), *Emmaus* can also be found elsewhere—and it is a crucial clue to some significant developments in print.

Christa in Theology

One of the places where a variant Garibay *Emmaus* is to be found is on the cover of Nicola Slee's amazing book, *Seeking the Risen Christa*.[21] This is for the most part a collection of poetry but also includes prayer relating to Christa. The book's notes complement a task that Slee articulates in her introduction, that is, sketching a wider context for her contribution on Christa by "look[ing] backwards over the history of Christian tradition to demonstrate that the idea of a female Christ is nothing new, but a very ancient idea rooted in scripture, tradition, and Christian practice down the centuries,"[22] of "noble and ancient pedigree,"[23] "with serious spiritual and theological intent."[24] One of the key points that her sketch reveals is a preponderance of thought about Christa in relation to crucifixion. For all that it may be recognized that images of a crucified Christa have provoked a range of responses (recall, for example, the sense of persons finding themselves via this image, "close to Christ"), but Slee's contribution pushes the image into new dimensions. In Slee, we find a distinctly fresh emphasis on

---

18. Tansey's "Deterrence" is the focus of Stephen Burns, "Deterrence: Crucified People," in Rebekah Pryor and Stephen Burns, eds., *Feminist Theologies: Interstices and Fractures* (Lanham: Lexington, 2023), 179–198.

19. See Emmanuel Garibay, *Where God Is* (New Haven: OMSC, 2011).

20. Rod Pattenden, "Recognizing the Stranger: The Art of Emmanuel Garibay," *Image* 68 (https://imagejournal.org/article/recognizing-the-stranger/).

21. Nicola Slee, *Seeking the Risen Christa* (London: SPCK, 2011).

22. Slee, *Seeking*, 4.

23. Slee, *Seeking*, 22.

24. Slee, *Seeking*, 22.

happy and "risen" Christas, in the mood of her chapter on joy and celebration in her earlier book *Praying Like a Woman*, "all golden peach."[25]

The reasons for the more common tilt of the image to crucifixion are perhaps both ancient and modern: modern, in recognition of myriad forms of suffering of women in contemporary contexts, from Canadian classrooms to Bosnian villages and beyond, but also ancient, in that early beginnings of a distinctive association of Christ and women are to be found in nascent Christian literature. Among these, the *Acts of the Martyrs of Lyons and Vienne*'s presentation of the death of Blandina is paradigmatic. The story of her death in 177 AD—when Blandina was given as food to wild beasts by suspending her from a stake—is depicted in the *Acts of the Martyrs* as an occasion on which it was possible for others to "encounter Christ *in the form of our sister*."[26] According to the tale, Blandina prayed "cross-wise," in earnest, as she was mauled. As she did so, those who watched her die "beheld with their outward eyes *in the form of their sister the One who was crucified for them*."[27]

The narrative of Blandina's death is vital in Rosemary Radford Ruether's pioneering feminist "systematics" of 1983, *Sexism and God-talk*, which locates Blandina's martyrdom as one of either androgenous or "spirit" Christologies in the tradition. But for Ruether, they contest "the patriarchalization of Christology," the opposite of which she proposes in the imaginative exercise that sits at the opening of her book. On the "kenosis of the Father," it retells the gospel story, and what the death of Jesus means is that "a new God is being born in our hearts to teach us to level the heavens and exalt the earth and create a new world without masters and slaves, [without] rulers and subjects, . . . [without] men first . . . women behind . . ."[28]

The aspects of the tradition which Ruether associates with Blandina's martyrdom in turn form part of Ruether's argument that "the maleness of Jesus is of no ultimate significance."[29] It involves a dynamic of distancing *Jesus* "in all his particularity as a first century Galilean Jew"[30] from *Christ* who comes to expression in others—"as *alteri Christi*," "other Christs"—when Jesus's "message and practice" is made manifest: "good news to the poor, the confrontation with systems of religion and society that incarnate oppressive privilege, and affirmation of the despised as loved and liberated by God."[31] In Ruether's view, while Jesus may be "the foundational representative" of this enacted good news, Jesus is by

---

25. Slee, *Praying Like a Woman*, 115–127, in the chapter title and in the poem at 117.

26. Rosemary Radford Ruether, *Sexism and God-talk* (London: SCM Press, 1983), 116. Emphasis in the original.

27. Ruether, *Sexism*, 110. Emphasis in the original.

28. Ruether, *Sexism*, 9.

29. Ruether, *Sexism*, 115.

30. Rosemary Radford Ruether, *Introducing Redemption in Christian Feminism* (Sheffield: Sheffield Academic Press, 1998), 93.

31. Ruether, *Introducing Redemption*, 93.

no means "its exclusive possibility."[32] *Sexism and God-talk*'s account of Blandina's "cross-wise" martyrdom seems to mean that crucifixion has been held in focus into further thought about "Christ in the form of our sister."

Carter Heyward also puts space between Jesus and Christ, saying for herself that Jesus was "a Jewish male with a particular relationship to his 'abba'" while Christ "may be for Christians the salvific implications of the Jesus story."[33] Hence Heyward's language of "the christic" in order to speak of "God taking shape among us"[34] as well as her suggestion that "God's incarnations are as many and varied as the persons who are driven by the power in relation to touch and be touched by sisters and brothers."[35]

For Rita Nakashima Brock too, Christa is coterminous with community—at least at its best, in certain ways—in a move she intends not only to "point[ ] away from sole identification of Christ with Jesus" but also to "shift the focus away from heroic individuals, male or female."[36] Lisa Isherwood draws attention to Brock's reserve to make the point that the identification between Christa and *any individual* may "not seem far enough removed from Christ to avoid lapses into old bad habits," while Isherwood adds that nonetheless Christa may be the means for some to find a "stepping-stone to totally new ways of imaging the divine."[37]

Nicola Slee in her turn searches others' perspectives in order to set them alongside those of Heyward and Brock. In *Seeking the Risen Christa*, Slee attends to white feminists like Heyward and herself, and to "black, womanist or Asian" voices. As none "speak of Christa as such," she assembles allusions—such as Kelly Brown Douglas' "black Christ," whose presence may be found "in the faces of the poorest Black women";[38] and Israel Selvanayagam's emphasis on the sacramentality of a "meal" of scraps fed hand to mouth by a mother to her baby in the context of "grinding poverty";[39] and Chung Hyun Kyung's incorporation into her own work of various Asian depictions of Jesus as mother, woman, and shaman.[40] Kyung's inclusions draw in Kwok Pui Lan's invocation of a weeping and pain-bearing mother, Park Soon Kyung's identification of Jesus as

---

32. Ruether, *Introducing Redemption*, 93.

33. References in Slee, *Seeking*, 8.

34. Heyward, *She Flies On* (New York: Church Publishing, 2017), 80.

35. Carter Heyward, *The Redemption of God: A Theology of Mutual Relation* (Lanham: University of America Press, 1989), 164.

36. Slee, *Seeking*, 9.

37. Lisa Isherwood, *Introducing Feminist Christologies* (Sheffield: Sheffield Academic Press, 1999), 103.

38. Slee, *Seeking*, 12, referring to Kelly Brown Douglas, *The Black Christ* (Maryknoll: Orbis, 1994).

39. Slee, *Seeking*, 12–13, referring to a story related by Donald Eadie, "More Than Eucharistic Liturgies and Eucharistic Living," in Stephen Burns, Nicola Slee and Michael N. Jagessar, eds, *The Edge of God* (Peterborough: Epworth, 2009).

40. Slee, *Seeking*, 13, referring to Chung Hyun Kyung, *Struggle to Be the Sun Again: Introducing Asian Women's Theology* (London: SCM Press, 1991).

"woman Messiah," and Choi Man Ja's claim that "women are the true praxis of messiah-Jesus in Korea."⁴¹

To all of these fragments related by Slee, hindsight suggests that more might have been added. While Kwok Pui Lan is mentioned, Kwok's work on "American Indian" notions of the corn mother who suffers on behalf of her children, drawn from George "Tink" Tinker's writings is not.⁴² Nor is Aruna Gnanadason's exploration of deities from Gnanadason's Indian context—especially Shakti, "the source and substance of all things."⁴³ And while it may be that none of those mentioned in her own discussion refer specifically to Christa, had Slee discovered Choan-Seng Song's work, she would have found Song's direct consideration of Christa in his *Jesus: The Crucified People*, a book, as its title betrays, very much focused on the crucifixion theme.⁴⁴

Also, while *Seeking the Risen Christa* does refer to Lisa Isherwood's *Fat Jesus*, it does not refer to Isherwood's *Introducing Feminist Christologies*, which includes numerous diverse references, as noted.⁴⁵ Like Kwok, Isherwood draws on Aruna Gnanadason's work on Shakti, and also leans on Clara Bingemer's insistence that women's bodies are Eucharistic, thereby providing ideas to ally to and expand Israel Selvanaganam's cited by Slee. Bingemer suggests that "[i]n the whole process of gestation, childbirth, protection and nourishing of a new life, the sacrament of the Eucharist, the divine act, happens anew."⁴⁶ And then, Isherwood also draws attention to Gabrielle Dietrich's association of Jesus' blood on the cross and women's menstrual blood.⁴⁷

Lisa Isherwood's introduction also incorporates a whole chapter on Sophia, whom she relates directly to Christa.⁴⁸ Isherwood's insightful discussion offers another clue as to why perhaps Christa has often been associated with the cross, in that she warns of a danger to be guarded against, "which is that women become totally associated with child-bearing and fecundity."⁴⁹ So the emphasis on crucifixion may be an attempt to avoid mother stereotypes when imagining Christa. At the same time, Isherwood underlines an important possibility in Elisabeth Shüssler Fiorenza's work on Sophia,⁵⁰ in that Schüssler Fiorenza argues

---

41. Slee, *Seeking*, 13.

42. Kwok Pui Lan, *Feminist Theology and Postcolonial Imagination* (London: SCM Press, 2005), 176–177. See also Slee, "Visualizing."

43. Kwok, *Postcolonial Imagination*, 178–179. See also Isherwood, *Introducing*, with credit to Ursula King, ed., *Feminist Theology from the Third World: A Reader* (London: SPCK, 1993), 351–360.

44. C.S. Song, *Jesus: The Crucified People* (Minneapolis: Fortress, 1993).

45. See Slee, *Seeking*, 141, 142.

46. Isherwood, *Introducing*, 63.

47. Isherwood, *Introducing*, 64–65.

48. Isherwood, *Introducing*, 103.

49. Isherwood, *Introducing*, 116–117.

50. Elisabeth Schüssler Fiorenza, *Jesus: Miriam's Child, Sophia's Prophet* (London: SCM Press, 1994).

"from the Q material" layered into some of the gospels, which is a source that "has no Passion narratives." Isherwood suggests that "thus women can engage with the death of Jesus in a more empowering way and not be guided to limited and devastating interpretations."[51] In short, a Q-inspired Sophia may dispense with any need for images of crucifixion—and I add, in making a link back to proper concern with *Christine on the Cross*, Fiorenza's path suggests a desirable outcome: no crosses at all, no unwitting focus in the Christian assembly on instruments of torture—or the violent killing of whomsoever.

Nicola Slee's concern is not so much to unlink the cross from Christa, as to enrich and expand the imagery around her, as can be discerned in the crafting of her book according to liturgical seasons: for example, with parts on "Come as a girl: Nativity and incarnation," "The table of women: Maundy Thursday," "The in-dom of Christ: Ascension and after." So while there is a chapter on "Christa crucified: Good Friday," this finds its place in a much wider schema. And the overall title highlights the special weight given to Easter, to Christa's "risen forms." The very first word of her first chapter is a question that suggests the focus she wants to broaden: "Why is the Christa always suffering, broken, dying?" (which is immediately followed up with another question, "Where is the risen Christa?").[52] She draws attention to two artistic contestations in which "almost all of the theological interest in the Christa . . . [has] centered on a *crucified* woman," and both already mentioned—Jill Ansell's reworking of Grünewald's Isenheim altarpiece, and Emmanuel Garibay's *Emmaus* which adorns the cover of Slee's book and about which she writes a poem.[53] She goes on to state that she is herself "in search of symbols of the feminine divine which can speak to and of women's risenness, strength, power, vitality and live-liness, our quest for life in all its fullness,"[54] invoking Mary Daly's castigation of "necrophiliac" religion—an invocation which reappears in her poetry.[55] Instead, she is especially interested in "biophiliac" alternatives, such as natality, flourishing. . . .

Essential in Nicola Slee's thinking in *Seeking the Risen Christa* is her employment of Ivone Gebara's idea of "everyday resurrections," which Gebara elaborates as a way of speaking about "a process of salvation . . . of recovering life and hope and justice," even as experience of justice and hope may be "frail and fleeting." Gebara suggests that everyday resurrections may include "a moment of peace and tenderness in the midst of daily violence, beautiful music that calms our spirit, a novel that keeps us company, a glass of beer or a cup of coffee shared,"

---

51. Isherwood, *Introducing*, 117.
52. Slee, *Seeking*, 1 (cf. 24).
53. Slee, *Seeking*, 121. See also Slee, "Visualizing," 77–79. Emphasis in the original.
54. Slee, *Seeking*, 24.
55. For example, Slee, *Seeking*, 114.

"a sentiment, a kiss, a piece of bread, a happy old woman."[56] At least some of these images are resonant with the way in which Ruether closes her book on redemption in feminist perspective, citing a "women's creed" prepared for a conference in Beijing in 1995:

> Bread. A clean sky. Active peace. A woman's voice singing somewhere. The army disbanded. The harvest abundant. The wound healed. The child wanted. The prisoner freed. The body's integrity honoured. The lover returned. . . . No hand raised in any gesture but greeting. Secure intentions—of heart, home and land. . . .[57]

In its own appropriation of these "everyday" hopes, *Seeking the Risen Christa* beautifully depicts risen forms of Christa bathing in spas, dancing, laughing, running across the grass, pouring Pimms and Tequilas, and cooking up extra food for unexpected guests. Christa is "in some bar . . . a little drunk," hitch-hiking across borders, listening to those who cannot speak or are usually ignored, embracing anxious bodies, reaching across "intolerable pain."[58]

Christa also continues in Slee's later writing, with *Fragments for Fractured Times*, a collection of essays, focusing on the last of its six parts on "a feminist practical theology of the Christa." There we find an emphasis on Advent (a season without a chapter in *Seeking the Risen Christa*), a re-evaluation of Christa crucified, a consideration of Sandys' *Christa* sculpture in relation to the #MeToo movement, and a final piece that expands one of the earlier poems on Christa as crone, "In Praise of God as Feisty Crone."[59]

But it is not that Christa is confined to this final part of *Fragments for Fractured Times*. One of the earlier places in which she may be glimpsed is in an essay on "Theological reflection *in extremis*," on a visit to Srebrenica, which finds further development in Slee's piece in the collection *Contemporary Feminist Theologies: Power, Authority, Love*.[60] These essays on her Bosnian experience are poignant because they represent a certain hesitation about "resurrection," formed in the face of the horrendous legacy of war in the Balkans of which Slee had "visceral experience" on a trip.[61]

Slee reminds us of the gendered nature of war, with women (though men as well) subject to rape as a weapon of war, and with more women than men

---

56. Slee, *Seeking*, 25.

57. Ruether, *Introducing Redemption*, 120.

58. Slee, *Seeking*, 124, 122, 121, 137, 128, 138, 122, 118, 144, 120, 131.

59. See Slee, *Seeking*, 126.

60. Nicola Slee, "Witnessing to What Remains, or the Power of Persisting: Power, Authority and Love in the Interim Spaces," in Kerrie Handasyde, Cathryn MacKinney and Rebekah Pryor, eds, *Contemporary Feminist Theologies: Power, Authority, Love* (Abingdon: Routledge, 2021), 28–37.

61. Slee, *Fragments*, 154.

"surviving" even though doing so "deeply scarred" by what happened to them.[62] She draws attention to the materiality of her visit, to how "little things" "undid" her, such as seeing streets of "pock-marked" buildings, confronting the "sweet, sickly smell of the morgue," being greeted with primrose and mint teas, coffees and cakes, everywhere she went, catching "the sadness in the eyes of survivors," and being wrapped up in their "strong embraces."[63]

Some poems in these later writings say more about what Slee saw, some focusing on particular women, such as Bakira Hasai,[64] who "refuses to keep silent" as she speaks of her shame—though it is not "she who has anything to be ashamed of"—having watched her daughter raped, and being raped herself, three times. Bakira "hunt[s] down war criminals," taking a camera everywhere, always urging testimony, and spending a quarter century amassing evidence to convict men who live with impunity all around.[65]

On a visit to a morgue, Slee meets another tenacious woman, the forensic anthropologist Dragana Vucetic, who matches fragments of broken bodies—"counting all the bones, storing every tear in her bottle"—in order to return remains to those who loved and lost the dear dead.[66] And in a parking lot next to a cemetery, where 8,500 bodies lie, she meets one of the fallen's mothers, "[i]n the kiosk selling souvenirs," overwhelmed by her "infinite gentleness."[67]

Slee suggests that these are people who "survive, who remain, who will not leave, who cannot forget; and God in them remains, remembers, retrieves, and refuses to give up."[68] In particular, Hasai is "an embodiment of the restless, justice-seeking imperative of the God who will not rest until righteousness is restored throughout the world," Vucetic is "an expression of divine attention to the detail of every human life and creature, even in death and dismemberment," and the souvenir-selling elder is a "compassionate face of our grandmother God."[69] And as if in echo of the like of Luke 13:20-21 and Luke 18:1–8, she suggests:

> we might say, "The kindom of God is like a woman who refuses to give up her search to bring war criminals to justice," or "The kindom of God is like a woman who goes to work every day to match fragments of bone from mass graves in order to identify the bodies of those mourned by relatives so that they may bury their loved ones in peace. . . ."[70]

---

62. Slee, *Fragments*, 155.
63. Slee, *Fragments*, 159.
64. There are alternative spellings of her name in *Fragments* and in "Witnessing . . ." and here I follow the latter.
65. Slee, *Fragments*, 161; Slee, "Witnessing," 32.
66. Slee, *Fragments*, 161–2; Slee, "Witnessing," 33.
67. Slee, *Fragments*, 162–3.
68. Slee, *Fragments*, 165.
69. Slee, *Fragments*, 164.
70. Slee, "Witnessing," 34.

Slee ends her reflections in recognition of "many questions," attentive to "what remains," "caught as [Bosnian women, and poems about them] are between death and resurrection in the middle space of Holy Saturday." It is notable that in these later poems she associates her subjects not with "risenness," with Easter, but rather with its eve, somewhat distinct in the liturgical calendar. What we find here is a development of Slee's Christa-thinking: Christa manifest not in the crucifixion, nor so readily in any mode of "resurrection," but embodied in fierce persistence, day in, day out.

Christa Queering Christian Worship

The travail of the Bosnian women about whom Slee writes might put into perspective some of the "battles" about women that happen in some churches, at least where there is no total acquiescence to ecclesial patriarchy. Even so, I want to return to church to note some work to do. The point is simply to note that despite there being decades of second-wave feminist theological reflection on Christa—to say nothing of Slee's conviction, noted earlier, that Christa is "nothing new" in the tradition—Christa remains unnamed in every official denominational resource of which I am aware. Indeed, in precious few such resources is it remotely clear that God is "beyond gender," let alone Christ.

By no means have many churches got as far as thinking, with Gail Ramshaw's suggestion, that "[w]ell-crafted prose can minimize masculine pronouns even in narratives about Jesus and avoid masculine language altogether when texts focus on Christ's divine nature."[71] So there is a long way to go.

At least one example where the heritage of scriptural maternal language does seem to have come home, however, is in the Uniting Church in Australia's official liturgies. One of its Eucharistic prayers depicts not God but Christ as mother:

> Blessed are you, O God;
> your Son our mother
> nourishes and sustains us
> with the pure milk of his very self. . . .[72]

An accompanying "bluebric" explains: "several spiritual writers have used the image of Jesus as mother: for example, Anselm, Archbishop of Canterbury (1033–1109) and Dame Julian of Norwich (c. 1342–1416)." *Uniting in Worship 2* also

---

71. Ramshaw, *God Beyond Gender*, 31.

72. Uniting Church in Australia, *Uniting in Worship 2* (Sydney: Uniting Church Press, 2005), CD-rom, SLD 3.

includes a "canticle of Christ's goodness" based on a prayer by Anselm addressed to Christ as mother.[73]

It is something of an open secret that the earlier drafts of *Uniting in Worship 2*'s invitation to communion, "This is the joyful feast of Jesus: bread for beloved children"[74] read "This is the joyful feast of Jesus-Sophia," but the reference to Sophia did not make it through to the final form. Had it, it would perhaps be the closest to Slee's proposals in an "old-line" "ecumenical-catholic" denomination.

Additionally, the "Wisdom" service which is bundled into *Uniting in Worship 2* is singled out among all of its resources as of a more experimental nature than the rest.[75] So as well as contextualizing the reserve about Jesus-Sophia that won-over when it came to the wording of the Eucharistic invitation, it suggests the wider struggle to include full-blooded feminist perspectives in the church's prayer. In any case, the image of Christ as mother on the one hand, and on the other a notion of either a disembodied or still male-imaged (that is, Jesus-) Sophia may each in their own way be (far?) less than fully encompassing of all that might be mediated by Christa. But these are at least a start—beginnings far too often entirely unmade.

For prayer to Christa as such, Nicola Slee's book includes manifold examples, including collects, though in fact, as she notes, "[she has] used the full range of Christian prayer forms to name and address the Christa."[76] All of this in *Seeking the Risen Christa* has earlier precedent in her *Praying Like a Woman*.[77] Slee avers that her prayers were crafted "in the hope that these might [ ] find their way into a range of liturgical contexts and help to shape Christian prayer that explicitly affirms the capacity of women to be in Christ/a and Christ/a to be in the form of a woman."[78] As yet, both the collects and the other forms are waiting to be welcomed into denominational resources.

A final matter also relates to Christian assembly. Traditions which refuse women a place as presider at table are by no means the only problem. For it is one thing for women to become priests/presbyters and another to catch a vision of a feminist ecclesiology; consequently, it is quite naïve to suppose that women being

---

73. Uniting Church in Australia, *Uniting in Worship 2*, CD-rom, canticle 30, adopted from multiple uses in the Church of England's *Common Worship* (London: CHP, 2000 [earlier in *Patterns for Worship* [London: CHP, 1989]).

74. Uniting Church in Australia, *Uniting in Worship 2*, e.g., 209.

75. See the introductory note: "*An unauthorised model service offered for trial use*" (Wisdom SLD, 1). Emphasis in the original.

76. Slee, "Visualizing," 86.

77. Slee, *Praying*, 124–125 for direct address to Christa in the earlier collection.

78. Slee, "Visualizing," 87.

"allowed" to preside in worship will necessarily lead to change toward a feminist practice of Christian assembly.[79] But somewhere along the line, women need to become presiders in church, especially at Eucharist:

> The church positively requires women's bodily presence in its lived expression of redemption, as unequivocal affirmation of the saving significance of "difference," and the enlargement of symbolic imagination as human persons re-explore their relationships to one another and to God.[80]

Hence I note that Christian feminism has produced a raft of excellent reflection on what is at stake in churches' failure to embrace "fully humanly inclusive" representation in liturgy. Tina Beattie,[81] Anita Monro,[82] Teresa Berger,[83] Karen O'Donnell,[84] and Bryan Cones[85] are among the most insightful. Beattie, Berger, and O'Donnell, however, concentrate their various tactics on the figure of Mary: Berger retrieving from the tradition suppressed elements that may yet be recovered—Eucharist as mother's milk, Mary's priestly womb and breasts, for instance; Beattie crafting a challenging "Marian narrative of women's salvation"; and O'Donnell focusing on a hyphenated "Annunciation-Incarnation Event" rather than the latter aspect alone.

Marian moves are hardly unanticipated, given scholarship such as Margaret Barker's that has illumined how the wisdom tradition may have its roots with the "lady in the temple," "the mother of Yahweh" in the Jerusalem temple, an aspect of early Hebrew religion trounced in the reforms of Josiah, but reappearing in transmuted mode in the early Christian Marian tradition.[86] The end of Schüssler Fiorenza's book on Sophia, *Jesus: Miriam's Child, Sophia's Prophet*, is just one example of a tempting slide from Christology to Mariology,[87] whereas Sally

---

79. Stephen Burns, "From Women Priests to Feminist Ecclesiology?" in Fredrica Harris Thompsett, ed., *Looking Forward, Looking Backward: 40 Years of Women's Ordination* (New York: Seabury, 2014), 99–110.

80. Ann Loades, "Unequivocal Affirmation of the Saving Significance of 'Difference', in Nicola Slee and Stephen Burns, eds., *Presiding Like a Woman* (London: SPCK, 2010), 77–86 at 85.

81. Tina Beattie, *God's Mother, Eve's Advocate: A Marian Narrative of Women's Salvation* (London: Continuum, 2002); Tina Beattie, "Vision and Vulnerabilty: The Significance of Sacramentality and the Woman Priest for Feminist Theology," in Natalie Watson and Stephen Burns, eds, *Exchanges of Grace: Essays in Honour of Ann Loades* (London: SCM Press, 2008), 235–249.

82. Anita Monro, "Ain't I a Woman," in Slee and Burns, eds, *Presiding Like a Woman*, 123-133.

83. Teresa Berger, *Gender Differences and the Making of Liturgical History: Lifting a Veil of Liturgy's Past* (Aldershot: Ashgate, 2011).

84. Karen O'Donnell, *Broken Bodies: Mary, the Eucharist and Trauma* (London: SCM Press, 2018).

85. Bryan Cones, *This Assembly of Believers: The Gift of Difference in the Church at Prayer* (London: SCM Press, 2020), 103–133.

86. See Margaret Barker, *The Mother of the Lord: Vol. 1—The Lady in the Temple* (London: SPCK, 2012).

87. Schüssler Fiorenza, *Jesus: Miriam's Child*, 163–190.

Douglas' *Early Christian Understandings of Jesus as Female* challenges that the focus of the wisdom tradition might best—and at the very least must also—rest on Jesus, "woman-wisdom." Douglas' study strikes me as profoundly important in connection with questions posed by the feminist "recovery" of Sophia, just as it does in relation to liturgical concerns. While Berger tracks "liturgical history," Douglas emphasizes the self-same imagery unearthed by Berger at different times and places but in scripture and in very early Christian sources. Note, as just one example, her discussion of Christ's breast milk as a New Testament image emerging "from, and for, the context of worship."[88]

For my own part, while in no way disparaging the efforts of those making a Marian turn in their liturgical arguments, I simply note that Christa seems still to be waiting to get in on the scene. And though I think there are reasons to encourage proceeding with care—I suggest reasons akin to Brock's refusal to identify Christ (or Christa) with any individual—it seems to me that a "Douglas route" is hopeful for a breakthrough, just as a door is ajar in the recent work of Sharon Jagger, focusing as it does on collision of Eucharistic themes and menstrual blood as women preside at table.[89]

I am deeply wary of the idea that the ordained or the presider in worship represents Christ. So I think that the *in persona Christi* tradition of ministerial representation is a major problem, though it might be reframed in terms of *in persona Christa/ae*.[90] I wonder, though, about searching for ways it might be linked to the *alter Christus* theme.[91]

Catherine of Siena is a bold exemplar of *alter Christus* idea, speaking in her prayers to God about "other Christs" who are "conformed to your only-begotten Son."[92] While Catherine applies this term to the ordained, she notably also turns it to those who are not. I suggest that the *alter Christus* tradition has some promise *if it can be linked to feminist moves that distinguish Jesus from Christ*—a move mentioned above not only in relation to Ruether, but as made by Brock and Heyward; and to add fuel to the fire at this point, I add some implications clearly articulated by Kwok: "the space between Jesus and Christ is unsettling and fluid, resisting easy categorization and closure."[93]

From feminist perspective, the *alter Christus* ideas will always need to be sifted carefully through the kind of scrutiny that insists that Christ/a is made manifest

---

88. Douglas, *Early Church Understandings*, 182–183.

89. Sharon Jagger, "Presiding Like a Woman: Menstruating at the Altar," in Ashley Cocksworth, Rachel Starr and Stephen Burns, eds, *From Shores of Silence: Explorations in Feminist Practical Theology* (London: SCM Press, 2023), 144–160.

90. For example, Stephen Burns, "Presiding Like a Woman: Feminist Gesture for Christian Assembly," *Feminist Theology* 21 (2009): 29–49; Bryan Cones, "'Evoking the Other': Toward Feminist Gesture for Any Assembly," *Feminist Theology* 28:2 (2020): 198–215.

91. Find it in Ruether in direct reference to Blandina, *Sexism and God-talk*, 110.

92. Suzanne Noffke, *The Prayers of Catherine of Siena*, 330.

93. Kwok, *Postcolonial Imagination*, 171; Slee, "Visualizing," 82.

in community. And I note that *at that very point*, conversation/confrontation emerges in relation to a commonplace, but all-too-often un-/underexamined mainstay of liturgical theology: that liturgy is "the work of the people," and therefore that participation is the key imperative for Christian assembly, the aim to be considered "above all else."[94] As *Uniting in Worship 2* has it, "the congregation is not an audience."[95] Aptly put, quite bluntly: "no participation, no liturgy"![96] So while I am not holding my breath for the liturgical mainstream/malestream to usher Christa to the table, I am clear that Sheezus Christa should cause a stir right around the room, queering every inch of liturgical space, and with respect to every role in the assembly.[97]

---

94. Vatican II's Sacrosanctum Concilium, #14. See David Lysik, ed., *The Liturgy Documents, Vol. 1: A Parish Resource* (Chicago: LTP, fourth edition 2004), 7.

95. *Uniting in Worship 2*, 131; *Methodist Worship Book*, Peterborough: Methodist Publishing House, 1999, vii.

96. See Stephen Burns, "No Participation, No Liturgy," in Bryan Cones and Stephen Burns, eds, *Fully Conscious, Fully Active* (Chicago: LTP, 2020), 2–11.

97. Note Bryan Cones's excellent remedies to the commonplace dearth of rubrics *for the assembly*: Bryan Cones, "Looking for the Body's Language," in Stephen Burns and Robert Gribben, eds, *When We Pray: The Future of Common* Prayer (Melbourne: Coventry Press, 2020), 257–275.

PART II
PRACTICING

we build our swayings on the hopes of generations past and coming
    shaping us with song and word
        movement and hosannas—oh the hosannas
the turns we take zip-zap into holy twirling
    that dares new imaginations of song and text
        art and ritual
and we pause or stop
    and open wide to the sweet spirit—the whole divine
    holy divine

CHAPTER SIX

"FORGIVE US OUR KERTERVERS"[1]

A Church of England Theological College as Queer Liturgical Space[2]

Susannah Cornwall and Joel Love

Introduction

At the end of January 2017, ordinands (trainee clergy) at Westcott House, a Church of England theological college in Cambridge, UK, led a service entitled "Polari Evening Prayer," held in anticipation of LGBT History Month. Subsequently, images of part of the order of service were shared online by an attendee. These included responsive prayers and Bible readings taken from the Polari Bible, which had been devised by the Sisters of Perpetual Indulgence in Manchester, UK.[3] Polari is a form of slang associated particularly with gay men's subculture in Britain prior to the decriminalization of sexual activity between men in the 1960s, but also used by some other countercultural communities. Gay men in Britain used Polari as a form of code in order to identify one another and to discuss topics that could otherwise have endangered them

---

1. "Forgive us our kertervers, as we forgive them that kerterver against us" is a line from the Lord's Prayer in Polari as used in the Polari Evensong. "Kertervers" is used as a synonym for "sins" throughout the Polari Bible.

2. We are grateful to Paul Baker for his useful comments on an earlier draft of this chapter.

3. The Polari Bible was created by a Manchester-based member of the Sisters of Perpetual Indulgence, Sister Matic de Bauchery (aka Tim Greening-Jackson), and can be found online at https://www.polaribible.org/. The Sisters, an order of "queer nuns," are celebrated for their "turning" of familiar religious imagery and language in the service of political activism and outreach to members of excluded communities, including those marginalized in faith settings because of their sexuality or gender. Greening-Jackson designed a computer program to "transduce" the authorized version, substituting particular vocabulary with its Polari rendering. See Tim Greening-Jackson, "Introduction and Credits," *Polari Bible*, 2015, https://www.polaribible.org/the-polari-bible-7th-edition-2/379-2/. Hard-copy versions of the Polari Bible were donated to the John Rylands Library in Manchester and exhibited alongside other manuscripts in the library's holdings such as Papyrus P52, a fragment of John's gospel which is the oldest surviving papyrus of a biblical text, dating from the second century CE. See Paul Baker, *Fabulosa! The Story of Polari, Britain's Secret Gay Language* (London: Reaktion Books, 2019), 266.

if overheard. The Polari Evensong at Westcott included lines such as "Fabeness be to the Auntie, and to the Homie Chavvie, and to the Fantabulosa Fairy; As it was in the beginning, is now, and ever shall be, world nanti end. Larlou." This, rendered in standard English, reads as "Glory be to the Father, and to the Son, and to the Holy Spirit; As it was in the beginning, is now and ever shall be, world without end. Amen."

News of the service created consternation within the college and beyond,[4] although the Westcott Polari Evensong was based on a similar service, devised by artist Erich Erving, that had taken place at Yale Divinity School earlier in 2017, which did not seem to have aroused such strong feeling. The then-principal of Westcott House, Rev'd Canon Chris Chivers, said publicly that the liturgy "was not an authorised act of worship in line with the college's procedures," and that "the contents of the service are at variance with the doctrine and teaching of the Church of England, and that is hugely regrettable."[5] A week after the service, Chivers said:

> The difficulty here is that Polari isn't a translation: it's a transgression. It's not like saying 'Let's do liturgy in French.' The point of Polari is it deliberately subverts. It's code language. I understand how it originated, but in the context of liturgy, that can never work, because that's not what worship is. It's not about transgression, but about finding language within which all can find themselves, because it's directed to God.[6]

Chivers added, "[The service was] far too horizontal. The question here is: where is the verticality in this? We understand ourselves only in the context of our worship of God, and, if we are spending all our time pointing to ourselves, we are missing the point."[7] Chivers spoke of the pain that had been caused to some attendees, and held that the "subversion" of worship had made it difficult for people to listen to one another.[8]

Conflicting assumptions about the space (Westcott chapel) and the freedom of students to experiment with its liturgy led to differing reactions to the

---

4. See, e.g., Robert Mendick and Abigail Frymann Rouch, "Leading Cambridge Theological College Apologises for 'Subverting the Teaching of Christ' in Church Service," *The Telegraph*, 3 February 2017, https://www.telegraph.co.uk/news/2017/02/03/cambridge-theological-college-sorry-for-subverting-teaching-christ-church-service/, and Katie Gibbons, "Gay Slang Service Angers the Faithful," *The Times*, 4 February 2017, https://www.thetimes.co.uk/article/gay-slang-service-angers-the-faithful-h82b2cn3t.

5. Quoted in Harriet Sherwood, "CofE College Apologizes for Students' Attempts to 'Queer Evening Prayer,'" *The Guardian*, 3 February 2017, https://www.theguardian.com/world/2017/feb/03/church-of-england-college-apologises-students-queer-evening-prayer.

6. Quoted in Madeleine Davies, "Polari a Transgression, says Westcott Principal," *Church Times*, 10 February 2017, https://www.churchtimes.co.uk/articles/2017/10-february/news/uk/polari-a-transgression-says-westcott-principal.

7. Davies, "Polari a Transgression."

8. Davies, "Polari a Transgression."

Polari Evensong. However, we note that although the Polari Evensong was publicly criticized for not being authorized liturgy, there were in fact other instances of unapproved liturgy used at Westcott around the same time which did not attract the same criticism. We suggest that Polari's self-consciously pro-gay angle was a source of the differential scrutiny which still attaches to LGBTQI+ people and their allies in the Church of England and undermines the Church of England's own commitments to "acknowledge prejudice; speak into silence; address ignorance; cast out fear; admit hypocrisy; pay attention to power."[9] We argue that the theological college is a queer space, a strange or odd institution that does not quite fit into the diocesan and synodical structures of the Church of England, and that, as such, it represents a possible location for the queering, questioning, and renewal of the church.

Queer can be defined as "the strange or odd, the thing that doesn't fit in."[10] As such, it speaks from the margins and complicates the narrative by asking awkward questions and by pointing out who or what is being excluded. Queer theology is a resource for the wider church because it identifies unrecognized inadequacies in the tradition. Queerness is an invitation to critical self-examination. Occasionally it achieves its ends through parody, flamboyance, and irony. In the case of the Westcott Evensong that we are exploring, the queer voices belonged to those students who wanted to experiment with language and liturgy, but also belonged to the academics and activists who reclaimed an LGBTQI+ argot and preserved it in a dictionary and the Bible. The queer voices of a subculture were being brought into prayer in a consecrated place of worship. Even if this took the form of parody or irony (or was vulnerable to being seen as such), the attempt represents a queer use of both the liturgy itself, and the language of LGBT ancestors.

Hierarchy and Contestation

In the Church of England, theological colleges fall outside regular organizational structures, and might be understood to maintain critical distance from them. Yet responses to the Polari Evensong showed that these spaces are in fact policed by power-structures within and beyond the church.

Westcott House is one of a number of Theological Education Institutions (TEIs) in England. TEIs exist as independent institutions with the role of forming students for ordination in the Church of England and, in some cases, other denominations via ecumenical partnerships. TEIs are reviewed periodically by the Church of England's National Ministry Team (formerly known as the Ministry Division), but receive most of their income through diocesan budgets

---

9. Pastoral Advisory Group (Church of England), *Pastoral Principles for Living Well Together* (London: Church House Publishing), 2019.

10. Gerard Loughlin (ed.), *Queer Theology: Rethinking the Western Body* (Oxford: Blackwell, 2007), 7.

when bishops and diocesan directors of ordinands (DDOs) decide to send them students.[11] These institutions are sometimes associated with secular universities with which they may have historic ties (or else through the Common Awards scheme which links them to the validating institution, currently the University of Durham). The status of Oxford-based institutions such as Wycliffe Hall and St Stephen's House is slightly different at the time of writing from that of Cambridge-based ones such as Westcott House. The former are Permanent Private Halls of the University of Oxford, while the latter are not constituent colleges of the University of Cambridge. The liminality of these institutions is visible in their funding structures and governance, and in their need to maintain relationships with their respective universities, the Church of England nationally, and individual dioceses.

At their ordination, and at every subsequent licensing to a parish or other diocesan role, Church of England clergy promise in their Declaration of Assent that "in public prayer and administration of the sacraments, I will use only the forms of service which are authorized or allowed by canon."[12] In practice this means that clergy must use the *Book of Common Prayer* (1662) or *Common Worship* (2000) or some other texts authorized by their ordinary, the bishop.[13] Diocesan bishops have the power within their diocese to authorize experimental forms of worship or to dispense with the requirements of canon law (for example, dispensing with the requirement that there be daily morning and evening prayer, and a public Eucharist in every benefice every Sunday, during the coronavirus lockdowns of 2020–2021).

From the point of view of canon law, however, the chapels of TEIs sit outside the jurisdiction of diocesan bishops. For the purposes of authorizing liturgy, the principal of each TEI is the "ordinary" of its chapel. In theory, this gives TEIs the freedom to experiment with liturgy and worship in ways that can help their students to explore the resonances and effects of the theology they are studying, or to blend theory and practice.

---

11. TEIs may generate additional income from independent students, short courses, and distance learning. Since 2017 and at the time of writing, funds for ordination training have been made as block grants to Church of England dioceses by the National Ministry Team. Dioceses make decisions about individual ordinands' training pathways based on factors including their age and any previous training. Dioceses then make a direct transfer to individual TEIs who invoice them each term for ordinands' fees. See Ministry Division (Church of England), *Resourcing Ministerial Education: A Guide to Financing Training for Ordination* (2019), 14; https://www.churchofengland.org/sites/default/files/2019-07/RME%20Handbook%202019.pdf. Ordinands on higher-cost programs such as the University of Cambridge Tripos may additionally have some fees covered by the central CofE Training for Ministry budget. See Ministry Division (Church of England), *Resourcing Ministerial Education*, 19.

12. Archbishops' Council (Church of England) (2007), "The Declaration of Assent" (from *Common Worship: Ordination Services*), https://www.churchofengland.org/prayer-and-worship/worship-texts-and-resources/common-worship/ministry/declaration-assent.

13. The regulations about authorized liturgy may be found in Section B of the Canon Law of the Church of England (Archbishops' Council 2016) and at https://www.churchofengland.org/about/leadership-and-governance/legal-services/canons-church-england/section-b.

As a matter of fact, the principals of Westcott House around the time of the Polari Evensong regularly authorized experimental forms of worship for use in the college chapel, at which one of us was present. On one occasion, an intervention was staged during Evening Prayer, just after the New Testament reading which happened to include 1 Timothy 2:12 ("I permit no woman to teach or to have authority over a man; she is to keep silent"). A large scroll was rolled down the aisle, with the names of the books of the Bible scrawled all over it. Worshippers were given felt-tipped pens and invited to write responses to the misogyny contained therein. The intercessions also reflected the feminist theology that this piece of experimental worship had been designed to showcase. On another occasion, a "rave mass" was held in the chapel, with strobe lighting and loud music. In lieu of intercessions, two ordinands jumped up and down in the middle of the chapel, while shouting words including "fuck." This service caused some consternation among the student body, but did not lead to articles in the national press or (to our knowledge) to any students being dismissed from the college or punished in any way.

The fact that an experimental service in an explicitly queer idiom, the Polari Evensong, received such a different reaction, seems suggestive. If nothing else, it demonstrates the need for the pastoral principles recently underpinning the *Living in Love and Faith* resources (2020). The principles comprise calls to counter six "pervading evils" via commitment to "acknowledge prejudice; speak into silence; address ignorance; cast out fear; admit hypocrisy; pay attention to power."[14]

There continues to be a certain paranoia in the Church of England about sexual matters. This is exacerbated by a long history of "don't ask, don't tell," as demonstrated by recent highlighting of the church's safeguarding failures over many years.[15] When behaviors are tolerated in practice but officially outlawed, it is harder to hold them up to appropriate scrutiny. Additionally, it is hard for those in authority to speak out lest they themselves attract opprobrium: it is quite understandable that bishops, college principals, and others should fear the British tabloid press given its track record. Yet those in authority do have pastoral and professional responsibility for those in their care, and a duty to create spaces in which sexual identities, desires, and relationships may be properly and appropriately interrogated in light of ministry and vocation.

The temerity of the Westcott students who sought to speak into silence (whether in Polari or plain English) was not met by an institution trying to cast out fear. If anything, this case study calls Christians to admit hypocrisy and especially

---

14. Pastoral Advisory Group (Church of England), *Pastoral Principles for Living Well Together* (London: Church House Publishing, 2019).

15. Alexis Jay, et al., *Independent Inquiry into Child Sexual Abuse (IICSA) Investigation Report: The Anglican Church: Case Studies: 1. The Diocese of Chichester; 2. The Response to Allegations Against Peter Ball* (London: Her Majesty's Stationery Office, 2019).

to pay attention to power. The response the Polari Evensong received from the national press[16] shows that there is still a need to address ignorance and acknowledge prejudice, both within the church and in wider society.

Polari as Anti-Language

Anti-languages like Polari, says linguistics scholar Paul Baker, "are used by people who are somehow apart from mainstream society, either residing on the edges of it, or hidden away or even criminalized, with attempts from the mainstream to expel or contain them."[17] Baker holds that Polari's "anti-language" status is obsolete in contexts where LGBTQI+ people are no longer an "anti-society" but assimilated into mainstream culture.[18] We suggest, however, that, in the Church of England, theological and ecclesial limits on LGBTQI+ people persist: reactions to the Polari Evensong, and distinctive institutional limits on their freedoms,[19] suggest that in the Church of England gay people *are* still an "anti-society."

Anti-languages do not just translate concepts like-for-like; they "encode something different, a kind of 'us-against-them' worldview."[20] Polari is associated with outsiders, those exiled from acceptable society. One possible disadvantage of using Polari liturgically, then, is that, in perpetuating the idea of queerness as outsiderhood (especially a particular kind of arch, camp, knowing outsiderhood), it allows institutions like the Church of England to maintain the fiction that there are no gay *insiders* in its ranks, using its workaday patterns of speech and practice in their lives and ministries. Another is that borrowing Polari so briefly might be understood to constitute cultural appropriation, using it playfully without adequately acknowledging the danger and threat lived by its erstwhile speakers.

As Baker notes, Polari is associated with an older generation of camp gay men, many of whom had already died by the time he started his Polari research in the 1990s.[21] Its anachronistic use at Westcott in 2017 was thus, arguably, less

---

16. See, e.g., Mendick and Rouch, "Leading Cambridge Theological College," and Gibbons, "Gay Slang Service."

17. Baker, *Fabulosa!*, 17.

18. Baker, *Fabulosa!*, 281.

19. Notably, Church of England clergy may neither marry their same-sex partners, nor be in openly sexually active relationships with their same-sex civil partners. Candidates for ministry who will not promise to conduct themselves in accordance with *Issues in Human Sexuality* (effectively recusing themselves from same-sex intimate relationships) may, depending on their diocese, find themselves not recommended for ordination: "The clergy cannot claim the liberty to enter into sexually active homophile relationships." Archbishops' Council (Church of England), *Issues in Human Sexuality: A Statement by the House of Bishops of the General Synod* (London: Church House Publishing, 1991), 45.

20. Baker, *Fabulosa!*, 18.

21. Paul Baker, *Polari – The Lost Language of Gay Men* (London: Routledge, 2002).

appropriation and more a conscious trying-on of something from a different time and place to see how it fits, with an explicit intention to honor and celebrate it and gay people, in the context of LGBT History Month (as the preface in the order of service makes clear).

Polari is in some sense artificial: probably no single speaker, notes Baker, would ever have used the full lexicon he collated, for it draws on a range of individuals' idiosyncratic usages. Yet this artificiality is hardly alien to liturgical contexts: indeed, the sometimes-unfamiliar language of liturgy heightens its capacity to hint at something beyond the everyday. Baker notes that in the 1990s, the Sisters of Perpetual Indulgence used Polari in their religious services (such as the "canonization" of Derek Jarman) precisely because it was at that point considered a "dead language" rather akin to Latin, so that its use invoked and heightened a sense of mysticism: the use of Polari at Westcott might thus be understood as being in continuity with that earlier religious-ceremonial usage.[22] Polari's playfulness and self-consciousness matter. Jem Bloomfield comments:

> All language about God is incomplete, an attempt to account in human words something which is beyond our capacity to capture in speech or writing. . . . Polari is as inadequate as standard English in this sense, but it might give another turn to the kaleidoscope and present another refracting vision of the glory.[23]

Polari's use at Westcott is thus double-edged. It consciously honors and makes visible certain individuals and subcultures often accepted implicitly but not explicitly within the Church of England. But it also risks repeating a sense that LGBTQI+ identity inevitably *is* or *should* be rebellious, countercultural, "beyond" the institution.

Liminal/Queer Space

In this section, we explore the potential queerness of theological colleges as liminal spaces, showing that as sites of experimentation they point to liturgy's capacity to disrupt and interrogate oppressive norms.

Church of England residential theological colleges are no longer set up or run by dioceses directly. They exist as separate institutions, sometimes housed within secular universities or sharing space with them. Ordinands are trained for ministry alongside students who may or may not share their religious traditions or affiliations, or who may belong to different denominations. Students in Church of England theological colleges are no longer part of their home (or "sending") parish,

---

22. Paul Baker, personal communication to the authors, 9 November 2021.

23. Jem Bloomfield, "Vada the Omi: On the Polari Evensong," 4 February 2017, https://quiteirregular.wordpress.com/2017/02/04/vada-the-omi-on-the-polari-evensong/.

nor are they still in the discernment process of their diocese. They have arrived at a new phase and location for what is called "formation." This makes the theological college a transitional environment existing at arm's length from diocesan structures and with a very specific purpose. It could not be a more liminal space and is perhaps one of the few such places within the structures of the national church.

Theological colleges describe their purpose in terms of "formation," which is understood as something more holistic than "education" or "training." One model of formation sees it as a process of "breaking" and "remaking" the individual, in which case their role is to submit and be transformed. This model is built on romantic or monastic ideas but in practice it has much in common with military training.[24] A more collaborative model of formation would see the student as an active participant, as suggested by language about "pathways," theological reflection, and module choices. In this case, the student can be understood as an agent within a changing network of relationships that includes their sending diocese, the National Ministry Team of the Church of England, the theological institution itself, other students, context placements, local, national, and global events, and of course the Holy Spirit.

From the authors' own experience, theological students do see themselves as active participants in their formation for ministry. Even where they are not encouraged to take this view, many bring this expectation with them from their previous careers and life experience anyway. Students find themselves in a stimulating environment where they encounter the variety of theological views available in the tradition and the academy. They are free of their home contexts and able to evaluate more critically some of the liturgical and doctrinal constraints within which they have grown up or been nurtured in the faith. This presents an opportunity especially for non-white, feminist, and LGBTQI+ students to explore what space there is for them in this niche that is somewhat protected from existing hierarchies and power structures. When theological colleges are housed in secular institutions or are multidenominational, there is even more reason for them to be safe spaces for experimentation.

A liminal situation like the one we have been describing is a potentially fertile place for the queering of liturgy. Like theological reflection, queerness is a work of interpretation. Language and imagery can be interrogated and subverted, and there is joy in this playfulness. A queer aesthetics combines elements from different places and registers (like Polari itself) or uses the symbols of power ironically (like ballroom queens). The Polari Evensong at Westcott House brought together the Polari Bible with the rhythms and setting of Anglican worship.

---

24. For a critique of this model of understanding of formation, see Brutus Green, "Being Called Out: Vocation as a Model of Anglican Ministerial Training and Priesthood," *Theology* 113 (2010): 114–122. See also further discussion in Susannah Cornwall, "Identity and Formation in Theological Education: The Occasion of Intersex," *Journal of Adult Theological Education* 12:1 (2015): 4–15.

Arun Arora, then the Church of England's director of communications, said in 2017:

> The principal of Westcott House has issued a statement where he says the service was "hugely regrettable" and that "theological colleges are places of experiment and inquiry where people do make mistakes." We would agree with both of those sentiments. The church should be a place which develops both risk-taking for the gospel and a no-blame culture.[25]

When and why, then, do particular risks feel *too* risky? We ourselves suggest that a theological college is precisely an appropriate space for experimentation, and we note that there were other instances of "risky" alternative worship at Westcott around the time of the Polari Evensong which suggests that such experiments were not unknown there. Indeed, risk-taking is, we suggest, an appropriate and even necessary part of liturgy, given that liturgy—as an interface of public and private prayer—also functions as a mix of the familiar and the strange, to draw worshippers to a God who continues to surprise.

Indeed, Bloomfield holds that there might be something *particularly* apposite about the use of Polari in a liturgical context, precisely because of its associations with outsiderhood:

> Just as the language of the Book of Common Prayer disrupts our modern language with its ingrained assumptions and patterns in one way, Polari seems likely to disrupt it from another angle. . . . Liturgical prayer seems ideal as a way to explore Polari prayer. It holds us in the tension between what we say privately in our own mind, in our everyday language, and the verbal shapes and emotional landscapes offered by the liturgy.[26]

Of course Polari is risky, he notes; but that is entirely appropriate for theological language, and utilizing discombobulating and unexpected forms of speech might remind worshipers of just what a risk they take when they speak of God by any means whatsoever. Polari, as a language from the underside, is especially fitting for use in a context which should be interruptive of ingrained patterns, assumptions, and modes of thought.

Of course, worshipers do not always allow liturgy to do its work of interruption, and this is perhaps particularly the case for those worshipers—like students in theological colleges—who engage with it day in and day out. In such instances, maybe it is even more important to ensure space for "irregular"

---

25. Arora quoted in Harriet Sherwood, "CofE College Apologizes for Students' Attempts to 'Queer Evening Prayer,'" *The Guardian*, 3 February 2017, https://www.theguardian.com/world/2017/feb/03/church-of-england-college-apologises-students-queer-evening-prayer.

26. Bloomfield, "Vada the Omi."

liturgical experiments, precisely because people very familiar with "regular" liturgy may lose touch with liturgy's capacity to be disruptive or strange.

Conclusion

Liturgy is profoundly embodied; thus, Bloomfield holds that a language so focused on bodies and body parts as Polari is might be understood as particularly, even peculiarly, suitable for liturgical use.[27] There are, of course, however, tensions here around individuals' bodies (and the sexual and gender identities they enact, publicly or otherwise) versus communal bodies: the worshiping body at a TEI like Westcott; the wider institution of the Church of England with all its sensitivities around power, reputation and establishment, and so on.

Chris Chivers held, as we saw above, that the Polari Evensong was too horizontal, not vertical enough: that is, we might gloss, that it was too much about those present, and not enough about God. It is worth noting, however, that the full order of service (an unpublished document shared with us privately by an attendee) shows the standard English text and the Polari text arranged side-by-side, so the objection that attendees might have been excluded from worship through not understanding what they were saying or hearing is moot. There are, in any case, sundry assumptions implicit in Chivers' statement which one might want to challenge: for example, that attention to one's fellow worshipers is not in itself a means of attention to God, as Christians encounter God in one another; or that the language of approved liturgy is by definition more successful at allowing for what Chivers calls "verticality" and does not itself frustrate people's capacity to connect with God in worship.

Sometimes things do not quite work out as hoped (cf. Arora, above), but this does not mean the experimentation was not worth the hazard. Innovation is risky by definition—but where better to take such risks than in a theological college chapel among other ordinands and members of the college community? Arguably, "failed" experiments are better carried out in such a "sandbox" space than in the context of a parish or other gathered community for which one has pastoral responsibility. Furthermore, even failures have their place. J. Halberstam's appeal to the queer art of failure is a reminder of the importance of calling into question the good of success by everyday standards.[28] Failing to live up to expectations which are themselves distorted or problematic can itself be a prophetic sign of the penultimacy and provisionality of many of the goods and norms taken for granted.

The Church of England's Pilling Report on human sexuality held that people, including clergy, should be able to talk openly and honestly about sexuality

---

27. Bloomfield, "Vada the Omi."
28. J. Halberstam, *The Queer Art of Failure* (Durham, NC: Duke University Press, 2011).

and to take full part in ongoing discernment processes about the Spirit's message to the church in changing times[29]—yet in 2017 at Westcott, there was clearly still anxiety about the presence of an avowedly LGBTQI+-affirming service. Polari's self-consciously LGBT-affirming history was, we suggest, part of the reason for the opposition the liturgy caused there when other experimental services had not. This signals the differential scrutiny which still attaches to LGBTQI+ people and their allies in the Church of England.

Baker's characterization of Polari as an "anti-language"[30] functioning to mark out a group from the mainstream parallels Christianity's characterization as community. Yet God's community is nonexclusive: Revelation 7:9 envisages, in the end times, "a great multitude that no one could number, from every nation, from all tribes and peoples and languages"—including the ironic ones. To quash such voices risks, we suggest, an unwillingness to uphold the pastoral principles to speak into silence and pay attention to power.

College chapels are, as we have seen, outside (that is, beyond, different from, or with some critical distance from) regular structures of the Church of England. Yet the Polari Evensong showed that these spaces *are* policed: by media outlets hosting pearl-clutching commentary, and by diocesan bishops withdrawing their students and/or funding. These are not, perhaps, unconnected: a long history of associations between sexual impropriety and moral "laxity" has left many clergy still in fear of what might happen if they were "outed" by the tabloids. The right-wing press in Britain has strong views on what the Church of England should do and should not, especially when it comes to sexual matters. This is exacerbated given the Church's own public expectations for its clergy's sexual conduct which frequently do not map onto what is tacitly allowed.

If a theological college cannot be understood as a queer space where there is space for risk, experimentation, and the celebration of diversity, then is there any such thing within the Church of England? We note that there are multitudinous queer experiments bubbling up in a range of parachurch contexts, as well as anecdotal instances of "unauthorized" liturgical innovation happening in ways not only tolerated but also commended by the Church of England's senior clergy. Nonetheless, we hold that there will also and crucially continue to be a key place for queer experimentation within theological colleges specifically. One line of argument runs that formation for ordained ministry is about initiating people into institutional norms and practices, so that going "off-piste" during training is, apart from anything else, a poor preparation for the more constrained environments in which they are actually likely to serve. Yet taken to its logical conclusions, this argument sets too much store by an institution's consistency and monolithic nature, when, in actual fact, the Church of England, just like many

---

29. Archbishops' Council (Church of England), *Report of the House of Bishops' Working Group on Human Sexuality (The Pilling Report)* (London: Church House Publishing, 2013), 102.

30. Paul Baker, *Fabulosa!*, 17.

other institutions, is a site of contestation, disagreement, and diversity of conviction. In the Church of England, like many other denominations, there are strikingly disparate views on matters such as women's leadership, gender transition, and same-sex marriage which are all held in good faith—as evidenced by responses to the Living in Love and Faith process and debates at General Synod since 2020. However, recognizing this diversity sometimes actually functions to close down movements for change. Why? Because however unsustainable holding together people with such disparate convictions might feel, the fact that the Church of England has already managed it for so long often serves as a kind of warrant to continue doing so.

When in late 2021, a discussion broke out on "Anglican Twitter" about *Issues in Human Sexuality*,[31] which had come to be the "official" line on human sexuality to which candidates for ordination were expected to give assent and which holds that Church of England clergy are not at liberty to enter into sexually active homophile relationships, it became clear that many clergy—including some of those involved in the ministry of discerning others' vocations—were only for the first time learning what it actually said. Some expressed shock at the outmoded and phobic accounts of bisexuality it contained, and at its apparent advocacy of sexual orientation conversion therapy,[32] something which the General Synod moved in July 2017 "has no place in the modern world, is unethical, potentially harmful and not supported by evidence."[33] But others articulated shock at their shock, hinting that the ability not to have known what it contained was a function of privilege, pertaining only to those (including heterosexuals) who had not had to promise to remain celibate in order to practice obedience to the ecclesial authorities and thereby be recommended for ordination. Evidently, many of those who *had* known what the document contained had taken for granted that everyone else was also aware, but that assumption had become a functional endorsement of the status quo.

Formation for ministry in such an institution therefore not only *should* but *must* be a queer formation. It must acknowledge the sheer impossibility of maintaining monolithic and univocal accounts of the divine and of humans' relationships to it. It should recognize and name the strangeness of the fact that LGBTQI+ people have found ways to thrive within an institution that continues to problematize them. Theological colleges are vital sites for this, existing as they do at the interstices.

---

31. Archbishops' Council (Church of England), *Issues in Human Sexuality: A Statement by the House of Bishops of the General Synod* (London: Church House Publishing, 1991).

32. Archbishops' Council (Church of England), *Issues in Human Sexuality*, 42.

33. Church of England. "General Synod Backs Ban on Conversion Therapy," 8 July 2017, https://www.churchofengland.org/news-and-media/news-and-statements/general-synod-backs-ban-conversion-therapy.

CHAPTER SEVEN

QUEERPENTECOSTAL WORSHIP

Karl Hand

When warm weather came, Baby Suggs, holy, followed by every black man, woman, and child who could make it through, took her great heart to the Clearing... Then she shouted, "Let the children come!" and they ran from the trees toward her.

"Let your mothers hear you laugh," she told them, and the woods rang. The adults looked on and could not help smiling.

Then "Let the grown men come," she shouted. They stepped out one by one from among the ringing trees.

"Let your wives and your children see you dance," she told them, and groundlife shuddered under their feet.

Finally she called the women to her. "Cry," she told them. "For the living and the dead. Just cry." And without covering their eyes the women let loose.

It started that way: laughing children, dancing men, crying women, and then it got mixed up. Women stopped crying and danced; men sat down and cried; children danced, women laughed, children cried until, exhausted and riven, all and each lay about the Clearing damp and gasping for breath. In the silence that followed, Baby Suggs, holy, offered up to them her great big heart.[1]

When I was a Fundamentalist Pentecostal teenager, the Christian revival known as the Toronto Blessing arrived in Blacktown, New South Wales. As an anxious and repressed homosexual teenager, I was not used to feeling any of my own emotions. I was terrified of them. But a few solid hours of weeping in the Holy Spirit changed who I was. I wept until my T-shirt was drenched in tears. Then I laughed until my sides hurt. I encountered my own emotions, and with them, my queerness.

---

1. Toni Morrison, *Beloved* (New York: Vintage Books, 2004), 102–103.

In those moments, I experienced the presence of God as physical touch. It was indistinguishable from any other physical sensation, and felt like a heavy blanket on my body, or a whole-body embrace. It was an experience of being deeply loved. This was the beginning of a complete turning point in my life. Queer children like me tend to experience self-hatred in environments hostile to queerness. Those feelings no longer made sense to me in the presence of this kind of love.

Certainly, that was not the outcome that the Pentecostal Church in the 1990s was hoping for. But it could not control the Holy Spirit. The manifestation of the Spirit disrupts and queers religious agendas.

It took five years for those experiences to emerge as a radical acceptance of my queer self, and it will take a lifetime of work to overcome ingrained prejudices and contempt for my own queerness. But I can trace it all back to those moments during the Toronto Blessing.

"Queerpentecostal"

I have chosen to describe this queerness of Pentecostal worship, ever-present yet unrecognized, as "Queerpentecostal." The term is modeled after Ashon T. Crawley's description of "Blackpentecostal Breath"—sonic events such as shouting praise during a sermon, or praying in tongues in the background, testifying, and holy laughter or weeping, that rely on disruption to function. They are "a disruptive force . . . grounded in the fact of the flesh."[2]

Crawley defines this compound term as: "If blackness is the tradition of resistance that inheres objects, and if Pentecostalism is the capacity for otherwise beginnings ongoingly, Blackpentecostalism is the capaciousness of otherwise resistance that rises to, while emerging from, the occasion of its genesis."[3]

Here, I cannot avoid the awkwardness of being a white Australian appropriating Black spirituality. The Pentecostalism I grew up in was always ethnically diverse. My church's congregation was filled with Islander and Indian Pentecostal worshipers and leaders. We frequently held combined services with Emmanuel Christian Family Church in Plumpton, where there was a significant Aboriginal population.

What was not obvious to me as a child was that, as a white Australian, I was a recipient of a distinctively Black spiritual experience. It was in fact, only when I was in my early 20s that I recognized that. The Blackness of Pentecostalism often remains invisible within Pentecostal churches. This reinforces the colonial myth of white folk "bringing the gospel" to other cultures. I visited the City of Refuge church in San Francisco, and encountered the preaching of Bishop Yvette

---

2. Ashon T. Crawley, *Blackpentecostal Breath: The Aesthetics of Possibility* (Fordham University Press: 2016), 4.

3. Crawley, *Blackpentecostal Breath*, 26.

Flunders. Through her ministry, I became aware my own spirituality was an appropriated Black spirituality, and that it had been such since I was too young to know better.

My hope is that the use of "Queerpentecostal" as a category creates a rewarding intersection with Crawley's idea. I am grateful that Crawley himself is frequently permissive and generous toward people like me enjoying the gift of Blackpentecostal Breath. He says that both Blackness and Pentecostalness are forces which "do not belong to any group, that *are* only insofar as they are given away."[4]

Crawley alludes to the close relationship of queerness and Blackpentecostal Breath, when he says that the latter exists "at the nexus of performance theory, queer theory, sound studies, literary theory, theological studies and continental philosophy,"[5] and that:

> If theology is "god talk," as is often colloquially offered, but talk in blackness is never categorically distinct or pure . . . Blackpentecostal Breath could not be offered into a conversation without the clearing work of those theologians black and womanist and mujerista and liberationist and queer, their work cleared ground through which I now move.[6]

Queerness as Radical Love Overcoming Boundaries

My use of "queer" follows the definition of Episcopal theologian Patrick Cheng. He defines queerness as Radical Love, especially as such love transgresses what is normal, and erases or deconstructs the boundaries set by binary understandings of sexuality, gender identity, and biological sex.[7] Cheng notes that Christian theology is a "fundamentally a queer exercise,"[8] because the story of Jesus is already a story of Radical Love overturning fixed and traditional categories. Cheng's "overturning of categories" overlaps with Crawley's understanding of the Blackpentecostal aesthetic. Pentecostal practices, he claims, urge against categorical distinctions since "the possibility for producing pure distinction is the grounds for racism, sexism, homo- and transphobia, classism, and the like."[9]

As the term Queerpentecostal suggests, Pentecostal worship is also queer by definition. The ecstatic encounter with the Holy Spirit is unavoidably an

---

4. Crawley, *Blackpentecostal Breath*, 26.

5. Crawley, *Blackpentecostal Breath*, 3.

6. Crawley, *Blackpentecostal Breath*, 20.

7. Patrick S. Cheng, *Radical Love: An Introduction to Queer Theology* (New York: Seabury Press, 2011), 2–11.

8. Cheng, *Radical Love*, 11.

9. Crawley, *Blackpentecostal Breath*, 5.

encounter with Radical Love which disturbs expectations and overcomes boundaries. It did that for me as a teenager.

Pentecostal worship is not only characterized by ecstatic worship, but also by the manifestation of spiritual gifts. I do not understand these as unavoidably queer, as the charismatic gifts can be and often are exercised in heteronormative ways. Feminist scholarship has already shown how such practices may disrupt and resist patriarchal norms. For instance, Janice McRandal draws on Andrea Hollingworth's model of a constructive Feminist Pentecostal pneumatology, and the experiences of Latin American Pentecostal women, who are "given voice" by the Holy Spirit within a traditionally *macho* home life, through the exercise of ecstatic utterance.[10]

Disruption of patriarchal norms, as well as the discovery of women's agency and subjectivity, are queer. This is really just to recognize that feminism itself is a queer practice, at least when it is intersectional feminism such as McRandal's.

Queerpentecostal Liturgical Studies

Queerpentecostal worship queers the discipline of liturgical studies. The use of this discipline to study what is sometimes called "non-liturgical" worship also transgresses boundaries and definitions. Estrelda Alexander, for instance, describes Pentecostalism as "devoid of liturgical structure, ritual enactment, or symbolic presence."[11] The title of her article ("Liturgy in Non-Liturgical Holiness-Pentecostalism") already seems to contradict itself. And yet the tools of liturgical studies are the most apt for the study of Queerpentecostal worship. Researching this chapter, I noticed with some irony that *queerness* is far from a strange topic in liturgical theology. The discussion of Pentecostalism, though, is rare in the literature. Pentecostalness is thus the queer thing about this chapter; queerness less so.

And surely, this is just how queerness works. Queer identities and experiences resist definitions. They refuse to be categorized, and yet they demand to be taken seriously. This demand is seen as "transgressive" because it undermines the way that identities are constructed (such as male/female, or in this case liturgy/not liturgy). Queer experience leads to a queering of the discipline itself, which is provoked to reassess its most basic categories.

Siobhan Garrigan's approach to queerness in liturgical studies is to describe the already-queerness of many practices of worship. Garrigan notes that "queer worship" is usually discussed in reaction to special moments in the lives of LGBT people, such as an ordination or a marriage. These are controversial, and the proper liturgical process is contested. But Garrigan worries (and I strongly agree

---

10. Janice McRandal, *Christian Doctrine and the Grammar of Difference: A Contribution to Feminist Systematic Theology* (Augsburg Fortress Publishers, 2015), 165–169.

11. Estrelda Y. Alexander, "Liturgy in Non-Liturgical Holiness-Pentecostalism," *Wesleyan Theological Journal* 32:3 (1997): 158.

with her), "that by concentrating on these occasional and extraordinary events within a person and a community's life as 'queer worship' (with its double sense of both 'unusual worship' and 'worship for LGBT people'), we are neglecting the myriad ways in which day-to-day ordinary worship is, and is not, queer."[12]

In the liturgical traditions, Garrigan is considering everyday worship is *not* queer when it lacks elements such as intercessions for issues which impact LGBT people, LGBT voices visible during prayers, and terminology outside of heterosexist binaries like "brothers and sisters."[13] But Garrigan also notices two claims which are frequently made about structural queerness inherent in liturgy. First, the physical and sensual nature of high church, Anglo-Catholic worship affirms the body and the senses. Second, because the liturgy is oriented toward an eschatological future in which society is radically transformed, it is inevitably queer.[14] Garrigan has some caution about these claims. She notes that the high church setting can be very male centered and even gynophobic toward the bodies of women. Eschatological countercultural worship may also run the risk of ignoring queer issues if it never talks about sexuality. So, Garrigan concludes that queering worship does involve recognizing the already-present queerness of liturgy, but it must also include the slow and hard work of the community, and is always a work in progress.[15]

"Oral Liturgy" or "Antiritual"

A common way of handling the problem of a non-liturgical liturgy seems to have originated with W. J. Hollenweger. He refers to Pentecostal worship as an *oral liturgy*, structurally comparable to jazz improvisation.[16] In this way, what we commonly think of as a "liturgy" is often used to refer to printed texts such as the Roman Missal, or the weekly Order of Worship in mainstream Protestant churches, and "non-liturgical" simply refers to the absence of such a written text.

In the recent collection *Historical Foundations of Worship*, Nicholas Wolterstorff similarly suggests that liturgy is a scripted activity, or that different historical worship traditions are examples of communities submitting to a common script.[17] In the case of Pentecostalism, the "script" is constituted by whatever the worship leader announces.[18]

---

12. Siobhan Garrigan, "Queer Worship," *Theology & Sexuality* 15:2 (2009): 214.
13. Garrigan, "Queer Worship," 215.
14. Garrigan, "Queer Worship," 223–225.
15. Garrigan, "Queer Worship," 228–229.
16. W. J. Hollenweger, "The Social and Ecumenical Significance of Pentecostal Liturgy" *Studia Liturgica* 8:4 (1971): 209–211.
17. Nicholas Wolterstorff, "Series Introduction," in *Historical Foundations of Worship: Catholic, Orthodox, and Protestant Perspectives*, eds. Melanie C. Ross and Mark A. Lamport (Grand Rapids, MI: Baker Publishing House, 2022), xiii.
18. Wolterstorff, "Series Introduction," xiv.

The oral liturgy approach, however, doesn't adequately account for the way that I have experienced Pentecostal worship. My own experience of being filled with the Holy Spirit was the exact opposite of what the worship leaders attempted to "script" for my life. The intention of the leader was a kind of inner purification which would eradicate any demonic strongholds such as homosexuality and (so-called) effeminacy, and convert people like myself into examples of traditional masculinity (or femininity) and heterosexuality. But the Holy Spirit simply had a different agenda. The Pentecostal experience wasn't in the "scripted activity"; it was in fact in the very disruption of that activity.

This is not to deny the existence of a flexible structure in Pentecostal worship. Praise is the typical way a worship service begins. One knows that an altar call and ministry is typically after the sermon at the end. The point is rather that, in the Pentecostal tradition, this structure is meant as a starting point, and the purpose was always for the Holy Spirit to interrupt what we are doing with a report of a miracle, a shout of praise, or a moment of deliverance. It is when the structure is interrupted that God is understood to have "shown up."

Bobby C. Alexander's approach to this issue seems to reflect my experience better than that of Hollenweger. Alexander undertook field work in a Pentecostal congregation. He suggested that what was happening there was best interpreted as what Victor Turner called "ritual anti-structure." The worship, he noticed, was "punctuated" with "ritualized ecstatic display,"[19] which he refers to as "possession," but Pentecostals typically call it the Baptism in the Holy Spirit, or being Spirit-Filled. As a Pentecostal myself, I will use the latter term.

Alexander suggests a Turnerian understanding of being filled with the Holy Spirit. He describes the experience as "ritual liminality" (the ability to "stand outside" of everyday life) and *communitas* (a direct, mutual, and egalitarian sense of belonging which emerges within the liminal space). For Pentecostal worshippers, these experiences take place, not in the structure, but in the interruption:

> In a rare reference to Pentecostals, Turner suggests that this movement is illustrative of groups attempting to legislate *communitas* as the norm. Any attempt to legislate *communitas* denatures, or perverts, it, however, since it has been "thoroughly domesticated, even corralled" by structure and its subversive capacity undercut.[20]

Queerpentecostal Disruptions

What follows are reflections on a small sample of Queerpentecostal disruptions, with examples of how their queerness is involved in their ability to create antiritual moments, in which Radical Love transgresses categorizing boundaries.

---

19. Bobby C. Alexander, "Pentecostal Ritual Reconsidered: Anti-structural Dimensions of Possession," *Journal of Ritual Studies* 3:1 (1989): 109–110.

20. Alexander, "Pentecostal Ritual," 120.

Queerpentecostal Testimony

Pentecostals testify in worship. This chapter began with a testimony, as a deliberate choice to model Queerpentecostal ways of knowing. James K. A. Smith has argued that Pentecostalism entails an affective and narrative epistemology—forms of knowing which are grounded in feeling and in story, rather than reductionistic or enlightenment modes of knowing rationalistically.[21] So, it is appropriate that the knowledge I share in this chapter be grounded in my own testimony; this is how Pentecostals know.

To pick up my testimony a few years after I left off earlier, after coming out around age 20, I moved away from Pentecostal churches and trained for ministry in a liturgical tradition with liberating theology, the Universal Fellowship of Metropolitan Community Churches (MCC). While MCC had a wide variety of ministry styles, the ones in my city ranged from mainstream liturgical to high church, and I did not encounter an "LGBT affirming" Pentecostal expression of worship until I visited City of Refuge in 2004. My plans were to operate in that tradition for my whole life. God had very different plans.

I'm somewhat embarrassed to admit what I was doing when God interrupted my plans, and revealed to me that I would need to radically change. I look back on some of my choices at these moments with embarrassment, not in the sense of shame, but with a cringe at my hapless attempts to find belonging and purpose in a disrupted life. God and I laugh together about that.

One example is when I took my first ministry placement in 2006. As I was trained for my role, I was told that a certain monthly worship service, "CRAVE Worship Night," was run by a group of younger people from Pentecostal backgrounds. I was informed that they didn't cooperate well with appropriate church leadership and didn't comply well with church policies and procedures. As a new minister, part of my job would be to build a positive relationship with this group, and firmly bring them back into harmony with the vision of the church as a whole.

But, as I was expected to wear liturgical attire to lead most worship services, I didn't know what to do about my first time at CRAVE worship. If I wore liturgical clothes, it could be perceived as disrespecting the Pentecostal style of worship. If I dressed more casually, it could appear that I wasn't taking that service seriously. The "worship wars" were so passionately contested in this church that I had significant anxiety about the choice. On the day, I decided to wear a suit and tie. I looked totally out of place the whole night!

In fact, I do not think anyone cared what I was wearing. But my feelings of foolishness made me vulnerable enough to be open to a spiritual experience which changed the course of my life. As I walked in, I saw a full band getting ready to rehearse. A woman (who I didn't know at the time) broke the silence with a simple sustained chord on the piano.

---

21. James K. A. Smith, *Thinking in Tongues: Pentecostal Contributions to Christian Philosophy* (Grand Rapids, MI/Cambridge UK: William B. Eerdmans Publishing Company, 2010), 48–85.

In my 6 years away from the Pentecostal church, I had still been aware of God's presence, but I had not experienced the power and glory I had known in my teenage years. I had started to write those experiences off as mere emotionalism. And pain from my rejection by my first faith community had also closed that door within me. But with this one chord, the door imploded. I was immersed in a sense of intense glory, accompanied with grief about the fact that I had missed out on this experience for six years. And I had to put on a brave face and act out the role of pastor. The CRAVE community ministered to *me* for my next 18 months.

This story is an example of what Smith claims, that Pentecostals think and learn in terms of narrative and feeling, rather than rationalistically. Smith does not go so far as to say it, but this is a queer way of knowing. Testimonies typically climax in a moment of divine intervention, which precipitates affective knowledge. Thus the knowledge is founded on a disruption of what is categorized as possible or impossible. As a teenager, and as a young minister, my own categories of who and what I could be were radically transformed by loving interventions of God.

Queerpentecostal Gifts of Utterance

Testimony often overlaps with what Pentecostal theologians have described as the "gifts of utterance," such as tongues, interpretation, and prophecy. As I mentioned earlier, feminist scholars have noted that such gifts allow women in male-dominated cultures to exercise their own voice. Janice McRandal suggests that Pentecostal experiences are an opportunity for agency and subjectivity to emerge among women. This is especially true in the manifestation of vocal gifts such as prophecy and tongues.[22]

Prophecy

I have already testified to the initial impact that Queerpentecostal worship had on me in the first months of my first ministry placement in 2006. This was only the beginning of disruptive manifestations of the Spirit in the coming years. One morning I was entering the church office. A congregational meeting was approaching during which the vision for the future of the church was being discussed, and I was praying about it, and seeking to discern God's will. It had been a long time since I operated in revelatory gifts. But as I walked, I heard the voice of God in my mind. The voice said, "whatever you decide about CRAVE, that will be your future."

What followed was a comedic misunderstanding based on double-entendre, such as the ones unspiritual characters in the Gospel of John (like Nicodemus

---

22. McRandal, *Christian Doctrine*, 161.

in John 3) were susceptible to. I thought the "you" in the revelation was a plural, referring to the whole church. Like a Johannine character, it was in struggling to understand the meaning of the words that I let go of my rationalistic way of knowing and surrendered to the wisdom of the Spirit. I realized that the word "you" was about me in particular, and I was being called to devote my life to this spirit-filled movement of queer-affirming believers emerging within the affirming churches in our city.

Tongues

It was also around this time that I simply allowed myself to pray in tongues again. I had been trained for some years now in spiritual direction and methods of contemplative prayer such as *lectio divina* and Ignatian exercises. There was a shock of realization that simple glossolalia was as effective and powerful as the other methods, but without the effort involved in practicing the correct technique. I asked myself, "Why did I ever *stop* doing this?" Just as with the comedic misunderstanding of my own prophecy, revelation came simply by letting go of what I thought was right.

McRandal is again helpful. She notes how, paradoxically, those who discover their own voice in this way may also overcome that new subjectivity, discovering through the Holy Spirit that selfhood is not fully autonomous or self-contained. This is particularly relevant in the practice of speaking in tongues.

The feminist practice of Pentecostal gifts is perhaps at its most obviously queer when it undermines the very logical structure of the language of binary gender and heteronormative sexuality. Citing James K. A. Smith's "Tongues as Resistant Discourse,"[23] McRandal notes that tongues signify the failure of rational discourse, and therefore tend to decrease in Assemblies of God congregations as those congregations increase in social class. In ecstatic speech, one's voice is surrendered to God, who prays through the worshiper. Speaking in tongues, McRandal claims, "does something with language that defies the rules and transgresses the boundaries—as one might expect if this is indeed the work of the Spirit of God without boundaries."[24]

Ashon Crawley's regard of glossolalic tongues as foundational for Black-pentecostal imagination is helpful in reflecting on why my experience has been so effortless and healing. Crawley makes a sharp distinction between "xenolalic" tongues, defined as the ability to speak another's language without knowledge of the language, and glossolalic tongues, which are "the eruption and enunciation

---

23. James K. A. Smith, "Tongues as Resistant Discourse: A Philosophical Perspective," in *Speaking in Tongues: Multi-Disciplinary Perspectives*, ed. Mark Cartledge (Carlisle, UK: Paternoster, 2006), 81.

24. McRandal, *Christian Doctrine*, 172–173.

of irreducible, nonlinguistic, nonrepresentational vocalizing, ecstatic language, the speechifying of nothingness."[25]

Xenolalic tongues, he argues, are based on a settler-colonial logic of wanting to speak to people who are "other," based on the desire for "mastery of the language of the Other" without even needing to understand it.[26] Glossolalia, on the other hand:

> —registering as nothing at all—is the movement into incoherence as a choreosonic form toward praise, toward divine encounter. Impurity is the grounds for such atheological-aphilosophical speechifying, incoherence allowed as praiseworthy.[27]

In other words, rather than seeking to control the Other, glossolalia allows incoherence and surrenders to communion with God without imposing rationality. It stops short of that "original violence" that Catherine Malabou accuses language of having worked by ripping apart words from that which they signify.[28] Crawley reflects on Malabou's original violence, and suggests that glossolalic tongues stop short of this violence and speak, "not words, but the very stuff, the materiality, from which words come."[29] To borrow again Cheng's definition of "queer," tongues are Radical Love not merely transgressing what is normal, but transgressing the very linguistic structure upon which every category of normality could ever be constructed.

Ecstatic Queerpentecostal Worship

Since that moment at the piano in 2006, the worship leader I now know as Pastor Elizabeth Plant has now ministered to me for almost two decades through her gifts of writing songs and leading worship. When I first read the scene on the Clearing from Toni Morrison's *Beloved*, I visualized Baby Suggs, holy, as Pastor Elizabeth leading a worship service.

In one particularly powerful worship service, I remember singing the classic 1970s worship song, *I Love You, Lord* by Laurie Klein. When we reached the line, "let me be a sweet, sweet sound in your ear," Pastor Elizabeth stopped. She began repeating the first half of that line over and over, "Let me be a sweet, sweet sound. Let me be a sweet, sweet sound. Let me be a sweet, sweet sound . . ." The whole gathered congregation built this line to a crescendo. I remember a note of near desperation in the voices—perhaps characteristic of

---

25. Crawley, *Blackpentecostal Breath*, 211.
26. Crawley, *Blackpentecostal Breath*, 216.
27. Crawley, *Blackpentecostal Breath*, 217.
28. Crawley, *Blackpentecostal Breath*, 222.
29. Crawley, *Blackpentecostal Breath*, 222–223.

the abject begging that characterizes King David in many of the Psalms. This is Queerpentecostal song.

Our experience that day was different from the queer-affirming and liberating style of hymnody that I had been trained in under such powerful leaders as Rev. Jim Mitulski in MCC in the 2000s. There, I encountered all kinds of queer Christian song, and songs which queered theology and liturgy. Important aspects of those expressions of Christian worship were inclusive and emancipatory language, such as Laurence G. Bernier's *Our God is Like an Eagle*, which affirmed nonbinary and omnigender God language, and Barry Wichmann's *Children of the Rainbow Promise*, which assertively claimed queer people's right to inherit God's blessing.

Pentecostal worship music, however, does not typically seek to teach theology through song. The Pentecostal understanding of worship is an intimate encounter with God's manifest presence. Pentecostalism is not taught, it is *caught*. It is transmitted through physical presence, and it is *felt*.

Pastor Elizabeth and I are now both queer ministers from Pentecostal backgrounds, leading similar churches in the same city. We frequently share conversations reflecting on these experiences. Our discussions focus on what we sense the Holy Spirit is doing in the church now. It was in these conversations that I became aware of what was happening in these moments. This is queer prophetic song writing, which I have also heard described as the ministry of the psalmist.

In contrast to the theological content of queer hymnody I had learned in the UFMCC, the first Queerpentecostal song I ever sang was *For Those Tears I Died*, written by Marsha Pino-Stevens during the Jesus Revival of the 1960s and 1970s. She would later join MCC, and it was my great privilege to meet her a number of times at our global conferences.

To call this song Queerpentecostal is more than just to acknowledge that this song was written in a Pentecostal style and by a person who later came out as a lesbian Christian. In this song, Jesus invites her to stand with him. He promises she will not be denied. She was not writing about her sexuality at the time, but the song delivers healing to people wounded by church rejection over issues of sexuality and gender.

For Those Tears I Died ministered Queerpentecostal experiences to me when I was a child who didn't yet know what queerness was, singing a song by someone who had not yet publicly identified as queer. The song speaks of Jesus promising those who cry alone in darkness that they are welcome to come and be with Jesus. It was already queerly including us without our conscious awareness or intent. The Holy Spirit, after all, begins a work of grace in people long before they recognize what is happening.

We Queerpentecostal worshipers pleading with God that day in 2006 were not theologically deconstructing or reflecting on our queerness. Like the followers of Baby Suggs, we were bringing our selves before God with all the scars of shame and self-hatred, and presenting them to God and *doing business with God* about them. Stopping and repeating the exact lyric which needed to be ministered to the congregation at that moment was an anti-ritual disruption of the song structure, allowing the ministry to occur.

And again, I am faced here with the problematic of appropriating Black spiritual genius. I cannot claim to have experienced or understood the spiritual power of the scene in the Clearing, where Blackpentecostal Breath rose up against the communal trauma of slavery. This is the power that William J. Seymour would draw on as he led the first Pentecostal revival at Azusa Street, and I also cannot deny what I received from these pioneers. To leave this unacknowledged would be a whitewashing of Pentecostal history.

Further Disruptions

In reflecting on my experiences of testimony, glossolalia, and ecstatic worship, I have deliberately not sought to describe distinctively Black expressions of Pentecostal worship, such as the shout tradition and whooping. Crawley has already discussed these at length in a way which reveals the queerness of these traditions. Although these forms of spiritual manifestation minister to my spirit, and I hope to experience them more fully someday, it would feel insincere for me to try to claim those as my own. There is an opportunity for a person of African descent, perhaps drawing on Crawley's work, to write about the queerness of these expressions of Pentecostal worship in the area of liturgical studies.

Conclusion

Queerpentecostal worship is the already-queerness of the manifestation of the Spirit characteristic of Pentecostal and charismatic worshipers. A form of ritual antistructure, its power comes from *disrupting* scripts. Thus, using Cheng's definition of "queer," it is the manifest Holy Spirit as Radical Love overcoming boundaries.

Three Pentecostal practices I have discussed here—testimony, gifts of utterance, and ecstatic worship—are each already queer, some unavoidably so. Where Pentecostal practices are unqueer, or even hostile and violent to queerness, Queerpentecostalism continues to disrupt the structure of the movement itself.

CHAPTER EIGHT

BROKEN READINGS— QUEER (M)ENDING

Bertram J. Schirr

Introduction

Discussions about queering worship routinely touch in general ways on the topics of preaching,[1] baptism, marriage, and presiding at Eucharist.[2] But what about looking into queering the engagement with scripture texts during worship? There are many things that continue to work against that engagement fulfilling its greater potential. In particular, a one-way, monologic delivery of what primarily are understood as static texts and formulas, along with simplistic promise-fulfilment schemes that link Old Testament and New Testament texts, exclude people from worship and work against God's Word becoming effective in the congregation.[3] This essay proposes ways for the encounter with scripture texts during worship to be inclusive, liberating, engaging, and interactive. Queer reading strategies, the identity plays performed by Bibliodrama, *Choose Your Own Adventure* books, and queer theories of embodiment and voice, propose new ways to proceed.

Inclusive lectionaries and translations work on the level of text, in many cases, are a positive development. Scripture readings during worship, however, are more than utterances of reconstructed or edited texts. This paper argues that the proclamation of the readings of the Liturgy of the Word can already be seen as somewhat queer, dramatized, and embodied performances. What if we further complicated, queered, and dramatized what is already a dramatization—and amplify the redeeming queerness of the Bible[4] in the practice of liturgical readings?

---

1. Jacob D. Myers, *Preaching Must Die! Troubling Homiletical Theology* (Minneapolis: Fortress Press, 2017).

2. Chris Greenough, *Queer Theologies, The Basics* (Oxford: Routledge, 2019).

3. See eds. Stephen Burns and Bryan Cones, *Liturgy with a Difference: Beyond Inclusion in the Christian Assembly* (London: SCM, 2019); David N. Power, *"The Word of the Lord": Liturgy's Use of Scripture* (Maryknoll, New York: Orbis Books, 2001).

4. See Elizabeth Stuart, "'Making No Sense': Liturgy as Queer Space," in *Dancing Theology in Fetish Boots: Essays in Honour of Marcella Althaus-Reid*, eds. Lisa Isherwood and Mark D. Jordan (London: SCM, 2009), 113–123; Siobhán Garrigan, "Queer Worship," *Theology and Sexuality* 15:2 (2009): 211–230.

Queer Reading Strategies

Queering texts—against their grain and against the intention of their authors—has produced spectacular insights and inclusionary effects. Eve Kosofsky Sedgwick[5] identifies several queer reading tactics. For Sedgwick, queer is "the open mesh of possibilities, gaps, overlaps, dissonances and resonances, lapses, and excesses of meaning when the constituent elements of anyone's gender, of anyone's sexuality aren't made (or can't be made) to signify monolithically."[6] This can also be applied to other categories of identity and to the narrative structure of texts as well. To reveal what is queer, Sedgwick first introduced the tactic of "paranoid reading": Text is worked over in search for those who are unheard, othered away, subdued and silenced, and for the influences of cultural contexts, power, and hegemony. She later adds the tactic of "reparative reading," which is a strategy of reading aimed at amending and repairing patriarchal damage and violence. Reparative reading is more suitable to connect to personal experience and affect, because it is "on the side of multiplicity, surprise, rich divergence, consolation, creativity, and love."[7] Following Siobhan Hawthorne,[8] paranoid readings, being ever vigilant and skeptical, assuming violence and hierarchy at every turn, avoid surprise and openness, safeguarding against manipulation, looking for ways of resistance. Reparative reading is at the heart of "queering" in that it is polydox and denies binarisms of oppression and liberation but promotes "tools and techniques for nondualistic thought and pedagogy."[9]

Sedgwick focuses on the practices of reading in literary-critical study, academic work, silent study, or the discussion of texts in groups. It is time that we extend the queering methodologies of reading to performances of corporeal reading out loud using hands and voices. I want to put Sedgwick's methodologies in place for out-loud reading during worship and thus help make visible the queerness that is in the texts. If we incorporate Sedgwick's methods, and modify current reading practices during worship, we can productively complicate the readings: The doubts, undecidedness, and fluid identities of the people in the scripture narratives and in the room can be surfaced. The menaces and the material realities of their contexts can be pointed toward, and the voices of the texts will be seen to be living words and not dead letters.

---

5. Eve Kosofsky Sedgwick, *Tendencies* (Durham, NC: Duke University Press, 1993); Eve Kosofsky Sedgwick, *Touching Feeling: Affect, Pedagogy, Performativity* (Durham, NC: Duke University Press, 2003).

6. Sedgwick, *Tendencies*, 8.

7. Heather Love, "Truth and Consequences: On Paranoid Reading and Reparative Reading," *Criticism 52* (2010): 235–241, 237.

8. Siobhan Hawthorne, "'Reparative Reading' as Queer Pedagogy," *Journal of Feminist Studies in Religion* 34:1 (2018): 155–160.

9. Sedgwick, *Touching Feeling*, 1.

Liturgical Order and Openings for Queering

My focus is on the readings from the Hebrew scriptures and the New Testament epistles and letters. In the mainline Lutheran and Reformed German traditions, readings from these sources open the second part of worship focused on proclamation. The *Evangelisches Gottesdienstbuch* outlines the Liturgy of the Word as follows:

> [The second part of a worship service] encompasses the reading of Biblical texts and the sermon that refers to them, furthermore creed, offertory, and intercessions as a response to the proclamation. In addition, there are congregational singing and liturgical antiphony as well as vocal or instrumental music. As a rule, readings, in the succession of Old Testament, Epistle, Gospel, follow the order of the liturgical year (according to the current lectionary). . . .[10] Lay readers recite the readings, the congregation responds with song. . . . Readings—particularly difficult texts—can be amended with a brief introduction (*Präfamen*). The reading should be ended with an established phrase to encourage the congregation to participate. . . . Readings can be performed as motets.[11]

The *Gottesdienstbuch*, by its own terms, admits into its order of worship openings for the work of queering, of tricksters or coyotes.[12] We are even encouraged to change the readings through brief amendatory introductions to "particularly difficult texts" (*Präfamen*), responses, and transfers to other performance modes such as a motet, which implies (but does not require) a multiple splitting of reading voices.

Repetition and Change

For many people, a meaningful part of Christmas worship is hearing the proclamation of Luke's nativity story in the German translation of Martin Luther, preferably read by the same person each year, in the same setting. There would likely be some protest if this activity were changed even ever so slightly. However, multiple readings of a text could never be the same, never identical copies of each other. Each iteration is unique because each one is influenced by constraints, by a myriad of factors in the immediate context: body movements, voice quality, precedent events, echoes, coincidences, ambient sounds, and others.

---

10. Kirchenleitung der Vereinigten Evangelisch-Lutherischen Kirche Deutschlands, Rat der Kirchenkanzlei der Evangelischen Kirche der Union (eds.), *Evangelisches Gottesdienstbuch, Agende für die Evangelische Kirche der Union und für die Vereinigte Evangelisch-Lutherische Kirche Deutschlands* (Berlin: Evangelische Haupt-Bibelgesellschaft und von Cansteinsche Bibelanstalt Berlin, 2003), 32–33.

11. *Gottesdienstbuch*, 41, author's translation.

12. Garrigan, "Queer Worship", 225–226. See Gordon Lathrop, "*Ordo* and Coyote: Further Reflections on Order, Disorder, and Meaning in Christian Worship," *Worship*, 80:3 (2006): 194–212.

Following Judith Butler's and Jacques Derrida's theory of reiteration,[13] text and signs by their nature never directly signify an original: There is no copy without blurring, no recitation or reading without adding and losing something. Every repetition is cut off from any original context and creates new meaning by deviation. Misalignment between original text and repetition are the performative powers that fuel not only such queer performances as drag or cross-dressing, postcolonial mimicry, or caricature, but are also required for any meaning to emerge. Speech acts and texts are not bound to the intention of their original author/producer, but rely on being supplemented, reapplied, and changed by those who re-perform or hear them.

In other words, if every proclamation of the same text of scripture was not different from every earlier proclamation of the same text, it would not mean anything. What would be the point of repeatedly proclaiming God's Word if there is no human interaction, supplementation, application, and in short, change. Liturgical readings as performance are never clean repetition, but always, and in a literary sense, subversive and changing.

With the *Gottesdienstbuch*, Derrida, and Butler we encounter different kinds of change. There are changes of biblical text *per se*, for example by *Präfamen* or amendment. Then, there is the change that stems from the repeated performance. Indebted to the second type of change, there is also a third kind that lies in the physicality of "doing" the reading. In the next part of this essay, I will address this final type of change, and turn from the text and its structure to its embodiment.

The Elvis Christ Theorem—Doing the Jesus Voice

There is one reader I know, Karen, who employs a soft and high voice when she reads words which she identifies as those of Jesus Christ, for instance his *logia* in the Sermon on the Mount, Matthew 5. Sometimes, however, she would forget to differentiate voices or to "do the/her Jesus voice." Her Jesus does not have a stable, unchanging voice. Karen's voice production highlights how the Liturgy of the Word is an act of imitation. It can be seen as something much like the exercises of immersion or role-taking suggested by Thomas à Kempis or Ignatius of Loyola. On the physical level, Karen imitates the Messiah, a performance in which an original voice and its capacities are mimicked.

In that regard, the voice of Jesus in the Liturgy of the Word is like that of Elvis Presley.[14] I am drawing this comparison because it highlights the

---

13. Jacques Derrida, "Signature, Event, Context," in Jacques Derrida, *Limited Inc.* (Evanston: Northwestern University Press, 1998), 1–24.

14. See the satire: Robert Offerman, *The Good News of Elvis Christ, Savior and King of Rock and Roll* (Washington: Lulu.com, 2012). Offerman changes the names of the biblical prophets and the messiah to the names of the prophets and messiahs of popular culture.

qualities of the embodied voice as a queer kind of salvific experience, as it is in Elvis' cult. Many people followed Elvis because of his voice. Much like in the case of Christ, Elvis' original voice, even though recorded, is beyond recovery. It is covered by copies and imitations, reverberating the physical dimension of Derrida's and Butler's reiteration theory: "[This] increasingly erased Presley as a point of origin, and Elvis impersonators are as much enacting an impersonation of other Elvis impersonators as they are attempting to impersonate 'Elvis' (in itself already an idea that functions at a distance from Presley)," especially since many female imitators' voices are mixed into the blend.[15]

As part of liturgical reading, human voices like Karen's or that of any other Sunday morning Jesus or Bible-character impersonator, re-embody in "sonic drag" original sound producers without being able to reproduce them fully. That cannot be helped even by people who do not discern or dramatize scripture voices but "only" employ their own reading voice. If we scrutinize liturgical readings as impersonation, not only of "Jesus voices" but also of Bible voices, it becomes evident how queer they really can be on the level of drama. The oral embodiment of text in the Liturgy of the Word must be reframed as paranoid, reparative, and polydox.

Queer Vocal Bodies

Lending one's voice in performing a liturgical reading means supplying and placing at public disposal one's own body as a surrogate. It is a queer giving birth done by nonbinaries, men and women alike, providing life and material to what is otherwise ink on a page. The image of giving birth conveys the idea of altering the world by use of one's body.[16] God's own body is in pain when liberation is born, when God cries giving birth (Isaiah 42:14), gasping for air, like all creation in labor, sighing together (Romans 8:22–23). Giving voice is giving birth.

The voice has its own intrinsically queer intangible materiality.[17] Queer theorist Freya Jarman-Ivens argues that voices are nothing but dramatized incoherencies:

> . . . if voice categories are naturalized rather than natural as such, the naturalness of the voice itself must be called into question, as the voice has a performative function more than it is a direct marker of

---

15. Freyq Jarman-Ivens, *Queer Voices* (New York: Palgrace Macmillan, 2011), 51; Francesca Brittan, "Women Who 'Do Elvis': Authenticity, Masculinity, and Masquerade," *Popular Music* 18:2 (2006): 167–190.

16. Beth. M. Stovell, "The Birthing Spirit, the Childbearing God," in *Making Sense of Motherhood*, ed. Beth M. Stovell (Eugene: Wipf & Stock, 2010), 27–44.

17. Bertram J. Schirr, "The Body We Sing, Reclaiming the Queer Materiality of Vocal Bodies," in *Queering Freedom, Music Identity and Spirituality*, ed. June Boyce-Tilman (Oxford et al.: Peter Lang, 2018), 35–52.

a stable, fixed, or inherent nature. Certainly, the ideology of the natural voice is a powerful one, and it is intimately bound to two other important ideologies of the voice—that it is a signifier of a very core of the speaker, and that it is individual, a unique sonic fingerprint."[18]

Voices can be added to Judith Butler's concept of gendered identity performance. They, too, are "the repeated stylization of the body, a set of repeated acts within a highly rigid regulatory frame that congeal over time to produce the appearance of substance, of a natural sort of being."[19] The voice in reading is nobody's, not the reader's anymore, not the Bible's anymore, but obscure and meandering physical layers of deviating, misaligning queerness (consider hearing your recorded voice). In liturgical readings, the voice itself is complicating fixed identities or the untarnished transmission of meaning. Readers birth what queer theorist Steven Connor calls "vocalic bodies": "Voices are produced by bodies: but can also themselves produce bodies."[20] Voices can produce other bodies, in another layer of strange, sonic surrogate pregnancy and birth, when they develop their own materiality and affect the hearer's bodies. Choosing the human voice to transport God's Word is accepting derivation and obscurity. It is revelatory to understand that lending voices to biblical texts and people is a queer experiment, already a weird motet of vocal births, in which through a unique human body a biblical entity is provided with a vocalic body, changing gender, sexuality and other identity categories repeatedly and fluidly.

This queerness of the voice is part of its ritual capacities and roots in Jewish and early Christian embodiment concepts. Oral religious storytelling always made the storytellers change their identity, become different for the liminal time of ritual, sometimes heightened by make-up or other changes of appearance, but most important by changing voices and thereby embodying several beings at the same time. Codified liturgical traditions like the collectively performed psalmodies of the Hebrew Bible are helpful for people to transcend identities and bodies, ascending, for instance, to the sphere of divine beings and angelic hosts in Psalm 118.

With the beginning of Christianity, with its Eucharistic origins, dominant ideas of embodiment and storytelling are radically disrupted. The resurrection of Christ changes any religious story of God and the way early Christians understand bodies and community break with Roman concepts of the free male abled body being the only one considered relevant and worthy of civil rights or inclusion. Christian body concepts and practices of embodiment have been queer and queering from the beginning. Differentiations of free bodies and slave

---

18. Jarman-Ivens, *Queer Voices*, 19.

19. Judith Butler, *Gender Trouble: Feminism and the Subversion of Identity* (Abingdon: Routledge, 2011), 45.

20. Steven Connor, *Dumbstruck: A Cultural History of Ventriloquism* (Oxford: Oxford University Press, 2000), 35.

bodies, identifications by gender or religion are liquefied in the body metaphor of egalitarian reciprocity (Romans 12; 1 Corinthians 12).[21] With Lisa Isherwood, it can be argued that encountering God's Word in worship is never a monadic activity of individuals.[22] Rather it is the divine and diverse body of Christ of the congregation that incorporates one body into others, making individual creatures porous and open for others.

In early Christian phases of reiterating tradition, performing what was to become the Liturgy of the Word must have been experimental. After the order of synagogue practice and observance was disrupted, so was the order of reading scripture. Therefore, it is likely that scripture readings for early Christians were mixture of storytelling and live Bible study, improv, and drama. Hymnodic and oral traditions must have been formed collectively from what was passed on by the first witnesses. It must have become an entirely different performance altogether to lend a voice to Jesus of Nazareth, knowing that his body was not what it seemed, but fully God and now present in the bodies of the congregation. From the priestly functions of pronouncing and performing divine dictum, whoever spoke the words of Christ did so adding another layer of identity, another split, another queering of embodiment, at the roots of the Liturgy of the Word.

In the next part of the essay I want to address the queering and changing of text in the Liturgy of the Word.

Queering the Text—Dramatizing the Dramatic

As we have developed, the substance of the Liturgy of the Word is not the transmission of unchanging text. It deals with multiple changing voices and bodies. Liturgical reading carries traces of a queer public work, paranoid, reparative, and polydox. In hearing and reading scripture together, people choose and change subject positions, fragment and rebuild storylines, mix their thoughts and their lives into the goings-on, fix or ignore unintelligible parts. They imagine alternatives. Is that not what queering does? Worshipers in the Liturgy of the Word fluidly navigate the "in between"[23] between culturally and performatively fixed norms and positions, mixing and diverting, complicating sequence alignments, exploring and surviving, finding alternative endings and futures, and above all new hope in old wineskins.[24] But all of this fragility, adding, repairing, done by the people "doing liturgical reading" is always left unspoken, un-proclaimed. But that can change.

---

21. See Ulrike Auga, Bertram J. Schirr, "Do Not Conform to the Patterns of this World! A Postcolonial Investigation of Performativity, Metamorphoses and Bodily Materiality in Romans 12," *Feminist Theology* 23:1 (2014): 37–54.

22. Lisa Isherwood, "Queering Christ: Outrageous Acts and Theological Rebellions," *Literature & Theology* 15:3 (2001): 249–261, 252–253.

23. See the reflections on queer in-betweenness in José Esteban Muñoz, *Cruising Utopia* (New York, London: New York University Press, 2009).

24. Muñoz, *Cruising Utopia*, 3–9.

Methodically Queering the Bible

This example from my ministry introduces a method for queering readings: improv.[25]

> In an alternative worship service, an improv youth group in my church performed biblical stories using improv methods. Two performers, a young person identifying as female and another one who identifies as nonbinary, informed worshipers that they would ask for a story from the Bible. They marked out spaces in front of the altar as opposites, demarcating the different emotional states they would go through. "Name a story," one asked and a parishioner yelled, "David and Goliath!" "Okay," she said, "and what emotions do David and Goliath go through?" Another person shouted, "Sadness and love." Moving in between the two marked spaces representing emotional states, one person identifying as female and one as male, her playing David, and him playing a rather small and scrawny Goliath, further and further approximated the neutral middle zone, where they set their differences aside and made peace. The congregation cheered.

Afterward, I had to schedule numerous meetings with conservative Elders. They complained that it was against God's will to change the Bible. They felt that this betrayal of biblical characters, this reparative live reading, would not fulfil the text's purpose. Really? Granted, in a little gender swap a young woman played David and a nonbinary person Goliath. But that is not unusual for modern or classical theater. But complaints about who portrayed whom were surpassed by the references to the insolence of those who would change the outcome of a biblical text. Can you do that?

Fortschreibung and Midrash

The method of midrash, or expansive Jewish biblical exegesis, is a distinct cooperative and collective practice in the Rabbinic tradition, sometimes asking readers questions, sometimes giving multiple answers, sometimes digressing extensively, less paranoid, more reparative and polydox, at times not at all dissimilar to improv. Amending and adding to the text is a practice that traditional old school German exegetes call *Fortschreibung*. "[*Fortschreibungen*] are distinct additions, that cannot simply be understood as independent units of tradition, but unmistakably pursue the theme struck upon by the fundamental word. Therein lies a process of successive enrichment of the core element."[26] The text and its

---

25. See Bertram J. Schirr, "Improvisieren für mehr Beteiligung am Gottesdienst?," *International Journal of Practical Theology* 23:2 (2019): 242–256.

26. Walther Zimmerli, *Biblischer Kommentar Altes Testament: Ezechiel* (Neukirchen: Neukirchener Verlag, 1979), 106, author's translation.

host of meanings are never depleted. I want to argue that *Fortschreibung* and the methods and multilingualism of the Talmud suggest another textual openness for polydoxy, a changeability of Scripture that can support the project of queering liturgical reading. Emerging from midrashic practice it entails situational and collective dramatized wrestling with Bible texts, with the addition of glosses and explanations, questions and interaction.

Queering Bibliodrama

Dramatizing biblical texts combining midrashic methods and drama theory has become a prevailing method in the German-speaking theological and religious pedagogical world. Peter Pitzele is the inventor of Bibliodrama, a type of dramatic live Bible interpretation including all recipients, who take on those roles the text offers and share ideas and feelings. Bibliodrama came from secular Judaism, applied psychodrama to the interpretation of scripture and reconnected it with Jewish tradition.[27] Bibliodrama is now seen as a prevalent midrashic method, introducing drama and games into collective Bible interpretation, moving from the proclamatory, educative, and edificatory effect to individual and group experience within the confines of biblical narrative.

Bibliodrama and Bibliolog (which is more densely structured by a trainer than Bibliodrama) build on the idea of late-antiquity Jewish exegesis that the Torah was written on parchment as "white fire," its letters "black fire, fire surrounded by fire, written in fire, given to fire with flaming fire in His right hand" (Jerusalem Talmud, Sota 8, 3, 37a.). In the medieval midrash *Aseret ha Dibrot*, this was extended to profound interest in what could be found in between and around the letters of scripture. With striking queer imagery, the white of scripture is identified as the unseen and unheard female voice or as the mystic body of God.

In Bibliodrama and Bibliolog, trainers will identify breaks and openings in the text—"shifts"—that strategically interrupt and invite participants to identify with a biblical figure, and, using the role as mask and protection, to utter I-messages, paranoid or reparative thoughts, doubts, and feelings. Identities given by the black fire of written scripture are used as demarcation and participants begin to explore polydox in-betweenness—and that can also be a queering collective and live movement in the white fire of midrashic reflection.[28]

In an increasing number of alternative German-language worship services, Bibliodrama and Bibliolog are used instead of liturgical readings. I would prefer that they are used as full-blown Liturgy of the Word, but with a little more queering involved. Because in the method of Bibliolog and Bibliodrama,

---

27. Peter A. Pitzele: *Scripture Windows. Toward a Practice of Bibliodrama* (Los Angeles: Alef Design Group, 1998).

28. Uta Pohl-Patalong, *Bibliolog* (Stuttgart: Kohlhammer, 2003).

black fire always triumphs. A Bibliodrama or Bibliolog trainer will close the story, eradicate polydox digression, reparative differing decision, paranoid questioning, and return to the one official ending of a biblical narrative. Of course, all new insights live on in the memory and experience of those involved. Yet they never become public and official expressions of faith in acts of worship, as they should. My suggestion here is to grasp what is already a process of queering underway in Bibliodrama and push it by allowing for polydoxy, for a multitude of identities and alternative endings as an official part of public and collective worship.

Choose Your Own Queer Adventure

The multitudinous and subversive narrative structures of Choose Your Own Adventure Books (CYOABs) offer further insights. CYOABs were created in 1976 by Edward Packard, who developed the idea of telling a story not in a straight line but rather using rhizomatic turns and reversals. Like liturgical readings and written Bible texts, CYOABs began with oral storytelling. Packard told his small daughter Andrea made-up good night stories that centered around Pete, an alternative male identity for her. His invention was fueled by gender frustration with conventional reading materials in which only boys were strong heroes, made decisions and enjoyed freedom. Packard's storytelling depends on ancient storytelling techniques, in which audience and storyteller interact, like psalmody or liturgical antiphons, similar to the old hymnodic nucleus of biblical narratives. Just like Bibliodrama "shifts," Packard frequently stopped the story and asked where Pete should go or what he should do, and he followed every decision. His other daughter, too, got to have her own endings to make the story her own.[29]

With CYOABs, "wearing brave-person drag,"[30] you can immerse yourself in another person in one run-through and then do it again differently, more and more embracing what is usually forbidden and extracted in paranoid readings: taboos, danger, impurity, and so on. You can test a multitude of identities, turns and endings. CYOABs, with their inherent narrative structure of choice and change, are queering in the sense of uncovering polydox and reparative multiplicity of identities that can lie in any story.

Using this method of storytelling, liturgical readings as well can be changed according to the interaction of the audience to questions, ideas, and responses, thus allowing intersections of perspectives and ideas and multiple endings. Non-linear, intersubjective, digressing, questing ways of liturgical reading help to participate in the queer center of worship, to embrace queer identities and polydoxy.

---

29. Leslie Jamison, "The Enduring Allure of Choose Your Own Adventure Books," *The New Yorker*, September 12, 2022.

30. Jamison, "The Enduring Allure."

This cannot fill the gaps of the subaltern or subdued bodies lost in scripture, but can mark their absence, celebrate, and bring before God their existence left out by the writing down of God's Word. Worshipers themselves—once they are involved again—can find and experience firsthand in the multinarrative, that is, the Bible the empowering change from an eternally fixed categorization or monolithic system.

Conclusions and Suggestions

When we practice liturgical reading according to the ideas offered above, we faithfully submit to the unexpectedness, the reversal, the play of identities, the surprises, and the power of the text to change us. We allow the text to queer us, and to liberate us, incorporating paranoia and doubt, repairing what is broken and celebrating what is manyfold, complicating, extending, and multiplying proclamation.

My suggestion is to re-interpret the Liturgy of the Word as a cooperative and experimental work on Bible texts. Liturgy does not simply receive unchangeable biblical narratives, chosen by ordained ministers or liturgical committees elsewhere and at other times. Every reading is a public work that is an ongoing struggle that is lovingly reparative, critically paranoid, and inclusively polydox. The Liturgy of the Word needs to be made more clearly the interactive work of the people again, as situational Bible study; it needs to get back to the roots of oral storytelling, and these techniques can be of help:

- Make methods like single-speaker motets, improvisation, Bibliodrama/Bibliolog or CYOA part of liturgical practice. Break open and segment the narrative and offer decisions to worshipers, but instead of deferring to the original narrative, proclaim the alternative endings, decisions, doubts, and feelings in an equal rights public expression of faith.
- Append alternative beginnings, endings and/or perspectives, excursions, and incursions. Interweave impromptu reactions, making them part of the liturgical act of reading; for example, ". . . and maybe the prodigal son came to the idea to also do something for the prostitutes and starving people he left behind," or ". . . and you could think this was when his older brother decided to go and waste his heritage, too."
- Highlight the interplay of the reader and the biblical character by announcing role changes with phrases like "I, Mary Levenson, will now lend my voice to bring to life for you the prophet Isaiah." Or note the act of lending a different voice: ". . . but standing before the Throne, maybe Isaiah sounded more like this."
- Ask liturgical practitioners and/or worshipers to paraphrase readings in their own words as part of proclamation.

- In liturgical and biblical pedagogy, prepare readings with the laity by combining Bibliodrama, or even role playing, and then reading their expressions of faith during the public liturgy.
- Train lay and ordained people to understand and practice liturgical reading as a cooperative and collective exploration with feelings and challenges, and to immerse themselves imaginatively into the identities in the text, focusing on their doubts, their situation, their changes of mind, their fluidities, rather than focusing on perfect transmission of one meaning.

CHAPTER NINE

REDEEMING PLEASURE IN WORSHIP

An Annotated Liturgical Play

Lis Valle-Ruiz

The Back Story

Lis Valle-Ruiz, born and raised in Puerto Rico, has been an actress since she was in her mother's womb. Back then, her mother, Elisabel Ruiz-Quirós, and father, Oscar Valle-Irizarry, would perform in plays at the Iglesia Presbiteriana Unida en Rincón that the pastor, José Roberto Colón-Rodríguez, wrote as sermons.[1] Ever since Lis has memory, she has been an actress. Lis felt called by God to share the good news of the gospel through theater, studied theater in college, founded a rolling theater troupe to preach the gospel in public spaces, went to seminary, moved to the continental USA, completed a Th.M., and started her doctoral degree in 2013. When Lis moved to the continental USA, she found that the tradition of church theater is hard to find here. Thus, every year since Lis moved to the USA in 2008, she has joined or produced a performance, to keep both her tradition and her sanity alive.

Sara Green (stage name, Dirty Magnolia) introduced Lis to burlesque. In the fall of 2016, as a peer student in Vanderbilt Divinity School, Sara invited Lis to join a burlesque workshop that Sara would offer and to attend a burlesque show with theological content, which Sara called "Alter Call." Those were Lis' first encounters with the art of burlesque. Later, Lis enrolled in a burlesque class that Sara offered.

The path to generate the burlesque piece "Less Fear, More Piña (Gozo)" was organic and serendipitous. There was going to be a recital to close the burlesque course in December 2016 and the group selected "The Nutcracker" as the theme to inspire their individual burlesque dances.[2] Lis' decolonial sensibilities kicked in and she decided to start her piece as required but then morph it into Puerto

---

1. The author of this essay makes the political choice of not italicizing words in Spanish because that would mark them as foreign, when in reality it is the English language that is foreign to her. Similarly, the author makes the choice of referring to Lis as the provider of testimonies that constitute the raw material for this essay. In contradistinction, the author of this essay is performing a social role as scholar and performing distance between scholar and actress through writing in third person.

2. Ballet by Russian composer Pyotr Tchaikovsky, which was first performed in December 1892. See, Betsy Schwarm, "The Nutcracker Ballet by Tchaikovsky," *Encyclopaedia Britannica*, last modified December 11, 2022, https://www.britannica.com/topic/The-Nutcracker.

Rican Christmas. She also decided that her piece needed to preach because her theater art is not for entertainment. She made her art sacred as a child, when she learned a reformed definition of sacred as separated and/or dedicated to God. The recital did not happen but by then Lis was too committed to her burlesque piece designed to serve as a sermon. Lis decided to invite her close friends to witness her sermon and to design a liturgy to nest the sermon.

The liturgy was intended to be a coming out ritual integrating knowledge about coming out processes and about healing from trauma to design both the liturgy and the sermon. Lis used what she had learned about the stages of the coming out process from a trans woman at a Theopoetics conference held in Boston in the spring of 2016. At the time of generating the liturgical play, what Lis heard about the stages of the coming out process was fresh on her mind. Lis also incorporated basic concepts from trauma theory, which she first encountered through Judith Lewis Herman's *Trauma and Recovery*.[3] According to Herman, part of the healing process includes re-framing one's story, changing the narrative, and sharing the new narrative with a community that would believe the new narrative.[4] This is why it was important for Lis to perform the sermon (her changed narrative) in front of an audience of loved ones. It was part of her healing process. It was part of healing from the purity culture that raised and hurt her. It was part of healing from colonization as perpetrated in the collusion of state and church since colonial times generating historic and generational trauma.

The liturgical play *Recovering Evangelical Coming Out* synthesizes, consciously and unconsciously, the knowledge that Lis acquired during her doctoral studies up to that point. She adapted the typical liturgical form of her faith tradition, queering it with the intention of having the form match the content. As an ordained minister in the Presbyterian Church (USA), Lis used the typical order for a worship service in said denomination.[5] It was a worship service to bless the coming out of Lis Valle-Ruiz as indecent theologian and of her stage persona, Sofía Divinatrix, as a polyamorous xenophilic.

Lis Valle-Ruiz's coming out as indecent theologian honors the influence of theologian Marcella Althaus-Reid, who wrote about indecent theology and a queer God.[6] Sofía Divinatrix is Lis' burlesque stage name, an alter ego, a character that Lis created to be able to perform burlesque beyond this first piece without being recognized. Several theological concepts are blended in this character. The name Sofía honors the female personification of the wisdom of

---

3. Judith Lewis Herman, *Trauma and Recovery*, rev. ed. (New York: BasicBooks, 1997).

4. See the chapters, "Remembrance and Mourning" and "Reconnection," Herman, *Trauma and Recovery*, 175–213.

5. *Book of Common Worship, Pastoral Edition* (Louisville: Westminster/John Knox Press, 1993).

6. See Marcella Althaus-Reid, *From Feminist Theology to Indecent Theology: Readings on Poverty, Sexual Identity and God* (London: SCM Press, 2004). See also, Marcella Althaus-Reid, *The Queer God* (London: Routledge, 2003).

God, Lady Wisdom as found in Proverbs 8. Divinatrix is a combination of divine and dominatrix in honor of the dominatrices who bear the light of life and the image and likeness of the Divine. Sofía Divinatrix is polyamorous thanks to what Lis learned from interactions with other queer students at Vanderbilt Divinity School. Sofía is xenophilic thanks to an article about xenophilia and xenophobia by theologian Luis N. Rivera-Pagán.[7]

In the following pages you will read an annotated script of the liturgical play. The annotations provided here reveal the scholarship that both shaped the liturgical play and that the liturgical play communicates. The script provided here in block quotes is a combination of a script format and a worship service liturgy. The worship service liturgy is further adapted including notes for actions and gestures and the script of the bodily expressions for the sermon.

The choice for the liturgical play genre, if such a genre exists, intends to blur the lines between theater and the ritual that Christian worship is by doing both and neither. The first time Lis heard the term "drama litúrgico," which Lis translated into "liturgical play," was when she directed the liturgical play "Siete Palabras" (Seven Words) written by Rev. Marissa Galván and performed by *Decisiones Rolling Theater*. This experience was in Puerto Rico, during Holy Week of 2003, if Lis remembers correctly. The liturgical play genre seemed a great fit for the blending of theater and ritual worship. After Lis started her doctoral studies, she read several books about theater and religion and became convinced that Christian worship is a religious ritual that shares characteristics with many other religious and non-religious rituals, that rituals tend to be the enactment of a myth (of a sacred story that contains truth for the community enacting the story), and that the actions in ritual are common actions that become ritualized by performing them differently.[8] Lis pushed the boundaries further by blending show and worship service, a pair typically disliked

---

7. Luis N. Rivera-Pagan, "Xenophilia or Xenophobia: Towards a Theology of Migration," *The Ecumenical Review* 64.4 (2012): 575–589.

8. The most important resources where I read these arguments include, Lance Gharavi, *Religion, Theatre, and Performance: Acts of Faith* (New York: Routledge, 2012); Victor Turner, *From Ritual to Theatre: The Human Seriousness of Play* (New York: Performing Arts Journal Publications, 1982); Richard Schechner, *Performance Studies: An Introduction*, 3rd ed. (New York: Routledge, 2013); Catherine M. Bell, *Ritual: Perspectives and Dimensions* (Cary: Oxford University Press, Incorporated, 1997); and Catherine M. Bell, *Ritual Theory, Ritual Practice* (Oxford: Oxford University Press, 2009). Other books that Lis read helped her realize the disdain that many homileticians have for theater and for comparing worship with theater, a disdain mostly based on the understanding of acting or performing as unauthentic or false. Nonetheless, there has been growth in the field of homiletics in the USA accepting the similarities between theater and liturgies as those books explain and demonstrate. See for example, Jana Childers, *Performing the Word: Preaching as Theater* (Nashville: Abingdon Press, 1998); and Jana Childers and Clayton J. Schmit, *Performance in Preaching: Bringing the Sermon to Life* (Grand Rapids: Baker Academic, 2008). More recent publications confirm the growth of acceptance of theater for homiletic reflection. See for example, Alyce McKenzie, *Making a Scene in the Pulpit: Vivid Preaching for Visual Learners* (Louisville: Westminster John Knox Press, 2018); Anna Carter Florence, *Rehearsing Scripture: Discovering God's Word in Community* (Grand Rapids: William B. Eerdmans Publishing Company, 2018); Jacob D. Myers, *Stand-Up Preaching: Homiletical Insights from Contemporary Comedians* (Eugene, OR: Cascade Books, 2022).

even by those who use theater in worship. Generating a show/worship service, that is, a liturgical play, is to experiment with blurring the lines between theater and Christian worship, and it leads to enacting that third space of which postcolonial theories talk about and the ambiguity that queer theories embrace. Choosing to write/do a liturgical play is one way to queer Christian worship.

Choosing explicit sexual language and sexualized performance for a Christian worship event, joining a centuries old tradition of erotic mysticism, redeems pleasure in Christian worship. Sharing in writing a script of a liturgical play that resembles both a theater play and a worship liturgy, nesting it in written critical reflection that begins and ends as scholars do, and writing more scholarship in the footnotes that in the body of the text are some ways to queer scholarship. Once again, the aim is for the means to match the message, for the content and its shape to align.

Recovering Evangelical Coming Out embodies ideas that Mark D. Jordan discusses in "Redeeming Pleasures," chapter seven of his book, *The Ethics of Sex*.[9] There, Jordan explores Christian speech around sex that has a long tradition of setting opposites against each other: for example, the virgin/whore. The liturgical play also embodies Audre Lorde's notion of "the erotic as power." The ritual journey of the worship service was fear, play, desire, and connection. Lis focused on the function of each part of the worship service to decide how to queer it. Challenging and deconstructing binaries, and enacting transfigurative union in Christ of apparent opposites, this worship service deconstructs the misuses of the power of the erotic and contributes to heal the wounds caused by the disconnection with one's own erotic power.[10] If Carter Heyward is correct in affirming that "our erotic power is the same life force that we call God," it is then appropriate to use the power of the erotic in Christian worship.[11]

The Script

Liturgical Play: Recovering Evangelical Coming Out

> This liturgical play constitutes a rite of passage for a person coming out of the cave where she has been studying in isolation. Her goal is to take off colonization from church and state, coming to terms with Fear (the main tool of the colonizers to keep her "in her place"). She will make peace with Fear through play, expressing and exposing her erotic self: Sofía Divinatrix, The High Priestess Unrobed.

---

9. Mark D. Jordan, *The Ethics of Sex* (Oxford: Blackwell Publishers, 2002), 155–172.

10. See, Audre Lorde, "Uses of the Erotic: The Erotic as Power," in *Sister Outsider: Essays and Speeches by Audre Lorde* (Berkeley: Crossing Press, 2007), 56–57.

11. See, Olive Elaine Hinnant, *God Comes Out: A Queer Homiletic* (Cleveland: The Pilgrim Press, 2007), 95; referencing Carter Heyward, *Touching Our Strength: The Erotic as Power and the Love of God* (San Francisco: Harper & Row, 1989).

Redeeming Pleasure in Worship   127

Proclamation Statement: God's power is in us helping us to play with Fear so we can risk vulnerability in order to be free to interconnect. El Verdadero Amor echa fuera el temor.

Design for the space (See illustration 1)

Set up 36 chairs in three sides of rows forming a square with the stage as the fourth side. Each side of rows will have 12 chairs arranged in two rows of six each and an aisle in the middle, between seats three and four, like airplane seating that looks like the double six domino from bird's-eye view. To generate a sense that it is a house, the two corners opposite to the stage side will have end tables like the ones one would find in a living room. On the end tables, there will be photos framed. In the feminine side three photos, one of Sofía Divinatrix, one of Lis Valle-Ruiz, and one of Jesus taking down from the uterus/cross the crucified woman. The image was a combination of a woman crucified to a uterus and Jesus trying to take her down from that cross.[12] On the masculine side, a photocomposition of portraits of Jesus of different ethnicities and also laughing.

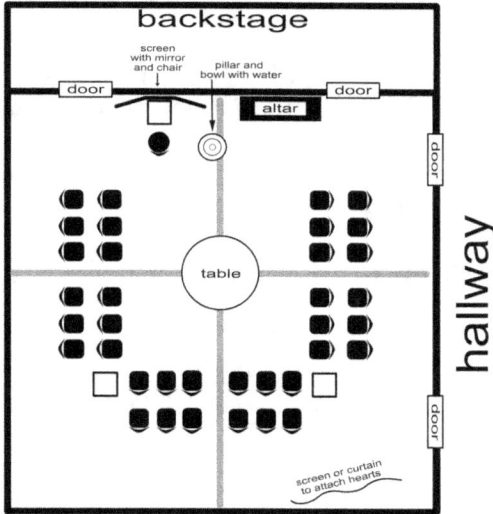

Illustration 1: Set design for the worship performance

---

12. The inspiration came from Eric Drooker, "Crucifixion," Ink on Scratchboard, 7" × 7", accessed April 1, 2023, https://www.drooker.com/original-art; and the book cover of Comisión Teológica Internacional de la Asociación Ecuménica de Teólogos/as del Tercer Mundo, Vigil J. Ma, editor, *Bajar de la cruz a los pobres: cristología de la liberación* (México D.F: DABAR, 2007). The cover art is by Maximino Cerezo Barredo. You may see it at https://liberationtheology.org/library/EATWOT GettingThePoorDown.pdf.

Set design (See illustration 1)

> Folding screen with mirror on center section of the screen; the sides of the screen will have pictures with images of what is desirable in female image and gender performance, it will be set up showing the tensions between beauty ideals of different communities, for example beauty industry vs. evangelical church. Small table, in lieu of bedroom furniture, simulating one of those dressers that have a mirror and you sit in front of it. Chair in front of the mirror and table to simulate a dresser. Pillar about three feet tall with a bowl full of water on top, like a baptismal font. Altar with designated areas for symbols of Taíno, Yoruba, and Christian religions.

Annotation: A dominant narrative in Puerto Rico is that Puerto Ricans emerge out of the encounter of Taínos (the indigenous people inhabiting the archipelago Borikén prior to the arrival of the conquistadores), Spanish, and West Africans. Each group contributed their religion to the Puerto Rican culture. Nonetheless, unlike music and food that have been the product of intermingling of the three cultures, religion has been kept separate and the religions of Borikén and West Africa have been demonized, the latter more than the former.

> Setting the table
>
> Ahead of time, during set up: Use duct tape to divide the space in four (left, right, back, front / feminine, masculine, day, night). Place a table where the two lines that divide the space meet, in the middle of the room. Dress the table with cloths, red prom dress, ding bowl, wine bottle opener, and a small bottle of frankincense.

The Worship Bulletin (scripted and annotated)

Liturgical Play
Recovering Evangelical Coming Out
All Faith Chapel, Vanderbilt Divinity School
Nashville, Tennessee | February 17, 2017

Play-lude

> (congregation will hold hands in a circle and sing as in children's round games)

// We have gathered here today
to celebrate life again //
// Life is sacred
and so we are //
// That's why we're gathered here today. //

Annotation: Lis Valle-Ruiz wrote the lyrics using the tune of a popular children's round game in Puerto Rico. Play is intrinsically related to ritual and theater. Performance is common to all three: play, ritual, and theater.[13]

Lighting of the candle

"Setting the Table," Scene 1

> (Actress 1 dings the bowl.)
> I have a date tonight . . .
> (The song "Ten Thousand Charms" by Sherry Cothran serves as romantic music in the background while Actress 1 sets the table for communion: adds bread at the center and around it a wine bottle, two cups of wine, a bunch of wheat spikes, and grapes, a Bible, an oil lamp, anointing oil, and ashes.)[14]
>
> Charge
> Mery: No vuelvas de allá hablando raro. Mantente humilde y siempre predicando en arroz y habichuelas.
> Hiramcito: Eres bendecida para bendecir.
> Translation: Do not come back from there talking weird. Be humble and always preaching using everyday language. You are blessed to bless.

Annotation: An attendee read these words from Lis' aunt and a friend. When Lis was accepted to the PhD in Homiletics and Liturgics at the Department of Religion of the Graduate School of Vanderbilt University, her aunt, María E. Ruiz-Quirós, charged her to keep her way of preaching and talking, a difficult task considering that words are the indicators that academia uses to determine if a doctoral student has learned, and thus deserves the title of doctor of philosophy. Mery, as her family calls her, said these words to Lis in person in Puerto Rico, near the day that Lis was traveling to Nashville, Tennessee, to begin her program. Similar to Mery, upon Lis announcing the news on social media, Lis' friend, Hiram A. Pérez-Cordero (or Hiramcito as Lis knew him from summer camps, when he was a child and Lis a teenager), responded with a charge reminding Lis that she is blessed to be a blessing. The phrase is common among Christians in Puerto Rico and yet, that day it took particular weight as Lis was going to gain a degree for her community, not just for herself. The words were read in Spanish as Mery and Hiram originally shared them and then read in English for other attendees at the liturgical play "Recovering Evangelical Coming Out" to understand.

---

13. See, Richard Schechner, *Performance Theory* (New York: Routledge Classics, 2003), 66–71, 108, 129–135.

14. Sherry Cothran, "Ten Thousand Charms," accessed April 1, 2023, song, 4:22, https://soundcloud.com/sherrycothran/ten-thousand-charms?in=sherrycothran/sets/sunland-album&utm_source=clipboard&utm_medium=text&utm_campaign=social_sharing.

Poem "Erotic, Mystic" by Lis Valle[15]

I would like to feel your flesh inside of mine, eventually.
I would like to taste the flavor of your most delicate skin, eventually.
I would like for you to kiss, lick, suck the petals of my flower, eventually.
I would like for you to do to me whatever you want, eventually.
I would like for us to do with each other whatever we want, eventually.
I would like for you to let me do to you whatever I want, eventually.
I would like to map you all, to feel your skin, kiss every pore, eventually.
I would like to feel your breath
over my neck,
over my ears,
over my face,
eventually.
I would like to taste those lips,
those very luscious lips,
eventually
And I would like for you to taste my lips,
all of my lips,
eventually.
I drink your milk,
You drink my water;
Cannibalism[16]; Eucharist; Communion.
We take in someone else's flesh.
We give ourselves and share our flesh.
It's so erotic.
It is so mystic.
Mystic. Erotic. What's the difference?
We enjoy God-given gifts.
We reach the point of praise;
we have to exclaim,
"O, God!
O, God!
O, God! O, God! O, God!
O, Goooooooooooooooood!" [sigh]
Erotic. Mystic. There is no difference.
We pray. We fuck. We praise. We love.
We share. We are. We become.[17]

---

15. © 2017 by Lis Valle. Reprinted with permission.

16. A sermon by Kyle Brooks, at the time a peer in the Homiletics and Liturgics program, raised Lis' awareness to cannibalism in communion.

17. The use of the word "become" in this poem, and later "becoming" in the message of gratitude is probably related to the fact that ethicist theologian Roberto Che Espinoza and Lis were housemates

You and I, would that ever be?
Maybe not
Or perhaps . . . eventually.

Annotation: In imitation of the Song of Songs and emboldened by Marcella Althaus-Reid's indecent theology, Lis wrote this poem combining sexual desire and desire for mystical union with God through communion. This poem is also a continuation of the language of erotic mysticism. In *The Ethics of Sex*, Jordan proposes a recovery and continuation of the language of erotic mysticism to reverse rhetorical choices in earlier theologies of sex. His aim is a moral theology that does not emphasize dichotomies, but rather emphasizes "the transfigurative union in Christ of apparent opposites."[18] The poem "Erotic, Mystic" challenges the virgin/whore binary and shows union of mysticism and sexuality.

Prayer for Illumination: Song "Come, Holy Spirit"[19]

Scripture Readings: Gen. 1:26–28, 31; 2:7, 22 (Accounts of Creation) and Psalm 139:13–16 (The Inescapable God)

Musical Message

Scripture Readings: I Corinthians 6:12–20 (Glorify God in Body and Spirit) and John 1:1, 14a; 3:8 (The Word Became Flesh)

Annotation: One of the many theologians in the room, though Lis cannot remember who, told Lis after the service that the selection of the readings, the juxtapositions, and the order was in itself queer.

Excerpt from "Loa" for the auto sacramental "El Divino Narciso," by Sor Juana Inés de la Cruz[20]

Annotation: The Loa stages an allegorical confrontation between two opposing parties: on one side stand America and her consort Occident (both natives); on the other are Religion (a Spanish lady) and Zeal (a Spanish captain). Through these characters in poetic dialog, Sor Juana offers an ingenious reflection on the colonial predicament and the erasure of indigenous religions. Religion and Zeal make evident their collusion to convert the natives out of their "idolatry" and into Christianity, Zeal through sword and valor, Religion through persuasion and mercy.

---

and Roberto spoke a lot about "becoming" as a theological concept because it was a key concept in Roberto's dissertation.

18. Jordan, *The Ethics of Sex*, 172.

19. John L. Bell, "Come, Holy Spirit," accessed April 1, 2023, song, https://hymnary.org/tune/come_holy_spirit_bell.

20. Sor Juana Inés de la Cruz, *The Divine Narcissus: El Divino Narciso*, translated and annotated by Patricia A. Peters and Renée Domeier, O.S.B. (Albuquerque: University of New Mexico Press, 1998), 8–19.

Burlesque-esque Message

Title: Less Fear, More Piña (Gozo)
Music: March 2, from "The Nutcracker"[21]; transitions into Afro-Caribbean music – instrumental; ends with shamanic music for healing.
Preacher: Sofía Divinatrix, The High Priestess Unrobed
Characters: Fearful Ginger Bread Soldier; Jiggly Tembleque; Delicious Piña Colada; Lis at the beach.

Annotation: The original worship bulletin stated "Burlesque Message." Members of the audience who were experienced in the art of burlesque provided feedback regarding the need to take more clothes off if this message was to be called burlesque. Since the message also included symbolic art, symbolic objects, and a theological framework related to the Christian traditions of Holy Fools, Lis decided to make plain that her choice of genre was inspired by and used the basic grammar of burlesque but not quite burlesque, thus the addition of "-esque."[22]

The idea of addressing fear fearlessly came to Lis as the result of participating in fear+less conversations, Forum for Theological Exploration, in Atlanta, Georgia, during the summer of 2016, facilitated by Gregory C. Ellison.[23] Lis chose joy as the destination out of fear. The association of joy (gozo) and pineapples comes from a childhood memory. The childhood memory consists of an artistic representation of the fruits of the Spirit, each fruit written on a tile with the drawing of a fruit. The fruit gozo/joy was represented by a pineapple. The artwork was at El Guacio Camp and Conference Center, San Sebastián, Puerto Rico. In addition, pineapples represent hospitality, an important value in Lis' life. The phrase piña "(gozo)" alludes also to joy, another important value in Lis' life.

When Afro-Caribbean instrumental music displaced the music from "The Nutcracker," the instruments were mostly drums. The choice intends to counter demonization of African cultures in the Christian traditions in Puerto Rico and to recover African heritage as sacred, as in Cuban santería, which evolves out of the Yoruba traditions. The choice for instrumental is because the absence of words

---

21. Tchaikovsky, "The Nutcracker." This was the agreement by majority of the group taking the class.

22. See Lis Valle-Ruiz, "Non-Preaching? Unmasking (White) Preaching Through Negation" in *Unmasking White Preaching: Racial Hegemony, Resistance, and Possibilities in Homiletics*, Lis Valle-Ruiz and Andrew Wymer, co-editors (Lanham: Lexington Books, 2022), 205–220. The message is available to watch at, Lis Valle, "The Sermon," Published June 24, 2022, performance video, 10:46, https://youtu.be/MCyxfFtAQTs.

23. See Ellison's book, *Fearless Dialogues: A New Movement for Justice* (Louisville: Westminster John Knox Press, 2017).

may convey the message better to speakers of any given language. The choice for shamanic music for healing responds to the aim of the play and the nature of the character. The aim of the liturgical play *Recovering Evangelical Coming Out* is healing and the character Sofía Divinatrix is a shaman, a seer, a healer, a high priestess.

The choice to preach through an alter ego responds to several reasons and purposes. On the one hand, the initial assignment (a recital at the end of a burlesque course) required a stage persona with its own name and tagline. On the other hand, for Lis, Sofía Divinatrix serves multiple roles: it is an alter ego that creates distance for purposes of critical engagement to protect Lis' "real" identity, and to remember that Lis is wearing someone else's shoes temporarily. The presupposition is that members of the audience can identify better with that character than with the actress. Lis remains aware that members of the queer and kink communities have more reason than her to fear coming out or living out as queer because Lis risks ostracism but they also face unemployment or death. Sofía is a name in Spanish that sounds the same in English and is also one of the names assigned to God's wisdom. Divinatrix is a combination of Divine and dominatrix: divine, to complete the reference to God's wisdom; dominatrix because the first few costume designs came out looking like a dominatrix. Lis tried to portray a soldier. The first two persons who saw Lis' costume design, both queer persons of color, interpreted the drawing/character as a dominatrix. Furthermore, the character embodies a transfigurative union of apparent opposites by combining a dominatrix with a high priestess, and reiterates union of mysticism and sexuality.[24]

Sofía Divinatrix is a character that plays other characters. Through the dance, Sofía plays a new character with every new costume disclosed to the audience/congregation. The first character, Fearful Ginger Bread Soldier, represents the way that Lis imagines fear as a person. Lis imagines fear as a bodyguard, a protector, or a soldier because the function of fear is to warn human beings when we are in danger. The first outfit that Sofía removes combines military and ecclesial powers, inspired by Sor Juana Inés de la Cruz's Loa to *El Divino Narciso*. The soldier that Sofía plays is a gingerbread soldier from "The Nutcracker" with added symbols to communicate the collusion of state and church.

The next two characters substitute the Russian culture of "The Nutcracker." The second character is Jiggly Tembleque. Tembleque is a jiggly coconut custard made in Puerto Rico mostly during Christmas. Being afraid makes Lis tremble, like tembleque does. Also, tembleque is from Lis' culture, a popular dessert during Christmas, unlike the nutcracker. Nonetheless, due to colonization and globalization, "The Nutcracker" is known and performed in Puerto Rico. The third character is Delicious Piña Colada. Piña colada is a drink from Lis'

---

24. See, Jordan, *The Ethics of Sex*.

culture but recognizable in other many cultures. Lis noticed after the performance that the characters moved from solid, to jiggly, to liquid. Lis was reflecting in therapy around that time that the most resilient swords are the nimblest and most flexible ones. She was also watching the TV series *Heroes*, which featured a woman that turned into water. Lis was learning that the more flexible a person is, the more resilient the person is, and consequently, the stronger the person is. It is a paradox.

The fourth character that Sofía Divinatrix plays is not a character at all. After Sofía plays the roles of soldier, tembleque, and piña colada, she becomes Lis at the beach. The "real" Lis is at her favorite sacred place in the world. Lis, as actress, changes into this outfit after the call to join the cloud of witnesses. She had traveled through history with her body, from colonial times of Spanish conquistadores and proselytizing church blended with the Russian culture of "The Nutcracker," shed to become Puerto Rican dessert and drink, shed to become herself. In fact, the audience never saw Sofía Divinatrix as a High Priestess, but only as an actress who played and shed three characters in order to let Lis come through and back to herself.

Props

> big candy cane (as rifle); big ginger man cookie plush toy (as shield); hazelnuts (nuts to crack, of course); sunscreen lotion.

Scripture Passage: 1 John 4:18

> which relates to love that casts out fear.

Proclamation Statement

> The power of the Divine Source of all life is in us helping us to play with fear so we can risk vulnerability in order to be free to interconnect.

Annotation: The props are loaded with references and symbolisms. The big candy cane is long and used as a rifle. It references traditional Christmas candy, sweet, weapon for the soldier, and phallic shape. The shield in the shape of a big ginger man cookie plush toy constitutes a connection between Lis' psyche and the agreement of the students in the burlesque course. Lis imagines her fear as a bodyguard, which matches well the gingerbread soldiers in "The Nutcracker." During the production, the shield ended up looking like Lis, teaching her that she is the only one that can protect herself from her fears. At least, that is what positivism and the industry of motivational speakers advance in the United States. The hazelnuts and nuts were represented with two big golden eggs. "The Nutcracker" is supposed to crack nuts. Lis took advantage of that to try and challenge manhood and masculinity. However, it did not happen in the presentation. The sunscreen lotion is a very appropriate object to have at the beach. Lis' decision intended including people from the audience as active participants in body, not only cognition, and to practice human touch as one of the values that Lis wants to highlight and transfer.[25] Lis does not remember it happening during the presentation.

For a sermon without words, the proclamation statement has a lot of words. The proclamation was based on 1 John 4:18a, which states that "perfect love casts out fear." Jerusha Neal suggests developing a sermon-play as one would a sermon, which is consistent with the way that Lis' pastor and playwright, José Roberto Colón-Rodríguez, does it and that Lis learned intuitively from him once she started a master of divinity.[26] As final step in the exegetical process, Thomas Long suggests finding the [biblical] "text's claim upon the hearers."[27] In preaching classes, the late practical theologian and homiletician Dale P. Andrews used to call this process, generating a proclamation statement.

Story line (burlesque-esque dance without words)

- Fearful Ginger Bread Soldier enters marching with the big ginger man cookie plush toy as shield facing the audience. Soldier walks to border of stage, shakes knees scared, peeks and hides behind the shield, runs to hide behind the chair, places the shield sitting on the chair.
- Shy to come out, Soldier hides and shows her face a few times and realizes that it can be a game. Soldier starts playing peek-a-boo with the audience.
- Soldier begins doing soldiery things: marches; succeeds; shows off being a soldier: plays with the candy cane—licks it.

Annotation: The initial intention of the sermon was to exorcise fear. During the rehearsal process, the peek-a-boo game just happened without planning or intentionality. Soldier's realization that hiding from and facing fear can become a game worked as heuristic hermeneutics. In time, Lis realized that play is an important way to face fears, to do healing work, to do research, and to produce new knowledge. It has always been part of her family's life. Play theory is intertwined in Lis' work.[28] Playing with the candy cane, turning it into a deadly

---

25. About the transfer of knowledge through performance, see Diana Taylor, *The Archive and the Repertoire: Performing Cultural Memory in the Americas* (Durham: Duke University Press, 2003).

26. Jerusha Matsen Neal, *Blessed: Monologues for Mary* (Eugene, OR: Cascade Books, 2013), 63.

27. Thomas G. Long, *The Witness of Preaching*, Third Edition (Louisville: Presbyterian Publishing Corporation, 2016), 93.

28. For play theory in the work of Lis, see, Lis Valle-Ruiz, "The Power of Divine Play at Sophia's Theme Park," *The Presbyterian Outlook*, 203: 12 (October 5, 2021), updated May 11, 2022, https://pres-outlook.org/2021/10/the-power-of-divine-play-at-sophias-theme-park/; and also, "Sophia's

rifle and licking it as a phallus, conveys an implicit connection between the art of war and the art of seduction or of sex.

- Soldier walks up stage, chimi-buttocks while opens military coat.
- Music changes. Soldier removes military uniform and clergy collar and blouse. Soldier is gone when that outfit is gone. Now Jiggly Tembleque is dancing.
- Tembleque dances and removes clothes (white short dress, coconut bra outside the dress, brown dots that simulate the cinnamon sprinkled over tembleque form a smile shape). Tembleque is gone when that outfit is gone. Now Piña Colada is dancing.
- Piña Colada (now wears a bra that shows yellow circles simulating pineapple rings with a cherry on top, the previous short dress has been changed into an even shorter skirt) dances until she finds her image in the mirror and screams in horror.
- Interruption. Music changes to shamanic healing music.
- Piña Colada starts cleaning the ugly parts of her body and ends up baptizing them and accepting her whole imperfect body. She is humming the song "al mirar la sonrisa de un niño al pasar" (when I see the smile of a kid passing by)[29] during the baptism.
- She sings "al mirar la sonrisa de un niño al pasar" while posting pictures of her sons in the borders of the mirror.

Response to the Word: Cloud of Witnesses

Piña Colada picks up a small chest and starts taking out small pictures and trinkets. For each picture, she says, "I perceive beauty in . . ." [the trickster, the nurturer, the collaborator, etc.], starting with Lis' "dead" ancestors and continuing with her current support system. She then invites attendees to write their names in the small red heart they received when they entered the room and to add it to the tree silhouette (in reality a shower curtain) on the other side of the room. While spect-actors[30] build the cloud of witnesses Piña Colada changes

---

Theme Park," *Open Plaza Podcast*, accessed April 1, 2023, 51:59, https://www.htiopenplaza.org/content/sofias-theme-park.

29. The song talks about finding God's presence in beauty, everywhere, seeing God in the face of a child, in the face of an-Other. It is a short worship song (corito) that Lis memorized as a child, part of oral tradition in Christian church in Puerto Rico. At the time of writing this essay, Lis has not found the lyrics or the author.

30. Spect-actors are the members of the audience, when they stop being passive spectators and engage in shaping the action of an artistic performance like actors do. See, Augusto Boal, *Theatre of the Oppressed*, translated by Charles A. and María-Odilia Leal McBride (New York: Theatre Communications Group, 1985).

clothes into Lis in swimming suit and royal blue wrapper. Meanwhile, a singer leads in communal song "Beautiful Things."³¹

Annotation: After the sermon, as a response to the Word, Lis invites the audience/congregation to join her cloud of witnesses. The intention was to have people join in the homiletical task of witnessing, in body as well as cognitively. Lis' blue wrapper is royal blue as in the color of the ocean that Lis sees from her sacred place, and is also the color of the throat/fifth chakra, which represents the voice, the ability to speak and communicate clearly. In this burlesque-esque message, it represents both the ocean and also Lis finding herself and her voice.

Lis' Affirmation of Faith: Do Not Be Afraid

One: What did God say to Hagar
when she thought
Ishmael would die in the desert?
Many: Do not be afraid.
What did Isaiah tell Jacob and Israel
when he assured them
that rivers would not overwhelm them
nor fire consume them?
One: Do not be afraid.
What did God tell Jeremiah
when he thought he was not fit
to be a prophet to the nations?
Many: Do not be afraid.
What did the angel say to Mary
when the birth of Jesus was foretold?
One: Do not be afraid.
Two: Beloved, let us love one another,
if we love one another, . . . love is perfected in us.
All: There is no fear in love,
but perfect love casts out fear.

Sofia's Affirmation of Beliefs

One: When a child is afraid
to get close to the cauldron to stir the potion,
what do we say?

---

31. Written by: Lisa Gungor, Michael Gungor. Lyrics © BMG Rights Management, Sony/ATV Music Publishing LLC. Lyrics Licensed and Provided by LyricFind. You may read the lyrics and listen to the song at https://www.lyrics.com/lyric/27740480/Beautiful+Things. Watch the music video, Gungor, "Beautiful Things," *Relevant* youtube channel, April 30, 2010, music video, 4:59, https://youtu.be/oyPBtExE4W0.

Many:	It's gonna be OK.
	When our friends are taking exams
	that will determine the direction
	of their future, what do we say?
One:	You got this!
	When a loved one is going into surgery,
	What do we say?
Many:	Don't be scared!
	When our people are anxious
	about upcoming trips to cross borders,
	what do we say?
One:	You can do it!
Two:	Beloved, let us love one another,
	if we love one another, . . . love is perfected in us.
All:	There is no fear in love,
	but perfect love casts out fear. (1 John 4:18a).

Annotation: There are two affirmations because there are two personas coming out, Lis and Sofía. More importantly, Lis' affirmation of faith is unapologetically Christian, whereas Sofía's affirmation of beliefs is mostly secular or humanist. This was an intentional decision to welcome those members of the audience who do not identify as Christians or as religious or who have been hurt by Christian supremacy. One of these members of the audience read the part of "One" of Sofía's affirmation of beliefs during the liturgical play.

Meal Ritual

Invitation to the table: "Setting the Table," Scene 2
(Lis and Actress 1 enter with the coconut milk and the honey.)
Lis: [reads Song of Solomon 2:5c; 1:2–3; 5:4–5]

Actress 1: [reads Song of Solomon 4:10–11]
(Lis and Actress 1 put the honey and milk on the table)
(Actress 1 continues speaking, while Lis touches the dress on the table, then smells the frankincense)

Lis: [reads Song of Solomon 4:16]

Communal Song: "For Everyone Born" (stanzas 1 and 2)[32]

---

32. Words: Shirley Erena Murray, "For Everyone Born," alt. music: Daniel Charles Damon, words © 1998 Hope Publishing Company, Carol Stream, IL 60188, all rights reserved; music © 2022 Hope Publishing Company, Carol Stream, IL 60188, all rights reserved, accessed April 1, 2023, hymn lyrics, https://www.hopepublishing.com/find-hymns-hw/hw342.aspx.

Prayer of Thanksgiving
This is a joyful feast
and we are grateful that we have access to it!

Blessing (unison)

Our Queer Parent que estás en todas partes,
promiscuizados sean tus nombres.
Thy Eros come.
Your love be made on earth,
As it is in heaven.
Give us each day our daily pleasure.
Forgive us our-isms,
as we forgive them that exclude us.
And lead us not into suicidal thoughts,
but deliver us from heterosexism and binary thinking.
For ours is the kinship, the power, and the glory.
For ever and ever. Amen.

Breaking the bread
Alimento para la lucha . . .
Nourishment for staying strong in the struggle . . .
The gifts of G*d for the people of G*d
The gifts we share with one another
in the beloved community.

Annotation: Alba Onofrio and Lis Valle-Ruiz coined the phrase "alimento para la lucha" for Alba's ordination. These were the words used to serve the elements of communion at Alba's ordination, an adaptation of the "Mujerista Liturgy" in *Mujerista Theology: A Theology for The Twenty-First Century* by Ada María Isasi-Díaz.[33] The words are not in the mujerista ritual but honor the spirit of it. Alba's ordination was held prior to the performance of *Recovering Evangelical Coming Out*. In this liturgical play, the sacred meal ritual did not use the mujerista liturgy but rather a disordered selection of texts from Song of Songs because the emphasis was on sexuality more than gender, on queer and indecent theology more than mujerista theology. Nonetheless, the mujerista spirit that proclaims in bread and milk with honey, "Alimento para la lucha/nourishment for staying strong in the struggle" is equally needed, helpful, and powerful here.

Before we eat together, we need to do one more thing: we need to get
rid of the binaries. Let's remove these divisions marked on the floor.

---

33. Ada María Isasi-Díaz, *Mujerista Theology: A Theology for the Twenty-First Century* (Maryknoll: Orbis Books, 1996), 170–191.

> (Liturgists and attendees remove the duct tape that was dividing the space.)
>
>> Giving, nourishment for the struggle
>> *Setting the Table*, Scene 3
>> Song of Solomon 5:1
>> *(People share the meal)*
>>
>> Thanksgiving
>> > Psalm 30: 11–12
>> > Communal Song: "For Everyone Born" (stanza 5)[34]

Sending Forth the Community:

> Poem *For Freedom,* by John O'Donohue
> Poem reader: And those who agreed said, . . .
> **Community: . . . Amen**

Sending forth the light

Post mortem

> A facilitator invites the audience to stay for conversation to analyze the liturgical play and share their experiences of it.

About the Preacher

> Sofía Divinatrix, through uncontrollable erotic power, disciplines harmful systems, binds dictatorship and tyranny, and unbinds humans for flourishing. She is from Matinino, an inaccessible Caribbean Island of taíno women, descendants of the Amazons. She has an insatiable thirst for knowledge and every time she gets into her system a new book, "o G*d, o yes, o yes, yes, yes!!!"
>
> She conceived this performance as a one-woman show, but she couldn't help herself because her life philosophy is "the more the merrier." In her own words, "Why play with yourself when you can play with many others? Let's **do** something together! It's gonna be amazing!"

Thanks

> The producer, Lis Valle-Ruiz, thanks all those who gathered for this celebration today, and those who made preparations for this performance,

---

34. Murray, "For Everyone Born," Words © 1998 Hope Publishing Company.

Redeeming Pleasure in Worship 141

particularly those named on the program, who offered their leadership gifts. Lis also thanks the student organizations Poiesis and Latinx Sems for sponsoring the event. Special thanks to Lyndsey Godwin, Elisabel Ruiz, and Brittney Jackson for hosting the reception. Many thanks to Steve Stone for the promo and to Scout for the awesome pictures for the promo and for being the camera person today. Thanks to Shaie (Sharon Dively) for being the stage manager. Thanks to many other people and institutions that have played a key role in the formation of my identity and that continue to do so because I am a work in progress, always becoming.

Annotation: The use of the word "becoming" in this message of gratitude, and previously the word "become" in the "Erotic, Mystic" poem, is probably related to the fact that Roberto Che Espinoza (though back then Roberto had a different name) and Lis were housemates. During those times, Roberto spoke frequently about becoming as a theological concept because it was a key concept in Roberto's dissertation.

Illustration 2: Folded worship bulletin

Note: The worship bulletin was folded and, in the front, had the picture of the closed back of an envelope with a kiss mark where the flap ends. The intention was to generate the feeling in each attendee that they were receiving a love letter. (See illustration 2.)

Some Feedback after the Liturgical Play Ended

No one sat down for a postmortem. It is probable that the community was tired and hungry after two hours of liturgy. There was tembleque, piña colada, and other typical snacks from Puerto Rico available to partake, and people stayed chatting and informally reacting to the liturgical play. At the door, while exiting, as it is typical in Sunday morning worship services, some folks gave Lis feedback as they walked out of the worship space and into the fellowship halls. People shared two main insights: (1) that the play helped them realize that they do not have to end a relationship with God just because their church ostracized them, excluded them, or expelled them for being queer, and (2) that they do not have to get rid of everything they learned from the faith traditions that raised/hurt them and/or expelled them. The service did not include any of these messages explicitly but these messages were driving the design of the liturgy and the sermon in intentional ways.

Post-Ludic

The liturgical play *Recovering Evangelical Coming Out* constitutes an example of queering worship so that the queer and performance theories that inform the content, also inform the shape of the rituals and messages. The ambiguity of genre in the show/liturgy, burlesque-esque sermon, and this annotated script/ essay as well as the sexualized language employed in worship are some ways in which this liturgical play queers Christian worship. In addition, by joining the erotic mysticism tradition as well as the Holy Fools Christian tradition, the preacher, Sofía Divinatrix, is able to play/pray, perform, enjoy sensuality and sexuality, decolonize herself, minister the word and sacrament, and seek mystical union with God and with God's people. While Sofía Divinatrix does not speak, her messages were transferred clearly. The liturgical play redeemed pleasure in worship allowing attendees to find redeeming pleasures in this queer Christian worship service.

CHAPTER TEN

UNDER THE PREACHER'S ROBES
A Queer Embodied Homiletic

Lucas Hergert

Queer theology is body theology. It reaches for God in the fleshiness of human life. As Marcella Althaus-Reid puts it, "the starting point of queering theology is always the body."[1] It is no surprise, then, that her book *The Queer God* begins with bodies doing concrete, specific things. One body is praying to a saint or to the Virgin Mary. The other is going to a bar to find a lover. And then the experiences of the two bodies begin to mingle and collide. The rosary used to pray to the Virgin is in the back pocket of the person dancing at the bar. The person going to church to kneel has a letter from their lover in their bag. Althaus-Reid's description of these venues and activities is memorable: "Now suppose," she writes, "that in your mind the church and the Latina bar somehow get mixed up with fragments of memories of the Nicaean creed and of a Christ who died of love for you some time ago contesting the fact that nobody else seems to be dying of love for you anymore."[2] Here queer theology is about the mixing up of seemingly contradictory practices and spaces. And it is about bodies. Bodies dancing, kneeling, praying, fingering rosaries and lovers, reciting creeds and love letters, initiate a midnight liaison with God and neighbor.

The act of preaching also involves bodies. Every word of the sermon is given and received with flesh and breath. As Todd Farley writes, "How can we offer our 'spiritual worship' if not through the body?"[3] Farley has in mind the performative dimension which includes the preacher's use of speech, gesture, and expression. Both early and recent homiletics manuals address this topic. But the history of preaching is also the history of ambivalence about the body and its presentation in worship. As just one example from Christendom, part of the early Reformed

---

1. Marcella Althaus-Reid, "Feetishism: The Scent of a Latin American Body Theology," in *Towards a Theology of Eros: Transfiguring Passion at the Limits of Discipline*, eds. Virginia Burrus and Catherine Keller (Fordham, NY: Fordham University Press, 2007), 134–152, at 136.

2. Marcella Althaus-Reid, *The Queer God* (New York : Routledge, 2003), 1.

3. Todd Farley, "The Use of the Body in the Performance of Proclamation," in *Performance in Preaching*, eds. Jana Childers and Clayton J. Schmit (Grand Rapids, MI: Baker Publishing Group, 2008), 156–185, at 157.

church regulated ministers' attire. It insisted that "the good Word of God" not be "slandered" by the "immoderateness" of the preacher's presentation.[4] This was partly a reaction to the extravagance of some Roman vestments. And it demonstrated a preference to conceal bodily presentation that might otherwise distract from the word. Homiletics can sometimes function as a theoretical robe, tucking away the parts of embodied existence it finds distracting, extravagant, or unworthy. But the body does not vanish simply because the preacher covers it in "comelie and decent apparel."[5] Whither, then, desire, sexuality, and longing in the pulpit?

A queer homiletic feels under the preacher's robes. Knowing there is no neat separation between the body's desires and holy activities, it relishes the moments when these get mixed up. A queer homiletic savors love letters the preacher has in their back pocket, phrases of the sermon written at the gay bar, the injunction to love one's neighbor all the way to their home, and closet devotions that yoke the homo-erotic, the transgressive, and the sacred. This meander through desire, this twist and turn through viscera, invites the preacher to follow queer trajectories. As I argue in this essay, attending to the body and its desires reshapes the preaching experience. It encourages modes of delivery and uses of language that center embodiment and intensify pleasure. It measures the success of preaching not in terms of piety or changed behavior, but in terms of amplified satisfaction. It grounds its authority in the body's knowledge beyond cultural and theological horizons. And it finds its prophetic edge against the pain and limits of the present. The queer word is always spoken in the context of the life-negating and pleasure-denying, which is precisely what makes it good news.

Those who inhabit queer lives know that the body is not (only) a pleasurable utopia. As Jose Muñoz puts it in *Cruising Utopia: The Then and There of Queer Futurity:* "The here and now is a prison house."[6] While many strive for a future where it gets better, queer people can never simply cruise past the pain of the present. It is a truth that twists down in the guts and touches deep personal histories. For instance, I came out the same year two men hung Matthew Shepard's body on a fence post. The press speculated that he had probably approached his killers for a hook up. And what happened to his body because of this approach looked terribly like a crucifixion. Seeing the images of Matthew Shepard's body incited fear that collapsed my shoulders, making me reticent to speak the truth of my desire. When I climbed into the pulpit for the first time (which also happened to be that same year), I swallowed the advice not to "preach queer." And so, the body of

---

4. These regulations are from the 1575 General Assembly of the Church of Scotland, quoted in R.A.S. Macalister, *Ecclesiastical Vestments: Their Development and History* (London, UK: Eliot Stock, 1896), 209.

5. The 1575 General Assembly of the Church of Scotland, quoted in Macalister, *Ecclesiastical Vestments*, 209.

6. Jose Muñoz, *Cruising Utopia: The Then and There of Queer Futurity*, 10th anniv. ed. (New York: New York University Press, 2019), 1.

the queer preacher also carries these challenges. It bears the scars of bashing, the hesitations over respectability and decorum, the velvet rage from absorbing abuse, the gestures disciplined to appear less feminine or masculine, the brow furrowed by lingering worries about God's love, and the church's embrace.

The commandment not to "preach queer" is a snare. For many congregations, simply being queer is preaching queer. Olive Elaine Hinnant, in her book *God Comes Out: A Queer Homiletic*, puts it this way, "When I was told not to preach about 'it' anymore in my church, I realized that as out gay and lesbian preachers we embodied the very thing people were afraid might split their church, encroach on their values, hurt their children, or tarnish their image."[7] In other words, simply being out in the pulpit provokes discomfort for some hearers. It is notable that Hinnant uses the word embodied here. The body can be a persistent reminder of one's queerness; it has a givenness whether or not the preacher and the hearer approve. Observers read and interpret its signals. The limp wrist, the butch haircut, the manicured hand; the earring, the pride bracelet, the pink shirt, the masculine cut of the pants; the lisp, the vocal fry, the voice too high or too deep; the tears, the laugh, the walk. The audience feasts on signals and makes of them what it will. And it is not uncommon for an audience to make much of them. As the homiletics scholar Leonora Tubbs Tisdale recalls, "A lesbian woman of my acquaintance was actually asked by someone on a pulpit search committee if she would consider changing her hairstyle and mode of dress to make her look less, well, lesbian."[8] In these moments the clerical collar can feel especially tight.

Queer preachers also know about the subtle negotiation that happens when talking about one's embodied experiences. This can make preaching feel close to coming out, provoking a host of questions. Who is in the audience today? How will they receive a particular message? Does the preacher feel fear or excitement at the prospect of naming a truth? Will the preacher share their identity and orientation? What risk is the preacher willing to take, not knowing how it will be received? What word has been crossed out, added back, crossed out, and added yet again? In a sermon about the body being a beautiful part of God's creation, will the preacher say the word clitoris? erection? orgasm? Will the preacher claim that a story is about a lover or pretend that the lover is a friend? Many sweat the answers. Concealing one's experience can amputate a preacher's sense of integrity and authenticity. At the same time, the expectation to share, such as the expectation that trans people will share medical details, can be aggressive and abusive. A queer preacher's negotiation of embodied experience is work—work that can easily go unappreciated by cisgendered and heterosexual colleagues.

---

7. Olive Elaine Hinnant, *God Comes Out: A Queer Homiletic* (Cleveland, OH: Pilgrim Press, 2007), 165.

8. Leonora Tubbs Tisdale, *How Women Transform Preaching* (Nashville, TN: Abingdon Press, 2021), 55.

The authority to preach exists in the breathing space between the pulpit and the pew. It does not result only from formal station and title. Nor does it rest on the eloquence, correctness, or sincerity of the message. The power lives with the hearers who grant and withdraw approval. David Buttrick's masterpiece *Homiletic: Moves and Structures* addresses this issue. He argues that the sermon stands or falls not on the independent validity of the message but rather on the understandings of the congregation. "We are never talking of ideas 'out there,' ideas that stand in pure isolation from the stuff of human consciousness. Instead," he writes, "we speak ideas that are tangled up with human responses."[9] They exist in relation to assumptions, attitudes, and emotions that are rooted in the culture and lifeworld of the hearer. Because of this, preachers are granted authority to the extent that they can negotiate the intersecting layers of understandings in the pews. This includes engaging the proliferation of theological explanations and alternative secular and political accounts. Religion is not the only interpretive frame for hearers, but rather one among many. And most hearers come with awareness of the psychological, political, and sociological explanations that challenge or buttress theological claims.[10] Hence, it no longer works—if it ever did—for the preacher to declare that something is so and be it so. Nor does it work to say, "Do this because the Bible says it." Many hearers are aware enough to ask, why interpret the Bible in that way? Does that interpretation fit or not fit with other theological understandings? What about alternative frames?

Traditional religious groups express nostalgia for a simpler time, one in which institutional authority encountered fewer challenges. Queer and trans people know, however, that such a time was no utopia. It was, to quote Muñoz, another "prison house." Today, queer preachers find ways to leverage the changing landscape to survive and flourish. The dispersion of authority into multiple domains can bolster the legitimacy of preachers whose identities and approaches challenge traditional theological assumptions. This dispersion can, in other words, support the capacity to "preach queer." The fact that hearers arrive with secular psychological and sociological frameworks unfolds a space for negotiation with scripture and tradition. For progressive congregations, it will not do to insist simply that cultural understandings bend to conservative Biblical interpretations. Indeed, alternative secular understandings may disarm the "clobber passages" used against LGBTQ people. The changing landscape can also invigorate and legitimize forgotten histories in Christianity that affirm different shapes of devotion

---

9. David Buttrick, *Homiletic: Moves and Structures* (Philadelphia, PA: Fortress, 1987), 27–28.

10. Charles Taylor is one of the most careful observers of the historical change that I am describing. As he puts it in *A Secular Age*: "the change I want to define and trace is one which takes us from a society in which it was virtually impossible not to believe in God, to one in which faith, even for the staunchest believer, is one human possibility among others." Charles Taylor, *A Secular Age* (Cambridge, MA: Belknap Press, 2018), 3.

and desire.[11] Far from being lamentable, these changes offer queer preachers liberty to reposition sexuality in the pulpit and in life.

Buttrick does not fully appreciate the complexity of authority negotiation. This becomes obvious when he discusses homosexuality as a social "situation" the preacher may be called upon to address.[12] He proposes three alternative theological options for understanding homosexuality. The first is an argument from creation, that God created men and women and thus ordained heterosexuality. The second option is that "persistent homosexuality" is a sin and a refusal of the mercy of Jesus Christ. The third option takes the interpretive angle that God does not rank sin. Therefore, straight Christians have no ground to criticize their homosexual siblings. The author defines the latter position as one of "radical inclusion"—which makes one wonder what standard inclusion looks like. Anything close to the idea that God created, ordained, and blessed sexuality apart from heterosexual relations remains unthought within his text. Now, I have little interest in judging Buttrick's 1987 *Homiletic* from the standards of today's sexual ethics. However, his framing of these three responses highlights an analytic gap. Cultural horizons may limit both secular and religious responses, even the ones that (supposedly) represent inclusion and affirmation. The preacher may need to reach for other tools to negotiate a response.

This brings us back under the preacher's robes. Perhaps what is needed is the outlaw pleasure/knowledge informed by the erotic longings and closet devotions of the preacher. In the Christian imagination, sexuality and knowledge are deeply entwined, beginning with the mythical tree in Eden. Likewise, there is a present and concrete way that erotics can provide insight. Our bodies may offer the knowledge that something is good and desirable even when the surrounding cultural messages insist it is not.[13] As queer people know well, it takes courage to listen to the body's affirmations and refuse prohibitions. Responses to such refusals are not uncomplicated: preaching a message rooted in embodied experience can invite the congregation's displeasure. But doing so can also lead to liberation and joy. Indeed, the preacher may discover a newfound authority that accords with embodied knowledge. Sometimes the congregation is simply

---

11. I am thinking especially of Richard Rambuss's *Closet Devotions*. By analyzing the extensive history of erotic devotion to Christ, he shows "how religion has made use of the body and the passions in signifying, even amplifying, devotion [and also] how the erotic conversely—perversely?—uses the religious to enhance its own affects." Richard Rambuss, *Closet Devotions* (Durham, NC: Duke University Press, 1998), 3.

12. Buttrick, *Homiletic*, 429.

13. Social conservatives will, no doubt, rehearse a list of rebuttals. What happens when desire becomes destructive or harmful? While coercion, self-destruction, and violence can enmesh with pleasure, this fact need not translate into an inherent suspicion of the erotic. Instead, it means that desire and sexual practice ought to be examined for problematic motives and social forces (racism, patriarchy, capitalism) that contaminate all human goods and relationships. For a fuller discussion, see Marvin Ellison, "Reimagining Good Sex: The Eroticizing of Mutual Respect and Pleasure," in *Erotic Justice: A Liberating Ethic of Sexuality* (Louisville, KY: Westminster John Knox, 1993), 76–93.

waiting for permission to think and feel anew, to experience not a here and now but a *"then* and *there."*[14] In that instance, the preacher is prophet, heralding a world beyond the pain of the present.

A queer-embodied homiletic does not wear itself out chatting about LGBTQ issues. Preaching is not tutorial. Instead, the sermon translates sensuality and experience into language. And this requires intention and method, as Fred Craddock carefully explores. In his landmark book *As One without Authority*, he does this by inverting the way the sermon had customarily been written. Previously, a deductive expository sermon began with a thesis or idea the preacher then argued. Experience, narrative, and image were used to "illustrate" the main concept. Often, images were treated as embroidery or ornamentation—dispensable so long as the idea was well-crafted. Craddock argues this approach is not sustainable; people no longer come to church to be taught about ideas. Instead, they come for a fresh experience of faith. He thus proposes an inductive model of sermon preparation that begins not with conclusions but experience. It brings hearers along an imaginative journey. If the hearer assents to a message, it is only because they have found the path there persuasive. And this will stand or fall on the preacher's ability to describe, interact with, and imagine the bodies and lives that populate the sermon. The images must be palpable, real, and vital to the message. As Craddock puts it, "Images are not, in fact, to be regarded as illustrative but rather as essential to the form and inseparable from the content of the entire sermon."[15] The message of the sermon, in other words, must pass through the doors of the particular and the concrete.

Such preaching requires different language. A homiletic grammar is the linguistic translation and shaping of embodied experience. It highlights interactions with bodies in space and time, using the senses of one's own body to facilitate the experience for hearers. This approach stresses the language of sense impression above the language of idea and abstraction, for the hearer does not experience a concept or an idea. Instead, one perceives particularities drawn in vivid color. For instance, one does not experience a Pride festival in general. Instead, they have a particular experience of their senses in space and time ("The artificial cherry smell wafted from the condensation-weeping red Dixie cups as a six-foot Drag Queen in glittering sequined angel wings belted out Ariana Grande's *God Is a Woman* in an unconvincing falsetto that sounded akin to a muffler scratching pavement"). This fills in the color of the empty conceptual category of Pride. The concept is vacuous without embodiment, of bodies interacting with bodies. Bodies at Pride, bodies of lovers, bodies in church, bodies in hospitals, bodies on the subway, bodies at the bar, bodies of Christ, even the bodies of the dead are given second life with sensate language.

---

14. Muñoz, *Cruising Utopia*, 1.
15. Fred Craddock, *As One without Authority*, rev. ed. (Nashville, TN: Abingdon, 2001), 65.

This homiletic grammar emerges from under the preacher's robes. It is the preacher's physical senses touching and interpreting bodies that form the substrate of the enfleshed word. As Fred Craddock famously puts it: "Preaching is the concerted engagement of one's faculties of body, mind, and spirit."[16] In other words, the preacher's bodily faculties, their uses of sense experience, are crucial for sermon crafting. The olfactive, aural, gustatory, tactical, and visual powers alchemized into language quicken the sermon's pulse and give it life. The preacher relies on embodiment and is called over and over to the experiential. It is the preacher's bodily senses touching the skin of the world that give basic shape to the message. And while this touching of bodies into language does not necessitate an amorous engagement, it makes such engagement possible. Through sensate language the preacher can awaken a rush of love for the world. As the queer poet and preacher James Baldwin put it, "love is the purpose of the human voice."[17] The preacher finds this purpose by translating their own concrete experience into language. This engagement stands as invitation for the hearer to desire the world anew.

Can a sermon survive without the contours of sense and embodiment? Can it survive without color and sound? Without texture and taste? Perhaps. But should it? As Laurel Schneider and Thelathia Nikki Young write, "Queer creativity reveals over and over again the important distinction between existing and living."[18] A sermon that merely survives or exists, that limps into the pulpit without light and texture, fails to live up to the potentials of enfleshed life. Unable to share in the vividness of living, it may do the bare minimum to get through another Sunday. But a sermon that stays in the closet, shut off from the sensuality of the lifeworld, offers vitality to few. Schneider and Young continue, "Living is what happens when one is able to feel, connect, desire, enjoy, and flourish in one's embodied existence—in one's skin and nerves, breath and bones."[19] A sermon that touches flesh, celebrates embodied existence, ignites the senses—that is a sermon that comes out and *lives*. This sharing of life, the felt celebration of enfleshed existence communicated through the word makes the pulse of preacher and hearer quicken. Without such language the sermon becomes airy, see-through, "merely spectral."[20] The flesh of the word goes cold.

Content is not the only part of sermon-crafting that touches the body. Form has sensual and even erotic prospects as well. Buttrick makes this point,

---

16. Fred Craddock, *Preaching*, 25th anniv. ed. (Nashville, TN: Abingdon Press, 2010), 17.

17. James Baldwin, "For A.," in his *Jimmy's Blues and Other Poems* (Boston, MA: Beacon Press, 2014), 87-88, at 88.

18. Laurel Schneider and Thelathia Nikki Young, *Queer Soul and Queer Theology: Ethics and Redemption in Real Life* (New York, NY: Routledge, 2023), 49.

19. Schneider and Young, *Queer Soul*, 49.

20. I quote here Emerson's famous commentary on preaching. Ralph Waldo Emerson, "An Address," in *The Complete Essays and Other Writings of Ralph Waldo Emerson*, ed. Brooks Atkinson (New York: Random House, 1950), 67–86, at 76.

though he appears to pathologize such attempts. "Sometimes the movement of a plot," he writes, "may be determined by a teller's own psyche—how often is a climax/catharsis pattern read into stories out of an author's own sexuality, or a problems-without-solutions plot formed as an enactment of an author's own depressive frustrations? Sermons may well demonstrate the same enactments."[21] By aligning sexuality with depression, Buttrick seems unimpressed with the use of erotics in sermon structure. He fails to envision how a preacher might intentionally engage a sensual form rather than unconsciously enact it. But that betrays a lack of imagination on Buttrick's part. Scholars of literature have long noticed the erotic play of narrative. As the literary theorist Robert Scholes writes, "In the sophisticated forms of fiction, as in the sophisticated practice of sex, much of the art consists of delaying climax within the framework of desire in order to prolong the pleasurable act itself."[22] It seems unusual that sermon writing would exclude itself from the use of this pervasive narrative technique. Indeed, other homiletic theorists explicitly claim and utilize narrative genre.

This is the point of Eugene Lowry's *The Homiletical Plot: The Sermon as Narrative Art Form*.[23] As the subtitle suggests, it expounds the use of narrative for sermon structure. The author's contention is that sermons are more effective when they are told like stories. And as he notes, stories are about the buildup, climax, and release of tension. Lowry's narrative structure engages a series of segments in the sermon (what he calls the "Lowry Loop"). The first is to take a commonly held belief or idea and to upset its equilibrium, the second is to analyze the discrepancy or tension, the third is to provide a clue to its resolution, the fourth is to experience the good news of its resolution, and the fifth is to analyze consequences. The sensual is just beneath the surface. The form's success is measured when it can stoke—yet delay—tension, releasing it only at the appropriate moment.[24] Premature relief kills the mood, as does overworking the climax.[25] But by stoking tension that begs to be resolved, the hearers stay attuned to the sermon because they desire cathartic relief. They feel the tumescent swell, the peaking tension, and the satisfaction of the spent word.

Jane Alison accuses most traditional narrative structures (of which I would count Lowry's) as being especially masculine. "Is this how I experience sex?" she asks. "It is not."[26] The point of her book is that many different narrative structures

---

21. Buttrick, *Homiletic*, 292.

22. Robert Scholes, *Fabulation and Metafiction* (Urbana, IL: University of Illinois Press, 1979), 26.

23. Eugene Lowry, *The Homiletical Plot: The Sermon as Narrative Art Form*, rev. ed. (Louisville, KY: Westminster John Knox Press, 2007).

24. Here climax and release come when the mounting tension is resolved through a gospel solution.

25. Lowry, *The Homiletical Plot*, 37, 52.

26. Jane Alison, *Meander, Spiral, Explode: Design and Pattern in Narrative* (New York: Catapult, 2019), 13.

can provoke and allure; they do not all need to build up to a single peak or climax. I cannot help but agree with her conclusion. At the same time, I also read her other narrative suggestions as undeniably sensual and even erotic. She speaks of "Dispersed patterning, a sense of ripple or oscillation, little ups and downs . . ." and "a firecracker spraying a shower of color, petals spoking from a gerbera's heart, or rays of light flaring from the sun . . ." and "a core of energy [that] radiates outward . . ." and, finally, "[a force] pulling me deeper and deeper into a vortex until I say enough. . . ."[27] She favorably quotes Ben Marcus, who calls the best stories "stun guns" that hold the reader "paralyzed on the outside but very nearly spasming within."[28] There is something undeniably sensual about her narrative suggestions—an erotics that is diffuse, open, and pulsing in life and literature. And is this not a part of the dynamics of queer play? An embrace of bodies and their pleasures in their kaleidoscopic diversity? The same could be introduced into sermon writing if the preacher risks promiscuity with form.

And then there is the question of delivery. The celebrative sermon in the African American preaching tradition is attuned to climactic release.[29] Part of this relates to form. As Frank Thomas puts it, "Celebrative design has a natural order and movement that establishes proper placement and sequencing of sermonic materials so that the sermon culminates in the celebrative moment."[30] But it does not abandon the sermon at the level of conceptual ordering. It instead gives flesh to the ways climactic release is embodied in preaching delivery. Simply because one has arranged the sermon to culminate in a climax does not mean that the climax will be experienced in the preaching moment. Its delivery requires intention. The celebrative moment or climax must be communicated energetically by the preacher. This is accomplished through the content, cadence, and rhythm of speech and movement of body that facilitate cathartic expression. Such celebrative expression becomes contagious and is felt by the congregation. It is only when the experience of climactic celebration is exhausted that the preacher retires. When this delivery style is done well, there is a unique satisfaction for the preacher and hearer. As I once heard a nonsmoking congregant put it after a sermon, "I feel like I need a cigarette."

This experience of satisfaction has worried some homiletic theorists. Does needing a hypothetical cigarette after a sermon enough? Is satisfaction the ultimate goal of the preaching effort? In *Rethinking Celebration: From Rhetoric*

---

27. Alison, *Meander*, 95, 165.
28. Quoted in Alison, *Meander*, 44.
29. The interplay of African American preaching and queer identity deserves its own treatment. While this area is beyond the scope of this essay, Terrence Dean offers an important starting place by analyzing the preaching of James Baldwin. See Terrence Dean, "A Queer Homiletic Futurity: The Radical Sexuality of James Baldwin," *Black Theology* 19.3 (2021): 249–267.
30. Frank Thomas, *They Like to Never Quit Praisin' God: The Role of Celebration in Preaching*, rev. ed. (Cleveland, OH: Pilgrim Press, 2013), 68.

to Praise in African American Preaching, Cleophus LaRue makes a pointed argument that it is not. As he writes, "We are emphasizing emotional rejoicing too much and substantive content in our sermons too little."[31] He suggests that too much preaching terminates not only in satisfaction but also self-satisfaction. It is too at ease in Zion. He worries that the celebrative moment in the sermon is grounded in festivity and self-serving pleasure. It fails to promote changed behavior in the lives of hearers. As he notes, festivity, carnival, and entertainment have no other end but themselves. They are not designed to change lives or the world but are rather attuned to the pleasure of the moment. For LaRue, the point of the sermon is to praise God and have lives changed accordingly. But even if a preacher views the purpose of the craft differently, LaRue's point is well taken. With the multiple intersecting crises of the social world (white supremacy, climate injustice, trans and queer erasure), it is easy to worry that church folks are simply entertaining themselves to death.

At the same time, there are grounds to defend satisfaction, even to celebrate the sermon as nonproductive enjoyment. This would indeed be a queer thing, for same-sex relationships are often dismissed as non(re)productive, selfish, and pleasure-seeking. But in a context where religious and political leaders continue to harm trans and queer people, festivity has the flavor of defiance. The ecstasy carved out on a Sunday morning may offer a *yes* that reverberates in the queer soul. By savoring the pleasures of the moment, such a homiletic affirms that the sensual should not be judged or shamed but relished instead. It blesses the love letter in the sanctuary, the prayer at the gay bar, and the devotion that stirs desire. It amorously returns to the world the senses, of bodies interacting with bodies, to source its content. And it greets those experiences in the sermon, shaping form and delivery into new and better pleasures. This homiletic reveals that preachers and hearers can rely on the sensuality of existence; the taste and touch of language; the arcs, pulses, and spasms of the erotic; and the enjoyment of the body. By getting lost in the senses, the preacher finds the message. Love for God and neighbor swells, peaks. Word is, again, made flesh.

---

31. Cleophus LaRue, *Rethinking Celebration: From Rhetoric to Praise in African American Preaching* (Louisville, KY: Westminster John Knox Press, 2016), ix.

CHAPTER ELEVEN

QUEER CONGREGATIONAL SONG

Past Celebrations, Current Resources, and Hopes for the Future

Stephanie A. Budwey

Introduction

Siobhan Garrigan asks, "As you sing with the faithful in all times and all places, how often have you sang in terms that were not based on heterosexist binaries—father and mother, male and female? And are you invited to sing as 'sopranos and altos/tenors and basses' or just as 'women/men,' regardless of the voice God gave you?"[1] She raises further questions, such as how often the binary language of "brothers and sisters" or "gay and straight" is used, and if intersex and bisexual people are recognized in worship.[2] Garrigan explains that in her experience with LGBT people, "they can count on one hand the number of times in their whole lives, if ever, that their particular way of being in the world was reflected in an ordinary worship service, and many report that they have never encountered any form of recognition of their sexuality or affirmation of their gender behavior in church at all."[3]

Garrigan's article points to the reality that those who are lesbian, gay, bisexual, transgender, queer, questioning, intersex, asexual, two-spirit, and all those who identify outside of "normative" understandings of sex, gender, and sexual orientation (LGBTQIA2S+)[4] are often made to feel invisible, excluded, and erased from worship because they are either outright told they are not

---

1. Siobhan Garrigan, "Queer Worship," *Theology & Sexuality* 15:2 (2009): 211–230 at 215, https://doi.org/10.1558/tse.v15i2.211.

2. Garrigan, "Queer Worship," 215.

3. Garrigan, "Queer Worship," 215.

4. A "normative" understanding of biological sex is that all humans are either clearly "female" or clearly "male," thereby excluding intersex people. A "normative" understanding of gender identity and expression is that all humans are either women or men, thereby excluding nonbinary, genderfluid, and bigender people among others. This includes the assumption that all humans are cisgender, meaning their gender conforms to the "normative" association with their sex assigned at birth (i.e., all females identify as women and all males identify as men), thereby excluding transgender people. A "normative"

welcome and/or there are no prayers, texts, or songs that specifically name them and reflect their lives. As Cameron Partridge writes, "being able to resonate with a worshipful text, to hear one's humanity echoed and not erased in liturgical language that articulates—that indeed 'performs humanity' in a real sense—is an aspect of 'inclusive' that is indeed crucial and powerful."[5]

Congregational song is one place in worship where LGBTQIA2S+ people can—in the words of Partridge—hear their humanity echoed, making them feel included rather than erased from worship. Dan Landes highlights the power of hymns in doing this work: "a single hymn is often more comforting and assuring than ten sermons. It has often been said that the average church goer gets more theology from the hymns that are sung than from the sermons that are preached. . . . Hymns can be used to change people's hearts and minds."[6] It is therefore imperative that congregations sing songs that disrupt "normative" understandings of sex, gender, and sexual orientation by naming and affirming LGBTQIA2S+ people as children of God who are good, holy, beloved, and made in God's image.

In a previously published article, I discussed five categories of queer hymns: (1) hymns that have been reclaimed as queer; (2) hymns written by queer poets and musicians; (3) hymns that speak of inclusion and acceptance; (4) hymns that specifically name LGBTQIA2S+ people; and (5) hymns written for queer life experiences.[7] In this chapter, queer congregational song is defined as songs and hymns "by, for, or about the LGBTQIA2S+ community."[8] The chapter begins with an exploration of past celebrations, looking at specific songs, hymnals, and hymn festivals that were pioneers in queer congregational song. Next is a survey of some of the current resources that are available, including song collections and composers who are contributing to queer congregational song. The chapter concludes by naming some hopes for the future of queer congregational song.

---

understanding of sexual orientation is that all people are only sexually or romantically attracted to those of the opposite sex or gender, thereby excluding lesbian, gay, bisexual, and asexual people, among others.

5. Cameron Partridge, "Very Members Incorporate: Expansive Common Prayer," in *In Spirit and Truth: A Vision of Episcopal Worship*, eds. Stephanie A. Budwey, Kevin Moroney, Sylvia Sweeney, and Samuel Torvend (New York: Church Publishing, Inc., 2020), 167–180 at 174.

6. W. Daniel Landes, ed., *Sing and Be Glad: A Collection of Hymns for Open and Affirming Congregations* (Nashville, TN: Smith Creek Music, 2001/2018), vi.

7. Stephanie A. Budwey, "'Draw a Wider Circle—or, Perhaps, Erase': Queer(ing) Hymnody," *The Hymn: A Journal of Congregational Song* 67:2 (Spring 2016): 21–26, https://www.academia.edu/24559437/_Draw_a_Wider_Circle_or_Perhaps_Erase_Queer_ing_Hymnody.

8. The Hymn Society in the United States and Canada, *Songs for the Holy Other: Hymns Affirming the LGBTQIA2S+ Community* (2019), 2, accessed March 10, 2023, https://thehymnsociety.org/resources/songs-for-the-holy-other/. While this chapter focuses on the music itself, many members of the LGBTQIA2S+ community are also musicians who lead congregational singing. See Patrick E. Johnson, "The Gospel According to the Gays: Queering the Roots of Gospel Music," in *The Oxford Handbook of Music and Queerness*, eds. Fred Everett Maus and Sheila Whiteley (Oxford: Oxford University Press, 2022), 81–92, https://doi.org/10.1093/oxfordhb/9780199793525.013.98; and Alisha Lola Jones, *Flaming?: The Peculiar Theopolitics of Fire and Desire in Black Male Gospel Performance* (New York, NY: Oxford University Press, 2020).

I want to recognize that many of the songs and resources in this chapter come from a predominantly white, North American context. While I have done my best to include examples from diverse communities from around the world, the reality is that in many cultures and countries the members of the LGBTQIA2S+ community continue to live in fear for their lives, with some countries putting them in jail and even to death simply for being who they are. I hope for the day when they may live their lives openly and freely and sing their queer congregational songs.

Past Celebrations

Much of the history of queer congregational song in the last thirty or so years of the twentieth century is related to the Metropolitan Community Church (MCC), founded in 1968 by Troy Perry as a church that welcomes LGBTQIA2S+ Christians.[9] Their "witness to 'God's all-inclusive love'" was often not reflected in the congregational songs that already existed, and this led to the altering of existing texts as well as the composition of new texts.[10] Laurence Bernier, who served as pastor of MCC Boston, wrote the song "When Israel camped in Sinai (Our God is like an eagle)" (1974) which boldly proclaims "We shout and sing, With joy we bring / God's all-inclusive love."[11] Drawing from the book of Exodus, the text speaks to the struggles of liberation around "gender parity and gay inclusion."[12] It was common in the MCC "to use evangelical hymn tunes and pair them with liberation texts," and here Bernier's text is paired with the tune WEBB, associated with the familiar evangelical hymn "Stand up, stand up for Jesus."[13] The text is an example of the MCC's commitment "to use inclusive language in worship when referring to God and God's people"[14] as it says in stanza four, "Our God is not a woman; / our God is not a man. / Our God is both and neither; / our God is who I am."[15]

---

9. For more on the history of the MCC, see Lynne Gerber, "We Who Must Die Demand a Miracle: Christmas 1989 at the Metropolitan Community Church of San Francisco," in *Devotions and Desires: Histories of Sexuality and Religion in the Twentieth-Century United States*, eds. Gillian A. Frank, Bethany Moreton, and Heather R. White (Chapel Hill, NC: The University of North Carolina Press, 2018), 253–276, especially 254–258.

10. Metropolitan Community Church, "A Companion to the MCC Statement of Faith" (2016), 49, accessed March 15, 2023, https://mccchurch.org/files/2016/08/Companion-Guide-to-the-2016-MCC-Statement-of-Faith-1.pdf.

11. Jim Mitulski and Donna Hamilton, "A Heart to Praise Our God: Celebrating Lesbian and Gay Poets and Composers: A Hymn Festival," *The Hymn: A Journal of Congregational Song* 62:3 (Autumn 2011): 28–42, https://babel.hathitrust.org/cgi/pt?id=mdp.39015080966453&view=1up&seq=196. The full text of the song is found on page 32. Most of the songs mentioned in this chapter are also available at Hymnary.org: A Comprehensive Index of Hymns and Hymnals, accessed March 15, 2023, hymnary.org.

12. Mitulski and Hamilton, "A Heart to Praise," 31.

13. Mitulski and Hamilton, "A Heart to Praise," 31.

14. Metropolitan Community Church, "A Companion to the MCC Statement of Faith," 49. This commitment was voted on in 1981.

15. For a theology of "both/neither," see Stephanie A. Budwey, *Religion and Intersex: Perspectives from Science, Law, Culture, and Theology* (London and New York: Routledge, 2023), 150–157.

As more songs like "When Israel camped in Sinai (Our God is like an eagle)" were written and existing texts were altered to be inclusive, the MCC compiled the *Trial Hymnal* (1981) under the leadership of Dick Follett and Jim Mitulski.[16] Shortly thereafter, Mitulski and Dwayne Best[17] led the *Metropolitan Community Church Hymnal Project* (1988–1993)[18] to "distribute a broad range of worship resources: both altered texts and original texts, tunes, and musical arrangements."[19] The importance of having a hymnal with these songs of liberation and inclusion can be seen in the need for the creation of a "Rite of Blessing: For the Dedication of New Hymnals" written by Nancy Wilson.[20] These hymnals were vital as they "express[ed] the new theology, ethic, and 'spiritual culture' . . . emerging through the lesbian/gay movement."[21]

For congregations like MCC San Francisco (MCCSF), "a congregation trying to affirm the faith of people often ostracized from Christian community, singing became a way to affirm the legitimacy—and, at times, the salvation—of LGBTQ Christian believers."[22] The style of music varied widely, ranging from traditional hymns such as "Abide with me" to "songs sacred to the gay and lesbian community" such as folk singer Cris Williamson's "Open mine eyes (Song of the soul)" (1975).[23] Additionally, the act of singing as a community "joined their disparate voices together to proclaim their hopes and bolster their faith," particularly during the extraordinarily difficult times at the height of the AIDS pandemic in the United States.[24] One song that was especially meaningful during

---

16. The Universal Fellowship of Metropolitan Community Churches, *Trial Hymnal* (UFMCC Hymnody Committee, Los Angeles, CA, 1981). "When Israel camped in Sinai (Our God is like an eagle)" is #38 and the entire hymnal may be viewed at "UFMCC Trial Hymnal 1981," California Revealed, accessed March 15, 2023, https://californiarevealed.org/islandora/object/cavpp%3A69398.

17. Metropolitan Community Church, "A Companion to the MCC Statement of Faith," 49. This document lists ten hymns that have been important in the life of the MCC (49–52).

18. Metropolitan Community Church, *Metropolitan Community Church Hymnal Project* (San Francisco, CA: Metropolitan Community Church, 1993). I am incredibly grateful to Kittredge Cherry and Dwayne Best for their helpful conversations about this hymnal. Special thanks to Kitt for sharing her personal experiences and for pointing me to many of the resources cited in this section regarding the MCC and its music. Many of the songs in this section can be found at Kittredge Cherry, "What's Your Favorite LGBT Hymn?" Jesus in Love Blog, June 12, 2010, https://jesusinlove.blogspot.com/2010/06/whats-your-favorite-lgbt-hymn.html.

19. Metropolitan Community Church, "A Companion to the MCC Statement of Faith," 49.

20. Nancy Wilson, "Rite of Blessing: For the Dedication of New Hymnals," in *Equal Rites: Lesbian and Gay Worship, Ceremonies, and Celebrations*, eds. Kittredge Cherry and Zalmon Sherwood (Louisville, KY: Westminster John Knox Press, 1995), 67–69. This book also includes hymns, including adapted and new texts by Chris Glaser.

21. Wilson, "Rite of Blessing," 68.

22. Lynne Gerber, Siri Colom, and Ariana Nedelman, "The Pink and Purple Church in the Castro" (2021), 7, accessed March 15, 2023, https://gallery.religioussounds.osu.edu/mccsf-exhibit-main/.

23. Gerber, Colom, Nedelman, "The Pink and Purple Church," 8–10, with a live recording of this song at MCCSF (10).

24. Gerber, Colom, Nedelman, "The Pink and Purple Church," 7.

this time was "We are the Church Alive" (1980), written by MCC ministers Jack Hoggatt-St. John and David Pelletier.[25] Often sung at AIDS healing services at MCCSF, the third stanza cries out "We are the Church Alive, / the body must be healed; / Where strife has bruised and battered us, / God's wholeness is revealed."

Mitulski, who served as pastor at MCCSF from 1986 to 2000, and Donna Hamilton led the hymn festival "A Heart to Praise Our God: Celebrating Lesbian & Gay Poets & Composers" at the 2011 conference of The Hymn Society in the United States and Canada.[26] This festival included "We are the Church Alive" along with other examples of queer congregational song. "Once we were not a people" (1987) was written by J. Thomas Sopko for a gay pride service and "is one of the earliest hymns written specifically for gay people" that includes the words "lesbian" and "gay."[27] Julian Rush's "In the midst of new dimensions (Ours the journey)" (1985), a hymn written to "celebrate diversity," also includes the words "lesbian" and "gay," yet the stanza with these words has been taken out when it has been published in hymnals.[28] Marsha Stevens' "You said You'd come and share all my sorrows (For those tears I died)" (1969) was included in the hymnal *Hymns for the Family of God* (1976),[29] yet after she came out, people literally tore her song out of the hymnal and mailed it to her, and this song that describes her "inner turmoil around struggling with her emerging lesbian identity" was not included in future editions of the hymnal.[30] One song that does include the word "gay" and is found in the Unitarian Universalist Association's (UUA) hymnal *Singing the Living Tradition* (1993) is Holly Near's "We are a gentle, angry people (Singing for our lives)."[31] Near "received" this song "at a rally after the 1978 assassinations of activist Harvey Milk and Mayor George Moscone in San Francisco," and since then it has become

---

25. For the musical score see Mitulski and Hamilton, "A Heart to Praise Our God," 42.

26. For the script, commentary, and music, see Mitulski and Hamilton.

27. Mitulski and Hamilton, "A Heart to Praise Our God," 29, musical score at 36.

28. Mitulski and Hamilton, "A Heart to Praise Our God," 34, and Donna Hamilton, "'Ours the Journey': Complete at Last," *The Hymn: A Journal of Congregational Song* 61:3 (Summer 2010): 41–43 at 41, https://babel.hathitrust.org/cgi/pt?id=mdp.39015080918306&view=1up&seq=187. Hamilton's article includes the complete text.

29. Fred Bock, ed., *Hymns for the Family of God* (Nashville, TN: Paragon Associates, 1976), 436. This was "[t]he most popular hymnal used in gay churches in the 1970s and 1980s" as "evangelical church music has been the style most frequently sung in these houses of worship" (Mitulski and Hamilton, "A Heart to Praise Our God," 32). For a discussion of the relationship between gay men and evangelical music, see Edward R. Gray and Scott Thumma, "The Gospel Hour: Liminality, Identity, and Religion in a Gay Bar," in *Gay Religion*, eds. Scott Thumma and Edward R. Gray (Lanham, MD: AltaMira Press, 2005), 285–301; and Douglas Harrison, "Southern Gospel Sissies: Evangelical Music, Queer Spirituality, and the Plays of Del Shores," *Journal of Men, Masculinities and Spirituality* 3:2 (2009): 123–141.

30. Mitulski and Hamilton, "A Heart to Praise Our God," 32 (includes full text of song).

31. Unitarian Universalist Association, *Singing the Living Tradition* (Boston, MA: Unitarian Universalist Association, 1993), 170. Another version includes the stanza "We are a gay and lesbian people" (Mitulski and Hamilton, "A Heart to Praise Our God," 41).

"a secular anthem for the LGBT civil rights movement," sung both inside and outside of church walls.[32] These are just a few examples from the rich history of queer congregational song, many of which continue to be sung today. There are also many new and exciting resources, and this chapter now turns to look at them.

Current Resources

Dan Damon and Eileen Johnson gave the plenary address "A Cry for Justice in Hymnody" at the 2010 Hymn Society conference, asking the question, "What are we already singing about justice?"[33] In order to answer this question, they surveyed the topical indexes of twenty North American hymnals for different entries related to justice, including justice for LGBT people.[34] The only hymnal that included the topic of LGBT justice was the UUA hymnal, *Singing the Living Tradition*. In its topical index, "Gay and Lesbian Pride Day" includes "We are a gentle, angry people" at #170 and "Marriage and Services of Union" includes Brian Wren's "Love makes a bridge" (1983) at #325.[35] The lack of attention to LGBT justice led Damon and Johnson to write that "hymnal editors have an opportunity to address this justice issue in their forthcoming collections."[36] Since the writing of their article in 2010, I am not aware of any other denominational hymnals that have included this topic in their index. While the Mennonite Church USA and Mennonite Church Canada's hymnal *Voices Together* (2020)[37] does not include this topic in their index, they do offer an online resource that lists songs from their hymnal which are appropriate for Pride Month.[38]

The reality is that while hymnals might include general songs of inclusion, most queer congregational songs are not found in denominational hymnals outside of the MCC and UUA, or if they are included, they are altered, as "In the midst of new dimensions" was. As a result, these songs are often only found in specific collections. One of these is *Sing and Be Glad: A Collection of Hymns for*

---

32. Metropolitan Community Church, "A Companion to the MCC Statement of Faith," 50.

33. Dan Damon and Eileen M. Johnson, "A Cry for Justice in Hymnody: A Plenary Address to The Hymn Society in the United States and Canada," *The Hymn: A Journal of Congregational Song* 61:4 (Autumn 2010): 8–16 at 8, https://babel.hathitrust.org/cgi/pt?id=mdp.39015080918306&view=1up&seq=214.

34. Eileen M. Johnson, "Tally of Topical Index Entries: A Cry for Justice in Hymnody," *The Hymn: A Journal of Congregational Song* 61:4 (Autumn 2010): 17–22, https://babel.hathitrust.org/cgi/pt?id=mdp.39015080918306&view=1up&seq=223.

35. The text can be found at Brian Wren, "Love makes a bridge," Hope Publishing, accessed April 7, 2023, https://www.hopepublishing.com/find-hymns-hw/hw2722.aspx.

36. Damon and Johnson, "A Cry for Justice in Hymnody," 12.

37. MennoMedia, *Voices Together* (Harrisonburg, VA: MennoMedia, 2020).

38. Katie Graber and Anneli Loepp Thiessen, "Pride Month: Resources for Worship," Mennonite Church USA, June 2, 2022, https://www.mennoniteusa.org/menno-snapshots/pride-month-resources-for-worship/. See also Katie J. Graber, "Pink Menno Hymn Sings: Queerness, Inclusivity, and the Mennonite Church," in *At the Crossroads of Music and Social Justice*, eds. Brenda M. Romero, Susan M. Asai, David A. McDonald, Andrew G. Snyder, and Katelyn E. Best (Bloomington, IN: Indiana University Press, 2023), 105–122.

Open and Affirming Congregations, edited by Daniel Landes (2001/2018). In the introduction to the 2018 edition, Landes explains that in 2001 when the collection was first compiled, it was "meant to give comfort and guidance as well as state openly and plainly what many Christians were feeling in their hearts but lacked the words to express."[39] While there has been progress regarding the rights and acceptance of LGBTQIA2S+ people from 2001 to 2018, "there is still a need for congregations to have such a resource" because there are hymnal publishers that are not comfortable printing hymns such as Brian Wren's "Great Love, your loveliness is signed" (1996), "which states boldly in the fifth stanza: 'Because the Word has graced our flesh, we celebrate today the givenness and giftedness of lesbian and gay.'"[40] In addition to Landes' setting of service music, this collection is comprised of thirty-two hymns that speak to a wide range of topics such as Diversity, the Church's Position Challenged, Fear of Change, Coming Out, Justice, Holy Union, and Sexuality. The texts—many set to tunes by Landes—are written by contemporary hymn writers, including Ruth Duck, Fred Pratt Green, Fred Kaan, Edward Moran, Shirley Erena Murray, Thomas Troeger, and Brian Wren, whose texts focus on inclusion and social justice.

Another resource is *Songs for the Holy Other: Hymns Affirming the LGBTQIA2S+ Community* (2019), a free online collection from The Hymn Society in the United States and Canada.[41] These forty-eight "queer hymns"—"hymns by, for, or about the LGBTQIA2S+ community"[42]—represent a wide range of musical styles while covering many topics from AIDS to same-sex/gender marriage to queer youth suicide.[43] The collection is meant to fill a gap as these songs are for the most part not included in denominational hymnals. There are multiple songs that boldly have the word "queer" in their title including Edward Moran's "God of queer, transgressive spaces" (2007/2019),[44] Amanda Udis-Kessler's "Queerly beloved" (2019) and "The Kingdom of God is the queerest of nations" (2019),[45] and Adam Tice's "Quirky, queer, and wonderful" (2015/2018), here set to THE Q TUNE by Sally Ann Morris.[46]

---

39. Landes, *Sing and Be Glad*, v.

40. Landes, *Sing and Be Glad*, v. Wren's hymn is #9 in the collection and can also be found at Brian Wren, "Great Love, your loveliness is signed," Hope Publishing, accessed March 19, 2023, https://www.hopepublishing.com/find-hymns-hw/hw2650.aspx.

41. See footnote eight for the full citation including the link where it can be downloaded. I was a member of the working group that compiled the collection. As of March 2023, the collection has been downloaded over 6,300 times (Steven Blondo, email message to the author, March 15, 2023).

42. The Hymn Society in the United States and Canada, *Songs for the Holy Other*, 2. The table of contents notes the authors and composers who self-identify as part of the LGBTQIA2S+ community.

43. Matthew Puddister, "Queer Hymn Collection Offers 'Much-Needed' Resource for LGBTQ+ Anglicans and Allies," *Anglican Journal*, October 24, 2019, https://anglicanjournal.com/queer-hymn-collection-offers-much-needed-resource-for-lgbtq-anglicans-and-allies/.

44. The Hymn Society in the United States and Canada, *Songs for the Holy Other*, 24–25.

45. Hymn Society, *Songs for the Holy Other*, 51–52 and 73–74. For more of Udis-Kessler's compositions, see Amanda Udis-Kessler, "Queer Sacred Music," accessed April 7, 2023, https://queersacredmusic.com/.

46. Hymn Society, *Songs for the Holy Other*, 53–55.

The title *Songs for the Holy Other* refers to how members of the LGBTQIA2S+ community "have been labeled as 'wholly other,'" and so this collection is a "self-conscious claiming of otherness as holy and beloved of God."[47] Many of the songs therefore speak of affirmation and the "rainbow diversity of God's creation,"[48] such as Carl P. Daw, Jr.'s "All the colors of the rainbow" (2016),[49] Paul Vasile's "God calls you good" (2017),[50] and Mary Louise Bringle's "Sing a new world into being" (2006).[51] There are songs of lament, for example Elaine Romanelli's "Hearts beating hard with freedom (Rest in power)" (2018) which commemorates those killed in the 2016 Pulse nightclub shooting,[52] Jeannette Lindholm's "Love's rage and grief" (2017),[53] and "We are the hidden" by Slats Toole and Megan Coiley (2019).[54] At the time of the writing of this chapter, Q Worship Collective[55] was recording some of the songs in the collection so they are more widely available, and there are plans to compile a second volume of *Songs for the Holy Other*. Additionally, Cedar Klassen, who was the coordinator of *Songs for the Holy Other*, has created a queer hymns database.[56]

Outside of the North American context, the European Forum of LGBT Christian Groups created a *Songbook* for their 2021 conference "Strong Voices."[57] Also used by Rainbow Pilgrims of Faith, "a collective of LGBTIQ+ Christian networks, churches, allies and activists working across five continents,"[58] this resource contains thirteen diverse songs, including "Nog is de uittocht niet volbracht" by Sytze de Vries (2019),[59] "God of life" by Geonyong Lee (2013),[60] and "Eat this bread"

---

47. Hymn Society, *Songs for the Holy Other*, 2.

48. Hymn Society, *Songs for the Holy Other*, 2.

49. Hymn Society, *Songs for the Holy Other*, 9. I am incredibly grateful to Carl for his wisdom and insight in the writing of this chapter. I am also grateful to Brittney Stephan for reading a draft of this chapter and offering helpful feedback.

50. Hymn Society, *Songs for the Holy Other*, 19.

51. Hymn Society, *Songs for the Holy Other*, 67–70.

52. Hymn Society, *Songs for the Holy Other*, 56–61.

53. Hymn Society, *Songs for the Holy Other*, 43. This is also included in Jeannette M. Lindholm, *Love Astounding: Hymns of Jeanette M. Lindholm* (Minneapolis, MN: Augsburg Fortress Press, 2023), a collection of hymns which focus on using nongendered language for the Divine.

54. Hymn Society, *Songs for the Holy Other*, 85–86.

55. Q Worship Collective, accessed March 10, 2023, https://www.qworshipcollective.com/.

56. Cedar Klassen, "Queer Hymns," QueerHymns.org, accessed March 10, 2023, http://queerhymns.org/all.php.

57. European Forum of LGBT Christian Groups, *Songbook* (2021). For more information on this group, see European Forum of LGBT Christian Groups, accessed April 7, 2023, https://www.lgbtchristians.eu/.

58. Rainbow Pilgrims of Faith, accessed April, 7, 2023, https://www.facebook.com/groups/rainbowpilgrimsoffaith. I am incredibly grateful to Axel Schwaigert for sharing this resource with me and to Kitt Cherry for connecting us.

59. European Forum of LGBT Christian Groups, *Songbook*, 9.

60. European Forum of LGBT Christian Groups, *Songbook*, 7.

(1984) from the Taizé community.⁶¹ Kittredge Cherry, who led Taizé services at MCCSF and MCC Los Angeles, speaks to the popularity of Taizé music with the LGBTQIA2S+ community "because it is multilingual and decentralized, embodying the queer values of diversity, internationalism, and equality."⁶²

A wonderful resource from Latin America is Red Crearte, "a network of liturgists and musicians whose main interest is the permanent liturgical and musical renewal of communities of faith in Latin America."⁶³ Coordinated by Gerardo Oberman, their "main goal is to promote composers and songwriters not only to create new contextual related songs but also to use as much as possible inclusive language."⁶⁴ In "Santo, Santa, Sante, ¡Santo/a/e! (Trina diversidad/ Triune diversity)" by Gerardo Oberman and Horacio Vivares (2021), they show their commitment to inclusive language as they "explicitly use three ways to call the Trinity as male [Santo], female [Santa] and in non-binary pronouns [Sante]."⁶⁵ "Diversidad divina (Inclusiva divinidad/Divine diversity)" by Gerardo Oberman and Jorge Vilchez Santisteban (2021) talks "about the diversity in the divine" as well as the Divine's "inclusive embrace."⁶⁶ Pablo Sosa, a strong supporter of Red Crearte whose music was included in their first songbook, wrote "No es lo que parece, pero sí, lo es (Villancico del Dios transformado / Carol of the transformed God)" (1998).⁶⁷ Sosa "was asked to write Christmas songs from the perspective of those on the margins," and this particular song is written "from the perspective of a transgender prostitute."⁶⁸ While the third stanza speaks of inclusion and there being space in the manger for the narrator, it underscores the reality that many transgender people are excluded from church, asking Jesus "please don't let anyone tell me: / 'You're not welcome here.'"

---

61. European Forum of LGBT Christian Groups, *Songbook*, 10.

62. Kittredge Cherry, email message to the author, March 15, 2023.

63. Gerardo Oberman, "Con ritmo liberador/With the rhythm of liberation," *The Hymn: A Journal of Congregational Song* 74:2 (Spring 2023): 31–33 at 33. See also Red Crearte, accessed April 7, 2023, https://redcrearte.org.ar/. I am incredibly grateful to Gerardo Oberman for sharing information about Red Crearte and their songs with me and to Brian Hehn for connecting us.

64. Gerardo Oberman, email message to the author, March 21, 2023.

65. Oberman, e-mail message to the author. The song can be listened to at Red Crearte, "Trina Diversidad," YouTube video, 1:28, May 26, 2021, https://www.youtube.com/watch?v=wYsoG_pl6us.

66. Oberman, email message to the author. The song can be listened to at Red Crearte, "Inclusiva divinidad," YouTube video, 2:17, November, 29, 2021, https://www.youtube.com/watch?v=_41y7xYkOks. The text is also included in Maren C. Tirabassi and Maria Mankin, eds., *Pitching Our Tents: Poetry of Hospitality* (Maren C. Tirabassi and Maria Mankin, 2021).

67. The song can be listened to at ¡Arriba los Corazones!, "Villancico del Dios transformado-L y M: Pablo Sosa," YouTube video, 3:52, December 27, 2021, https://www.youtube.com/watch?v=87vH2T-jktho. It is found in Spanish and English at #69 in Andrew Donaldson, ed. *Hosanna! Ecumenical Songs for Peace and Justice* (Geneva, Switzerland: WCC Publications, 2016). Thank you to Gerardo for suggesting this song and to Andrew for sharing the score with me.

68. Terry MacArthur, "In Memory of Pablo Sosa," World Council of Churches, January 21, 2020, https://www.oikoumene.org/blog/in-memory-of-pablo-sosa.

Returning to the North American context, many of Mark Miller's songs have become anthems for the LGBTQIA2S+ community particularly in their struggle for acceptance in churches that continue to tell them "You're not welcome here."[69] His 2008 musical setting of Gordon Light's 1994 text of inclusion, "Draw the circle wide," is found in The United Methodist Church's hymnal supplement *Worship & Song* (2011).[70] Also included in *Worship & Song* is "Christ has broken down the wall" (2011),[71] a song originally written in 2005 that he "later revised and published after the 2010 death of Tyler Clementi."[72] The second stanza states, "We're accepted as we are," and Miller writes, "when I lead youth or young adult choirs in singing it, talking about Tyler's death and that despite homophobic/transphobic bullying, I wanted them to know and feel that message of acceptance."[73] Miller "believes that everyone is a Child of God and that music is instrumental in healing in the world. He also adheres to Cornel West's belief that 'Justice is what love looks like in public.'"[74] This conviction is found in "No matter what people say (Child of God)" (2014), which boldly proclaims that regardless of what people, the world, and the church say, "You are a child, a child of God!"[75] Additionally, Miller's musical setting of Lindy Thompson's text "Who you are" (2020) is "a powerful statement of giving people the respect of naming themselves."[76]

Naming is incredibly important to the LGBTQIA2S+ community, especially for those who choose a name and pronouns that reflect their identity. It is similarly vital in worship and congregational song—as pointed out by Garrigan and Partridge—that people hear and sing the words "lesbian," "gay," "bisexual," "transgender," "queer," "intersex," "asexual," and "two-spirit." In 2022,

---

69. Joseph Rossell, "We Will Tear Down the Walls," Juicy Ecumenism, April 28, 2017, https://juicyecumenism.com/2017/04/28/lgbtq-activists-vigil-judicial-council/.

70. The United Methodist Church, *Worship & Song* (Nashville, TN: Abingdon Press, 2011), #3154. The song can be listened to at Break into Song at East End United, "Church Choir Sings 'Draw the Circle Wide' (Gordon Light, Mark Miller) Eastminster United Church," YouTube video, 4:38, April 13, 2018, https://www.youtube.com/watch?v=PcIQrWOYug8.

71. The United Methodist Church, *Worship & Song*, #3122. The song (with musical score) can be listened to at Choristers Guild, "CGA1224 Christ Has Broken Down the Wall-Mark A. Miller," YouTube video, 2:39, March 16, 2022, https://www.youtube.com/watch?v=-EBAWB4snXo.

72. Mark Miller, e-mail message to the author, March 20, 2023. I am incredibly grateful to Mark for his suggestions and conversation about his work.

73. Miller, e-mail message to the author. Clementi, who was gay, died by suicide at age eighteen after being the victim of cyber harassment. See Tyler Clementi Foundation, "Tyler Clementi's Story," accessed April 9, 2023, https://tylerclementi.org/tylers-story-3/.

74. Yale University, "Mark Miller," Institute of Sacred Music, accessed April 9, 2023, https://ism.yale.edu/people/mark-miller.

75. The song (with musical score) can be listened to at Choristers Guild, "CGA1425 Child of God-Mark A. Miller," YouTube video, 2:59, June 29, 2020, https://www.youtube.com/watch?v=MYZ79kSC6_I. The score is in Mark A. Miller, *Roll Down Justice! Sacred Songs and Social Justice* (Dallas, TX: Choristers Guild, 2015), 26–28.

76. Miller, email message to the author. The score is in Mark A. Miller, *Revolution of the Heart* (Chicago, IL: GIA Publications, Inc., 2022), 122–123.

I gave a presentation at the Hymn Society Conference titled "Decolonizing Binary Language: Incorporating Intersex People in Congregational Song."[77] In that talk, I discussed my interviews with intersex people from my book *Religion and Intersex: Perspectives from Science, Law, Culture, and Theology*[78] and the need for congregational song that includes inclusive and expansive language for God and for humans. I furthermore raised the need for songs that explicitly name intersex people as made in God's image. Hymn writer Dan Damon attended my presentation and shortly thereafter he wrote to me saying he "left the conference with a more open heart and a desire to write a hymn that would celebrate intersex people."[79] Together with the input of Marissa Adams, an intersex woman, advocate, and educator, Damon wrote two hymns that specifically use the word "intersex," "Intersex people" and "O God, you share your beauty."[80] In reflecting on these hymns—which I believe are the first published hymns to ever include the word "intersex"—Damon says,

> In my writing I try to give voice to those whose voice has been denied or rejected. In 1986 at the Franciscan School of Theology in Berkeley, California, I took some Bible courses from Michael Guinan, OFM. He spoke for three days about Genesis 1, teaching that the rhetorical device "the heavens and the earth" implies that God also made everything in between. He said, "This is as true now as it was the first time it was spoken." As we learn to see the whole spectrum, we begin to celebrate the variety of creation in new ways. I believe the scripture teaches that God made male and female and all that lies between.[81]

Damon continues to write hymns that celebrate the diversity of humans along the spectrum of creation with "We celebrate today with joy," a text which uses the word "transgender" and declares that transgender people are "made and known and loved by God."[82] This chapter concludes by exploring the need for more texts

---

77. The Hymn Society, "Sectional: 'Decolonizing Binary Language: Incorporating Intersex People in Congregational Song," YouTube video, 1:16:41, September 20, 2022, https://www.youtube.com/watch?v=nHeoJDzPvK0.

78. See footnote 15 for the full citation.

79. Daniel Charles Damon, FHS, with Eileen M. Johnson, "'For everyone born': A Hymnwriter Struggles to Address All People," *The Hymn: A Journal of Congregational Song* 74:3 (Summer 2023): 30–34 at 31. I am incredibly grateful to Dan for sharing drafts of this article with me.

80. Dan Damon, *Look at the Light: Hymns and Songs for Worship* (Carol Stream, IL: Hope Publishing Company, 2032), #31 and #44. This collection also includes "A eunuch, trusted by my queen," #1, written from the perspective of the Ethiopian eunuch in Acts 8:26–40. These hymns may also be found at: Daniel Charles Damon, "Intersex people," Hope Publishing, accessed August 14, 2023, https://www.hopepublishing.com/find-hymns-hw/hw9159_31.aspx; Daniel Charles Damon, "O God, you share your beauty," Hope Publishing, accessed August 14, 2023, https://www.hopepublishing.com/find-hymns-hw/hw9159_44.aspx; and Daniel Charles Damon, "A eunuch, trusted by my queen," Hope Publishing, accessed August 14, 2023, https://www.hopepublishing.com/find-hymns-hw/hw9159_01.aspx.

81. Damon, *Look at the Light*, 102–103.

82. Damon, *Look at the Light*, #54. The hymn may also be found at Daniel Charles Damon, "We celebrate today with joy," Hope Publishing, accessed August 14, 2023, https://www.hopepublishing.com/find-hymns-hw/hw9159_54.aspx.

that move away from a binary understanding of and language for humans and move toward this spectrum.

Conclusion: Hopes for the Future

The MCC and hymn writers such as Ruth Duck were pioneers in changing existing texts and writing new ones that employed inclusive language, radically expanding the heteropatriarchal language of the time. While the addition of "sisters" to "brothers" and "gay" to "straight" has helped to include those who identify as women and gay, this binary language—which is meant to be inclusive—still excludes a large group of people who do not fit into these restrictive binaries. Partridge points out that this language "can feel like the farthest thing from inclusive" as it "can underrecognize or even define people out of existence."[83] It is not only language about humans that can be exclusive; Jann Aldredge-Clanton[84] and Mark Cartledge[85] have conducted studies that show the harmful effects of only using masculine language of God, supporting my assertion that "a limited vision of God leads to a limited image of humanity."[86] Christians are taught that they are made in God's image, and if that image is of an endosex,[87] cisgender, heterosexual (and usually white) man, all those who do not fit into these categories are excluded and made to feel that they are not made in God's image. As Patricia Beattie Jung writes, "people can only really understand who they are in light of who God is."[88] It is vital for future queer congregational song to not only use inclusive language (language for/about humans) but also expansive language (language for/about God) in order to include *all* members of the LGBTQIA2S+ community as children of God who are good, holy, beloved, and made in God's image.[89]

---

83. Partridge, "Very Members Incorporate," 172.

84. Jann Aldredge-Clanton, *In Whose Image? God and Gender*, revised and expanded (New York: Crossroad, 2001). Aldredge-Clanton is also a hymnwriter. Her most recent collection includes feminine language and they/them pronouns for the Divine. See Jann Aldredge-Clanton, with McKenzie Brown and Larry E. Schultz, *Inclusive Songs from the Heart of the Gospel* (Fort Worth, TX: Eakin Press, 2022).

85. Mark J. Cartledge, "God, Gender and Social Roles: A Study in Relation to Empirical-Theological Models of the Trinity," *Journal of Empirical Theology* 22:2 (2009): 117–141.

86. Budwey, *Religion and Intersex*, 139.

87. Someone who is endosex "has sexual or reproductive anatomy such that their body does fit the typical definitions of 'female' or 'male,'" while someone who is intersex does not fit these typical definitions" (Budwey, *Religion and Intersex*, 4).

88. Patricia Beattie Jung, "Christianity and Human Sexual Polymorphism: Are They Compatible?" in *Ethics and Intersex*, ed. Sharon E. Sytsma (Dordrecht: Springer, 2006): 293–309 at 302.

89. This definition of inclusive and expansive language draws from Task Force on Liturgical and Prayer Book Revision, "Guidelines for Expansive and Inclusive Language," Reports to the 80th General Convention (2022), 20–24, https://extranet.generalconvention.org/staff/files/download/29991.

While I have written about this topic elsewhere,[90] it is important here to highlight those who are taking up this crucial work of acknowledging the need to move beyond the binary and toward the spectrum in the language of congregational song. Adam Tice and Sarah Johnson talk about the formative nature of language—for relationships with ourself, each other, and God—and the corresponding need for inclusive and expansive language in relation to their work in editing the hymnal *Voices Together*.[91] Slats Toole offers helpful insights into reasons for the need to move beyond the binary and resources for how to do so, such as adding "siblings" to "sisters and brothers."[92] Paul Vasile is the Executive Director of Music that Makes Community,[93] a group with "many queer leaders" that is "queering practices of congregational singing" with "a commitment to expansive language for God and God's people."[94]

As has been the case since the work was begun by the MCC, this is not only about writing new texts but also finding ways to revise existing texts. One example is the work that Damon and Daw, Jr. have done to update Shirley Erena Murray's text "For everyone born, a place at the table" (1998).[95] Damon describes how:

> Murray's idea and intention was to write a text that imagines all people at the great feast. She thought she had listed everyone, only to realize that some groups had not been named. So she later wrote another verse for gay and straight people. But this binary naming still leaves out portions of the human race. What about bisexual, pansexual, or asexual people? When we try to list the people invited to the great feast, we inevitably leave someone out.[96]

---

90. See Budwey, *Religion and Intersex* (especially chapter 5); Stephanie A. Budwey, "Letting the Entire Body of Christ Speak: Moving Beyond the Female/Male Binary in Liturgy," in «Der Kunst ausgesetzt». Beiträge des 5. Internationalen Kongresses für Kirchenmusik, 21.–25. Oktober 2015 in Bern, eds. Thomas Gartman and Andreas Marti (Bern: Peter Lang Verlag, 2017), 189–199; and Stephanie A. Budwey, "What We Think is New is in Fact Very Old!," in *In Spirit and Truth: A Vision of Episcopal Worship*, eds. Stephanie A. Budwey, Kevin Moroney, Sylvia Sweeney, and Samuel Torvend (New York: Church Publishing, Inc., 2020), 157–168.

91. Sarah Kathleen Johnson and Adam M. L. Tice, "Our Journey with Just and Faithful Language: The Story of a Twenty-First Century Mennonite Hymnal and Worship Book," *The Hymn: A Journal of Congregational Song* 73, no. 2 (Spring 2022): 17–27.

92. Slats Toole, "Gendered Language and Congregational Song," Presentation at The Hymn Society in the United States and Canada Annual Conference, online, July 13, 2021, accessed April 9, 2023, https://www.dropbox.com/sh/90t277gdvb1000z/AACYhN3AtFTGqrQ5jwkK_mKca?dl=0&preview=Hymn+Society+July+2021.pdf.

93. Music that Makes Community, https://www.musicthatmakescommunity.org/.

94. Paul Vasile, e-mail message to the author, March 24, 2023. I am incredibly grateful to Paul for our conversation.

95. The revised version may be found at Shirley Erena Murray, alt., "For everyone born, a place at the table," Hope Publishing, accessed August 14, 2023, https://www.hopepublishing.com/find-hymns-hw/hw9159_16.aspx. The original version may be found at Shirley Erena Murray, "For everyone born, a place at the table," Hope Publishing, accessed August 14, 2023, https://www.hopepublishing.com/find-hymns-hw/hw9008_37.aspx#.

96. Damon and Johnson, "For Everyone Born," 32.

The binary language of woman/man was therefore changed to "all who share life" and gay/straight was changed to "all who have breath," thus moving beyond the binary to include the entire spectrum of humanity. This change highlights the tension between naming those who have previously been unnamed and made invisible in worship (i.e., women and gay people) and using inclusive language that includes everyone.

My hope for the future of queer congregational song is for more texts and tunes written by LGBTQIA2S+ people that voice their particular experiences. I also hope that queer congregational song will speak both to the diversity of humanity and the unfathomable nature of God by naming LGBTQIA2S+ people and using masculine, feminine, and nongendered language for God to show that the Divine encompasses *all* sexes, genders, and sexual orientations. How powerful would this be for LGBTQIA2S+ to know that they are made in God's image? And how powerful would this be for endosex, cisgender, and straight people to know that their LBGTQIA2S+ siblings are beloved and made in God's image and therefore should be treated with dignity, love, and respect so that they might live their lives freely, openly, and without fear? May it be so.

CHAPTER TWELVE

THE QUEER ART OF WORSHIP

Rod Pattenden

Queer folks in the assembly will bring discord, disruption, and disappointment. It is not simply a matter of celebrating diversity through the inclusion of another marginalized group. What occurs is a more fundamental disturbance to the underlying parameters of what is considered normal found in the eschatological aspiration that through liturgical ritual we touch heaven on earth, whereby we in turn find God's order of things. Words and actions of inclusion drive the process of recognizing the lives of lesbian, gay, bisexual, transgender, and intersex people among worshiping communities. Expanding the vocabulary and actions found in worship is to intentionally welcome such diversity, and to extend our sense of what it is to be human, and to test the edges of what is considered normative. This may bring with it a sense of liberation as definitions and assumptions are expanded, but it will also arrive with reactions that generate conflict and threaten the apparent unity of values that holds a community together. We may ask whether worship that gathers a community through word and action, and that builds values and regulates behaviors, can also be a form resilient enough to welcome diversity and negotiate the tensions that difference brings.

There is already a substantial history of liturgical innovation in response to the visibility of queer folks. Liturgical experiments from the 1980s onward offered pastoral responses to key life passages experienced by queer people, such as "coming out," and the acknowledgement of relationships. There was an early recognition that such "liturgy is dangerous" because it unsettled the inherent power relations present in liturgical forms.[1] This liturgical innovation was generated through an effort to be inclusive and was concerned with apologetics, claiming queer persons to also being subject to the love of God. As Cherry and Sherwood explain: "Lesbians and gay men are starved for words of life, for symbolic forms that wholeheartedly affirm their personhood."[2] In addition to giving voice and visibility to the experience of gay and lesbian people, such efforts

---

1. Elizabeth Stuart, ed., *Daring to Speak Love's Name, A Gay and Lesbian Prayer Book* (London: Hamish Hamilton, 1992), xi.

2. Kittredge Cherry and Zalmon Sherwood, eds., *Equal Rites: Lesbian and Gay Worship, Ceremonies, and Celebrations* (Westminster: John Knox Press, 1995), xv.

also reflected on the values of majority communities and their ability to exercise tolerance and welcome. The presence of otherwise marginal individuals within a diverse community is itself a sign of a community's ability to be tolerant and loving. As an out gay minister in a mainline denomination, I often experience such processes of naming my presence as a sign, or badge of honor, for the progressive nature of the wider denomination. My difference makes them normal.

Linn Marie Tonstad names the queer element more sharply: "Queer theology is not about apologetics for the inclusion of sexual and gender minorities in Christianity, but about visions of sociopolitical transformation that alter practices of distinction harming gender and sexual minorities."[3] Such visions bring a sense of crisis and tension into play within the space for worship. Michael Jagessar in a discussion about race and gender states: "The challenge and opportunity before us is the entrenched depth of our inherited deposit of faith, which is largely male-shaped-embodied and heteronormative."[4] This analysis results in Jagessar making "a plea to evoke and imagine participatory and subversive spaces that will contribute to the implosion of the dominant liturgical edifice."[5]

Queer perspectives are not simply add-ons to the normal order of things, they are a calling into disarray the power and effect of the "normal." Queer things disrupt and disturb, they frustrate the desire for completion and perfection. Can worship, then, be ordered in such a manner that allows for more fluid experimentation, provisional states, temporary habitations, and for holding complexity in a creative state that moves toward life-giving love? This is the threat and promise of any perspective on queer worship.

Queerness disturbs the appearance of things. It illuminates awareness, for what had appeared to be normal is now seen to be an illusion. Queer worship makes plain the patriarchal assumptions that lie behind the language, action, dress, gesture, and material culture of liturgical forms. Instead of the smooth surface of normalcy, queer worship creates shock, disjuncture, and disappointment. Part of the process is to disrupt if not split open comfortable phrases and actions that hide prejudice and power. What seems natural is exposed as a cultural construction, an inheritance of forms that oppress and limit human thriving. Linn Marie Tonstad describes this moment of apprehension where viewers become aware of this disjunction of seeing. "Denaturalization renders visible the cultural constructed nature of our basic organising categories, thus limiting their power and efficacy."[6] The gift of queer worship is to allow for moments where people are confronted with the shock of the new, through which they become aware of

---

3. Linn Marie Tonstad, *Queer Theology: Beyond Apologetics* (Eugene, OR: Cascade Books, 2018), 3.

4. Michael Jagessar, "beyond words, gestures and spaces: evoking and imagining liturgical *contradictions*," in eds. Stephen Burns and Bryan Cones, *Liturgy with a Difference: Beyond Inclusion in the Christian Assembly* (London: SCM, 2019), 133.

5. Jagessar, "beyond words," 127.

6. Tonstad, *Queer Theology*, 56.

how they have been enamored and held captive to ideas that limit if not enslave them. These forms no longer look or sound normal, but become strange, archaic or simply redundant.

To illuminate this necessary process of denaturalization, I wish to turn in the following discussion to the resources of visual culture. This choice is not about introducing an approach that is novel, but because worship is fundamentally a process of seeing, apprehending, and mapping the embodied experience of hope and freedom. Visual and spatial awareness provide a playground where theory and embodied practice come together. This is more crucial given that we inhabit a cultural moment where visuality has become the prime organizer of meaning and communication systems. This is a recognition that has had limited attention in the formation of the worship experience, but one that describes processes of seeing, as a form of insight, that include gesture, space and embodiment. Rather than art being about decoration and illustration, it belongs to this more fundamental category of seeing. I have referred elsewhere to the value of vision to understanding how worship works for participants.[7] The notions of "mapping" points to the manner in which vision is able to deal with multilayering, complexity, and even incongruity, as a form or territory of orientation toward meaning, and a reciprocal sense of discernment where viewers choose images vibrant enough to live by.[8] But this is best explored through inviting the current reader to become a sympathetic and insightful viewer.

The work by Braddon Snape, *altar/d Cloud*, 2018, was installed in the Adamstown Uniting Church as part of a series of six art installations over six months, where artists placed work that had the potential to intersect, disturb, and renew the activity of worship.[9] The intent was not to add in art as decoration, but to treat this activity as an installation that challenged and spoke to the whole physical space and the manner in which worshipers moved through and interacted with its elements. The artists addressed a range of concerns, such as human relationships to the environment, attitudes toward indigenous peoples, states of nakedness and vulnerability, passion and ecstasy, as well as hierarchies of gender, and the privilege of speech in the space.[10] Snape's work appeared like a "pop art" cloud in the space, alien and shiny, electric with mirrored reflections, like a startling exclamation mark. The form of the cloud invited viewers to search for connections to biblical accounts of the appearance of clouds, such as the cloud

---

7. Rod Pattenden, "Mapping the Liturgy: Seeing Sacred Spaces," in eds. Stephen Burns and Anita Monro, *Christian Worship in Australia: Inculturating the Liturgical Tradition* (Strathfield, NSW: St Pauls Publications 2009), 211–219.

8. Rod Pattenden, "Worship with Eyes Wide Open: Seeing God in an Age of Visuality," in ed. Stephen Burns, *The Art of Tentmaking: Making Space for Worship* (Norwich, UK: Canterbury Press, 2012), 73–90.

9. *Altar/d Cloud,* Adamstown Uniting Church, 2018.

10. Video interview with Rod Pattenden discussing the works, https://vimeo.com/299148159.

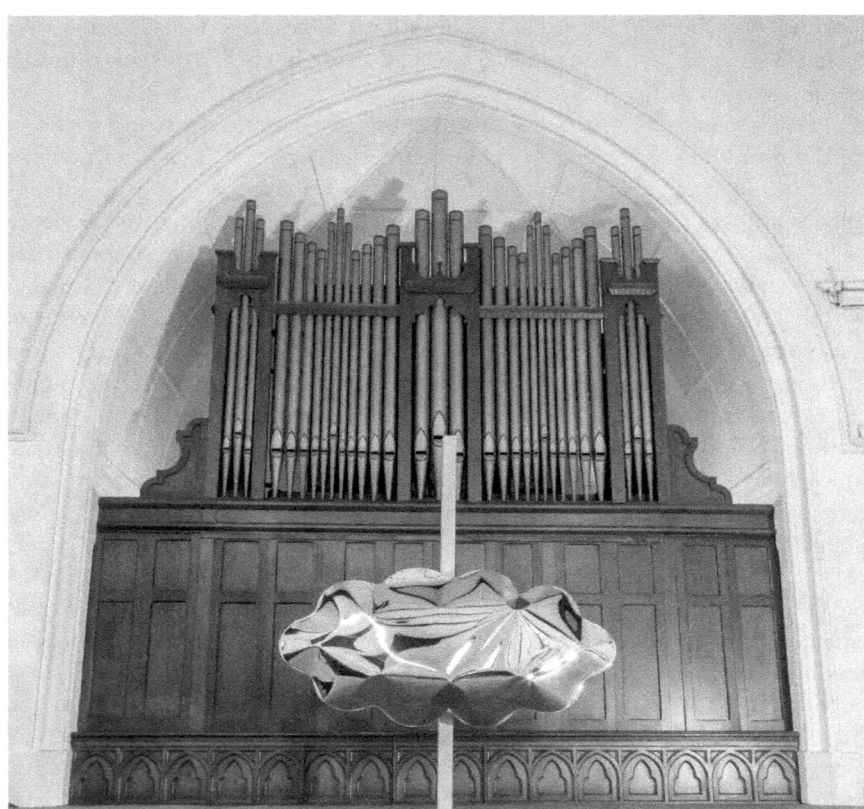

Braddon Snape, *altar/d Cloud*, 2018, welded, mirror polished and inflated stainless steel, painted wood and steel, H 109.5, W 87, D 15 inches. Collection of the artist. Photograph by John Cliff. Used with permission.

on the mountain where Moses receives the Ten Commandments, the cloud that accompanies the forty-year journey in the desert, the cloud at the transfiguration, or the gathered cloud of witnesses. Images always create anxiety until they are accommodated in the mental library of vision where they are given meaning and ordered through the imagination. But this particular form of a cloud contained other qualities that defy this process, and that went on to create a more fluid and unsettling presence in the space.

A close up of the shiny mirrored surface of the cloud form (as illustrated on the front cover of this volume) indicates an increasing slippery surface, mercury thick, that turns the firm architectural features of the interior of the church into a fluid play of light. This moment of seeing is akin to the gift of queer worship where things that provide order and stability are perceived as playfully provisional and able to be questioned and engaged. This sense of vision is not one that conveys destruction or vandalism, but rather visualizes the possibility of being able to bend the straightened lines to allow for better human habitation. While some might anticipate a loss of firm structures, what is welcome for the whole assembly is a sense of play and provisionality. As Rachel Mann affirms, "Queer is more concerned with metaphor, play and possibility, with going astray from that which is received."[11] Rather than destruction and demolition, there is a space for a visual sense of discernment to develop where choices are wider, and outcomes better suited to the diversity of a community. This shiny liquid space visualizes the opportunity and gift found in queer worship where there is permission for human experiment and liturgical play that orders the diverse nature of the body of Christ.

This is a space that is provisional. It is always under refinement and amendment, according to the current challenges a community might be facing. This is the ability to manage conflict and find space for discernment in community. This liquid state suspends sequential time, and then creates time and space to play, experiment, and find solutions that are birthed in this liminal moment. This is not the space of the temple but rather of the tent. What is reflected in this work is not the firm Romanesque geometry of the sacred, but a temporary habitation useful for long journeys. This is the tent of meeting, the mobile temporary space signifying the presence of God in the desert. It is also the space of Sukkot—The Feast of Tabernacles or Booths, where faithful Jews build temporary structures on their verandas and in backyards to remind them of their identity as pilgrims, and that tents were used on that journey. Architectural edifices that construct the appearance of permanence and immobility tend to reward the view of the dominant culture that produces monochrome authorized speech and action. This is played out in liturgical forms that are not only considered correct, but that are used as "correctives," and applied to human lives irrespective of their difference. Worship then engenders violence and causes injury to people who embody signifiers of race, ability, gender and power that are different.

This shiny cloud radiates the freedom of impermanence and justice making. Religious "observance" moves from an attention to boundary codes, correct speech, authorized actions and roles, to the opportunity of taking responsibility for one's freedom in community, and celebrating that in word, action, and image, mapping out a cartography of grace and human embodiment. As Susannah Cornwall affirms, "Queerness in liturgy involves highlighting contingency."[12] Such fluid states offer better hospitality to queer folk, as well as the diverse nature of the body of Christ. They also keep open the need for continuing discernment and adjustment due to ongoing changes, and the shifting human movement of

---

11. Rachel Mann, "'The Performance of Queerness': Trans Priesthood as Gesture towards a Queered Liturgical Assembly," in *Liturgy with a Difference*, 40.

12. Susannah Cornwall, "All Things to All? Requeering Stuart's Eucharistic Erasure of Priestly Sex," in *Liturgy with a Difference*, 51.

people who assemble in one place. The human community is always undergoing change, such as new birth and aging, the shifting of roles, new patters of migration. This needs to be reflected in the way worship is conducted so that it may respond to the fluid nature of human community. The goal of worship is not an eschatological one that reaches for a defined expression of transcendent beauty, but rather the beauty that comes through a fitness for purpose; the who we are is found in how we are.

Marcella Althaus-Reid observes: "Truth, manifested in a desire for harmonious and orderly forms, denied the chaos of sexuality, and the chaotic God which emerged from it."[13] God is mostly linked to markers of impermanence and unchangeability, as if these, in turn, create order and control over existence. This pushes divinity away from the flesh toward disembodied states that in turn discipline the body. Queer perspectives plunge us back into the flesh to value its knowing and its desire, its desire for justice and its passion for love. Queer worship loves human flesh. It allows for a space for experiment and play, a fluid space for exploring what it is to be truly human. In and through such activity the assembly glorifies God by being an icon or image of human and diverse community. What some may see as chaos, from the comfort of their staid but comfortable certainty, is rather more a space for creativity and experiment, workshopping new conclusions to the ethical and moral challenges we face as embodied communities of grace. What emerges as the gift for the community is the recreative possibilities of openness and play, rather than closure and confinement, through the demarkation of lines based on gender, sexual expression, clothing, speech, color or ability.

But there is more to see. Braddon Snape's work does not hide the fact that it is manufactured through steel and wood. It has a material presence. But it also allows us to stretch our imagination to take in its magic and playful permission as an object that has somehow landed in the space. It is both ordinary stuff like the ordinariness of our daily lives, but also allows for the capacity of wonder and surprise. This is when you take in or expire air, and then hold your breath in surprise. And of course, this is how the work itself has been created. With the shiny stainless steel being welded together and then pumped up with a pneumatic compressor. The object in front of us is formed by compressed air, like a rib cage or a balloon. It is made by breath or air, and we anticipate that it floats before us, and that we in turn are kept alive by the gentle rhythm of our own breathing, in and out. There is a common process of creation through air and breath. This work is an invitation to look, and see, to breathe and to wonder. This work gives permission for curiosity to be the basis for seeing and the forming of faith through an embodied sense of self.

David Morgan's discussion of "visual piety" has done much to draw attention to the material nature of religion, and in turn the implications for the practice

---

13. Marcella Althaus-Reid, *The Queer God* (London: Routledge, 2003), 40.

and study of forms of worship. Morgan draws attention to the social function that objects and images play in the formation of personal piety and a sense of self in a religious community. Morgan is particularly interested in accounting for the effective power and influence of images. This is not just the expected symbols of the cross, but images that display feminine purity, masculine strength, mothers and their dependent child, repeated roles based on gender that teach us how to live a pious life in the social sphere. Through repetition and amplification, in both domestic and public life, such images reinforce the appearance of a natural horizon for a stable identity, a firm sense of self that is reflected through consistent images. In contrast to these repeated images which appear to display a horizon of order and naturalness, he points to the role of contemporary art as one that challenges and subverts the status quo, working "to destabilise our expectations about the visual systems of value and representation to which we have become attached."[14] The intention of this process of dismantling, or denaturalization, is not one of destruction or negation but "a willingness to call into question everything that has been learned and to begin again."[15]

Engaging seeing through contemporary art alerts us to our ingrained cultural habits of sight; we see what we expect to see. The capacity of contemporary art to bring insight into seeing is a rich resource for the environment of worship that in turn creates a means of playful discernment and choice making. Jonathan Koestle-Cate's study of the success and failure of projects that have sought to exhibit contemporary art in churches offers an affirmation of the role of art in worship. He sees the value of art "as an ecumenical language of religion, able to cross borders and traditions, but also, more significantly, able to operate both artistically and liturgically."[16] His study points to projects (like the *altar/d* project) that succeed as art installations and at the same time support enabling worship and the movement of meaning in the space. Visuality offers this space for consideration, a time to the side that allows complexity, chaos, and creative potential, with potency to hold in positive tension the disruptive effect of queer perspectives. Worship as a liberative human activity that sustains healthy community needs to be defined in queer ways. As Linn Marie Tonstad states: "If we recognise that the body of Christ (the actually existing church) is made up of persons of all sexes, genders and sexualities, then the body of Christ (symbolic and real) will no longer be masculine; it will be queer. Once we recognise that the body of Christ is queer, queers can then be included into the fluid and diverse body."[17] Queer worship is not a term that demands special pleading for apologetic inclusion but

---

14. David Morgan, *Visual Piety: A History and Theory of Popular Religious Images* (Berkeley: University of California Press, 1998), 150.

15. Morgan, *Visual Piety*, 151.

16. Jonathan Koestle-Cate, *Art and the Church: A Fractious Embrace. Ecclesiastical Encounters with Contemporary Art* (London: Routledge, 2016), 134.

17. Tonstad, *Queer Theology*, 91–92.

Lottie Consalvo, *How Much*, 2017, acrylic on board, H 71 x W 192 inches. Collection of the artist. Photograph John Cliff. Used with permission.

offers a denaturalizing awareness toward a more fluid and dynamic sense of being. The anxiety toward regulating what is normal becomes redundant.

Lottie Consalvo's work *How Much* is another of the works installed as part of the *altar/d* series. It provides a way to further explore the resources of the visual to queer seeing and provides a visual conclusion to this discussion. Consalvo's work is a vast gestural abstract painting, 16 feet long. It was installed on the front wall of the church, under the organ pipes, and in a position that embraces the Eucharistic table. It has sufficient scale to directly take on the architectural volume of the whole space and to address it in challenging ways. This work is part of a series by the artist that has concerned itself with articulating spaces that express an intuitive sense of intimate support, in what might be considered a physical expression of grace. The artist has been exploring a simple set of forms that reminds the viewer of altars, hills, valleys, and containers—places where one is kept safe, and where there is intimate if not spiritual connection. When installing this work, there was a stark and obvious contrast between the gestural and organic lines in the work, and the clearly defined geometric vocabulary of the church's architecture, based on the Romanesque play with perfect forms, such as circles and squares. This vast fluid and gestural work by a female artist subverts this dominant language of perfect forms. This is particularly disruptive given that the language of perfect forms has always been aligned with a more masculine and rational vocabulary that admires order and control. This work speaks to us with other tongues, ones that are fluid and open ended, that allow for the filling up of spaces for diverse ways of human habitation.

The reception of the work presented a challenge to members of the congregation, some of whom may have had no background in contemporary abstract art. Many eyes wanted to quickly nail down what the work represented, what it stood for, wanting to stabilize its meaning. Abstract art requires a stepping back from such rapid labeling, and allowing for the time needed for a conversation that brings forth memories, intuitive knowing and deeper life experience.

I was interested by one conversation with a woman who recounted her youthful participation in athletic events, and in particular, the activity of running over hurdles. For her, the work conveyed this sense of going over and under that such running requires. In her wisdom she noted that life in general also requires such skills of negotiation. We are always needing to weave in and around, under and over, trying to find rest and a sense of arrival, to find grace, to be still. I think she is clearly in the sort of territory of knowing that this work invites us to remember. It would be like closing one's eyes in our own familiar domestic space, and navigating through our fingertips a safe passage through the territory of these nurturing spaces. Such memories are not abstract or conceptual, but are most often stored under our skin, and at the end of our eye lashes!

This work carries the record of mark-making and painterly gestures, which are labored and human in origin. They carry a sense of tentative and investigative unfolding; they are not perfect, confident, or brash in their expression. They reveal the process of their execution and construction; there are splashes and paint marks in the detail. The work does not hide the signs of its manufacture over time. This is as an essential part of its final form. We might expect the central visual focus of the church to have been populated by a confident vision of transcendent signifiers, with heroic figures with beautifully perfect faces, surrounded by a photoshopped scenario of heaven on earth, with an off-the-shelf baroque pink and blue sky. Rather than an elevated site for transcendent perfection that is out of reach of human hands, Consalvo occupies this vast terrain with an incessant nervous and edgy thick line that she is pushing through the mud-like surface. It is humble, without grand claims, or transcendent horizons. And yet there is a sense of grandeur, grace, and possibility. Through its individual and idiosyncratic gestures, it carries a delicate and fragile sense of humanity into the assembly, bringing a sense of gratefulness and graceful enclosure.

Queer worship needs to be seen. The attention to visual forms invites interaction with wider cultural forms that affirm the embodied and imaginative lives of those who worship. As Linn Marie Tonstad comments, "Queer theology is often done in and through engagement with artistic and cultural forms."[18] This affirms the life of the body and the role of the imagination enabling us to fully inhabit a particular cultural moment, both to affirm values and to allow for exploration and expression. An awareness of contemporary art, theater, and dance provides a rich resource for the renewal of the way a community worships, celebrates its life, negotiates change, and manages points of tension. The arts in worship allow for the engagement of fluid and recreative states of play. Worship is not an edifice, but a temporary place to hold the complexity and changing nature of a community. Visual strategies highlight this aspect of the assembly in being a space that is temporary and recreative. It is a space both to welcome and to say goodbye to our favorite icons. Over time, all our most loved icons become tired and ossified and end up looking more like idols. A lively assembly needs to choose images worthy of a full and queer life.

---

18. Tonstad, *Queer Theology*, 126.

CHAPTER THIRTEEN

UNTITLED (HOLY MYSTERIES)

Motifs of Containment, Presence, and Reservation in Liturgical Imagination

Rebekah Pryor

It felt strange, crossing myself like that. But there I was, in the middle of a Catholic church, instinctively moving with the late morning masses who seemed to do it without even a second thought. It felt strange, but I liked it—a kind of wordless, creedal choreography that surprised me and unsettled what I thought were, at least until then, my well-reasoned reservations. I was a visitor and while the Mass followed a familiar liturgical rhythm, it also bore the curiosities of a world I hadn't seen before. I had soaked up a heady blend of Protestant ecumenism over the course of my life (Baptist, Uniting and Anglican flavors, mostly) but wasn't so ecumenical as to have experienced or identified much with Catholicism. (My "low church" formation paired with my feminist convictions had, by now I thought, rendered me a bit too radical!) This sacramental ritual of self-blessing intrigued me though—the way (at least) two distinct traditions seemed to breach containment lines to intersect with me in that moment; the way that instinctive gesture drew me into something new *and* returned me to myself at the same time. It made me think about how porosity—brought about by the gaps or intervals between certain things (theologies, traditions, liturgies, to name a few examples)—gives way to encounters of divine presence in, between and beyond us. It made me think, too, about how tensile containment (of theologies, traditions, liturgies) is.

The dance between containment, presence, and reservation I sensed that day confounded me but also returned me to the materials, including my own body, to which I had access. I already knew how to stretch materials and meanings, how to hold things in tension. Part of that knowledge comes simply from navigating life as a body (and, for some at certain life stages, as a maternal body) in relation to human and nonhuman others. Visual art practice in combination with feminist theology also compels you to test the limits of things. I remember making the photograph *Manet's Milkbar* (2013) (Figure 1) in response to feelings of periodic boredom and frustrated agitation that came with my role as the mother of young children. The flat, near-defeat emotion Manet's barmaid expressed mirrored my experience well after he had painted his celebrated *A Bar at the Folies-Bergère* (1882). For maximum effect, my composition had to mimic and operate within Manet's formula of representation, and then exceed it. It had to make holes in his nineteenth-century impression of modern life—render it porous enough so that there was space for something (and someone, in the case of my own image) different to be seen, encountered, and wondered about.

Figure 1: Rebekah Pryor, *Manet's Milkbar*, 2013, photographic print on archival cotton rag, 96 × 130 cm © Rebekah Pryor. Image courtesy of the artist.

This process of exploration informs the discussion that follows. In this chapter, I focus on three motifs of containment that feature in the history of Christian imagination, devotion, and ritual practice: the *hortus conclusus* (enclosed garden), the *Theotokos* (Mother of God) icon, and the object of the tabernacle or Holy Mysteries. I explore the conceptual implications of these enduring motifs and, with reference to my own art practice, possible material perforations that might allow more space for worshiping bodies to move. Following Catherine Keller's lead toward the "routine carnality" of our "not-Jesus bodies" and their entanglement in and with the divine, I wonder, with presence and reservation, what fresh renderings of old motifs could mean for Christian assembly, its religious imaginary and liturgical practice.[1]

---

1. Catherine Keller, *Intercarnations: Exercises in Theological Possibility* (New York: Fordham University Press, 2017), 26.

Containment

The hortus conclusus

Gardens feature prominently in the Christian story: in the beginning, the paradisical Garden of Eden (Genesis 1); the Garden of Gethsemane, for Jesus, a site of prayer and, in time, his fateful arrest (Mark 14:32–51); the tomb garden where Jesus was buried (John 19:41–42) and, days later, rose from death and met Mary Magdalene (John 20:11–18); and, the heavenly allusions to garden-like landscapes in John of Patmos's Revelation (Revelation 22:1–2), echoed in such theology as that of Nicholas of Cusa who, in the fifteenth century, wrote, "Thou, Lord God, thou helpe of them that seeke thee, I see thee in the Garden of Paradise".[2]

Especially since medieval times, the enclosed garden has endured as a popular trope in art and architecture too. *Madonna del Roseto* (*Madonna of the Rose Garden*) is a fifteenth-century example that depicts the Virgin Mary seated in an enclosed garden, holding the Christ Child on her lap.[3] Highly decorative, the tempera-on-panel painting features flowers, angels and peacocks, as well as a font, indicating Mary as *fons gratiae* (fountain of grace), and the figure of St Catherine of Alexandria (apparently among the "most helpful saints in heaven"[4]), whose martyrdom is signified by a torture wheel and sword. This work follows the tradition of the *hortus conclusus*, a motif that grew in Christian significance from the time of the Western Roman Empire's fourth-century decline and coincided with the Islamic equivalent of the garden as Earthly Paradise. The *hortus conclusus* did not only signify for the Christian devotee a necessary separation of sacred space from the outside world. Bolstered by allusions to containment in poetic biblical texts, it also came to represent Mary's virginity, the enclosure of her womb:

> A garden locked is my sister, my bride,
> a garden locked, a fountain sealed.[5]

For her role as virginal mother of Jesus, Mary was imagined as the passage to Paradise, Cardinal John Henry Newman eventually naming her "the Gate of Heaven, because it was through her that our Lord passed from heaven to earth."[6]

---

2. Nicholas of Cusa, *The Vision of God* (Giles Randall: 1646), 72.

3. Stefano di Giovanni (also known as Stefano da Verona), *Madonna del Roseto*, c. 1420, tempera on panel, 130 × 95 cm, Castelvecchio Museum, Verona, Italy.

4. Leon Clugnet, "Catherine of Alexandria," in *The Catholic Encyclopedia: An international work of reference on the constitution, doctrine, discipline, and history of the Catholic Church*, eds. Charles G. Herbermann, Edward A. Pace, Condé B. Pallen, Thomas J. Shahan, John J. Wynne (New York: Robert Appleton Co., 1907–1912), 445–446, at 445.

5. Song of Songs 4:12 (*NRSV*).

6. John Henry Newman, "May the Month of Promise and of Joy: Janua Coeli," *Meditations and Devotions* (1893) in Fordham University, "Modern History Sourcebook: John Henry Newman on the Blessed Virgin Mary," last updated 18 April 2023, https://sourcebooks.fordham.edu/mod/newman-mary.asp.

From a critical feminist perspective, these kinds of categorizations of Mary's body prove problematic because they incidentally empty her of the subjectivity and agency proper to her embodiment. As I have written elsewhere, the traces of such conceptualizations linger still in contemporary Christian material cultures where they continue to serve and solidify patriarchal visions of sexuate and gendered bodies.[7] Even with the liberative opportunities Christianity offered (and arguably continues to offer) women—beyond salvific opportunities, the option to join ascetic and monastic communities, for example, enabled women in the Early Church new freedom of movement, thought, community and economic potential—as historian Carolyn L. Connor notes, "a highly patriarchal society does not give up on traditions easily, and gendered expectations of women's and men's roles were engrained from classical as well as biblical precedent."[8]

My artwork *Lament* (2016) (Figure 2), along with its precedent *Woman, Why Are You Weeping?* (2016), aim to resist the closures put on women by conveying something of their bodies' uncontainable excesses. In the case of these works, excess is materialized in part by salt, used as one sign of embodied grief and lament. These images reimagine the first moment of Mary Magdalene's encounter with Jesus after his resurrection (John 20:11–18). Inspired by Fra Angelico's fifteenth-century fresco *Noli Me Tangere* (1387–1455) but nevertheless motivated to produce something new, I sought to reference and stretch the typology of the enclosed garden (such features as its spectacle, its function as a place of order and ordering, and its role in facilitating contemplation, revelation and meaning-making).[9] For example, in *Woman, Why Are You Weeping?*, while the composition includes a concise horizon line combined with the verticality of trees as Fra Angelico's work does, my "garden" is without a fence to suggest and reserve some sense of limitlessness and unknowing. Unlike Fra Angelico's fresco, my image depicts only a single figure; the presence of another figure is indicated only by the subject's gaze. The gaze also ensures that the sense of intimacy characteristic of enclosed gardens is not lost. The closer framing of the figure in *Lament* helps to emphasize this proximity and sense of tension.[10] To exaggerate it further, on one occasion, I hung *Lament* over the once-domestic fireplace of the gallery space. The curatorial choice to locate the work in such an ordinary but intimate place helped to translate the enclosed garden motif for contemporary audiences while remaining true to its centrality and capacity to

---

7. See Rebekah Pryor, *Motherly: Reimagining the Maternal Body in Feminist Theology and Contemporary Art* (London: SCM Press, 2022).

8. Carolyn L. Connor, *Women of Byzantium* (New Haven, CT: Yale University Press, 2004), 1.

9. See Rob Aben and Saskia deWit, *The Enclosed Garden: History and Development of the Hortus Conclusus and Its Reintroduction into the Present-Day Urban Landscape* (Rotterdam: 010 Publishers, 1999), 37–55.

10. For more on how tension culminates in the resurrected Jesus's encounter with Mary Magdalene, see my chapter "Lament" in Pryor, *Motherly*.

"absorb the rhythms of the day," both features that made it so important to Cistercian architecture.[11]

Figure 2: Rebekah Pryor, Lament, 2016, photographic print on archival cotton rag, 79 × 110 cm © Rebekah Pryor. Image courtesy of the artist.

Architect and scholar Kate Baker describes the ambiguity of enclosed gardens, highlighting the way they can be "designed to have layers of enclosure, habitable porous zones that mediate between interior and exterior conditions."[12] The colonnade or cloister function in this way, acting as physical thresholds, "preparing us for either the interior or the exterior, to expand or contract into, or just to walk in."[13] Enclosed gardens are designed for shelter and solitude, but also for gathering and intimacy. Above all, they are active spaces of participation.

My surprise experience at the Mass suggested to me that, despite obvious closures, there exist enough pores or perforations in Christian liturgical traditions into and out of which multiple and alternative ways of seeing and meaningfully participating might be revealed. As my own contemporary art

---

11. Kate Baker, *Captured Landscape: The paradox of the enclosed garden* (Abingdon: Routledge, 2012), 106.

12. Baker, *Captured Landscape*, 15.

13. Baker, *Captured Landscape*, 15.

examples have so far indicated, despite the historical conflations and containments of the Virgin Mary (and inarguably all women thereafter), the spatial conceptualizations of motifs like the enclosed garden remain of interest and, especially through architectural and horticultural examples, offer evidence and some hope in the porosity of Christianity's material cultures and religious imaginary. In a way, this is no surprise, given the common ambiguity of both the enclosed garden and the relation with the sensible transcendent and vastly irreducible divine they mean to cultivate. Landscape architects Rob Aben and Saskia de Wit concisely state that, "In the enclosed garden this polarity emerges as its most distinctive quality: the paradox of the infinite in the finite, two extremes heightened by being present simultaneously."[14] The resonances of their summation with incarnational theology suggest that there is still so much for Christians to glean from the play of fields of experience and thought that today operate separately from the religious histories that have helped form them. In terms of this chapter's search for openings in Christian liturgy and worship, Aben and de Wit's speculative observations on the usefulness of "the tool kit of the enclosed garden" for large-scale public space, offer some wisdom and conceptual possibility:

> One quality of the enclosed garden is to couple programmatic freedom with spatial specificity. Brought to bear in the designs of urban landscapes, this would imply a radical about-turn: from merely adding together so many clearly defined programme components, to a field fixed in its spatial composition yet able to admit a galaxy of programmatic configurations.[15]

Architect and designer of the 2011 Serpentine Pavilion Peter Zumthor describes the idea more simply, in terms of feeling and relation:

> The *hortus conclusus* that I dream of is enclosed all around and open to the sky. Every time I imagine a garden in an architectural setting, it turns into a magical place. I think of gardens that I have seen, that I believe I have seen, that I long to see, surrounded by simple walls, columns, arcades or the façades of buildings—sheltered places of great intimacy where I want to stay for a long time.[16]

But it is this line in the architect's statement about the *hortus conclusus* that seems most useful to the present discussion: "something small has found sanctuary within something big."[17]

---

14. Aben and de Wit, *The Enclosed Garden*, 14.

15. Aben and de Wit, *The Enclosed Garden*, 244.

16. Peter Zumthor, "Architect's Statement," *Serpentine Galleries*, May 2011 https://www.serpentinegalleries.org/whats-on/serpentine-gallery-pavilion-2011-peter-zumthor/#downloads.

17. Zumthor, "Architect's Statement."

The Theotokos

I had tried this before; making something small find its belonging inside something big. In fact, I had devoted an entire exhibition to the cause. My 2015 *Cathedral* show, installed inside St. Paul's Cathedral, Melbourne, Australia, was an attempt to hold open enough space to position myself and my experience of divine life inside the ecclesiastical center of my Anglican tradition.[18] I wanted to cultivate an interval, akin to the one philosopher Luce Irigaray describes, wherein I and different others might meet each other, with irreducibility and freedom to collaborate in meaning-making and, in the process, encounter divine presence. According to Irigaray, this kind of interval or third space between (at least) two can be "a place suitable for our dwelling," intrinsically ethical because it is built on conjunctive rather than necessarily complementary relations.[19] She elaborates on what this means ontologically and communally:

> We then enter a space which no longer obeys the system of measurements to which we were accustomed. Expanses, distances, intervals and so on exist, or at least ought to exist, but they are not measurable in a way external to them, nor, what is more, by universal and constant mensurations. Expanses, distances, intervals where we are placed and which exist between us are created by our being in relation, and they change continually. Hence the challenge that the relationship between us represents. It reopens the space allotted to us by our historical and sociocultural belonging and opens up to another space for which estimations are yet lacking. We must build this space and build it together, at least in part.[20]

This was the kind of open space I was longing for. And so, I set about making art that somehow made new space inside existing space. I did this by resizing architectural dimensions, applying alternate surface treatments, and playing with pattern. *Portable Cathedral* (2015), *Dear Mr Butterfield* (2015), and *Fleur de Lis* (2015) were among the exhibited installations.[21] Each work invited some kind of active engagement: in the case of *Portable Cathedral*, to enter in; in *Dear Mr Butterfield*, to touch; and in *Fleur de Lis*, to see.

Prior to the *Cathedral* exhibition, I had made *Triptych* (2014) and generated a body of choreographic-note-like images called *Performing the Icon* (2015), all of which aimed to locate the moving maternal body in the Marian iconographic tradition.[22] The icons of Mary I was familiar with (the *Eleousa* [the Virgin of

---

18. See www.rebekahpryor.com/cathedral.

19. Luce Irigaray, *Sharing the Fire: Outline of a Dialectics of Sensitivity* (Cham, UK: Palgrave Macmillan, 2019), 13.

20. Irigaray, *Sharing the Fire*, 13–14.

21. View the *Cathedral* exhibition catalogue here: https://www.rebekahpryor.com/writing.

22. For more on these images in relation to the development of Marian icons in art, see my chapter "Performing the Icon" in Pryor, *Motherly*.

Tenderness] is one example) seemed to contain the maternal body so precisely as to limit the making of correlations between the Virgin and less tidy—read "virginal" and "virtuous"—motherly realities. I understood their function and purpose in devotional life (as far as my own Protestant-informed experience and imagination allowed, of course), but wondered about their apparent limits on how we imagine ourselves, our own bodies, in relation to the divine. I was looking for icons that allowed for stretch and spillage.

Iconographic attempts to account for and conceptualize Mary's maternal body have long proven controversial in the Church. Her status as the *Theotokos* (Mother of God), used since the third century, proved contentious enough to spark a gathering of Christian bishops to discuss its implications more robustly. On that occasion, at the ecumenical Council of Ephesus in 431 CE, they determined that the label was fit for purpose because it helped account for the joint human and divine natures of the historical Jesus, whom Mary had birthed. Thus, the doctrine of Mary as the *Theotokos* was upheld and, with it, the theology that made sense of the Incarnation: hypostatic union (in summary, the coming together of distinct human and divine natures in one personhood, by which Christ is understood as being fully human and fully divine). An authorized paradox. A holy mystery. Returning to Mary and her maternal body, while the *Theotokos* summarized a union of human and divine natures, the icon was not meant to render Mary herself as human and divine—in this schema, that status was preserved for Jesus Christ alone. The icon frames this concisely. It is doctrinal rather than allegorical and, as such, requires this limit or containment in order to function.

Theologian Maxine Walker invokes the *via media*—the middle way that helped distinguish Anglicanism in particular from other Christian traditions—to navigate her way to more open iconographic fields. In the same way that my *Fleur de Lis* (Figure 3), for example, tested and determined my own body's iconographic potential by "deepening the repetition" of the religious images I had inherited,[23] Walker explores the lives of Evelyn Underhill and Barbara Brown Taylor, both Anglican women writers, to find the body is itself the "open" icon, concluding that:

> The body as icon opens to the diverse ways grace is found, discovered, and experienced and tells a story whose ending remains open, even, postponed rather than defending a tradition or expounding dogmatic theology.[24]

---

23. This act of "deepening the repetition" is borrowed from Catherine Keller, who contends that, "as the third Christian millennium slouches forward," burdened by "quaint" versions of the same old apocalyptic imaginings, "perhaps there is nothing to do but *deepen the repetition*," with full expectation that by doing so, we might discover "another depth of 'God'" and the intimacy between us. Catherine Keller, *Face of the Deep: A Theology of Becoming* (London: Routledge, 2003), 229–230.

24. Maxine Walker, "Allegory and the Body as Icon: Evelyn Underhill and Barbara Brown Taylor," *Feminist Theology* 30:2 (2002): 179–196, at 179, 195.

Untitled (Holy Mysteries) 185

Figure 3: Rebekah Pryor, *Fleur de Lis*, 2015, digital printed wallpaper © Rebekah Pryor. Image courtesy of the artist.

Figure 4: Rebekah Pryor, *Portable Cathedral* (installation view), 2015, mixed media, 240 × 120 × 300 cm © Rebekah Pryor. Image courtesy of the artist.

Where the space I had made for my own and, I hoped, other different bodies in the form of *Portable Cathedral* (Figure 4) stopped and the sacred space denoted by the existing cathedral started was unclear; the porous walls of my installation had materially blurred the lines of distinction between them. A punctured paradox. A still holy mystery.

The Tabernacle

In keeping with the mystery, Christian imagination, devotion, and ritual in practice should properly bring the comfort of common conviction at the same time as it seeks to unsettle doctrinal certainties. How else are we to be led out into the wide open space of divine possibility and surprise? As I hope is by now apparent, art's capacity to materialize and maintain an interval between (at least) two different bodies, people, positions, and possible viewpoints may help us hold onto the best of our traditions while opening us up to new, more generously spacious ways of encountering the holy mysteries that operate in and between us. Much care is required for the task. We could risk confining holy mystery to one or another representation or become fixed on single revelations of divine life at the exclusion of others—a problem my work *Untitled (Holy Mysteries)* (2020) seeks to interrogate.

Figure 5: Rebekah Pryor, *Untitled (Holy Mysteries)*, 2020, reclaimed timber [*Eucalyptus obliqua*], iPad, cotton rag, brass hinges, glue, box: 29.5 w × 21.5 d × 15 h cm, digital video: 1 min, looped. © Rebekah Pryor. Image courtesy of the artist.

Untitled (Holy Mysteries) (Figure 5) is a mixed media work that combines digital video with a box made of *Eucalyptus obliqua* (Messmate Stringybark)—a widespread Australian species and reportedly the first Eucalypt to be classified. Inside the box, a vision of a wetland appears; its cacophony of birdsong and frog sound resonates and dampens as the box lid is opened and closed. The work soothes, like a music box, but it also unsettles. Here, life (and so mystery) is redacted and reduced, the moving image still signifying the real thing but never fully constituting it. *Untitled (Holy Mysteries)* is a containment of sorts, like a tabernacle designed to contain divine presence and, in sacramental terms, the Eucharistic bread. The space contained by the material object is a place where the divine is thought to dwell, but it is not the only place. By evoking the mysterious pattern of the tabernacle then, *Untitled (Holy Mysteries)* also acts as a provocation—to refuse religious fixations and open ourselves to revelations of divine presence, mystery and encounter beyond what we have come to know and experience already. We needn't necessarily be afraid of loosening our grip on the liturgical rubrics and doctrinal traditions we have loved until now. As I have suggested elsewhere,[25] the event of encounter *is* the holy mystery, since the divine springs up out of the interval we form together and between us, as Irigaray, through her notion of the sensible transcendental, has already identified.[26]

Presence and Reservation

Through her exploration of medieval cloister gardens and the role of trees in religious spiritual formation, historian Sara Ritchey highlights, "the capacity of the Christian religious imagination to kindle a sense of God's presence in the world. Conjuring the presence of God requires the imagination as well as the sensation of the material world."[27] In the material worlds represented by the motifs of the *hortus conclusus*, the *Theotokos* and that box of holy mysteries, the tabernacle, we are invited to venture in *and* out of bounds, past the usual certainties and exceptionalisms (including of Mother and Son) to the sometimes untidy and always "routine carnality" of our own "not-Jesus bodies" and their entanglements in and with the divine.[28] We are invited into divine life and into collaborations that cultivate it, where we can expect to come upon the queerest and most certain thing of all: "the amorous return of a divinity that had never left."[29]

---

25. See my chapter, "Materials in Tension: Assemblage and the Art of Revelation," in *Numinous Fields: Perceiving the Sacred in Nature, Landscape, and Art*, eds. Samer Akkach and John Powell (Abingdon: Routledge, forthcoming 2023).

26. Luce Irigaray, *An Ethics of Sexual Difference* (New York: Cornell University Press, 1993), 129.

27. Sara Ritchey, "Spiritual Arborescene: Trees in the Medieval Christian Imagination," *Spiritus* 8 (2008), 64–82, at 78.

28. Keller, *Intercarnations*, 26.

29. Keller, *Intercarnations*, 26.

By attending to the surprise movements of our bodies in worship and the other unexpected things that happen when we come together in difference and bear witness to each others' experiences of God, we open ourselves up to deeper, more imaginative repetitions of old images, motifs, and symbols. There is no doubt we will continue to face the "double bind" of accountability to and reinvention of our theological and liturgical traditions, as Keller anticipates.[30] Objects of art, devotion, and ritual can help us though. And artists, skilled and "insouciant" enough to handle the materials, can help lead us—if together we hold the old containment lines open long enough for new imaginings to emerge.[31]

---

30. Keller, *Face of the Deep*, 229.

31. Keller, *Face of the Deep*, 229.

PART III
PROPOSALS

there is a world that we are stirring into place
    where hope has gone and found a home
        with welcome table large and sturdy ... enough
            to hold joy and sorrow
            and never let any of us go
our horizons are only limited by our will to dare our way into feeling
    that divine urge to fully be
        face to face with love and justice
what spirit(s) we summon if open our hearts
    minds
    body
    souls

CHAPTER FOURTEEN

"HOLY ABOMINATION, BATMAN!"

Questions about Ordination from a Gay Lay Scholar

W. Scott Haldeman

As a professor of worship at a (liberal, Protestant, queer-friendly) Christian seminary, I teach students how to preside at worship on Sunday mornings (and other times too, of course). This necessitates not only teaching them about such things as Eucharist but also allowing them to try it out and to rehearse this central sacrament. There is always some reluctance on the part of some students, especially those with overly (in my opinion) scrupulous mentors and ordination committees. I'm not sure if the students (and those who may or may not ordain them) are more worried that "consecration" will not happen because these pastors-in-training are not fully authorized . . . or that it will. But the students usually report that they are worried that if they "play" at the Table, they will be reprimanded or even rejected from the ordination process for doing what the ordained alone are supposed to do.

This strikes me as bizarre: if we are training school bus drivers, do we send them out to drive a group of our precious children only after they have earned their license in a process that did not include any actual driving? Of course not! So, why then would we expect seminarians who are not yet ordained to lead a congregation in this central rite that is meant to nourish the body and serve as a portal of divine grace without ever practicing hosting at table? Do we want bad presiders? This is surely one way to guarantee this!

Or, do we want "Eucharistic virgins" to preside for the first time (magically?) only after we have laid hands on them?

Or, as I suspect is really the case, given our confused notions of how ordination really sets apart clergy from laity, are we afraid that ordination is fragile and paltry and must be protected and that the table is the last site about which we can say: "Clergy only!"?

I used to be able to "get away with" having not-yet-ordained students presiding at a table as a course exercise when we were together in one of our chapels on campus. Here, away from prying and overly protective eyes and ears, we could experiment, we could fail, and then improve. I would tell them that we were not "really" doing Eucharist and, instead, that we were practicing the words and gestures and attitudes and skills that efficacious celebration requires. And, it is also true that when doing these exercises, something sometimes would indeed happen, the Spirit would move, a presence felt (tasted?)—and we would all be left astonished. This too is preparation, of a different sort.

Now, however, I teach presiding online. My students are often at their theological field education sites when they chose to take the course. They send me video clips of themselves trying out various exercises and we discuss them. When we came to Eucharist week during this past semester, I had one student who asked their supervisor if they could assist at the communion table. The answer came: "Yes, but you can only do the cup. As pastor, I need to do the bread." Another student at another site was instructed: "You can only do the bread. As pastor, I need to do the cup." Really?! These contrary experiences seem to indicate some fear—of scandalizing the people perhaps. Perhaps of scandalizing God. They also seem to be about some confusion around ordination, sacrament, and consecration: Do these (my people) liberal Protestants really believe that the meal can properly be blessed only by those with "magic hands"? Or that we need to protect these "holy things for holy people"? These curiosities lead me to explore (or, at least, pose) troublesome queer questions about ordination. Given the focus of this collection on queering worship, I ask most pointedly: How do questions of "holiness" figure in the debates about the ordination of LGBTQIA+ folk? Can one serve at table if the body has declared it has no need of you, if one is in fact considered an abomination?

We proceed speculatively and informally. After two caveats, I ask three impertinent questions about wrong turns we may have made related to ordination. Then, I briefly consider three alternative models of queer ecclesial and liturgical leadership.

Two Caveats

Before proceeding to the questions, these are my caveats. First, of course, I understand that openly LGBTQIA+ folks are being ordained. The United Church of Christ, the denomination with which my school is associated, ordained Bill Johnson in 1972—the first openly gay man to be authorized for ministry among US Christians.[1] Even as we celebrate the affirmation of his call and the many who have followed and offered faithful service, here, in a strategic choice

---

1. The Rev. Dr. William R. Johnson was the first openly gay person ordained in the United Church of Christ (UCC) and the first such person ordained in the history of Christianity. His ordination took place on June 25, 1972, at the Community UCC in San Carlos, California, authorized by the Golden Gate Association of the Northern California/Nevada Conference UCC. See https://lgbtqreligiousarchives.org/profiles/william-r-johnson, accessed 12 April 2023.

parallel to the marriage equality movement, LGBTQIA+ folk sought and gained not a queering of ministry but access to a normalizing (some might say stifling) institutional status. Fifty years of visible queer ministry, we celebrate. But the task of reconsidering ordination itself in queer perspective remains.

Second, what is it "to queer"? To answer this question, in a recently published article in the *T&T Clark Handbook on Sacraments and Sacramentality*,[2] I turned to the work of Linn Tonstad. In her *Queer Theology: Beyond Apologetics*, Tonstad highlights three moves common to queer analysis and deconstruction: de-naturalization, anti-normativity, and anti-essentialism.[3] Far too briefly, let's take these in turn.

When someone asserts that a way of being (e.g., Aretha Franklin sings: "You make me feel like a natural woman!") or a structure (e.g., "marriage is between one man and one woman") is "natural," they are making a claim that things are "just the way things are," the way they are supposed to be. In the LGBTQ movement both sides make such claims. On the one hand, "God created Adam and Eve, not Adam and Steve," we hear again and again. Then, queer folk should not exist, right? On the other hand, we sing with Lady Gaga: "I was born this way." We recognize that claims that the way we want things to be are based not in certainty but are arguments, are claims of naturalness, which points to their mutability not solidity. They should change as our knowledge of the created world changes. Some cling to inherited models. Others follow evolving theological and scientific views of the cosmos. Creation appears not be fixed; it is dynamic. Is there a "natural" clerical identity or will we allow our views of religious leadership to change too?

Tonstad discusses the problem of constructing a normative subject against which the non-normative is measured through analysis of Justice Kennedy's majority opinion in *Obergefell v Hodges* (2015), the SCOTUS case that granted to same-sex couples a federal right to obtain a marriage license and be wed. She concludes:

> This normative subject is the one against whom, implicitly, nonnormative subjects of all kinds are measured and fall short (some more than others), even though in reality, it's not the case that some human beings are self-possessing, self-determining, autonomous subjects and others are not. In reality, all human beings experience loss, lack, and fragmentation. . . . [T]he imaginary vision of the truly free subject continues to haunt us as a specter of possibility against which different people fall short in different ways. . . . [E]ven the most "normative" human being can be made such only by a process of abstraction, a snapshot taken at a

---

2. W. Scott Haldeman, "Sacraments and Queer Theory," in eds. James W. Farwell and Martha Moore-Keish, *T&T Clark Handbook of Sacraments and Sacramentality* (London: T&T Clark, 2023), 392–406.

3. Linn Marie Tonstad, *Queer Theology: Beyond Apologetics* (Eugene, OR: Cascade Books, 2018).

specific moment that erases both particularity and the time across which human life takes place. Put differently: the normative subject is a fiction, but it's a destructive fiction. . . .[4]

Such a destabilization of norms helps us to unmask the ways in which we govern each other and parcel out the resources of our society (e.g., economic benefits and opportunity, certainly, but also liberty and civil protections) inequitably in order to re-make them. Naming the normative and non-normative is important both in society and in church if we are to include all equally and treat all justly.

Finally, after undermining claims of a fixed natural order and questioning our norms, many queer theories argue that our identity markers—gender and sexuality, among others—are not the manifestations of an inner core reality but instead "identities without an essence." My maleness, my gayness, my whiteness are constructions, scripts I accept and perform with greater or lesser comfort or sense of coercion. These constructions are not neutral but encourage dynamics of domination and submission, belonging and exclusion. They also are less stable than they first appear as, to use a term from Judith Butler, in each performance there is the possibility of "slippage." I can follow masculine norms and "pass" as straight, but eventually a clue (e.g., a gesture or a certain turn of phrase, perhaps) to my gayness will appear and (perhaps) put me in danger. Of course, slippages from an oppressive script can also be a window to freedom—as we discover a marvelous spectrum of ways to live as gendered selves. Perhaps we could also liberate pastor-types from the scripts they inherit and allow them to imagine and create—or, just stumble into—new ways of being a faith leader.

I hope this is sufficient to bolster the argument that there is much we assume about the "nature," "norms," and "essence" of ordination and the ordained at which we should look again and that these strategies can be useful to us in this work.

Three Impertinent Questions

1. Did we come wrongly to create a class of professional Christians, one which, for at least 1,000 years, was both exclusively male and either celibate or closeted?
2. Why are ordination and marriage the only two life-paths that get significant ritual attention?
3. Why does squeamishness around sexuality figure so significantly in debates about access to ordination?

---

4. Tonstad, *Queer Theology*, 27.

Ordination and the Rest of the Body

I have written elsewhere of the primacy of baptism in shaping the faithful life for all Christians. The essay, "Washed and Ready: Baptism as Call and Gift of Ministry," appeared in an issue of a Presbyterian worship journal on ordination and served as a foundational argument—that ordained ministry is simply one way to live out the baptismal vocation that we all share (albeit in different forms) and not something separate from this.[5] In branches of the churches where the priesthood of all and the dignity of the laity are affirmed, this should be obvious. Yet talk of the Pastor as someone special, as one with authority in spiritual matters, as one with an especially close relationship with the divine, always seems to arise. Certainly, liturgically, elaborate ceremonies of ordination and installation point us in this direction. Which else of our vocations (that all emerge from the font) is celebrated so distinctively? This is a real question with a real answer: the married life. We will return to reflection on the parallels between ordination and marriage below. For now, we note that these two are the paths in which we invest ritually.

Paul Bradshaw investigates the solidification of clergy as a class. He notes:

> These two third-century developments—the sharp distinction between clergy and laity and the idea of the ordained ministry as exercising a priesthood on behalf of the laity—gradually weakened the older view in which the ordained were understood to as those who presided within a priestly people.... Although thereafter some liturgical texts themselves might still carry the more ancient image of the common priesthood in which all Christians participated, both theological discourse and ecclesiastical practice instead came to view ordination rather than baptism as the decisive point of entry to the priestly life.[6]

And he thinks he knows why:

> This change of perspective is often interpreted as being largely the result of social pressures on the church . . . [because] in the ancient world a religion needed a priesthood . . . [but] Christian apologists were still insisting Christianity was not a religion like others. . . . It is perhaps more likely . . . that what caused Christianity to begin to regard its ministers as priests was the increasing importance that came to be attached to authoritative leadership in the church's struggle against heresy and schism.[7]

---

5. See "Washed and Ready: Baptism as Call and Gift of Ministry," *Call to Worship: Liturgy, Music, Preaching, and the Arts* 40:2 (November 2006): 1–8.

6. Paul F. Bradshaw, *Rites of Ordination: Their History and Theology* (Collegeville, MN: A Pueblo Book from The Liturgical Press, 2013), 44.

7. Bradshaw, *Rites*, 45.

The priest as symbol and vehicle of orthodoxy demonstrates the unity and purity of church teaching at the cost of lay agency. Conformity is made paramount and a class of self-perpetuating leaders comes to dominate what was supposed to be a community of equals.

Let us jump to the Reformation for a counterexample. Luther may have desired for us to celebrate all callings with equal dignity, but this principle does not seem to have taken root, at least, not liturgically. He is especially concerned when the clerical order is self-perpetuating, when it claims for itself the spiritual authority to identify new leaders and mark them as "unlike the laity." He emphasizes the font as the one true entry to the faith, into the body, and how we are all, then, equal in authority. He writes:

> It is pure invention that pope, bishops, priests and monks are to be called the "spiritual estate"; princes, lords, artisans, and farmers the "temporal estate." That is indeed a fine bit of lying and hypocrisy.... [T]hat a pope or a bishop anoints, confers tonsures; ordains, consecrates, or prescribes dress unlike that of the laity, this may make hypocrites and graven images, but it never makes a Christian or "spiritual" man. Through baptism all of us are consecrated to the priesthood, as St. Peter says in I Peter 2:9, "Ye are a royal priesthood, a priestly kingdom...."
>
> To make it still clearer. If a little group of pious Christian laymen were taken captive and set down in a wilderness, and had among them no priest consecrated by a bishop, and if there in the wilderness they were to agree in choosing one of themselves, married or unmarried, and were to charge him with the office of baptizing, saying mass, absolving and preaching, such a man would be as truly a priest as though all bishops and popes had consecrated him. That is why in cases of necessity any one can baptize and give absolution, which would be impossible unless we were all priests. This great grace and power of baptism and of the Christian Estate they have well-nigh destroyed and caused us to forget through the canon law. It was in the manner aforesaid that Christians in olden days chose from their number bishops and priests, who were afterwards confirmed by other bishops, without all the show which now obtains. It was thus that Saints Augustine, Ambrose, and Cyprian became bishops.[8]

In other words, what seems settled or "natural" about church orders is actually the result of a wrong turn in the historical trajectory of canon law. What is not, what needs to be. We can look to earlier eras for alternative models. We can also

---

8. Martin Luther, "An Open Letter to The Christian Nobility of the German Nation Concerning the Reform of the Christian Estate," (1520), in *Works of Martin Luther: with introduction and notes*, Volume II, introduction and translation by C. M. Jacobs (Philadelphia: A. J. Holman Company, 1915); accessed on 25 March 2023 at https://www.projectwittenberg.org/pub/resources/text/witten-berg/luther/web/nblty-03.html.

develop better theologies to reshape how the church understands itself, is structured, and operates. The ordained are members of the Body who are called out of the Body to be the Body's caretakers with one special responsibility and one distinctive support. On the one hand, the ordained are to live an interruptible life. They are meant to drop everything and head to the hospital when a member falls ill. On the other, they are supposed to be freed from the pressures of the workaday in order to pray and to study and to reflect and to imagine so that they can discern the needs of the body and provide nourishment and vision. That is all. But we do not actually free them; we do not pay them enough. And, they certainly have the right to a whole life, times when they are not interrupted and time for rest. They also have the right not to be put on pedestals so we can imagine their virtues and study their flaws. We cannot help ourselves, however, it seems. The received patterns remain pervasive. The Pastor is coming, take out the good china. The Pastor is nearby, watch your language. The Pastor is here, she/he/they should pray. Specialness, set apartness, and holiness appear endemic even in those ecclesial bodies with progressive, egalitarian, covenantal, lay-led polities.

The problem comes with the ways in which this set-apartness is woven into fabrics of social respectability. Fifty years ago, we might have spoken of social power. Men-(as it was back then—with important exceptions)-of-the-cloth had social caché. They could enter a room and expect some measure of deference. The pastor was tall and handsome and well-spoken, with a stained-glass voice. He had a wife who kept a neat house, organized potlucks, and either taught (unpaid, of course) Sunday school or accompanied the choir or both. They raised well-behaved children. This was (and in too many places still is) the ideal candidate to whom to offer a call. Yes, women have claimed their place[9] and a number of openly queer folk serve faithfully. But the specter of hetero-cis-gendered-male "Pastor" remains, claiming the normative space, the natural, the essential. It is precisely here that we need a queer troubling. Two observations: one cynical and one hopeful. First, it has only been with the waning of the social power of the pulpit that women and sexual minorities have found access. Second, we may be witnessing a time of renewal and reinvention—a different mode of leadership that is not about individual authority but fosters collective care and empowerment—and that women and queer clergy are leading the way.

Ordination and Marriage

We return to the relationship of ordination and marriage. The Christian ritual system is complex and ever-evolving but has some stable features. We have a rite of welcome, or initiation, that for most of us takes the form of baptizing babies.

---

9. Three examples may suffice: The Presbyterian Church (USA) began ordaining women as elders in 1930 and as Ministers of Word and Sacrament in 1956. In 1956, the Methodist Church in America granted ordination and full clergy rights to women. The Lutheran Church in America (which joined other Lutherans in the ELCA) ordained Elizabeth Platz in 1970.

In the West and certainly among Protestants, we have sliced off confirmation and first communion from the ancient and unified rite in which all three were experienced at once, using them instead as rites to mark a child's growing maturity toward full participation. That we welcome infants and (for the most part) ex-communicate them immediately is an example of some of the problems we have created for ourselves. And, of course, for most young people, confirmation serves as a kind of graduation from Sunday school; as we have little to offer them as youth, they disappear until they have children of their own that they wish to have baptized. The only two rites that commission us in an adult vocation are ordination and marriage. Rites of healing, confession and reconciliation, dying and death, and weekly worship with or without regular celebrations at the table round out the system as whole. But let's keep focus on the two (what I will call) vocational rites.

Both the wedding and an ordination include vow-taking, bestowing blessings, and sending. In the West, until Luther, they were alternatives. In effect, the oldest son would marry, inherit the family business, and raise another first son to carry on the legacy. The second son, without the need for a worldly vocation, would be given to the church, remain unmarried, and serve God in the wider community. "My boy, the priest," generations of mothers have said proudly. We passed by it quickly but now note that, in the quote from Luther above, the one chosen to fulfill "the office of baptizing, saying mass, absolving and preaching" could also be either married or unmarried. He makes possible the living out of these two vocations commencing with both of our two vocational rites for one man. But what about everyone else? Where do the rest of us take vows, receive blessings and support, and get sent to fulfill our committed singleness, our life with a chosen nontraditional family, our call to teach or advocate or organize. Our ritual poverty in the matter of adult Christian vocation helps to elevate ordained ministry as the true Christian vocation and the married life as the one faithful structure of Christian intimacies.

The ghost of the celibate priesthood focuses our attention on the pastor's relational life. In his book on discerning a call to the priesthood in the Episcopal Church, Gregory Milliken discusses the ordination of the first openly gay bishop within that denomination as a watershed, a making of space for his own call to grow. He also notes tellingly: "Gene Robinson was the people's choice to be the new Bishop [of New Hampshire] in 2003. He was openly gay and partnered at the time, a radical possibility for a candidate for the episcopate."[10] In a recent Zoom conversation, Milliken had a different emphasis—that it was important that Robinson was partnered to make him more palatable. So . . . radical, yes! but also recognizable, normal-adjacent. To be a bishop, Robinson had to move from outsider to insider, from the ostracized to the celebrated.

---

10. Gregory Millikan, *Being Called, Being Gay: Discernment for Ministry in the Episcopal* Church (New York: Church Publishing, 2018), 29.

That's a long way to go and he did it, in part, by being (in appearances at least) in a stable, committed relationship.

Ordination and Sexuality

This intertwining of ordination and the sexuality of the one ordained all leads back to ordination and sexuality. The shadow of Leviticus is long. The soon-to-be-ordained should exhibit holiness of life: faithful in marriage, chaste in singleness. Certainly, "the man who lies with another man as with a woman" cannot qualify as one who has been chosen by God to lead God's people (Leviticus 18:22 and 20:13). Such a man is an abomination. So, we hid. We fled our callings. And, we struggled for access, for affirmation, for recognition of our true selves and our vocations.

This is what it is, and the victories have come—seemingly taking forever but also with astonishing speed. The problem comes when we find ourselves conforming to traditional relational forms in order to gain access to the benefits of the institution of marriage and, then, we conform to traditional forms of marriage to gain access to the institution of the clergy.

I attended the diaconal ordination of Barry Stopfel, the first openly gay man to be ordained in The Episcopal Church in 1990. Barry and his partner, Will, lived across the hall from me in seminary housing at Union Theological Seminary. Bishop John Shelby Spong was a mentor and a sponsor to Barry. But it was retired Bishop William Righter who presided on this day. My memory is surely faulty, but I can still see the color of the face of a man who strode down the aisle when the liturgical question of whether there were objections to the proceedings was read out. He was an odd reddish purple color, matching the vile things that came out of his mouth about what Barry supposedly did with his body and how such disgusting practices should disqualify him from the priesthood. He looked as if he would explode. No one breathed for several moments. Then Bishop Righter assured the man that his objection had been heard, but that, given overwhelming affirmation of Barry and his call, we would proceed. The man stomped off. Righter would have to endure a heresy trial. Barry served a brave and perhaps naïve congregation in Maplewood, New Jersey.[11]

I tell the story because questions of ordination are questions of the real lives of real people. Vocations hang in the balance. Dreams come true but also are dashed. Calls are affirmed but also denied. The disgust that man felt was surely real—how does one come to change one's mind and heart? And, where does it lead? If the ordination of LGBTQIA+ candidates simply bolsters the institutions that previously excluded us, we have certainly made little progress. If we join the

---

11. For Will's account of the service and the larger story of the journey he and Barry took towards each other and to Barry's ordination, see Will Leckie and Barry Stopfel, *Courage to Love: A Gay Priest Stands Up for His Beliefs* (New York: Doubleday, 1997), especially pages 190–201.

ranks of clergy to empower all of the baptized, we are surely on a better path. If we dare to be clergy queerly, even better. But what might this look like?

A Trinity of Queer Models of Christian Leadership

I am currently contemplating three models; one from the real world and two from fiction. These are preliminary sketches to prompt conversation and expand elsewhere. Sorry for the tease, but I do enjoy the role of the tantalizer.

"To expiate stigmatic guilt and promulgate universal joy"

The Sisters of Perpetual Indulgence are a unique religious order, which was founded by gay men who don the habit, make vows, minister to at-risk populations, and enjoy sticking it to Roman Catholic authorities.[12] "To expiate stigmatic guilt and promulgate universal joy" is their mission. "Serious parody," as defined by Melissa Wilcox, is their *modus operandi*. She writes:

> Serious parody, as I conceive it, is a form of cultural protest in which a disempowered group parodies an oppressive social institution while simultaneously claiming for itself what it believes to be an equally good or superior enactment of one or more culturally respected aspects of that same institution. In the case of the Sisters, this means enacting parodies of Roman Catholic rituals and figures such as nuns and priests while also claiming in all seriousness to be nuns.[13]

Protest Masses with condoms for hosts is but one example of their activism to call the church to account for its part in perpetuating the HIV/AIDS crisis. Can one be ordained and still create enough distance to engage in serious parody of our own institutions? I'm not sure. But perhaps some measure of parody at our ordinations would help. Certainly, resistance to being parodied indicates exactly the problem we have been exploring—the role of Pastor and its fragile dignity. The queer religious leader is open to the ludic, to the camp of liturgy, and to re-imaginings of our common life so that we can better, all together, expiate guilt and promulgate joy.

"And as your last breath begins / Contently take it in / 'Cause we all get it in the End"

Julian Bond, host of the sex club known as Shortbus, in the film of the same name, sings the refrain that serves as our section header in the final scene as club members

---

12. I have met a couple of Sisters in passing, but only that; I am dependent here on the magisterial work of Melissa M. Wilcox: *Queer Nuns: Religion, Activism, and Serious Parody* (New York: New York University Press, 2018).

13. Wilcox, *Queer Nuns*, 70.

and visitors engage in intensifying intimacies of all kinds.[14] Andy Buechel finds here an image of heaven after the eschaton, the joyous rapture of life fully absorbed with Divine, our longings fulfilled.[15] But I want to contemplate Justin Bond as a queer religious leader. In the film, these writhing bodies have not undergone death and resurrection as Buechel has us imagine, to good theological ends. Instead, they are still very much alive and vulnerable and needy and sweaty and, eventually, satisfied. Bond sits on a stool, head and shoulders above the crowd, singing, just singing. But this presider has set the space, opened the doors. He subtly encourages each person to participate as they feel led, to reflect on their own secret desires and fulfill them. Fears are acknowledged and dissipate. Confessions are made and forgiveness offered. Pleasures of great variety abound. Healing abides. This is a sanctuary of love. May such places be known and multiply.

"uncalled, unrobed, unanointed"

Baby Suggs, holy, may be a surprising character to find at the end of this piece, but she occupies a uniquely apt role in her community. She has not joined the ranks of the clergy; she is "uncalled, unrobed, unanointed." In Toni Morrison's masterful telling, her people come to the Clearing for the empowerment and healing that she, with her great big heart, offers to those held in white supremacist bondage . . . "when the warm weather comes." Unlike Jesus, "she did not tell them they were the blessed of the earth, its inheriting meek or its glorybound pure."[16] She exhorts them instead simply to love their own flesh in the context of violent hatred and injustice. The Clearing is a space of temporary escape that they have claimed together and where they can dance and laugh and cry . . . and rest and touch and sing . . . under their own vine and fig tree. While careful not to claim this character who embodies the distinctive genius of African American spirituality as queer per se, Baby Suggs, holy, can perhaps serve us as a model of one who stands on the margins of institutional religion, avoiding being swallowed up by its expectations and able to lead the people in rites that recognize their full and complex humanity and the existential threats that surround them, while empowering them to survive and thrive in a social order that offers them only exploitation and death. For queer, and especially for trans folk, in our own day, such a style of leadership would not only be welcome, but is also sorely needed.

A Concluding Note

My hope for a queer re-ordering of church orders may be a fleeting dream. Any role with proximity to the Divine surely (properly?) entails some sense of being

---

14. John Cameron Mitchell, *Shortbus: A John Cameron Mitchell Film* (Fortissimo Films and Q Television, 2006).

15. See Andy Buechel, *That We Might Become God: The Queerness of Creedal Christianity* (Eugene, OR: Cascade Books, 2015), 137–146.

16. Toni Morrison, *Beloved: A Novel* (New York: Plume/Penguin Books, 1987), 87–89.

set apart. And, the duties of Pastor will always make for a quite different way of life from those members of the Body who are destined to pursue other vocations. Can we distinguish roles without bestowing a higher status? Probably not. But we can try. We can mine the riches of baptismal equality further; the depths of those waters are limitless.

I celebrate those queer folk whose calls have been recognized and affirmed. I also recognize that formation in ministry entails some measure of conformity professionally and theologically. I am a theological educator, after all. But this conformity must be about more than the repetition of inherited theologies and contributing to institutional maintenance. Current denominational discernment processes seem as much about grinding down any spirit of independence as they are about affirming (or denying) a candidate's sense of call. Beyond harm reduction and concern for liability (to which we need to attend, of course), we also must have leaders with bold imaginations and the courage to propose substantive and creative experimentation. In this moment, we need the "serious parody" of the Sisters to banish guilt and cultivate joy. We need "safe enough" spaces like the club Shortbus where shame dissolves, desires blossom, and healing touch is felt. We need Baby Suggs, holy, and her Clearing, where we can experience the great beating heart at the center of our faith, find sanctuary from the forces of death and captivity, love our own flesh deeply, and imagine a grace that is promised, which we will all inherit. May such so-called abominations lead us.

CHAPTER FIFTEEN

AN INDECENT PROPOSAL

Love Is Not Love

Bryan Cones

Since the legalization of same-gender marriage in the United States and some other countries in the last decade, theological reflection on marriage, and why it should be open to couples regardless of gender, has diminished. With "marriage equality" a legal reality, and many churches following suit by offering "church weddings" to couples regardless of gender, the fight for same-gender marriage appears settled. Left largely unaddressed is the resistance among queer activists and theologians to "marriage equality" who see it as a surrender to heteronormativity in the matter of relationship. Which households have been forgotten? And what might voices suspicious of "marriage" contribute to the current conversation and future practice? This essay will seek to recover the "indecency" of queer households and their various forms, including my own, and how they might appear in an assembly's practice of "marriage."

Few queer people likely lament the legal extension of marriage in the United States to couples regardless of gender. Thanks first to a US Supreme Court decision[1] and now partially codified by an act of the US Congress,[2] same-gender or gender-diverse couples in the United States now have access to the social and economic benefits once restricted to opposite-gender couples: joint tax returns, spousal health coverage, survivor benefits, legal recognition across state lines, government recognition and protection. At times preceding legal recognition, but now more often accompanying it, is the extension of religious rituals related to marriage in many communions.[3] For the most part, and with some exception,

---

1. Obergefell v. Hodges, https://www.supremecourt.gov/opinions/14pdf/14-556_3204.pdf [accessed 2 August 2017].

2. Congress passed the Respect for Marriage Act (RFMA), which provides "statutory authority for same-sex and interracial marriages," in December 2022. RFMA requires the federal and state governments to recognize the validity of same gender and interracial marriages performed in jurisdictions where it is allowed. https://www.congress.gov/bill/117th-congress/house-bill/8404 [accessed 12 December 2022].

3. In the United States, the LGBTQI+-identified Metropolitan Community Church was the first Christian denominational body to affirm religious same-gender marriage. See Heather White, "Gay Rites and Religious Rights: New York's First Same-Sex Marriage Controversy," in *Queer Christianities: Lived Religion in Transgressive Forms*, eds. Kathleen T. Talvacchia, Michael F. Pettinger, and Mark Larrimore (New York: New York University Press, 2015), 79–90. More recently, larger

these rituals are the same, or nearly the same, as those used for opposite gender couples for centuries, though now rendered in more contemporary language with a nod to the presumed equality of the partners.[4]

Taken together, these developments on both the civil and religious front (reflecting the hybrid civil-religious character of marriage in the US context)[5] have extended to once-excluded couples the benefits long enjoyed by the heterosexual majority. They arguably have not, however, "queered" marriage as an institution to any significant way other than to release it from a female-male gender binary, which is the only change to the civil law and religious practice in most places. The parallel religious rituals have also changed little except for a light editing of gendered references in most resources, and, perhaps, a more common exercise of the option to exclude the mention of children from the wedding ceremony, long a feature of resources for the weddings of opposite-gender couples.[6] "Marriage equality" may have been achieved; a more robust queering of

---

denominational bodies in the U.S. have extended their liturgies of marriage to same-gender couples. These include the United Church of Christ (2005), the Evangelical Lutheran Church in America (2009), The Episcopal Church (2015), and the Presbyterian Church U.S.A (2015), among others. See http://www.pewresearch.org/fact-tank/2015/12/21/where-christian-churches-stand-on-gay-marriage/ [accessed 13 December 2022].

4. The Episcopal Church, in which I am a presbyter, began a church-wide movement toward religious marriage equality with the provisional approval of "The Witnessing and Blessing of a Lifelong Covenant" [WBLC] in 2012 specifically for same-gender couples (and for such couples only) as part of its resource *I Will Bless You, and You Will Be a Blessing*. It is to my knowledge the only denominational resource created specifically for same-gender weddings. In 2015 the church's General Convention extended the Book of Common Prayer's "Celebration and Blessing of a Marriage" to couples of any gender, also permitting different-gender couples to use the materials prepared for same-gender couples with the consent of the local bishop. At the 2018 Convention, Resolution 2018-B012 directed that all couples regardless of gender have access to all wedding materials, in effect eliminating the authority of the local bishop to prevent a same-gender marriage. (Local clergy retain the right to decline to officiate at any wedding.) See Resolution 2015-A054, https://www.episcopalarchives.org/cgi-bin/acts/acts_generate_pdf.pl?resolution=2015-A054 [accessed 13 December 2022] and Resolution 2018-B012, https://www.episcopalarchives.org/cgi-bin/acts/acts_generate_pdf.pl?resolution=2018-B012 [accessed 13 December 2022].

5. While weddings sometimes take place in church contexts, the traditions of which impute theological meanings to the marriage created, they also affect civil marriages. Nor is the change in marriage practice limited to recent extensions of civil and religious forms of marriage to same-gender couples; on the contrary, that extension reflects progressive changes in the Western cultural understandings of marriage, as sociologist Stephanie Coontz has documented, for example, in her *Marriage: A History* (New York: Penguin Books, 2005). Kimberly Bracken Long's *From This Day Forward* (Louisville, KY: Westminster John Knox, 2016) extends Coontz and others' reflections on contemporary wedding practice to churches, particularly in light of the extension of legal marriage to same-gender couples.

6. I have tracked the appearance of gender in the Episcopal Church's rites of partnership, noting the shift from the Book of Common Prayer's "Celebration and Blessing of a Marriage," once restricted to opposite-gender couples, and "The Witnessing and Blessing of a Lifelong Covenant," originally created for same-gender couples. See my *This Assembly of Believers: The Gifts of Difference in the Church at Prayer* (London: SCM Press, 2020), especially 167–175.

committed relationships and the rituals to symbolize them has largely been left by the wayside.

This outcome is hardly surprising, given that marriage in its various forms has been the primary means by which a heteronormative family structure has been proposed and perpetuated. Prior to "marriage equality," Siobhan Garrigan highlighted the work of Janet Jakobsen and Ann Pellegrini, who argue that "[h]eteronormativity is embedded in American civic life just as, and perhaps because, it is embedded in American religious life and one of the main ways in which it is continuously embedding in American religious life is through worship," and in this case, through marriage.[7] It is hard to argue that same-gender marriage in either civil or religious form has done much to alter that fundamental "cult of normalcy," which Thomas Reynolds describes as "a set of rituals trained upon demarcating and policing the borders of a 'normal' way of being . . . so as to remediate and thus neutralize their deviances."[8] Whether intended or not, "marriage equality" at least implicitly legitimates one particular sexual and family structure as normative by joining it to one most often celebrated in the dominant heterosexual pattern.

While forthrightly acknowledging that queer marriage practice "submit[s] to (and enact[s]) particular norms of . . . gender, sexuality, race/ethnicity/culture, and class,"[9] W. Scott Haldeman goes on to aver, "My hunch is that queer bodies both enrich and challenge our liturgical thinking and doing—forcing us to contend with the underlying heteronormativity in our rites and revealing new dimensions of the blessings God desires to bestow upon all of us in and through our rites."[10] The current practice of marriage extended to couples regardless of gender both affirms Haldeman's conclusion and suggests further directions in need of exploration. With Haldeman, I want to affirm that same-gender couples can still "queer" the received script of marriage, at least for now. At the same time, with Marcella Althaus-Reid, I wonder if the struggle for the religious and civil right to marry has rendered queer relationships "decent" to such an extent that households that do not fit the light renovation of the historic marital heritage are once more rendered invisible or required to "pass" as straight-adjacent, my own among them. Althaus-Reid identifies some of the characteristics of a "decent" theology,

---

7. Garrigan, "Queer Worship," *Theology and Sexuality* 15:2 (2009): 211–230 at 217–218.

8. See Thomas Reynolds, *Vulnerable Communion: A Theology of Disability and Hospitality* (Grand Rapids, MI: Brazos Press, 2008), 60. Reynolds, though writing from a broadly systematic theological perspective without significant reference to liturgical practice, notes the power of the "cult of normalcy" to "ritualize normalcy" (74) and, later, to "ritualize consumerism" (95). While he applies it to impairment and disability, it surely applies also to the ritual affirmation of certain human relationships and the exclusion of others.

9. See W. Scott Haldeman, "The Queer Body in the Wedding," in *Liturgy with a Difference: Beyond Inclusion in the Liturgical Assembly*, eds. Stephen Burns and Bryan Cones (London: SCM Press, 2019), 61–78 at 65.

10. Haldeman, "The Queer Body," 66.

including relational exclusivity and the claim of a divine warrant, always intertwined with the dominant patriarchal economic system.[11] If, following Althaus-Reid, I was truthful about the "indecency" of my own relationship with my partner, David—its lack of sexual exclusivity, its refusal to seek ecclesiastical recognition, its rejection of heteronormative forms of address such as "husband,"[12] its openness to other relationships, among other things—would any assembly deem it worthy of recognition as a graced pattern of relationship? Would an assembly permit my partner and I to function as a symbol of life together in their meeting?[13] On the other hand, does our relationship's complicity with the "decent" economic order, explored below, erase any "indecency" it might propose?

The Received Script

The literature produced before and during the "marriage equality" debate tended to focus on the "definition" of marriage—particularly its restriction to "one man and one woman."[14] Lying beneath this feature were more fraught questions about sexuality, sexual expression, and sexual exclusivity, though these dimensions were often veiled in language of "fidelity" and "exclusivity," especially in denominational liturgical resources.[15] In effect, "marriage equality" troubled only the issue of gender; with

---

11. I will not be seeking to apply Althaus-Reid's methodology in this piece comprehensively; at the same time, I am guided by her attention to the intertwining of sexuality, theology, politics, and economics, with sexuality as an underappreciated medium for their negotiation. See, for example, Althaus-Reid's first chapter in *Indecent Theology*, "Indecent Proposals for Women Who Would Like to Do Theology Without Using Underwear" (Abingdon, UK: Routledge, 2000), 11–46.

12. See Bryan Cones, "With All Due Respect: He Ain't My Husband," in *Feminist Theologies: Interstices and Fractures*, eds. Rebekah Pryor and Stephen Burns (Lanham, MD: Lexington Books/Fortress Academic, 2023), 99–122.

13. I take it for granted that the primary symbol of liturgical celebration is the assembly itself enacting its *theologia prima*. In the celebration of marriage (however understood), the assembly, through its ministers (in this case, the parties to the relationship), is recognizing a particular pattern of relationship as revelatory of the encounter with the living God. Any marriage is, therefore, not just an act between or among the parties, but includes the assembly as a whole, and so in some way must be negotiated in relationship to the whole. See *This Assembly of Believers*, especially 70–102 and 162–196.

14. Norman Doe gathers various then-current denominational versions of the "definition" of marriage (both in the United States and beyond it) in his "Articulating the Christian Principles of Marriage," *Politics, Religion & Ideology* 17, no. 2–3 (June 2016): 306–310; doi:10.1080121567689.2016.1234745.

15. Denominational resources are generally circumspect in naming sexual exclusivity or sexuality in general as a feature of a marriage, preferring language of "fidelity" or "being faithful," or references to "one flesh" evoking Genesis 2. Two notable exceptions are the Church of England's *Common Worship: Marriage*, which refers to "the delight and tenderness of sexual union" in its preface, with an alternative preface naming "bodily union." See https://www.churchofengland.org/prayer-and-worship/worship-texts-and-resources/common-worship/marriage#na [accessed 13 December 2022]. In its 2006 revision of its marriage liturgy, which was modified to be available to couples regardless of gender, the United Church of Christ eliminated any reference to sexual exclusivity, though formulas include the promise to "love *him/her* faithfully." As W. Scott Haldeman of that denomination notes, "In the vows, the word 'covenant' appears in both of the two sentences; the assumption is that

few exceptions churches that now celebrate marriage without regard to the gender of the parties use the same liturgy for any couple. The rest of the marital trousseau remained largely intact and expressed ritually. This marital inheritance, detectable in both the initial consent and the vows, includes a presumption of sexual exclusivity, an implicit exchange of sexual access, and lifelong commitment.[16] The exchange or pledge of property, long a dimension of marriage across cultures though less commonly reflected upon in theological writings, also appears in the exchange of rings, though the objects can vary from culture to culture, and the exchange is not always mutual. These textual liturgical elements are accompanied by various ritual actions, which also vary from culture to culture, which themselves reinforce or intensify the dimensions of marriage noted above, including the clothing of the couple and their attendants, the manner of entrance, the value of the rings or other property exchanged, and the kiss signaling the marriage is complete.

The cumulative effect of texts and ritual elements together is the creative "performance"[17] of a new marital household, in many cases a repetition and citation of the "nuclear family" from which many couples were once excluded because of their gender or sexual orientation. Its religious expression further suggests that there is something divinely ordained in the arrangement, especially when the classic "pronouncement" includes the line: "What God has joined together let no one put asunder."[18] In effect these rites could perpetuate what Dale Martin has criticized as an "exclusionary technique," by which "modern churches legitimate one kind of social and intimate bonding and therefore declare illegitimate all others."[19]

While David and I are civilly married—for reasons explained below—we have never sought to symbolize our partnership through these received patterns. While we certainly see our partnership as a source of grace and a form of our

---

the relationship is life-long—however, no mention is made of sexual exclusivity." See United Church of Christ, "Order for Marriage," *Book of Worship* (Cleveland, OH: United Church of Christ, 2006), 323–46, and Haldeman, "The Queer Body," 71.

16. As opposed to received religious definitions, Bracken Long summarizes a contemporary Western understanding of marriage as "an egalitarian commitment between two people who love each other and depend on one another for romance, sexual fulfillment, mutual support, and happiness." See *From This Day Forward*, 89.

17. The use of "performance" (as articulated by Judith Butler) is particularly apropos to a wedding to the extent that it can be thought of as "willed performance[], consisting of conscious acts of performing. . . . Performativity, [Butler] suggests, is not a singular 'act,' but is always a reiteration of a special model of behaviour. Even more: it is a norm or convention of which it is a repetition." See Andrea Bieler and David Plüss, "In This Moment of Utter Vulnerability: Tracing Gender in Presiding," in *Presiding Like a Woman*, eds. Nicola Slee and Stephen Burns (London: SPCK, 2010), 112–122 at 115–116.

18. "The Celebration and Blessing of a Marriage," Book of Common Prayer (New York: Church Publishing, 1979), 428.

19. See Dale Martin, "Familiar Idolatry and the Christian Case Against Marriage," in *Authorizing Marriage? Canon, Tradition, and Critique in the Blessing of Same-Sex Unions*, ed. Mark D. Jordan with Meghan T. Sweeney and David M. Mellot (Princeton, NJ: Princeton University Press, 2006), 17–40 at 39.

common discipleship, the inescapable dimension of "acquisition"[20] embedded in most marriage liturgies is absolutely at odds with our own understanding of our life together. As I have written previously, celebrating a variation of any of these liturgies would not produce what Teresa Berger describes as a "truthful anamnesis"[21] of what the Holy One is doing and revealing in us in our lives together, and we could not serve as ministers embodying such a relational symbol.[22] In fact, to do so would be to embody an outright lie—and perhaps not only for us.[23]

Forsaking All Others

A hallmark of most wedding liturgies in the creation or recognition of "the couple" as the marital unit, around which marriage creates an exclusive boundary, not only in the matter of sex, but also more and more as the fundamental relationship of each member. In the secular world, spouses become "soul mates" or "best friends"; in the religious world they become expressions of the divine intention for human relationships, shaped in part by what Kimberly Bracken Long has called a "marriage canon" of biblical texts that have "formed the way Christians have thought about marriage for the last 2,000 years."[24] Liturgically this dimension

---

20. While not all couples, regardless of the genders of the parties, would accept the language of "acquisition"—or may well be shocked by it—the history of marriage and its related rituals suggest that such language captures at least a significant dimension of the institution. L. William Countryman devotes a significant portion of his *Dirt, Greed, and Sex: Sexual Ethics in the New Testament and Their Implications for Today* to conceptions of "property," including sexual property, in the contexts that shaped both the Hebrew scriptures and the New Testament. See *Dirt, Greed, and Sex*, revised edition (Minneapolis, MN: Fortress Press, 2007), 144–214. Steven Greenberg notes that, in traditional Jewish marriage liturgies, a woman is "acquired" by a man, albeit with strict limits, a practice judged by Jewish feminists as irretrievable from its patriarchal foundations. Greenberg suggests same-sex couples might appropriate it as an expression of mutual exchange that signifies sexual exclusivity rather than an exchange of property. See his "Contemplating a Jewish Ritual of Same-Sex Union: An Inquiry into the Meanings of Marriage," in *Authorizing Marriage?*, 88–89. John Witte has also traced the "contractual" dimensions of marriage beginning with biblical foundations through the Enlightenment. See his *From Sacrament to Contract: Marriage, Religion, and Law in Western Tradition*, second edition (Louisville, KY: Westminster John Knox Press, 2012), especially 35–38, 46–52, 87–91.

21. See, for example, her *Gender Differences in the Making of Liturgical History: Lifting the Veil on Liturgy's Past* (London: Ashgate, 2011), 33.

22. See Cones, "With All Due Respect," 115.

23. Non-monogamous relationship patterns among gay couples have long been studied; see, for example, Jeffrey T. Parsons, et al., "Alternatives to Monogamy among Gay Male Couples in a Community Survey: Implications for Mental Health and Sexual Risk," *Archives of Sexual Behavior* 42:2 (2013): 303–312. doi:10.1007/s10508-011-9885-3. Beyond such research, the topic is common in popular media across platforms.

24. These include Genesis 1:26–31 (creation of male and female, with the command to be fruitful and multiply); Genesis 2:18–24 (creation of "woman" from "the man," with the two becoming one flesh); 1 Corinthians 7:1–9 (Paul's exhortation to marry as a remedy for sexual desire); Ephesians 5:21–31 (household code, with the husband–wife relationship reflecting that of Christ and the church); Matthew 19:1–9 (Jesus' prohibition against divorce); John 2:1–11 (the wedding at Cana).

finds expression in the interplay between various promises to "forsake all others" and God as the author of the union.

Queer reflection on this dimension often celebrates this extension beyond the opposite-gender pair, but at what cost? On its face it reifies the dyad as the relational highpoint in the Christian assembly, especially since it is likely the only pattern of relationship regularly acknowledged in any assembly's practice. Further, in Christian contexts, it seems to seal off the couple from other kinds of relationships by creating a closed relational system that hardly reflects reality, tends toward codependence, and seems at odds with Christian mission, as Susannah Cornwall has pointed out.[25] Theologically, the reification of a dyad or pair seems inconsistent with the primary Christian image of God, which proposes a relational structure of three "persons" expressing the one God.[26] The basic binary begging to be queered is the reification of the pair itself, as if "twoness" is the *sine qua non* of relational patterns, with all others being exceptions at best, aberrations at worst.

It is likely that a neuralgic point is the question of sexuality and its use. Put bluntly by Bernard Cooke for his context, but still detectable in literature across denominations: "In modern times the Catholic Church has seen the substance of this contract to be the mutual exchange of exclusive rights to sexual intercourse as directed to procreation."[27] Marriage has provided socially acceptable access to sexual expression with one (opposite-gender) partner, with at least some openness to procreation, while the other household forms, monastic or religious life among them, generally forbid it completely, or at least provide no socially acceptable outlet for doing so. What rituals of committed relationship generally shared is a concern with regulating sexuality and thus propose a ritual structure to symbolize and enforce it. In effect, marriage liturgies propose a kind of "normal"—either you have sex with one other person, or you don't have it at all—and allow for no apparent variation, despite the fact that marriage long ago ceased to be the threshold of sexual activity and has never managed to contain sexual expression within its bounds anyway.

Bracken Long attempts a retrieval of these passages for contemporary Christian marriage while also suggesting an expansion of the "canon" to include such texts as Romans 12:9–18 (Paul's exhortation to the church to love one another); Colossians 3:12–14 (a hymn text exhorting hearers to "clothe yourselves with compassion"); and Song of Songs 7:6-13 and 8:6–7 (the more erotically robust sections of the ancient love poem). See Bracken Long, *From This Day Forward*, 90.

25. Cornwall's exploration of theological objections to consensual polyamory undermines any particular claim of the dyad as a fundamentally superior relational structure. See her "The Content of Marriage: Two and Only Two?" in *Un/familiar Theology: Reconceiving Sex, Reproduction and Generativity* (London: Bloomsbury Academic, 2017), 49–60.

26. Martín Hugo Córdova Quero and Joseph Nicholas Geok Lin Goh trace ancient accounts of the relations within the Trinity on the way to seeking a trinitarian grounding for polyamory. See their "More than a Divine Ménage à Trois: Friendship, Polyamory, and the Doctrine of the Trinity," in *Contemporary Theological Approaches to Sexuality*, eds. Lisa Isherwood and Dirk von der Horst (Abingdon, UK: Routledge, 2018), 289–312, esp. 292–302.

27. Cooke, "Historical Reflections," 42.

The repeated insistence on "exclusivity," "forsaking all others," suggests that Mark Jordan is right in arguing that, "To bless open relationships that will not agree to abide by the fiction [of monogamy] would undo the fiction for everyone. Queer relationships, so far as they are presumed to be 'open,' do destroy Christian marriage in this sense, that they destroy cherished fictions about what it has accomplished."[28] Jordan's insight has real-world manifestations: My own Episcopal Diocese of Chicago's early statements on blessing same-gender couples noted that it was "outside the moral vision of the Church to bless 'open' relationships or relationships with more than two partners."[29] This reflected the national church's anxiety expressed in its first openings to exploring the recognition of same-gender relationships. While affirming the possibility of "fidelity, monogamy, mutual affection and respect, careful, honest communication, and the holy love," it simultaneously denounced "promiscuity, exploitation, and abusiveness in the relationships of any of our members."[30]

Those in openly polyamorous or multipartner relationships have taken initial steps to disrupt what Althaus-Reid might call a "fetishization" or "thingification" of the pair,[31] using their own sexual stories as a place to do theology. These have begun to yield appeals to the Trinity as a model for a relationship beyond "the couple," with the divine perichoresis as a fruitful metaphor for relating beyond the dyad.[32] They are not alone in appealing to the Trinity: Duncan Reid draws on the Orthodox theology of John Zizioulas to suggest that such a relationship reflects "communion that allows the other to remain itself, but within relationship."[33] Reid in particular connects the communion of "otherness" in the Trinity as described by Zizioulas to human friendship rooted in the body as "a vehicle both of otherness and communion. Body here means a particular body, so that the other presents her-/[them-]/himself as a particular, human, personal other, not as a generalized abstraction."[34] For Reid, this suggests mature friendships that are truly public "open relationships" which "prepare[] the ground for a friendly world."[35]

---

28. Mark Jordan, *Blessing Same-Sex Unions: The Perils of Queer Romance and the Confusions of Christian Marriage* (Chicago: University of Chicago Press, 2005), 166.

29. Diocese of Chicago, "Guidelines for the Solemnization of Holy Union," 6, https://www.episcopalchicago.org/files/8613/2017/2408/Holy_Union_Guidelines_and_Liturgy.pdf [accessed 2 August 2017].

30. Task Force on the Study of Marriage, "Report to the 78th General Convention," 29–30, https://extranet.generalconvention.org/staff/files/download/12485 [accessed 14 August 2017]. This language remains current in the most recent edition of *I Will Bless You*, for example, in materials developed for the preparation of gender and sexual minority couples for their marriage or covenant. See *I Will Bless You*, 71.

31. See Althaus-Reid, *Indecent Theology*, 92.

32. See Quero and Goh, "More than a Divine Ménage," 289–312.

33. Duncan Reid, "Friends and Lovers, Friends and Others," in *Kaleidoscope of Pieces: Anglican Studies on Sexuality*, ed. Alan Cadwaller (Adelaide, SA: ATF Theology, 2016), 59–74 at 69.

34. Reid, "Friends and Lovers," 71.

35. Reid, "Friends and Lovers," 65; Reid quotes Jürgen Moltmann's *The Church in the Power of the Spirit*.

In the case of "the couple," then, a proper queering may at least be two-fold: First, to expand the variety of households recognized in assemblies, with attention to the biblical resonance of the term,[36] and second, to rethink the appearance of sexuality in any of them. After all, even the most sexually active households must still work, eat, organize their resources, and maintain life together. That does not mean excluding sexuality, but it could mean recognizing households whose foundation does not rest on a presumed sexual relationship between or among its members. That will require naming "of God" a range of relational possibilities Garrigan claims "need to be talked about": "LGBT dating and union-making, threesomes, bathhouses, periodic celibacy, open relationships, adoptive families, and self-insemination need to be talked about, just as straight dating and marriage, monogamy, nuclear families, nursing-home romance, and immaculate conceptions(!) are."[37] That does not mean individuals within the households do not practice or perform sexuality in some way; it could mean that their use of sexuality is not part of the household "contract."

Such a move would, of course, be a profound departure from inherited Christian practice, which in general still sees marriage as "the correct way to deal with human sexuality."[38] Yet there are signals that some churches may be rethinking this presumption: The Uniting Church in Australia, when debating the extension of marriage to same-gender couples, countenanced the possibility of couples for whom sexual expression in not a part of their union.[39] Without surrendering the fundamental sacramentality of queer sexual expressions,[40] might churches consider placing in brackets questions regarding sexuality and its use, as they now do with the expectation of children? Or, as Mary Hunt more trenchantly puts it: "How a friendship is sexual is the concern of those who are

---

36. Paul especially speaks of the assembly as an *oikos*, with himself as chief steward among the slaves. That detail also suggests caution in applying the model too directly. That said, the concept of household can claim at least as much biblical grounding as references to the duties of husbands and wives in the household codes, for example, in Colossians (3:12–21). See, for example, Mitchell Alexander Esswein, "The Οἶκος of the Lord and the Church at Corinth: Understanding Οἰκονόμος and Οἰκονομία in Paul's First Epistle to the Corinthians," *Biblische Notizen* 172 (2017): 87–110; and Arthur J. Dewey, "'House' as Root Image in Galatians," *Proceedings* 12 (1992): 195–203.

37. Garrigan, "Queer Worship," 227.

38. See Lisa Isherwood, "Marriage," in *Contemporary Theological Approaches to Sexuality*, 135–45 at 135.

39. Regarding sexuality within a marriage, the Uniting Church in Australia's 1997 Statement on Marriage avers, *"Where sexual union takes place*, the partners seek to express mutual delight, pleasure, and tenderness, thus strengthening the union of their lives together." See Peter Grayson-Weeks' reflections on the expansion of marriage in that church, "From Equality in Marriage to Marriage Equality," *Australian Journal of Liturgy* 18 (October 2022): 104–112 at 108.

40. See, for example, Alejandro Stephano Escalante, "Sacramental Sex/Uality," in *Contemporary Theological Approaches to Sexuality*, 313–323. While I concur that sexual expression can unveil divine encounter—that is, function sacramentally—not all such expressions necessarily need recognition in the assembly.

involved, not those who would seek to label."[41] Decoupling the presumption of sex from marriage might unveil new, queerer pathways to how assemblies recognize households among their number.

Such moves would surely require expanding the range of households that appear in an assembly's practice. W. Scott Haldeman documents his own (unsuccessful) attempt at including such possibilities in his denomination, the United Church of Christ.[42] Many commentators take up friendship as a more fruitful metaphor for marriage regardless of gender, a point reinforced with reference to the Trinity by Hugo Córdova Quero and Joseph Goh in their reflection on polyamory: "[F]rom a queer theological perspective, we suggest that polyamory can be imaginatively expressed as perichoretic friendship."[43] Mary Ann Tolbert suggests a more thorough reimagining of marriage, discarding marriage practices derived from various antiquities and replacing them with references to ancient practices of friendship, which included sharing things in common, mutuality and reciprocity, honesty and intimacy, the faithful keeping of secrets and confidences, among other things.[44] As Mark Jordan points out in his reflection on John Boswell's[45] and Alan Bray's[46] different exploration of rites of public friendship in Christian history, such proposals are hardly without warrant in Christian liturgical tradition, and in fact may be a recoverable "liturgical genealogy" for contemporary churches.[47]

In the case of David and me, a ritual appeal to some form of friendship might take steps toward that "truthful anamnesis." From that perspective, David describes our relationship as "closed" and so exclusive, in that there are dimensions of our friendship to which others do not have access. Nevertheless, we have each had significant relationships with other men that have been largely independent of (though honest about) our own. Our commitment to one another is not grounded in particular use or restriction of sex; to us it is but one way of relating among many, and we have never required exclusivity of each other. Beyond that, our household includes a long-time friend who has lived with us for more than a decade and who is also a presbyter—giving our home more the character of a religious community than a nuclear household. Could an assembly countenance witnessing the blessing of such a household, given that it would certainly be judged by many as "outside the moral vision of the Church"?

---

41. Mary Hunt, "Love Your Friends: Learning from the Ethics of Relationships," in *Queer Christianities: Lived Religion in Transgressive Forms*, 137–147 at 142.

42. See Haldeman, "The Queer Body," 72–75, and "Appendix I: Same-Gender Union," 165–170.

43. Córdova Quero and Goh, "More than a Divine Ménage à Trois," 307.

44. Tolbert, "Marriage and Friendship," in *Authorizing Marriage?*, 41–51 at 49–50.

45. *Same-Sex Unions in Premodern Europe* (New York: Villard Books, 1994).

46. *The Friend* (Chicago: University of Chicago Press, 2003).

47. Mark Jordan, "Arguing Liturgical Genealogies, or, the Ghosts of Weddings Past," in *Authorizing Marriage?*, 104–112.

All That I Have

Despite the fact that a household is also an economic unit, reflection on the economic dimensions of marriage—and the economic damages suffered by households excluded from its benefits—is sparse in debates about marriage equality, though not in some theological reflection.[48] Further (as my own partner has pointed out), civil marriage at its basic level is what he calls a "GAP": a Government Assistance Program granted to couples but denied to others, a policy reflecting a zero-sum outlook toward resources, necessitating their restriction to some household forms.[49] Why, he asks, are religious institutions so involved and eager to serve as agents of such a worldview? The unquestioned assumption that only households formed by couples are eligible for participation in the GAP of "marriage" is interesting. US law does not limit a medical, dental, legal, or professional partnership to just two members in order to qualify for benefits available to "legal partnerships." If the societal good sought is stable and enriching relationships, why are only couples admitted?

Given the hybrid, civil-religious nature of marriage in the US context, the GAP extends to church life as well: With same-gender marriage now canonically legislated and protected in The Episcopal Church, in which I serve as a presbyter, these prohibitions have economic impact: Whereas before "marriage equality," the Church Pension Group allowed clergy in same-gender partnerships to choose who might share their health and pension coverage without reference to marriage, the progressive extension of marriage rights brought a different policy. Where same-gender marriage was legal, same-gender couples were required to be married to cover another member of their household (only a spouse)—just like their different-gender counterparts. For that reason and to protect our then 15-year-old household, David and I were civilly married in 2014. Oddly, Roman Catholic institutions, such as the university where David once taught, allowed employees to cover any adult not related by blood, in effect to sidestep "recognizing" same-gender marriage. Which is queerer?

By and large religious commentators on marriage have shown primary interest in the fundamental equivalency between the love of partners to warrant entrance into the institution: "Love is love." Nonetheless, queer-identified voices warned of the complicity with injustice that extending the boundaries of marriage without including other households might entail. Writing before same-sex marriage was extended to couples throughout the United States, Haldeman argues:

---

48. See, for example, Isherwood, "Marriage," 140–144; and Althaus-Reid, *Indecent Theology*, 140–145.

49. Lisa Isherwood notes that the infamous US Defense of Marriage Act reinforced the GAP by encouraging the "state to offer financial benefits to middle-class couples if they were married from property tax exemptions to beneficial health care coverage." See Isherwood, "Marriage," 142.

> The real fight, the struggle to be engaged by people of faith . . . may be less to ensure that loving, stable same-sex couples and their children get social benefits as that all families, all people, are supported and have what they need in terms of health insurance, visitation privileges in hospitals, the distribution of their estate at death and so on. In this way, those who experiment in love may serve the increase of social justice.[50]

Echoing similar concerns, Mary Hunt is clear: "I remain unconvinced that the two-by-two model, whether a woman and a man, two women, or two men, will ever result in a society that favors the common good over the individual or the family."[51] The arrival of "marriage equality" has not blunted these critiques; on the contrary, households once excluded from marriage seem no less eager to reap the benefits built into the social contract for those able to tick the "married, filing jointly" box. Marriage is an economic arrangement favored by society with substantial economic benefits that are not enjoyed by those excluded from it. Religious celebrations of same-gender marriage have done little, nothing even, to disrupt this arrangement. Mary Hunt was right.

It is hard to identify how marriage might be "queered" in the matter of its economics. The texts of weddings liturgies are thin on the ground when addressing money, even though the secular liturgy that once accompanied it included an actual exchange of human and real property. As to the former, most weddings involving couples previously excluded from marriage preserve some form of procession by one of the parties that has historically suggested the living property being transferred. Only occasionally do partners enter the assembly together—though most denominational resources presume this possibility.[52] But that change alone would only signal an equality among the partners, not a commitment to equality among households, however constructed.

Queering marriage in this case may have less to do with disrupting a binary than with troubling a tautology: Love is love. The collapse of marriage into coupled romantic, companionate love, abetted by allies religious and secular, has veiled the economic dimensions of a household to such a degree that "marriage equality" sounds like justice. On the contrary, it did little to address, and in fact reinforced, a "marital privilege" both religious and secular that excludes many

---

50. Haldeman, "A Queer Fidelity," 151.

51. Mary E Hunt, Marvin Mahan Ellison, Emilie M. Townes, Patrick S. Cheng, Martha A. Ackelsberg, Judith Plaskow, and Angela Bauer-Levesque, "Roundtable Discussion: Same-Sex Marriage," *Journal of Feminist Studies in Religion* 20:2 (2004): 83–117 at 91.

52. See, for example, the Roman Catholic *Rite of Marriage*, no. 20: "If there is to be a procession to the altar, the ministers go first, followed by the priest, and then the bride and the bridegroom." See International Commission on English in the Liturgy, *The Rites of the Catholic Church* (New York: Pueblo, 1976), 539. While still common in weddings religious and secular, the separate entrance of the bride on the arm of her father or other male relative is commended by none of the denominational wedding resources I have consulted, though a separate entrance of at least one partner remains common.

households.⁵³ These include many whose members are queer or queer-identified but do not conform to requirements of what Haldeman has called "marriage and its policing."⁵⁴ On the contrary, Lisa Isherwood suggests that the expansion of marriage has confirmed Hunt's fears, noting that families are progressively seen as "a consumer unit, the pride of capitalism!"⁵⁵

Further, the current marriage liturgies of most denominations are so intensely couple-focused that even the prayers of the people are directed to the parties to the wedding. In rare cases, as in the Roman Catholic nuptial blessing for example, one catches a glimpse of a household's mission to the world around it, but such expressions are few and far between. Concurrent accounts of the "nuclear family" created in marriage (no matter the genders of the couple who heads it) that reflect little relationship with the community beyond it have already drawn critique from the theological reflection of opposite-sex married persons.⁵⁶

In addition to an expansion of the kinds of households a church liturgy might uphold as symbols of grace, the liturgies themselves would benefit from a thorough review of how they propose the role of the household as a unit of the common good. If David and I ever asked an assembly to recognize our own household, I would be hard-pressed to come up with a way to acknowledge the economic dimensions of our life together or the responsibilities that entails: that we co-own a house; that we hold most of our financial property in common; that we (or at least David) seek to produce our food; that our household has an obligation to the common good. We may signal that in the prayers of the people, in requests for donations in lieu of gifts, or in the manner of Eucharistic celebration—though these are at best indirect gestures. As two white men with no children, we sit atop the unjust economic pyramid, and our civil marriage further cements our position. Could we celebrate a liturgy that might both disrupt that order and shape us toward something new? Or would it be better to refrain from any "church wedding" at all?

---

53. A 2014 Pew research study noted that less than half of children lived with a couple in their first marriage, while just over a quarter lived with one parent. This trend has only accelerated in the intervening years. See Pew Research Center, "The American Family Today," 17 December 2015, https://www.pewresearch.org/social-trends/2015/12/17/1-the-american-family-today/ [accessed 28 February 2023]. Exploring queer family structures remains in early stages. See, for example, Jessica N. Fish and Stephen T Russell, "Queering Methodologies to Understand Queer Families," *Family Relations* 67:1 (2018): 12–25, https://doi-org.divinity.idm.oclc.org/10.1111/fare.12297.

54. W. Scott Haldeman, "A Queer Fidelity: Reinventing Christian Marriage," *Theology and Sexuality* 13:2 (2007): 150–151.

55. Isherwood, "Marriage," 143.

56. Lisa Sowle Cahill gathers the reflections of Roman Catholic married theologians, who hope "to find resources for resistance of cultural trends toward family fragmentation and consumerism." See her "Marriage: Developments in Catholic Theology and Ethics," *Theological Studies* 64 (2003): 78–105. See also Julie Hanlon Rubio, *A Christian Theology of Marriage and Family* (Mahwah, NJ: Paulist Press, 2003).

What God Has Joined

The fact that couples once excluded from Christian marriage practice now have access and have embraced it suggests both the desire to have a religious sanction and an underlying belief that God has something to do with "marriage." While the theological reflection emerging around the time of greater civil and religious recognition of same-gender marriage engaged claims around the "divine institution" of marriage, they focused their efforts on the question of gender rather than the institution itself. Since most denominational marriage liturgies have only been lightly edited for use with same-gender couples, the claim that "marriage," whatever the gender of the parties, is divinely ordained remains intact.

To the extent that binaries of any kind also embed hierarchies—male over female, husband over wife, parent over child, and so on—their extension to human relationships is no exception: Being married is still preferred—socially, economically, culturally—to being unmarried. A mere eight years after national recognition of same-gender marriage in the United States that hierarchy is already asserting itself in the expectation of marriage as the logical endpoint of any romantic relationship, mimicry in the matter of civil and religious celebration, and the eager adoption of gendered spousal titles of "husband" and "wife." Judith Butler's argument that privileging "long-term monogamous" pairs "breaks alliance with single people, with straight people outside of marriage, with single mothers or fathers, and with alternative forms of kinship which have their own dignity and importance" is not without merit.[57]

While resisting the powerful secular forces at work in marriage is probably beyond the churches, what they can do, finally, is repudiate any special theological claim for marriage as particularly divinely instituted. Instead, they can allow a variety of households, in whatever form or configuration, to be different experiments in Christian practice and mission, with none more exemplary of Christian living on its own than any other form. Beneath the umbrella of "household" might appear many shapes—indeed, they already do. The question is how liturgies recognizing households might develop in ways that are ritually honest to the way partners live their commitments now, rather than how they once (allegedly) did.

One underexplored resource for further adjustments to marriage practice is the long-held conviction in Western theological reflection about marriage that it is the couple (better, household) through their consent who are the "ministers" of the marriage, with the assembled church, through its designated presider, as an/the "official witness" of the union. As Christian liturgical practice of recognizing committed relationships or households continues to unfold, the persons or households themselves emerge as the primary interpreters of

---

57. Quoted in Isherwood, "Marriage," 16.

whatever commitment will be between or among them. Mark Jordan's assertion that "shared ritual agency" is when many same-gender partners become "a couple" is particularly apropos in this regard: "They are not 'being together,' they are doing together," whether their "doing" involves "sexual sharing or sexual exclusivity, financial compacts or joined households, care-taking or child-rearing."[58] Expanding the ritual vision to the household would take this contention a significant step further.

Taking the persons themselves as the "ministers" of marriage, along with their own interpretation of the symbol's contours of commitment, will require a more open-ended approach to "marriage" than can be captured in any canonical form. Sarah Bachelard argues that more practical dimensions of life as a household might be a more fruitful course than attempts at theological justification: "Increasingly . . . it is difficult to disregard the ordinary, incarnate criteria for discerning the human good (vitality, compassion for others, joyful participation in the common life of the community) in favor of arbitrary claims about what is allegedly 'ordained by God.'"[59] More promising, recognizing in the practice of assembly a more multivalent household symbol may allow a richer exploration of human relationship and its possibilities. Such expansive practice may open new lenses on the meanings of Christian life "together" as yet unexplored, while allowing theological reflection on marriage to remain, as Mark Jordan argues, appropriately incomplete.[60]

Although Charles Helfling has suggested that specialized liturgies for queer households may no longer be necessary as more and more churches accept same-gender marriage,[61] the opposite is true. The churches need more, not fewer, options for acknowledging the symbolic contour of human relationship in its many committed forms. That will mean taking seriously the reality of the contemporary moment, well described by Mary Hunt from her perspective as an ethicist, an insight that may well apply also to liturgists: "Variety is the name of the game. The task of postmodern Christian relational ethics seems to be to figure out how to create and sustain a just and welcoming society based on more, not fewer, options."[62]

Any of the above, of course, could be applied to the "traditional" marital couple; commentators on the reform of marriage have raised similar concerns, including whether marriage ought to be celebrated in churches at all, or at least

---

58. Jordan, *Blessing Same-Sex Unions*, 74.

59. Bachelard, "Marriage and the Sacred: Fragments Straight and Gay," in *Kaleidoscope of Pieces*, 43–58 at 57.

60. Jordan, *Blessing Same-Sex Unions*, 120.

61. Charles Hefling, "Variations on a Theological Theme: The Episcopal Church's Rites for Blessing a (Same-sex) Covenant," in *Encouraging Conversations: Resources for Talking About Same-Sex Blessings*, ed. Fredrica Harris Thompsett (New York: Morehouse Publishing, 2013), 71–79 at 75–76.

62. Hunt, "Love Your Friends," 146.

that their civil and religious dimensions should be separated.[63] To do so, however, would be to exclude from Christian liturgical practice the privileged encounter with the divine such households might propose, especially those once excluded, as well as mask the economic dimensions present in any wedding. As James Alison has argued on this matter: "a mistake about being gay is also a mistake about being straight. For being normative and being a large majority are two very different things, and the shifts in self-understanding which will flow from this are only just starting."[64] While Alison is in no way opposed to the expansion of civil protections to families made up of or headed by same-gender couples, he suggests the need for greater discernment in how they are lived out in the churches: "[W]e are going to have to trust that this same Holy Spirit which has opened up the truth of our *just being* this sort of thing [sexual minorities] is also going to show us over time what is the best and richest shape for our *living out of our just being* this sort of thing, giving us the human, social and ecclesial tools to create whatever signs of God's love we are asked to birth."[65]

Though couples regardless of gender have now been admitted to Alison's "very large [heteronormative] majority," a great many households remain excluded from the recognition same-gender couples have long sought. The gift of queer households may propose new patterns that liberate people of every relational tribe from that "cult of normalcy" into new ways of living together in love. If we need a scriptural warrant for such practice, it may be Matthew 18:18: "Truly I tell you, whatever you bind on earth will be bound in heaven, and whatever you loose on earth will be loosed in heaven." Assemblies and churches have the authority they need to determine how households will appear in their meetings, as some once demonstrated when they first began to recognize same-gender couples.

If David and I were to seek our own expression, the liturgy we would invite an assembly to celebrate would be simple indeed, likely taking place in the regular Sunday Eucharistic assembly. Its biblical "wedding canon" would likely consist of a rarely heard passage from Ecclesiastes (4:9–12) on friendship—"Two are better than one, because they have a good reward for their toil. . . . A threefold cord is not quickly broken"—in recognition that our lives are richer together and acknowledging that "third" strand that extends beyond our "two." A section of the appearance of the Risen One on the road to Emmaus (Luke 24:13–35) might offer further shape, an acknowledgment of incarnational accompaniment in our life together, and the hope that in us, somehow, others discover that presence. In place of vows "forsaking all others" would be a promise we could both make

---

63. I argued this myself some years ago. See Bryan Cones, "It's Time to Separate Church and State Marriages," *U.S. Catholic* 79:2 (February 2014), 40–43.

64. *Broken Hearts and New Creations: Intimations of a Great Reversal* (London: Darton, Longman, and Todd, 2010), 201.

65. Alison, *Broken Hearts*, 201.

(if not always keep) for life, one proposed by the late Jesuit priest Anthony De Mello (though not as a wedding vow) as an apt description of what it might mean to love another: "I leave you free to be yourself: to think your thoughts, indulge your tastes, follow your inclinations, behave in ways that you decide are to your liking."[66] We have found nothing better to capture what we are up to, and to us it reflects the non-possessive love proposed in the symbol of the Trinity. I wonder what assembly might be able to affirm such a vow.

---

66. Anthony De Mello, *The Way to Love: The Last Meditations of Anthony De Mello* (New York: Doubleday, 1992), 26.

CHAPTER SIXTEEN

FUNERALS AND VIGILS
Aspects of Queer Grief

Florence Häneke

*"The wounds this world left on my soul will all be healed and I'll be whole. . . .
And I will not be ashamed, for my savior knows my name."*
—Julie Miller

These lines from the song "All my tears" in the interpretation of Ane Brun remained in my head after a mourning ceremony for a close friend. She was a trans woman who could not bear the wounds this world inflicted on her soul any longer. The lines and the melody of the song offered comfort to us, a group of queer friends, who mourned for her.

As a pastor I talk to the bereaved, offer the consolation of the gospel, hold vigils and funerals.[1] Not only as a queer person myself, but as a queer pastor, I therefore ask: Is there such a thing as queer grief—and if so, what challenge and potential does it bring to the liturgies we hold around death? One purpose of mourning is to accompany the bereaved, to offer consolation, and to form community.[2] I want to analyze the challenges and potentials around Christian pastoral care and funerals for and with queer people—mourning the death of a queer person, as well as mourning by queer persons.

I begin by examining the difference between forms of *private* and *public* grief, with a queer-informed view on the private and public. I then look at queer experiences, practices of queer resistance, queer vulnerabilities and resources. Vigils and funerals, as the established places of *public* grief, play an important role in offering recognition and representation to queer Christians. I conclude that queer grief, because of the situational vulnerabilities of those grieving, can differ considerably from cis-heteronormative grieving.

---

1. By "bereaved" I mean to include all those who mourn for someone, not only those who had a legal or family connection with the deceased.

2. On the specific resource of a religious community in grief, cf. Kerstin Lammer, "Seelsorge mit trauernden Menschen," in *Seelsorge: Grundlagen - Handlungsfelder - Dimensionen*, ed. Ralph Kunz et al. (Gottingen, 2016), 116. Funeral homiletics is a field of its own, and not the focus of this article.

221

Grief and Mourning—Private and Public

Grief is not restricted to death.[3] Changes like gender transitions or relationship transitions can also be accompanied by grief.[4] People part from names, stories, role-models, fantasies about future, body parts, and much more. All those processes need articulation without the implication that grief would show wrong decisions, instead accepting the multiplicity of feelings, which enable change.[5] Transitioning is not a linear process and can be supported by pastoral care and rituals in order to enable a new way of relating.[6]

While grieving and mourning are not occasioned only by death but are reactions and responses to different kinds of losses, for the purpose of this article, I will focus on the loss of a person through death. The relationship of the one who is grieving to the person who has died does not need to be intimate, close, or intense; it is enough that the person stood in some relationship to the mourner.[7] People can grieve for those they strongly disliked or who treated them violently, sometimes accompanied by shame. People's grief can continue over extended periods of time or be a once for all time process. Whether someone was a friend, a lover, a metamour, someone met occasionally in the neighborhood café, or someone like a nurse, each unique role is a factor of how one grieves. In a heteronormative white patriarchal culture that focuses on two-person marriages and family structures, these hierarchies prolong mourning.[8] Openness to queer experiences, to subtle tones and general awareness of prejudice is needed, when pastors ask: "What was your relationship with the deceased?"

In her work on bereavement care, Kerstin Lammer distinguishes between grief, as the private practice and reaction, which is highly subjective, individual and existential, and mourning as the publicly visible behavior which is strongly shaped by cultural customs and expectations.[9] She further distinguishes the modes in which these different reactions need to be cared for.[10] Every grieving process needs a more private intimate approach, a close company as well as a public mourning

---

3. Cf. Stephanie Witt-Loers, *Trauernde begleiten: Eine Orientierungshilfe* (Göttingen, 2010), 16.

4. Such relationship change could be choosing polyamory.

5. Jonathan Kohlrausch and Né Fink, "Trans*-Sein und Transition: Impulse für Beratende: Ein Dialog," in Radbruch et al., *Anders leben, anders lieben, anders trauern. Leidfaden*, no. 3 (2021): 21–22.

6. Queer and trans groups wrote liturgical resources in order to accompany such moments. For the German background see the group "QuiKT – Queer in Kirche und Theologie."

7. Kerstin Lammer, *Trauer verstehen: Formen, Erklärungen, Hilfen* (Berlin, 2014), 36.

8. Cf. Laurel C. Schneider and Thelathia Nikki Young, *Queer Soul and Queer Theology* (London/New York, 2021), 90–109. Mathias Wirth, "Queer Families: Effect and Effectivity of a Reformed Theology," *Theology Today* 78, no. 2 (2021): 137.

9. Kerstin Lammer, *Den Tod begreifen: Neue Wege in der Trauerbegleitung* (Neukirchen-Vluyn, 2013), 37–38.

10. Lammer, *Den Tod begreifen*, 23.

ritual, in which the bereaved are getting recognition from the community.[11] In a Christian funeral, the pastor leads the ceremony and by doing so also represents the public. In the funeral, emotions and behaviors are controlled and orchestrated—to protect the people attending.[12] Both forms—pastoral care in private and in public—are significant and necessary. However, they serve different purposes.[13] The first is to give personal comfort and to accompany the bereaved; the second is to provide public recognition of the loss. Considering that recognition plays a vital role in queer liturgies, by publicly recognizing grief, the queer relationship and life itself is recognized.[14]

The distinction between private and public however, when looked at from a feminist and queer perspective, proves to be problematic, especially when a lived public relationship is rendered "private" after a death.[15] The public is not open to everyone and to all experiences; the public is a gated community.[16] "The closet" provides a vivid picture of this reality.[17] The private can be seen not only as a safe space, but also as a place people are asked to remain and remain invisible. If the private is the room of communities and family systems, it can offer safety, belonging, and comfort in times of mourning. It can, however, also be used to silence and politicize different affections, those deemed to be too intimate or that produce discomfort in society. The private is also the place of violence no one sees; the place of tears, no one dries; the place of kisses, no one acknowledges; the place of a sexual desire, which was shamed. Further to have the safety of a private space, which is not invaded but respected as a boundary, is a privilege not everyone shares.[18] People often disrespect the private boundaries of queer persons, leading to disturbing questions, such as those that trans and intersex people often experience about their gender identity. A harsh distinction between private and public in bereavement care must therefore be examined as to whether it offers the bereaved safety and comfort, or whether it silences their feelings and makes them invisible. And pastors

---

11. Carmen Berger-Zell, *Abwesend und doch präsent: Wandlungen der Trauerkultur in Deutschland* (Neukirchen-Vluyn, 2013), 240–241.

12. Cf. Lammer, *Den Tod begreifen*, 59.

13. Cf. Lammer, *Den Tod begreifen*, 18–19.

14. Sara Ahmed, *The Cultural Politics of Emotion* (Edinburgh, 2014), 156.

15. Lammer notes mixed forms: Lammer, *Den Tod begreifen*, 58. Cf. Francis Seeck, *Care trans_formieren: Eine ethnographische Studie zu trans und nicht-binärer Sorgearbeit* (Bielefeld, 2021).

16. Judith Butler, *Anmerkungen zu einer performativen Theorie der Versammlung* [*Notes Toward a Performative Theory of Assembly*] (Berlin, 2018), 58.

17. Eve Kosofsky Sedgwick, *Epistemology of the Closet* (Berkeley/London, 2008), 65–68. The closet is neither hermetically sealed, nor freely chosen, but a performance initiated by silencing and oppression. It is however also a space of safety, in contrast to a prison. Sara Ahmed, *Queer Phenomenology: Orientations, Objects, Others* (Durham/London, 2006), 175–176.

18. Cf. Ahmed, *Queer Phenomenology*, 10.

need to stay alert: if they appear as representatives of the public or the church, they become gatekeepers.[19]

Queer life in my understanding is a mode of perceiving *and* of being perceived, it is a form of belonging *and* of not-belonging; ambivalence and tension are part of being queer in a heteronormative, cisnormative, and mononormative society.[20] Queer life—and grief—includes the positive experiences of belonging, as well as the negative ones of neglect and exclusion. And these experiences are intertwined: Exclusion may lead to the formation of supporting communities, which offer a sense of belonging. Experiences of marginalization become a part of a person's daily life and movement in the world,[21] and inform where one feels safe, where one goes, and how one interacts with others.[22] I argue in the following pages that processes of neglect, as well as those of recognition, must be considered when examining queer liturgical expressions of grief and mourning.

Dealing with Vulnerability—The Loss of Recognition

Queer grief is a unique situational vulnerability.[23] Obviously, queer people do not *per se* grieve differently than nonqueer people. Further, queer people are not *per se* more vulnerable than nonqueer people. Vulnerability is on a sliding scale and depends on many factors.[24] However, LGBTIAQ+ people are at an increased risk to have experienced discrimination, and violence,[25] even more so if one adds in concurrent dimensions like racial, gender, age, and ability discrimination.

The cultural references to queer grief are innumerable. Maybe there is more queer art and literature about grief than about love, and surely those two are inseparable.[26] Queer history is stories of pride, survival, joy, and power—as well as stories of pain and loss.[27] However, there is a noticeable shift when the

---

19. Cf. Kenneth J. Doka, "Trauer, die nicht anerkannt wird: Aberkannte Trauer," in *Neue Wege in der Trauer- und Sterbebegleitung*, ed. Chris Paul (Gütersloh, 2011); Lammer *Den Tod begreifen*, 59.

20. Cf. Ahmed, *Queer Phenomenology*, 4.

21. Cf. Carolin Emcke, *Kollektive Identitäten: Sozialphilosophische Grundlagen* (Frankfurt, 2000), 246.

22. Chester Pierce introduced the term microaggressions for those daily negative impacts influencing behaviour. Chester M. Pierce, "Offensive Mechanisms," in *The Black Seventies*, ed. Floyd B. Barbour (Boston, 1970).

23. Bieler, *Verletzliches Leben: Horizonte einer Theologie der Seelsorge* (Göttingen, 2017), 47–53.

24. Judith Butler, *Anmerkungen*, 87–89.

25. ILGA Europe, *"Annual Review of the Human Rights Situation of Lesbian, Gay, Bisexual, Trans and Intersex People in Europe and Central Asia: Co-funded by the Rights Equality and Citizenship (REC) programme 2014-2020 of the European Union"* (2022). David Kasprowski, Mirjam Fischer et al., "Geringere Chancen auf ein gesundes Leben für LGBTQI*-Menschen," *DIW Wochenbericht* 88, no. 6 (2021).

26. To name just a few popular literature representations: Isherwood, "A Single Man"; Feinberg, "Stone Butch Blues", Taylor, "C+nto & Othered Poems"; Vuong, "On Earth We're briefly Gorgeous"; Winterson, "Why Be Happy When You Could Be Normal?"; Yanaghihara, "A Little Life".

27. "Queer activism has consequently been bound up with the politics of grief, with the question of what losses are counted as grievable." Ahmed, *Politics of Emotion*, 156.

focus is on the stories of pain and loss: it amplifies a notion of being and living queer as mainly tough, sad, or dangerous, instead of picturing being queer as joyful, powerful, or sometimes pretty boring.[28] The effect of that shift is a binary of possibility and impossibility, in which a queer life seems less desirable and livable. It is a dangerous shift as it *takes away* power and agency. Christian pastoral care, services and rituals, however, aim to *give* power and agency. Christian pastoral activities focus on life, on finding ways back to a livable life after a loss.

A focus on life does not mean that death and suffering are ignored. The losses, past and present, are measurable: queer people, especially Black and Indigenous trans and intersex people, and trans and intersex people of color, have shorter life spans and higher mortality rates in many societies.[29] Further, in a community with a high suicide rate (like the LGBTIAQ+ community), many people know someone who ended their own life.[30] To read and hear of violence against and within one's own community impacts mourning and grieving. Hearing about the deaths of other queer people can reactivate grief—even if the person was not a close companion. It can reactivate the knowledge of a prohibited existence.[31]

Recognition is achieved through social struggles and deemed necessary to act.[32] As recognition is required for agency, Axel Honneth argues that the *expectation of recognition* is a fundamental human experience.[33] Therefore neglect—as not meeting the expectation—has the potential to impede interactions and therefore for the individual losing the possibility to appear in the public context.[34] It is not only open hate toward queer people that is harming, but all direct or indirect ways in which individuals are prevented from coming into a self-relation, an existence and therefore a place in society and the possibility to appear.[35] Neglect, whether by law, by society, family, or institutions leads to a situational vulnerability.[36] The experience of rejection, the foreign gaze on the own body materializes again. Such grief about neglect and prevented full

---

28. Older mainstream productions that do not have positive outcomes would be *women love women* or *Philadelphia* (TriStar, 1993). Positive counter narratives are increasingly emerging.

29. Cf. footnote 24.

30. Cf. Cody J. Sanders, *Christianity, LGBTQ Suicide, and the Souls of Queer Folk* (Lanham, Maryland, 2020).

31. Cf. Judith Butler, *Hass Spricht: Zur Politik des Performativen* [*Excitable Speech. A Politics of the Performative*] (Frankfurt am Main, 2006), 196.

32. Axel Honneth, *Kampf um Anerkennung: Zur moralischen Grammatik sozialer Konflikte* (Frankfurt am Main, 2016), 264–266.

33. Honneth, *Kampf um Anerkennung*, 221–223.

34. Honneth, *Kampf um Anerkennung*, 310.

35. Butler, *Anmerkungen*, 55–58.

36. Bieler, *Verletzliches Leben*, 53–54.

existence is a specific form of loss.[37] It is the loss of a positive self-relation and the impossibility to be seen as a fully valid part of society. Therefore I understand neglect as a form of violence, even the inhibition of existence. Living as someone whom one is not is a mode of surviving, not existing. Yet we are called not into survival but into existence.[38]

Queer grief, then, presents as a unique situational vulnerability.[39] As such, it possibly adds to the vulnerability following an acute loss. Every loss stirs up memories; the situational vulnerability of queer grief can mean to bring back memories and emotions about the loss of the full potentiality of life and existence.[40] Given that grief generally holds the potential to lose one's social identity, it is necessary for pastors to play close attention to how identification is enabled or inhibited in church practices—in all its fragmented and paradox ways.[41] In order to support the bereaved to regain agency—coming into existence when life is stuck—the knowledge of situational and overlapping vulnerabilities forms a base for pastoral work, whether in the private or the public or in mixtures of both.[42]

An actual loss can also reopen the grief about what might have been. Examples could include a sermon about the beautiful marriage of the deceased that bring up the sorrow of not being able to marry or grief about not being able to share a room with same-gender partners in the home for the elderly. Some may feel the loss of youth because they were unable to come out at the time. Others may grieve the wounds done to one's body as an intersex-born baby. If those wounds and scars are due to institutional violence by the church or abuse by religious professionals, further reflection is necessary.[43]

All these forms of grief ask to be explicitly addressed and held visible; those wounds and scars press to the surface and demand space, even if the events are long passed and the grief is unexpected.[44] As Kenneth Doka states: unrecognized or even inhibited grief deepens and becomes stronger.[45] The relationship between

---

37. Cf. Judith Butler, *Gefährdetes Leben: Politische Essays* [*Precarious Life. The Politics of Mourning and Violence*] (Frankfurt am Main, 2005), 154–178.

38. "If livability points to a capacity to survive and possibly thrive within our shared physical world and to be recognized as both living and worthy of life, then un-livability is a state and experience of having those possibilities constantly threatened and ultimately foreclosed." Schneider and Young, *Queer Soul and Queer Theology*, 24.

39. Situational vulnerability is embedded in political context discourse: Bieler, *Verletzliches Leben*, 47–53.

40. Kohlrausch and Fink, "Trans*-Sein und Transition", 21.

41. Cf. Lammer, *Trauer verstehen*, 55. On "soul violence," and spiritual care: Sanders, *Christianity*.

42. On situational vulnerability in pastoral care: Bieler, *Verletzliches Leben*, 51.

43. Brooke N. Petersen, *Religious Trauma: Queer Stories in Estrangement and Return* (Lanham, MD: Lexington, 2022).

44. Cf. Traugott Roser, "Anders lieben. Anders trauern," in Radbruch et al., *Anders leben, anders lieben, anders trauern. Leidfaden*, no. 3 (2021): 15.

45. Doka, "Aberkannte Trauer."

recognition and grief has been highlighted by many scholars in queer studies.[46] "Simply put, queer lives have to be recognized as lives in order to be grieved."[47] This is to be extended to the diversity of queer lives, especially those which are not publicly visible or recognized by law.

Pastoral Care—Offering Recognition

One path to recognition lies in careful use of language and attention to gender performance. An example would include not to assume that a "gay couple" is made up of two binary men, and so using "partner" rather than "husband," or asking for the most appropriate form of address. A pastor may use "husband" from the wish to show respect for the gay relationship, but without further questions she may fail to recognize the nonbinary identity of a deceased. An awareness of the manifold queer identities does not mean to know everything, but it leads to fewer assumptions and more open questions about individuals and individual relationships. Therefore, in order to *queer* liturgies, working on basic knowledge is absolutely necessary—though mourning people should not have to carry the burden of educating. What is standard in palliative care, for example, includes knowledge about cancer types and developments so as not to worsen pain applies also to the care of grieving queer persons—and I consider funerals a dimension of that care.[48] If the individual bereaved is not only seen as grieving but recognized as a *queer* grieving person, with an openness to queer experiences, it can provide space for their authentic identification and recognition.[49]

Drawing from the work of Andrea Bieler, I understand pastoral care as aid to reestablish a narrative of flow. Christian narratives can help recover the lost stories of oneself without forcing a consistent narrative and accepting the ambiguous.[50] The stories of the Bible tell about times of suffering, accompanying those with stories of consolation and liberation.[51] It allows for movement: in the oscillation between autonomy and heteronomy.[52] With people who experience neglect while mourning—whether present, like when a spouse was not accepted due to hospital regulations or whether in triggered memories of neglect—the services we hold are an offer for consolation, a reminder of grace, the ultimate recognition lies in the hands of the Eternal.[53] Thus the liberating power of the gospel can take form.

---

46. Cf. Butler, *Gefährdetes Leben*.

47. Ahmed, *Politics of Emotion*, 156.

48. Cf. Francis Seeck, *Recht auf Trauer: Bestattungen aus machtkritischer Perspektive* (Münster, 2017).

49. Same goes for all experiences of positive self-relation as well as discrimination, like being a queer BIPoC and/or disabled person.

50. Bieler, *Verletzliches Leben*, 186–187.

51. Bieler, *Verletzliches Leben*, 73.

52. Bieler, *Verletzliches Leben*, 58–59.121. HyeRan Kim-Cragg, *Interdependence: A Postcolonial Feminist Practical Theology* (Eugene, OR: 2018), 10–12.

53. Cf. Bieler, *Verletzliches Leben*, 197. Roser, "Anders lieben," 12–13.

Knowing that many queer people experienced violence through religious narratives I focus on resources queer experience brings.[54] Given that old experiences come to surface anew, an authentic and credible proclamation includes acknowledgment of violence experienced through religion, including the pain and grief it produced. In his ethnological study on the narratives of suicide survivors and their experiences with violence by Christian religion, Sanders shows that both parts, wound and resource, are not to be separated and not interchangeable. Both form a part of the person's identity.[55] The interwoven structure is strength, combining queer and Christian knowledge, as memories of the AIDS crisis reinforce knowledge about chosen family structures and solidarity.[56] The past and its endured pain is acknowledged as a resource—without resolving or idolizing the pain.

Talking to the Dead—Relationship Transformation

Vigils and funerals are not about minimizing vulnerability or grief; instead they open space for transformation. Christian bereavement care strives to find new ways of relating to life, and for that matter also to the deceased.[57] Contrary to theories that understand grief as a process of letting go, I understand grief as transformational process.[58] The relationship itself is to be transformed into a new form and a new way of relating; relationships to the dead are possible, whereas differing to our relationships to living people.[59] The conversations with the dead people engage while sitting at graves seem, as Gutmann points out, to provide paths toward a transformed relationship.[60] Christian religion holds a vast variety of language and symbols for that task.[61] Grieving work therefore is to be understood as relationship work.[62] Queer grieving work is further also community work over the centuries, looking at those who lived before and our relatedness:

> Most of the queer ancestors we would invoke and honor didn't use the term "queer"—indeed the words, the names, and even the sexualities themselves morph and change over time with cultural meanings and social frames, and

---

54. Mathias Wirth, "Trans-Körper: Theologie im Gespräch mit Transhumanismus und Transsexualität," *Zeitschrift für evangelische Ethik* 62, no. 1 (2018): 22–25.

55. Sanders, *Christianity*.

56. Cf. Bieler, *Verletzliches Leben*, 197; Schneider and Young, *Queer Soul and Queer Theology*, 23–24; On pastoral care in the context of HIV as "transformational knowledge": Andrea Fröchtling, "Curriculum (vitae) - positiv leben lernen: Überlegungen zu einer HIV/AIDS-bezogenen Pastoraltheologie/-pädagogik," in *Gender-Religion-Kultur: Biblische, interreligiöse und ethische Aspekte*, ed. Renate Jost and Klaus Raschzok (Stuttgart, 2011), 163.

57. Cf. Hans-Martin Gutmann, *Mit den Toten leben - eine evangelische Perspektive* (Gütersloh, 2002), 156–57; Schneider and Young, *Queer Soul and Queer Theology*, 32.

58. Cf. Lammer, *Trauer verstehen*, 37. Berger-Zell, *Abwesend*, 36.

59. Cf. Schneider and Young, *Queer Soul and Queer Theology*, 20.

60. Gutmann, *Mit den Toten leben*, 156–157.

61. Berger-Zell, *Abwesend*, 246.

62. Cf. Gutmann, *Mit den Toten leben*, 164; Berger-Zell, *Abwesend*, 182–183.

it is important to remember that, and respect it even as we make use of one word to gesture toward a vast horizon of difference. Yet, when we break the death grip by recognizing and touching each other, or when some of us talk to the queer deceased and tell their stories, or when some of us invoke Aztec traditions related to the deceased by lighting candles for and placing marigolds on and around the ofrenda; or when some of us vogue on the ball floor and hit a "death drop" like Willi Ninja; or, when some of us articulate the magical act of the Christian God enfleshing the Holy Spirit through the Incarnation, we all testify to a divine breaking of the life-death/living-dead boundary and give voice to God's disidentification with the "limits" of death. In so doing, we attempt to put ourselves and all our relations back together.[63]

Pastoral care and funerals accompany these experiences, the assessment of the lost relationship and the transformation to the new relationship. The loss is not to be let go, but to be integrated into one's life.[64]

Resources for Transformation: Orientation

When confronted with death, one can lose all known systems of orientation, sometimes even one's basic orientation or place in the world.[65] The perception of the world as known is shaken. Death calls for a re-orientation of a kind, common to queer experience in other moments of life. One might even call it a queer skill: orientation and re-orientation, finding ways to relate in a world which is sometimes openly hostile, sometimes enshrining perceptions that exclude.[66]

At birth we are assigned one of two genders, and through constant (re) production the binary system materializes in the body itself.[67] Queer people re-orient themselves and re-inhabit their bodies in order to gain agency and to exist: In order to find her own way of being, her own orientation, a lesbian woman has to find her own interpretation of being a woman.[68] A nonbinary person has to find their very own way of being nonbinary —including whether and if or how this affects their appearance, name, pronouns and more.[69]

---

63. Schneider and Young, *Queer Soul and Queer Theology*, 26

64. Lammer, "Seelsorge," 124–125.

65. Gwyn Daniel, "Familienprobleme nach einem Trauerfall," in *Neue Wege in der Trauer- und Sterbebegleitung*, ed. Chris Paul (Gütersloh, 2011), 211.

66. Ahmed, *Queer Phenomenology*, 101.

67. Judith Butler, *Das Unbehagen der Geschlechter* [*Gender Trouble*] (Frankfurt am Main, 2012) 38–39. Butler, *Hass Spricht*, 197–198.

68. This says nothing about the fact if we talk about a cis or a trans woman and not every lesbian is a woman, but if a person is self-defining as lesbian woman, she needs to find her own meaning of the matter. Cf. Butler, *Unbehagen*, 182–183.

69. The topic of coming-out is still mainly theorized for gay and lesbian people: Helana Darwin, *Redoing Gender: How Nonbinary Gender Contributes Toward Social Change* (Cham, 2022), 19–20. Coming-out not as a singular act, but as a performative act, which has potential to harm, but also to gain recognition, however, is not to be understood as non-contigent truth. Cf. Sedgwick, *Epistemology*, 4.

So, what happens to the body if it is mis-assigned after death? Who is present, when the *deadname*, the name once applied to the dead but rejected by them in life, is uttered at a funeral?[70] Which corporeality, the dead body as an object, the soul?[71] It is possible to argue that it does not matter as only the dead body is present.[72] But doesn't such an approach neglect the arduous and painful re-inhabitation of the individual body that queer, inter, trans, and nonbinary people go through in a cis-centered world? Further: Is *deadnaming* the dead against their will not also affecting the people present and their orientation to the dead person? Does it not also reconfigure *their* self-perception?[73]

The parting is from the body—which has indeed to be let go in its very physical way.[74] The ritual accompanying this is the funeral. Though the dead person needs a new place, it is not bound to the body anymore. Perception and being perceived is an embodied experience.[75] Personal perceptions of and engagements with people are commonly bound to the experience of their bodies—or at least the possibility of them.[76] Even if knowing that the body is not the whole essence of the other, but confronted with death, we painfully come to realize how *much* the actual body means to us—and our sexual and gender orientation.[77] The identity of the bereaved can be existentially challenged by a loss. If this identity was hard to acquire, like a queer identity, it can even feel like a personal failure by those who grieve. Such challenge further derives from the ways we address—and interpret—persons, bodies, practices in rituals, and liturgies.

If grief is understood as a process—without a clear goal and end but irreversible—in order to find a new relationship to the dead, the queer experiences of orientation and queer relationship skills in finding own ways of relating can be a viable resource.[78] The experience of not having role models, which can be

---

70. Of course, not every person sees their birthname necessarily as deadname.

71. Cf. Maurice Merleau-Ponty, *Phenomenology of Perception* (London, 2005), 77–83.

72. Cf. Maurice Merleau-Ponty, *The Primacy of Perception: And Other Essays on Phenomenological Psychology, the Philosophy of Art, History and Politics* (Evanston, IL: Northwestern University Press, 1971), 15.

73. Cf. Traugott Roser, *Sexualität in Zeiten der Trauer: Wenn die Sehnsucht bleibt* (Göttingen, 2014), 30.

74. On the complexity of the body-death relation cf. Richard Coble, "The Body as Touch: Speaking Death and Dying in Queer Theory and Religion," *Pastoral Psychology* 64, no. 5 (2015), 621–634.

75. "External perception and the perception of one's own body vary in conjunction because they are the two facets of one and the same act." Merleau-Ponty, *Phenomenology of Perception*, 237.

76. On immanence and transcendence in perception cf. Merleau-Ponty, *Primacy of Perception*, 16.

77. Cf. Roser, *Sexualität*, 7.

78. Cf. Susannah Cornwall, *Un/familiar Theology: Reconceiving Sex, Reproduction, and Generativity* (London , 2017), 69. Queer families are an extensive understanding of systems of care. Ahmed therefore specifies that family is a practice: "Families are *a doing word and a word for doing*. Indeed, thinking of families as what people do in their intimate lives allows us to avoid positing queer families as an alternative ideal, [. . .]" Ahmed, *Politics of Emotion*, 153. On the diversity of families in Protestant theology, cf. Wirth, "Queer Families".

felt as destabilizing, can be resource, while also admitting feelings of pain. As Sara Ahmed writes:

> The absence of models that are appropriate does not mean an absence of models. In fact, it is in "not fitting" the model of the nuclear family that queer families can work to transform what it is that families can do. The non-fitting or discomfort opens up possibilities, an opening up which can be difficult and exciting.[79]

Embracing the uncertainty can be interpreted as a queer treasure of not only enduring the ambiguous, but to exploring and owning it, in order to live. Such knowledge includes the possibility of contextual identifications instead of firm identities, open to change and re-orientation.

> But "getting lost" still takes us somewhere; and being lost is a way of inhabiting space by registering what is not familiar: being lost can in its turn become a familiar feeling. . . . The familiar is an effect of inhabitance; we are not simply in the familiar, but rather the familiar is shaped by actions that reach out toward objects that are already within reach. . . . The work of inhabiting space involves a dynamic negotiation between what is familiar unfamiliar. . . .[80]

The re-orientation to the dead and the familiar/unfamiliar might be seen as a similar experience. To give an example with a Bible verse commonly used in funerals in Germany: "For here have we no continuing city, but we seek one to come" (Hebrews 13:14).[81] The text is a typical example of holding the ambiguity; it tells of an experience of loss and not-belonging, yet includes the freedom to seek places to settle. Queer experiences of moving in the ambiguous between the binaries can be uphold as a great treasure in orienting between the no longer existing poles of life and death challenged by the resurrection of Christ.[82]

Resources for Transformation: Intelligibility

If queer experiences are further seen as a resource and comfort in times of grief also the problems of intelligibility can teach us. In a cis- and heteronormative world, people can struggle to find explanations to make their own experience understandable to others. Sometimes relieving solidarity can be found between those who experience similarly. There can be joy, even fun, in embracing the

---

79. Ahmed, *Politics of Emotion*, 154.

80. Ahmed, *Queer Phenomenology*, 7.

81. The verse is one suggestion in the standardised liturgy proposed for funerals, and also the Epistle for Good Friday in the Evangelical Church in Germany.

82. Schneider and Young, *Queer Soul and Queer Theology*, 27.

unintelligibility of resisting what is proposed as normative and celebrating its transgression, necessarily contrasting experiences of neglect.[83] To make my point, many have been called *queer,* meaning of strange and perverted, have learned to embrace it. Perhaps they can also learn to allow themselves to be queerly "strange" while mourning,[84] rather than wasting further energy trying to fit into a norm of how grieving and funerals are to be done "properly." Empowerment and encouragement can arise from the strange.

Grieving people search for words and might struggle to express their feelings—as their experience appears strange in a world which centers around the living.[85] Their connection to the dead does not fit. Just as every gender and desire have the right to appear without regard to its intelligibility, every form of mourning also has the right to be expressed *this way* and to be recognized to yield a liveable grief, a grief that integrates into life.[86] In the very end the debate centers again around the fundamental question of who appears as grievable. As Schneider and Young put it:

> Talking to the dead is an attempt to correct such a dismissal and to bridge the divide between what is and is not recognized as having life within the cosmos, between what can and cannot affectively or intelligibly exist herein.[87]

Funerals

Incarnation theology ruptures the distinction between God and human, all-comprehending love challenges the distinction between bodies, eschatology questions human-made hierarchies, and resurrection the everlasting parting between love and death.[88] Christianity lives from breaking taboos and welcoming challenging thoughts.[89]

So what about funerals with drag performances inside the chapel? Would that not cross a line? I consider performances of queerness at funerals (drag is only an example) as a very conscious appropriation of one's own belonging and being-in-the-world, which is to be encouraged from a Christian perspective. The search for one's own space and rituals as a fitting way to work with the pain can be a source

---

83. Roser, "Anders lieben," 13.

84. Cf. Butler, *Hass Spricht*, 251.

85. Grieving people can act "strangely" or fear to be "strange": Lammer, *Trauer verstehen*, 82–83.

86. Butler, *Anmerkungen*, 55–76.

87. Schneider and Young, *Queer Soul and Queer Theology*, 19.

88. "As with the case of queer theory, it is in Jesus Christ that all of these seemingly fixed binary categories are ultimately challenged and collapsed." See Patrick S. Cheng, *Radical Love: An Introduction to Queer Theology* (New York, 2011), 11.

89. Cf. 1 Corinthians 1,23; on the breaking of taboos in Christianity and queer practices: Mathias Wirth, "Auf ‚queer' kann man sich beziehen wie auf ‚protestantisch': Zur ethischen Bedeutung des q-p-Bezugs für familiale Praxen," in *Protestantisches Familienbild? Theologische und sozialphilosophische Reflexionen auf ein strittiges Konzept*, ed. Bastian König and Marcel Kreft (Leipzig, 2021), 176.

of power to endure grief. It is not a split from Christian tradition but a search for a place *in* it, a further way of seeking the city to come.[90] Such is the calling of "queer ancestors" and referencing queer relationships.[91]

Places where queer ancestors, queer dead are visible are powerful places to the community, like the lesbian cemetery or the "positHIV" memorial in Berlin as well as LGBTIAQ+ grieving groups. Such public places are important because they publicly show that their grief exists. They form bridges between church and queer communities, enabling space for queer grief and for queer Christian believers. They are a tangible objection to religious queer-hostility—the dead are not gone, they are not suddenly straight or cis, they are queer and present:

> And, because we believe that the dead are not dead and instead live still within our shared cosmos, the practice of talking to the dead allows and perhaps forces us to disavow the idea of death as punishment for perversion.[92]

Therefore, funerals might hold both private and public, which are not in every case easily separated, as in public vigils for prominent queer people, or after attacks or accidents, after public suicides. All those deaths provoke dismay not only for the people who did know the deceased personally but for those who experience it vicariously.[93] As a public liturgy, funerals are therefore an expression of recognition politics:

> In such a politics, recognition does still matter, not of the other's grief, but of the other as a griever, as the subject rather than the object of grief, a subject that is not alone in its grief, since grief is both about and directed to others.
>
> It is because of the refusal to recognize queer loss (let alone queer grief), that it is important to find ways of sharing queer grief with others.[94]

If grief gets worse when not recognized, it is necessary for a community that is too often called to be less "loud," "visible," "extravagant"—in short to stay in the private—to hold a public ceremony, offering words and acts that recognize *queer* grief. Therefore, queer funerals—in all their variety—may offer exactly the recognition needed in order to transform the loss into a new part of life. Death and funerals do not call for decency but for remembrance and transformation.

---

90. Like practices of indecent theology, cf. Marcella Althaus-Reid, *Indecent Theology: Theological Perversions in Sex, Gender and Politics* (London, New York, 2000), 181.

91. Schneider and Young, *Queer Soul and Queer Theology*, 20.

92. Schneider and Young, *Queer Soul and Queer Theology*, 25.

93. Stuart already wrote already in the year 2000 about the phenomenon: Elizabeth Stuart, "A Queer Death: The Funeral of Diana, Princess of Wales," *Theology & Sexuality*, no. 13 (2000), 77–91. The impact of violent deaths can be drastically seen in the aftermath of attacks, like the nightclub shooting in Orlando in 2016 or in Oslo 2022; or systemic violence, like after a trans woman, who fled from Iran to Germany, 2021 publicly burnt herself at Alexanderplatz in Berlin.

94. Ahmed, *Politics of Emotion*, 161.

Funerals do not stay in the cemetery but look toward life. Queer Christian funerals are representations of queer Christian belief in the public space:[95] As a cultural tradition the funeral enables the socially integrated farewell and supports that people can see themselves and their dead in the light of the Gospel—seen by the Eternal.

It can however be necessary to offer more than one service—for some might need a queer vigil and some might need exactly *not* that. Such practice would welcome differences and recognize individual perceptions, milieus and needs. If those diverse needs meet, moments of estrangement might happen. In the argument of enabling transformation such estranging moments need not to be ignored, judged or be ashamed of, but in the light of our differences be taken seriously, warmly connecting the spaces in all their ambivalence and taking a risk.

Reification—I Called You by Your Name

Based on research done in gender studies it is to be assumed that many funerals resignify gender and gender performances.[96] Especially queer, inter, nonbinary, and trans people might not be on the horizon of many pastors and priests.[97] The use of self-chosen names, pronouns, and relationship titles in the funeral offers recognition to the queer dead person, as well as to those oriented toward their queer existence.[98] It can, however, lead to conflicts with people who do not respect the chosen name. The liturgist then slips into the role of a mediator, explaining the importance of naming to the deceased while also accompanying them in their loss and their transformation process. Clarity and serenity from liturgist and liturgy create space for resonance; enabling both parts, the sorrow, pain, and discomfort of those who cannot or want not to accept the current name of the dead person while still clearly siding with the inter, trans or nonbinary people, instead of acting into an either–or situation. Both, those who knew the person by their birthname, as well as those who knew the person by their chosen name, mourn; they might, however, mourn for a different personality. Seeing each other, such confrontation might provoke a further pain, like feeling to have missed out an aspect of the life of the dead person. Complicated situations arise if those creating the funeral were not made aware of the new name and only informed of

---

95. Cf. Berger-Zell, *Mit den Toten leben*, 240–241.

96. Cf. Karen Ellwanger et al., *Das "letzte Hemd": Zur Konstruktion von Tod und Geschlecht in der materiellen und visuellen Kultur* (Bielefeld, 2010); Seeck, *Recht auf Trauer*, 86–87.

97. Cf. Mathias Wirth, "Demand for Space: Elderly Transgender and Gender Nonconforming People, Healthcare, and Theological Ethics," *Journal of Religion and Health* 60, no. 3 (2021). With enough financial and social capacities, the bereaved can look for a queer mortician and church. However mostly the next available ones are called, and the people rely and depend on the general awareness. Queer theology needs to look at the margins and capitalism affects every part of our life—and death. Practices of recognition (a decent grave, music at the funeral) are expensive.

98. This is not restricted to names of daily use but could also mean to use the drag name of the dead.

the birthname/deadname. This is a dilemma that calls—as all funerals and care work—for a sensitive recognition of the systems present.[99]

Such situations can produce unintended hurting and therefore might call for retroactive care, for which the Christian tradition can offer images. God knows our name and already recognized every person with their very own name. The eschatological hope and trust ritualized in the baptism is a strong covenant we hold and can remember in times of grief and at the funeral.[100] The baptism is not bound to worldly binaries and not bound to the name one was given by their parents. But on the very contrary: To be baptized into Christ's death (Romans 6: 3–4) overcomes the binary of life and dead, the binaries of differences between people and worldly hierarchies and genders (Galatians 3: 27–28). Further Christians are baptized all in but one name, the Father, Son, and Holy Spirit (Matthew 28:19).

Conclusion

Queer grief is not in itself special grief; it is grief caught in cis-straight-centered societies. Therefore, queer grief is one form of situational vulnerability with a risk of neglect and of losing the possibility to grieve. Recognition is given by addressing the bereaved not only as bereaved but also as *queer* bereaved and the dead as *queer* dead. In all the individuality of their experiences but with the recognition and awareness of specific experiences. If such collective experiences aren't explicitly focused and spoken out, it leads to a circle of silencing, the opposite of the desire to recognize the unique life experiences and grief of queer people. At the same time, the search for a kind of "neutrality" toward queer persons, treating them as any other bereaved persons, might fail to offer a necessary specific recognition and acknowledge a specific demand. In order to look out for God's traces in bereavement care, the violence and exclusion experienced by some queer people in church contexts must be acknowledged. As spaces of public recognition, funerals and vigils can name religious violence, provide a public objection, and begin the process of working through its impact.

For liturgists, one consequence is to learn the basics of queer life. This is similar to learning clinical skills in pastoral care, by knowing the surrounding conditions, legal and social, as well as basic vocabulary of sexual orientation and gender identity, and the correlation between recognition and neglect. This might mean adapting through queer-sensitive training the common bereavement care knowledge that every loss triggers memory of old losses, including the loss of recognition, and therefore one's sense of identity and the ability to exist as oneself.

---

99. On systemic approaches in bereavement care: Daniel, "Familienprobleme."
100. Cf. Wirth, "Trans-Körper," 25.

Recognition is enabled by openness toward the other and careful reflection on one's own presumptions and biases. Such approach sees queer individuals rather than stereotypes, while still acknowledging common experiences of exclusion and pain. Such basic knowledge combined with openness and sensitivity toward other ways life and self-designation can help mourners find their own ways of grieving in both public and private, and encourage and empower them to seek the assistance they need. Such care can restore the queer potential of Christianity to question all binaries and to know that the ultimate recognition is happening *coram deo* and not *coram mundo*.

Christian belief and action challenge the hegemonies of our world, racial, financial, social, gender and sex, and many more. In all liturgies we renew this certainty, as we are certain that man-made normativity cannot separate us from the love of Christ (Romans 8:35–39). The immense treasure of Christian liturgies and pastoral care is to not bind our existence to human standards and norms. Funeral liturgies therefore act as agents to the knowledge that in life and death to exist and to be fundamentally recognized is not dependent on gender, sexuality and performance as solely out of grace we live.

CHAPTER SEVENTEEN

BURY ME IN THE STRUGGLE FOR FREEDOM

Lament as the Queer Apophatic Practice of Failure toward a New World

Sharon R. Fennema

> "Bury me in the struggle for freedom
> In the arms of those who know my name
> Cover me in love as the struggle it goes on
> And say my name till something beautiful is born."[1]

Proposal 1: To queer or to be queer is to always be practicing failure in the face of white supremacist, heteropatriarchal, capitalist and colonizing empire.

Considerations:

1. What forms of success have you been trained to desire?
2. In *The Queer Art of Failure*, J. Halberstam argues that queer failure names practices that refuse the privileging of certain ways of living associated with success, mastery and profit. Failure is the art of unbecoming when to become means to achieve coherence in systems of normativity.[2] How are you unbecoming normal? Where do you witness queer practices of failure and what are they unraveling?
3. In your community, how is Christian worship failing and succeeding?

Our Sanctuary: Club Q and TDOR
November 20, 2022
each time hate pours
into our queer bodyfulljoy

---

1. "Bury Me," track 4 on Tracy Howe, *Things That Grow,* Just Love Music, 2019, compact disc.
2. J. Halberstam, *The Queer Art of Failure* (Durham and London: Duke University Press, 2011), 96.

> I wonder if they know
> that they are shooting up
> a sanctuary
> this place where God dances
> where we swim in belovedness
> where every turn of the head
> reveals a new vision of divine
> and a new version of home
>
> sometimes I wish that they would call it
> a church shooting
> because this joy we have
> is sacred
> the world didn't give it
> and a gun can't take it away

Proposal 2: Theologically, we can understand the queer brilliance of failing, of becoming incoherent to normativity, as apophatic practice.

Considerations:

1. Imagine or remember your own experience of queer failure. What is being failed at? What does that failing show you about what it means to be made in the image of God, to be queerly beloved?

2. When visual and graphic artists talk about working with "negative space" they generally refer to rendering a subject by relying on the space that surrounds it to supply shape and meaning. Negative space can reveal a subject by showing everything around it, but not the subject itself. In Christian theology, a similar kind of theological modality has been called "apophatic," pointing toward who and what God is by showing who and what God is not. Apophatic theological practice and discourse approaches obliquely that which is beyond all knowledge, occupying the spaces around and between, gesturing toward but never fully grasping or articulating. What do you know God is not? What desires for humanity and the earth does God not have? How does the queer practice of failure help you answer these questions?

3. In *Immemorial Silence*, Karmen MacKendrick suggests that, for apophatic or negative theologians, theology itself is doomed to failure. If "success" means making positive, even systematic claims about who God is and how God operates in connection with human beings and the world, then apophatic theologians embrace failure *as* theology, relying instead on what cannot be positively claimed or named with regard to the unnameable. As MacKendrick finds in her analysis of the theology of Meister Eckhart, failure may be

inherent in theology because to speak about God, that is, to theologize, is to speak wrongly; it is to fail at speaking altogether. But, it is only by speaking wrongly, through failure, that God emerges in the world, because the ineffable God who exceeds language, knowledge and articulation, is there unspoken, more silence than speech.[3] When have you known theology to speak wrongly, especially in and through Christian worship? What has that revealed to you about humanity, creation and the Holy?

Making Love after Ferguson
August 2015

I don't remember what bodies felt like
before the street where his body lay
for four hours
was under my skin

I don't remember what hands looked like
before they rested on guns
eager to "keep the peace"
death so close
to so much tender flesh

I don't remember what lips tasted like
before they swallowed the words
of throbbing hearts
nothing to lose but our chains

I only remember

police barricades pressed into my thighs
as your hands grasping my flesh
or the way your voice sounds like air
excavated from lungs
crying I can't breathe
please [don't] stop
or the way protest chants are the love songs
my tongue sings to yours

making love after Ferguson is
eating and drinking
sweating and crying
wailing and moaning
drumming and dancing
a revolution

---

3. Karmen MacKendrick, *Immemorial Silence* (Albany: State University of New York Press, 2001), 84.

>   that loves and fucks
>   like mouths on fire
>   fists in the air
>   fingers on skin
>   that has bodies underneath it
>   lying in streets
>   that soak up blood
>   and give birth to a family
>   of skins that crawl
>   with freedom

Proposal 3: In Christian worship, lament is a quintessential queer apophatic practice of failure.

Considerations:

1. What do you know of forsakenness (Psalm 22)? How have tears been your food (Psalm 42)? What depths have you cried out from (Psalm 130)? What do your personal lament psalms and the biblical lament psalms reveal about the patterns, languages, and structures of queer apophatic failure?
2. At their heart, laments, especially scriptural ones, express the breach of a covenant. They articulate, show, and point toward the ways in which the promises we understand as inherent in the relationship between humans and God, and humans and each other and the earth, are being broken. They show us who God is and what God desires for humans and the earthy by giving voice to God's and our failures. How might your laments be queer in the ways they reveal to us a God who fails to be the god of white supremacist, heteropatriarchal, capitalist and colonizing empire? How might your laments be apophatic in the ways they reveal breeches that open up a negative space of understanding or knowing who God is and what God desires for humans and the earth?
3. Theologian Patrick D. Miller reminds us that the first lament in the Hebrew scriptures is the voice of one who is already murdered, already dead. It is the blood of Abel crying out from the ground after he has been murdered by his brother Cain in Genesis 4.[4] How does Christian worship in your community queerly cry out from the ground?

A Prayer for When You Can't Remember What He Smelled Like
World AIDS Day 2020

>   it was like leaves
>   becoming earth

---

4. Patrick D. Miller, "Heaven's Prisoners: The Lament as Christian Prayer," in eds. Sally A. Brown and Patrick D. Miller, *Lament: Reclaiming Practices in Pulpit, Pew and Public Square* (Louisville: Westminster John Knox Press, 2005), 16.

right there on the sidewalk

do this in remembrance of me

it was like earth
rising up like incense
as rain soaked asphalt

do this in remembrance of me

it was like rain-
soaked leather
on feet becoming prophets in the streets

do this in remembrance of me

it was like leather
that only you could ever taste
in the wine

do this in remembrance of me

it was like wine
pouring out our joy
like so much bread

do this in remembrance of me

it was like bread
breaking
breaking
breaking
to be given away

Holy One,
whose goodness I can taste and see,
make of these prayers straining across time and loss
a memory
make of the memory I can no longer taste and see
a prayer
until,
like incense,
the scent of this absence
rises before you
the lifting up of my hands
as a long-night
sacrifice.

Proposal 4: Lament, as an apophatically queer practice of failure, points toward/gives shape to the new realm of Love, God's commonwealth of peace and freedom, the kin-dom we are building on earth as it is in heaven.

Considerations:

1. For failure to be queer, it must also inhabit visions of alternative modes; it is negativity linked to creative critique and a new kind of antipolitics. What if, as Halberstam suggests, the techniques of failure often characteristic of queer lives offer generative strategies for unthinking and unraveling the disciplinary norms that make life unlivable for those who find themselves outside the norms of society?[5] What are these generative strategies and where do you witness them?
2. In her essay collection *Rebellious Mourning: The Collective Work of Grief*, Cindy Millstein argues that collective works of public grief, like laments in Christian worship, interweave mourning with "the fight for truth and freedom."[6] When our grief becomes mourning or lamenting by becoming public and collective, then it opens up space for contesting the status quo and, in turn, reimagining it through "intervulnerability and strength, empathy and solidarity."[7] "It can," Millstein suggests, "discomfort the stories told from above that would have us believe we aren't human or disserving of life-affirming lives . . ." even as it shows us new stories.[8] Lament is a crack in the wall of the system, to use an image from Subcomandante Galeano. Keeping that crack open, expanding and deepening it is the common struggle we can engage in: "one that transforms pain into rage, rage into rebellion and rebellion into tomorrow."[9] What tomorrow are your laments, your rebellious mourning, giving rise to?
3. How can queer lament as an experience with failure, when embraced as a way of (un)being in the world, become a path out of the circular logics of power and mutually-reinforcing performances of normativity, or in other words, a way to lose our way, and in so doing, find other methods of making meaning, other sources of knowledge, other styles of life?

It is Finished
with homage to "Imagine the Angels of Bread" by Martín Espada[10]
Good Friday 2022

---

5. Halberstam, *The Queer Art of Failure*, 89.

6. Cindy Millstein, "Prologue: Cracks in the Wall," in ed. Cindy Millstein, *Rebellious Mourning: The Collective Work of Grief* (Chico, California: AK Press, 2017), 6.

7. Millstein, "Prologue," 8–9.

8. Millstein, "Prologue," 9.

9. Millstein, "Prologue," 3.

10. Martín Espada, "Imagine the Angels of Bread," in Martín Espada, *Alabanza: New and Selected Poems 1982–2002* (New York and London: W. W. Norton & Company, 2004).

When Jesus said
it is finished
what if he was saying
we know what it means to be done
there will be a time when this will no longer be the case
this work will be complete

When Jesus said
it is finished
what if he was saying
there will be an end
to the powers and principalities
that steal our very breath

there will be an end
to the violence that the state can meet out
to blood soaked ground
and non-indictments
to soul-killing legislation
and fearmongering bans
to the handwashing complicity of the powerful
and the handwringing guilt of the bystander

there will be an end
to the culture of fear
to all the ways we die to ourselves and each other

When Jesus said
it is finished
what if he was saying
if abolition begins
when we can no longer abide people in chains
in cages
on crosses
and we stop believing that punishment is justice
that vengeance will heal us
then
it is finished

if restoration begins
when we stop believing we can own the land
and erase the people
and the bones of the ancestors escape from museums
to dance in the grasses that know their names
and no one will accept that invading armies come as gods
with a divine right
a sacred mandate

then
it is finished

if freedom begins
when we can no longer stand the taste of supremacy in our mouths
and the myth of superiority turns to dust in our hands
when we unlearn the color of good and evil
and how skin is somehow
is the measure of a man
then
it is finished

if repair begins
when the apology comes with keys
and redlines are knit together into welcome mats
when closed doors fall from their hinges
because disuse has rusted the metal locks from the inside out
and the attic smells like trees and moss
instead of the cold ice of glass ceilings
and equity is the song the children sing
as they jump rope in the driveway
then
it is finished

if community begins
when the illusion of our separateness washes away
like so much haze in the storm
leaving the sky clear and sparkling behind it
and we cannot help but know ourselves connected
sinew to sinew
heart to heart
breath to breath
filling our lungs with the knowledge that we belong to each other
and in our we and us, there is home
then
it is finished

if resurrection begins
when we are no longer invested in the power of death
begins with the women who will not let him die alone
who will not let the murder be unseen
who will remain close by his wounds
and say his name
until the sky is torn in two
then
it is finished

INDEX

abomination, 192, 199, 202
Aboriginal, 72, 100; *see also* indigenous
abundance, 62
abuse, 70, 145, 226
activism, 10, 14, 48, 200
adoption, 42, 53
advocacy groups, 12, 40
AIDS, v, 4, 8, 17, 156–7, 200, 228, 240
Anglican, v, vii, 19, 36, 95, 177, 183, 184; *see also* Episcopal
anti-language, 92–3, 97
anti-ritual, 110
apophatic theology, vi, 237–43
architecture, 175, 179, 181
art, 69–73, 169, 174, 179, 180, 188, 238

baptism, v, 9, 13, 19, 20, 22, 40, 46, 49, 111, 136, 195, 196, 202, 235
beauty/-iful, 21, 27, 30, 33, 61, 128, 136, 163, 226, 237
beloved, 54, 81, 137–8, 154, 164, 166, 238
bibliodrama, 111, 119–20, 122
binary thinking, 139
birth, 24, 53, 61, 76, 229, 240
black, vi, 7, 8, 30, 59, 75, 93, 100, 101, 107, 110, 225
blessed, 16, 39, 53, 80, 129, 147, 201
body, vi, 8, 12, 20, 36, 50, 52–3, 57–8, 60, 69–72, 78, 103, 116, 117, 131, 135, 143–4, 145, 147, 149, 152, 172, 176–7, 184, 187, 191, 199, 210, 225, 230
    body of Christ, 9, 19, 20, 53, 60, 61, 62, 63, 117, 171, 173
"bodyfulljoy," 237

boundary, 25, 61, 65, 101–2, 102, 104, 107, 110, 125, 223
bread, 16, 55, 61, 64, 67, 78, 81, 129, 139, 160, 187, 192, 241, 242
buggery, 36
burlesque, 123, 124, 132–5, 137, 142

capitalism, 66, 213, 237, 240
Catholic (Roman), 42, 52, 98, 194, 198
"ceremonial break," 3, 30, 32, 36, 37
"choose your own adventure," 111, 120
Christ, *see* incarnation
    passion of Christ, 65
Christa, 18, 20, 69–84
Christx, 20
Church of England, *see* Anglican
climate injustice, 152
clobber passages, 146
collusion of church and state, 124, 133
colonization, 8, 124, 126, 133
coming out (coming-out), 5, 11, 13, 16, 40–2, 47, 105, 124, 126, 133, 138, 145, 159, 167
congregational song, 153–166
covering, 46, 48, 49, 50
Coyote, v, 21–38, 113
crucifixion, 73–6, 77, 80, 144

darkness, 14, 16, 82, 109
death, 19, 30, 36, 52, 64–5, 68, 74, 79, 155, 162, 198, 201–2, 214, 221–236, 244
Deep, the, 63
denaturalization, 168, 169, 173, 174
disruption, v, 16, 17–20, 100, 103, 104, 106, 110, 167
"draw a line," 36
dunamis, 56–8, 61, 62, 64, 66, 67

245

Easter, 23, 70, 77, 80
ecumenism, 21, 40, 45, 89, 173, 177, 184
Eden, 147, 179
embodiment, 14, 55, 60, 111, 116–7, 144, 148, 149, 169, 171, 180
Episcopal, 3, 12, 16, 32, 62, 69, 70, 101, 198, 199, 210, 213; *see also* Anglican
equality, 6, 12, 49, 65, 167, 204
  baptismal equality, 202
eucharist, 11, 19, 23, 32, 55, 58, 60–5, 67, 73, 76, 80, 81, 82, 83, 90, 11, 130, 187, 191, 192, 218
"eucharistic virgin," 191
exousia, 56
experimentation, 81, 88, 89, 90, 91, 94, 97, 116, 117, 121, 126, 167, 171, 172, 192, 202, 214

failure, iv, vi, 17, 33, 82, 91, 96, 107, 230, 237–43
fear, 89, 91, 123, 126, 127, 133, 135, 137–8, 144, 155, 159, 166, 192, 201
feminism, v, 82, 102
flourishing, 64, 65, 77, 140, 149
fluidity, 112, 122
formation, 94, 97, 98, 187, 202

garden, 18, 178, 179, 180, 181, 182, 187
global South, vii, 43
glory, 61, 65, 93, 106
glossalia, *see* speaking in tongues
"godding," 62
grace, 20, 34, 54, 109, 171, 172, 175, 176, 179, 184, 191, 196, 202, 207, 215, 226, 227
gynophobia, 57, 103

healing, 13, 30, 36, 109, 124, 133, 135, 157, 167, 198, 201, 202

heteronormative, 5, 6, 43, 45, 49, 50, 53, 102, 107, 168, 203, 205–6, 218
heteropatriarchal, 164
hierarchy, v, 3, 47, 48, 89–92, 112, 169, 216, 222, 232, 235
holiness, 192, 197, 199
holy fools, 132, 142
horse, 62
household, vi, 203, 207, 209, 211–4, 216–8
hunger, 65

image of God, 154, 163, 164, 166, 238
imagination, 44, 59, 82, 107, 147, 150, 170, 172, 176, 178, 186, 187, 202
impermanence, 172
incarnation, 56–9, 61–5, 67, 75, 77, 82, 182, 184, 229, 232
inclusion, 11–17, 44, 55, 60, 65, 67, 112, 116, 147, 154, 156, 158, 161, 162, 168, 173
indigenous, 11, 128, 131, 169, 225; *see also* Aboriginal
intersectionality, 4, 8, 18, 20, 102, 120, 201
intersex, 3, 53, 163, 167, 223, 226

joy, 7, 23 24, 58, 74, 94, 132, 147, 155, 200, 202, 223, 231, 238, 241
juxtaposition, 26, 33, 52, 131

kaleidoscopic, 61, 63, 151

lament, v, 26, 160, 180, 203, 237–244
liberation, 7, 9, 11, 18, 112, 115, 147, 155, 167, 227
  liberation theology, 6, 67
liminality, 90, 104
liturgy of the word, 111–122
Lutheran, 22, 28, 33, 113
"made larger," 27
mapping, 3–20, 169, 171

marriage, 10, 11, 13, 15, 16, 18, 39, 41, 52, 72, 98, 102. 111, 158, 193, 194, 195, 197–9, 203–20, 222, 226
marital privilege, 214
Mary, 82–3, 137, 143, 179, 180, 182, 183; *see also* Theotokos
material cultures, 168, 180, 182
messy, 56
Metropolitan Community Church (MCC), 105, 109, 155, 156, 164, 167
milk and honey, 157
monogamy, 52, 210, 211
most vulnerable, 46
Mother Earth, 30
 Earth Mother, 72
mourning, 221–236
Muslim, 36, 71
muting, 46

nonbinary, 161
normal/normalcy, 4, 17, 47, 49, 51, 54, 59, 101, 108, 167, 168, 174, 193, 198, 209, 237
 "cult of normalcy," 203, 218
North American Academy of Liturgy (NAAL), 20, 37

ordination, 45, 89, 90, 98, 102, 139, 191–202
ordo, 9, 26, 31, 33, 33, 52
open relationship, 210, 211

parables, 28, 29
parody, 77, 89
 serious parody, 200, 202
pastor, 22, 26, 33, 46, 50, 108, 123, 135, 191, 194, 197, 200, 202, 221, 223, 226, 234
pastoral principles, 91, 97
patriarchy, 50, 67, 80
Pentecostal, vii, 99–110
performance theory, 101, 147

play, 94, 151, 168, 171, 176, 191
Polari, vi, 87–98
polyamory, 125, 210, 212
poverty, 53, 75
presbyter, 81, 212, 213
Presbyterian, 124, 195
presiding, 17, 18, 33, 81–3, 191, 195, 201, 216
priest, 18, 19, 62, 65, 81, 82, 117, 196, 198, 200, 219, 234
primary symbol, 18, 206
proclamation, vi, 111, 113–4, 121, 134–5, 228
prophecy, 106, 107

queer theory, vii, xi, 4, 8, 17, 19, 81, 101

"real people," 199
Reformed, vii, 113, 143
religious ecstacy, 101, 104, 110
risk, 49, 53, 68, 73, 95, 127, 134, 145, 186, 200, 224, 234

script, 17, 19, 103, 104, 110, 194, 205, 206–8
sermon, vi, 10, 32, 41, 43, 100, 104, 123–5, 135, 137, 143–52, 226
 Sermon on the Mount, 114
shame, 3, 79, 105, 109, 152, 202, 221, 222
shout tradition, 110
silence, 26, 89, 91, 97, 105, 238
slippage, 194
social justice 23, 159, 214
sonic drag, 115
Sophia, 76–7, 81, 82–3
speaking in tongues, 107
Spirit, vii, 34, 35, 36, 50, 51, 88, 94, 97, 99, 100, 104, 106, 107, 109, 110, 131, 132, 192, 218, 229, 235
spiritual gifts, 102
sweet sound, 108
symbol, 21, 35, 60, 77, 82, 94, 132, 173, 196, 206, 208, 215, 217, 219

testimony, 79, 105–6, 110
thanks, 26, 62, 139
theological education, 89
Theotokos, 178, 183–6
thingification, 210
tohu vobolu, 62
Toronto Blessing, 99, 100
transgender, 3, 4, 8, 14, 15, 16, 17, 39, 42, 72, 153, 161, 163
tree, 99, 136, 147, 180, 187, 201, 244
Trickster, 28, 29, 33, 36, 113, 136
truthful anamnesis, 212
Trinity, 11, 27, 34, 56, 161, 210, 212, 219
  Three in One, 53

Uniting (Church in Australia), 73, 80, 81, 109, 177, 211

ugliness, 30, 32, 136

violence, 3, 5, 51, 52, 71, 77, 108, 112, 171, 223, 224, 225, 228, 235, 243
visuality, 173
war, 34, 36, 78, 79, 136
wedding canon, 218
weeping, 23, 33, 75, 99, 110, 180
welcome, 13, 23, 36, 39 45, 46, 47, 55, 109, 168, 176, 189, 197, 198, 201, 234, 244
white supremacy, 152, 201, 237, 240
wine, 16, 64, 66, 67, 241
wisdom, 6, 31, 32, 34, 81, 82–3, 107, 124, 125, 133, 182
work of a group, 54
work of the people, 84, 121

www.ingramcontent.com/pod-product-compliance
Lightning Source LLC
Chambersburg PA
CBHW070324240426
43671CB00013BA/2359